Wish

Let me be the one to realize your wish.

2

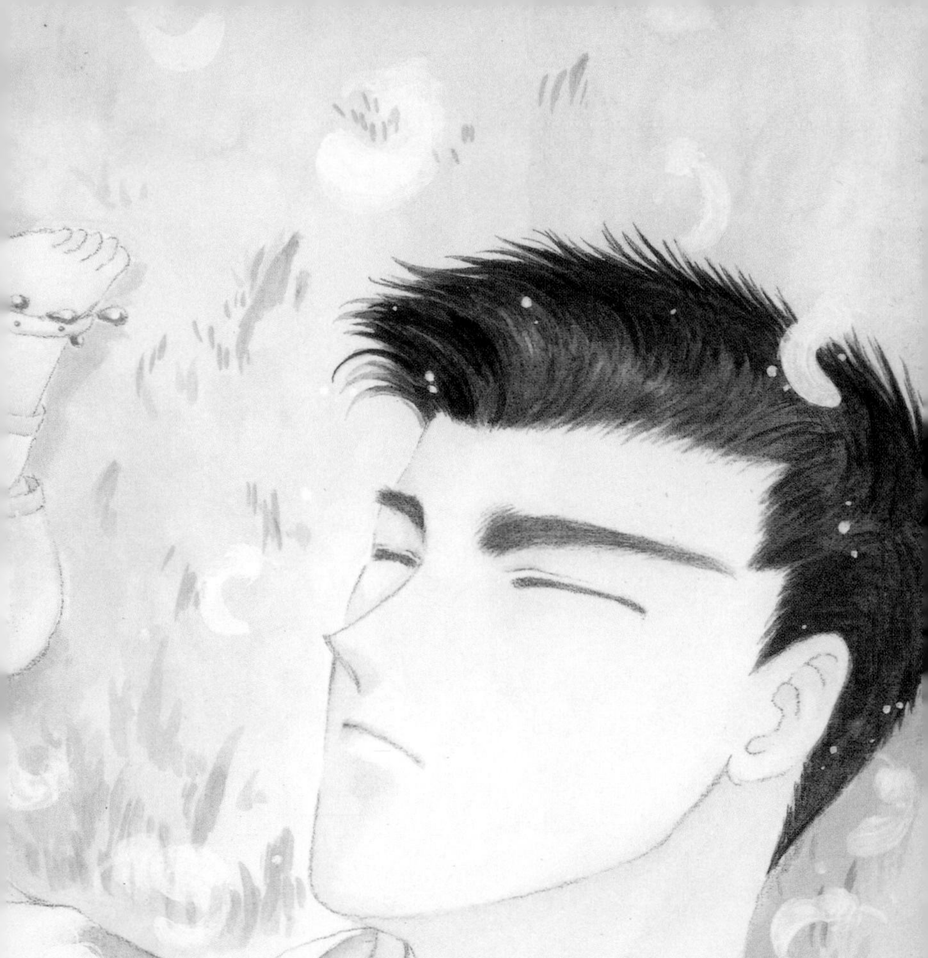

A TOKYOPOP Manga
TOKYOPOP ® is an imprint of Mixx Entertainment Inc.
5900 Wilshire Blvd., Ste. 2000, Los Angeles, CA 90036
Come visit us online at www.TOKYOPOP.com
Email: editor@TOKYOPOP.com

ISBN: 1-59182-060-X

First TOKYOPOP Printing: October 2002

10 9 8 7 6 5 4 3 2 1

Manufactured in Canada

Translator – Ray Yoshimoto; English Adaptation – Jamie S. Rich; Graphic Designer – Gary Shum; Retouch and Lettering – Fawn Lau; Editor – Jake Forbes; Art Director – Matt Alford; Production Manager – Anna Kernbaum; VP Production – Ron Klamert; Publisher – Stuart Levy

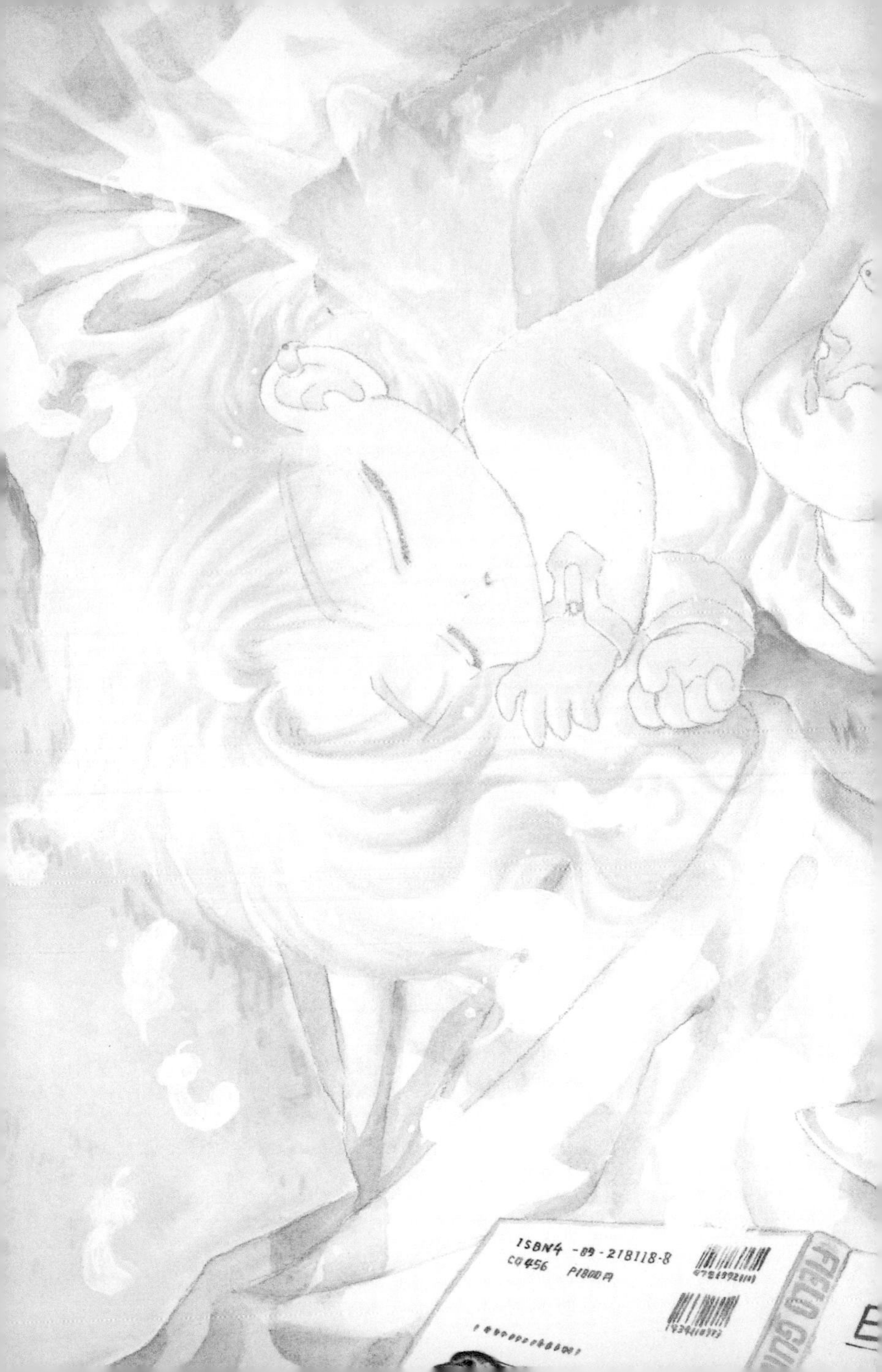
ISBN4 -89-21B118-8
C0456 P1800円

contents

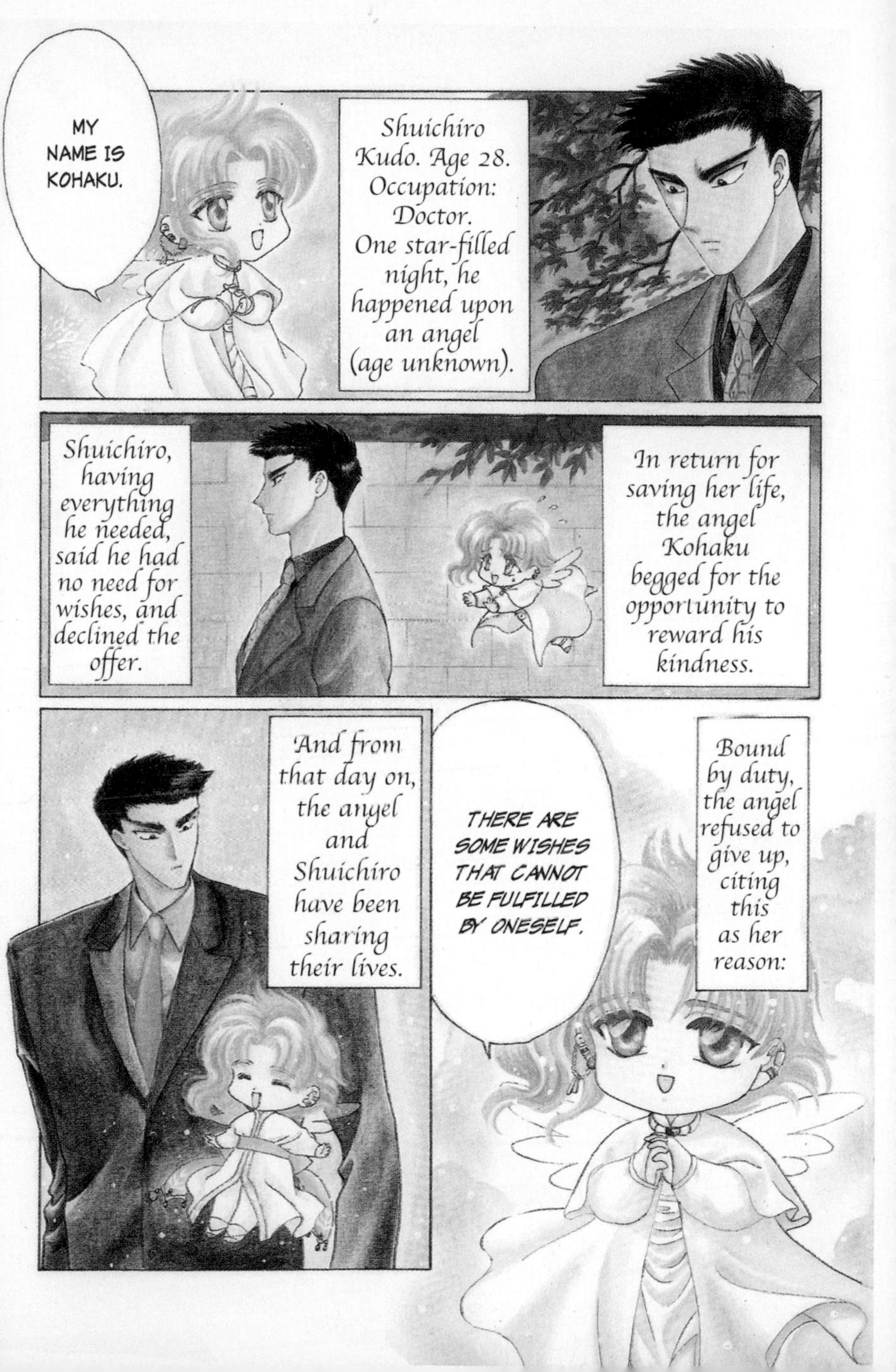
Shuichiro Kudo. Age 28. Occupation: Doctor. One star-filled night, he happened upon an angel (age unknown).
MY NAME IS KOHAKU.
In return for saving her life, the angel Kohaku begged for the opportunity to reward his kindness.
Shuichiro, having everything he needed, said he had no need for wishes, and declined the offer.
Bound by duty, the angel refused to give up, citing this as her reason:
THERE ARE SOME WISHES THAT CANNOT BE FULFILLED BY ONESELF.
And from that day on, the angel and Shuichiro have been sharing their lives.

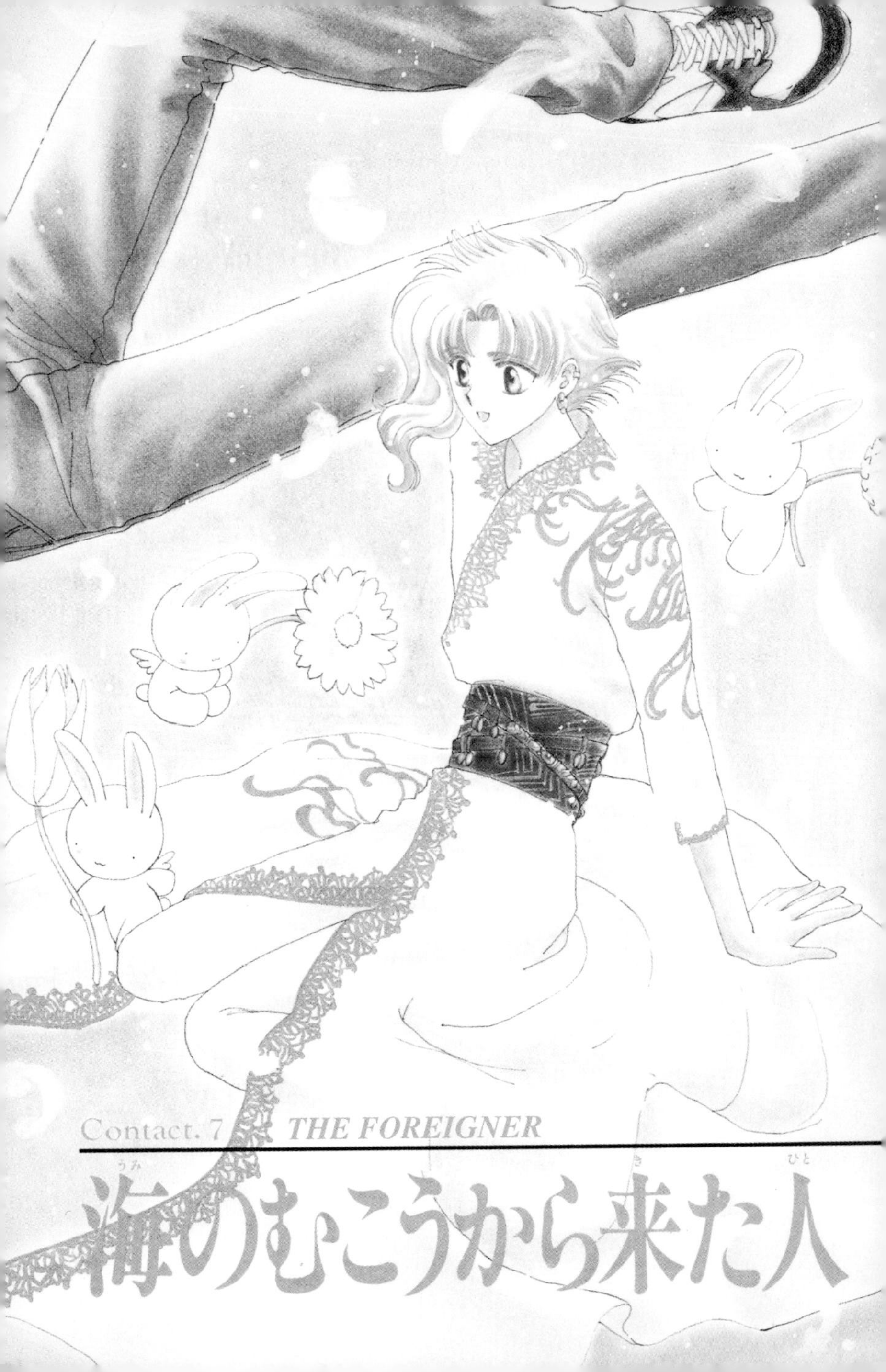
Contact. 7 THE FOREIGNER
海のむこうから来た人

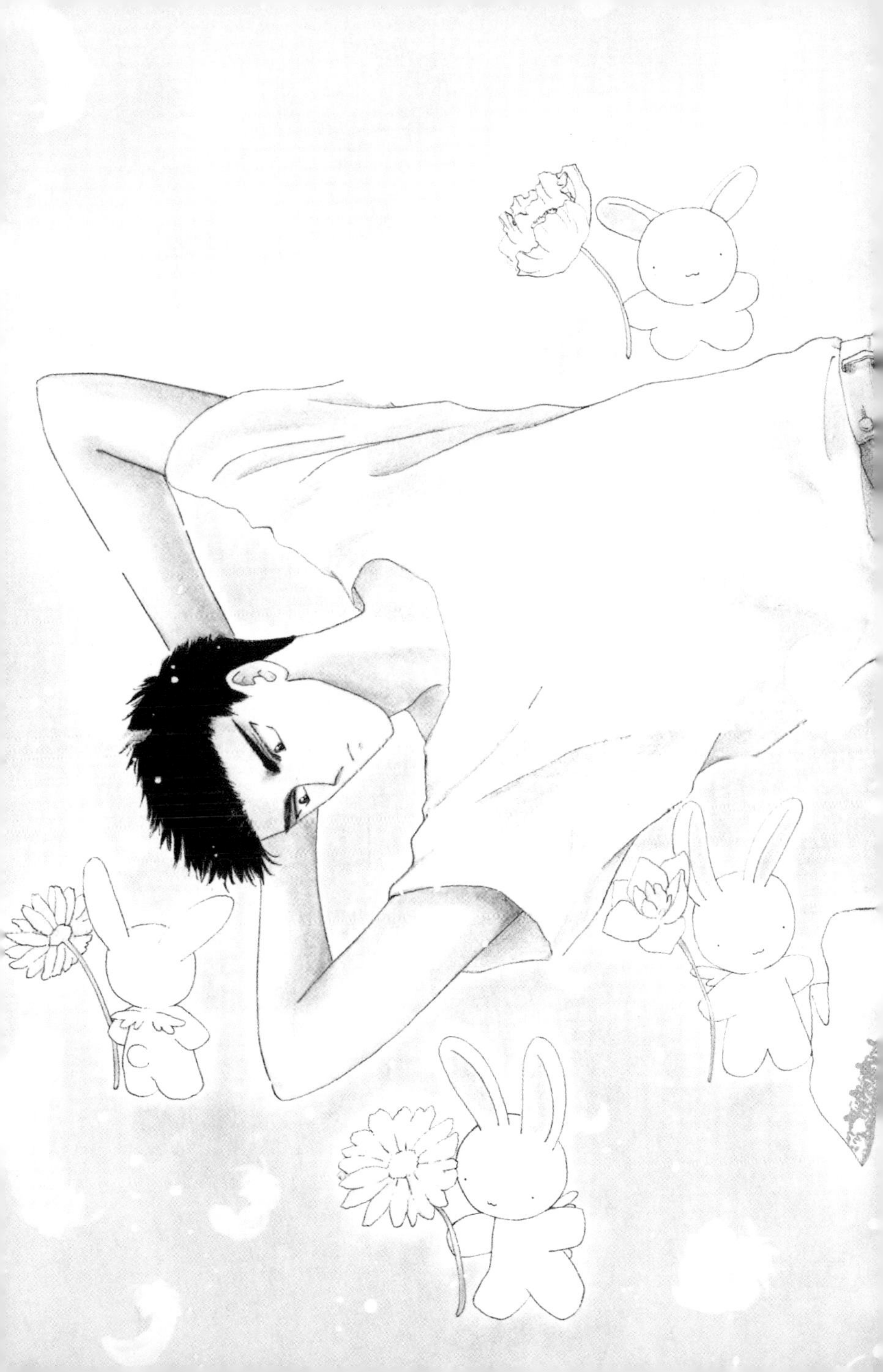

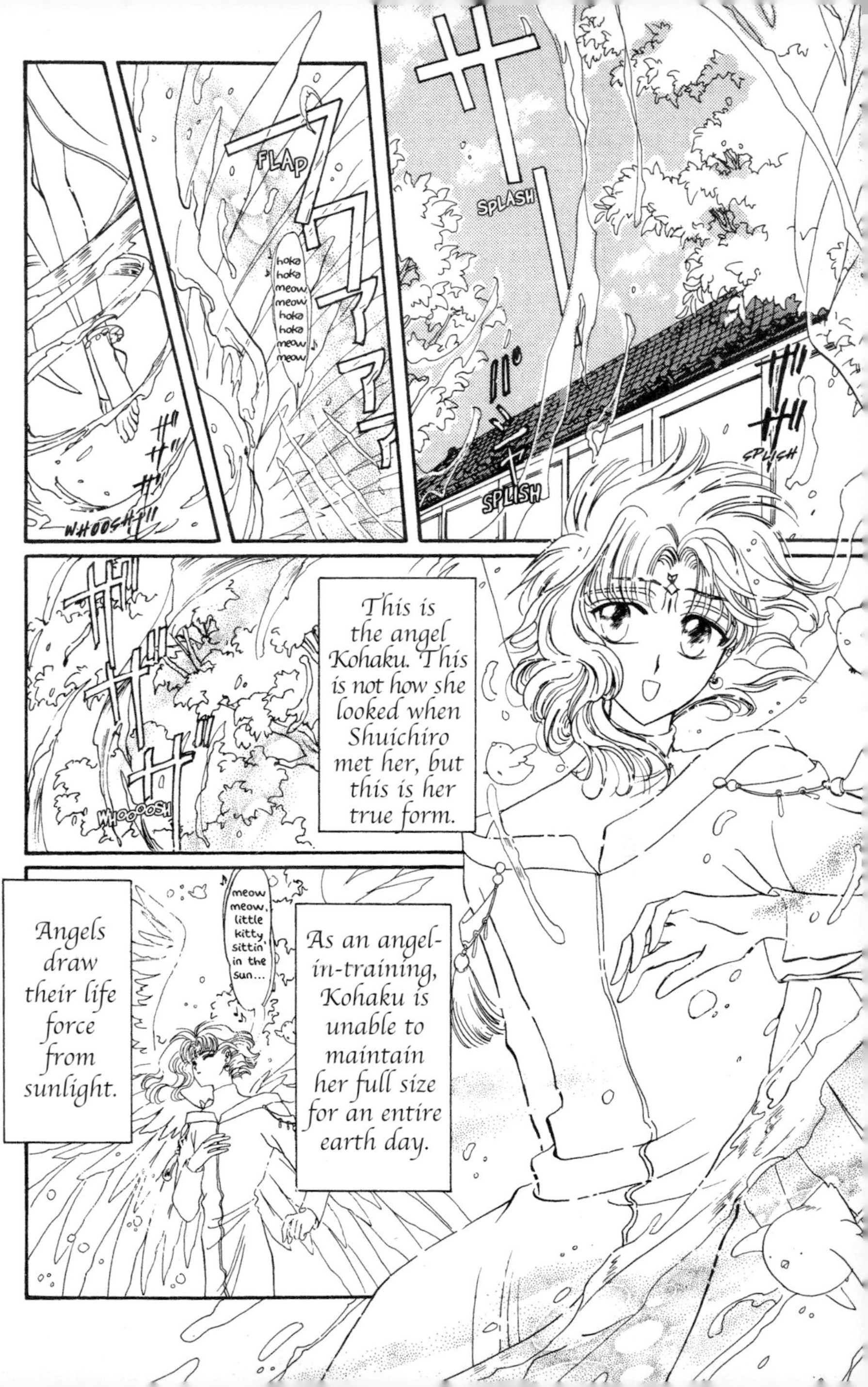
SPLASH
SPLISH
SPLISH
FLAP
hoka hoka meow meow hoka hoka meow meow
WHOOSH!!
This is the angel Kohaku. This is not how she looked when Shuichiro met her, but this is her true form.
WHOOOOSH
As an angel-in-training, Kohaku is unable to maintain her full size for an entire earth day.
meow meow, little kitty sittin' in the sun...
Angels draw their life force from sunlight.

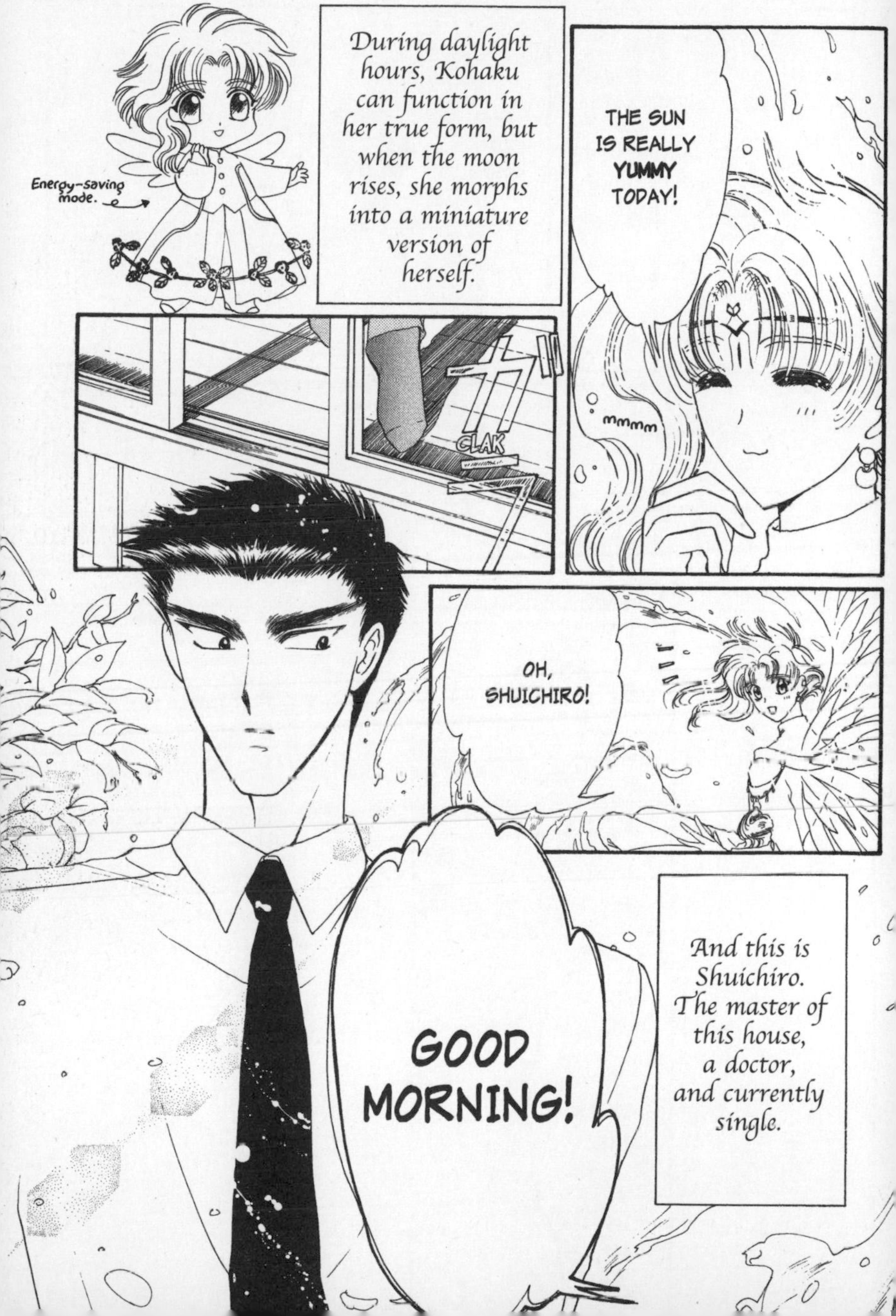
THE SUN IS REALLY YUMMY TODAY!
mmmm
During daylight hours, Kohaku can function in her true form, but when the moon rises, she morphs into a miniature version of herself.
Energy-saving mode.
CLAK
OH, SHUICHIRO!
And this is Shuichiro. The master of this house, a doctor, and currently single.
GOOD MORNING!

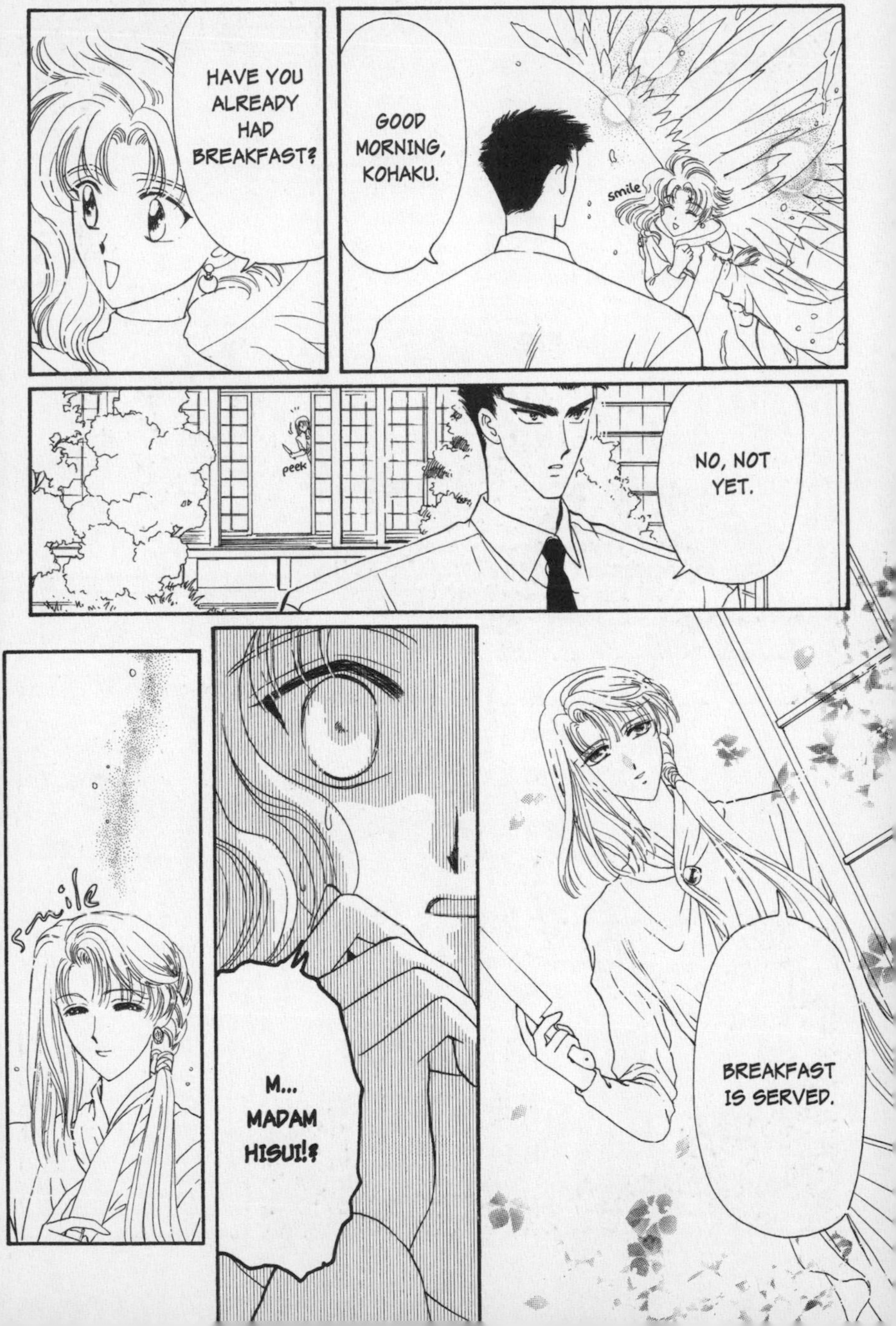
GOOD MORNING, KOHAKU.
smile
HAVE YOU ALREADY HAD BREAKFAST?
NO, NOT YET.
peek
BREAKFAST IS SERVED.
M... MADAM HISUI!?
smile

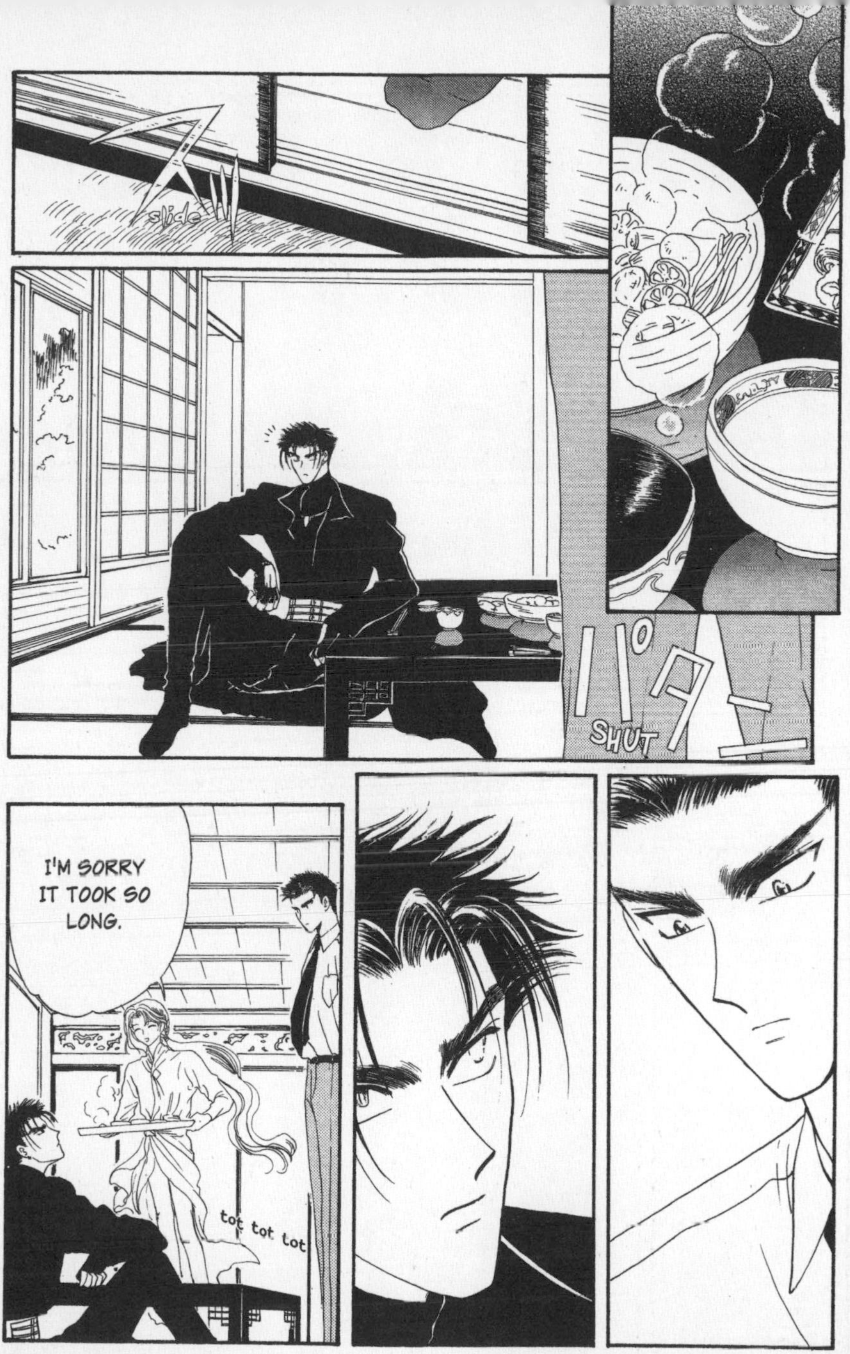
slide
SHUT
I'M SORRY IT TOOK SO LONG.
tot tot tot

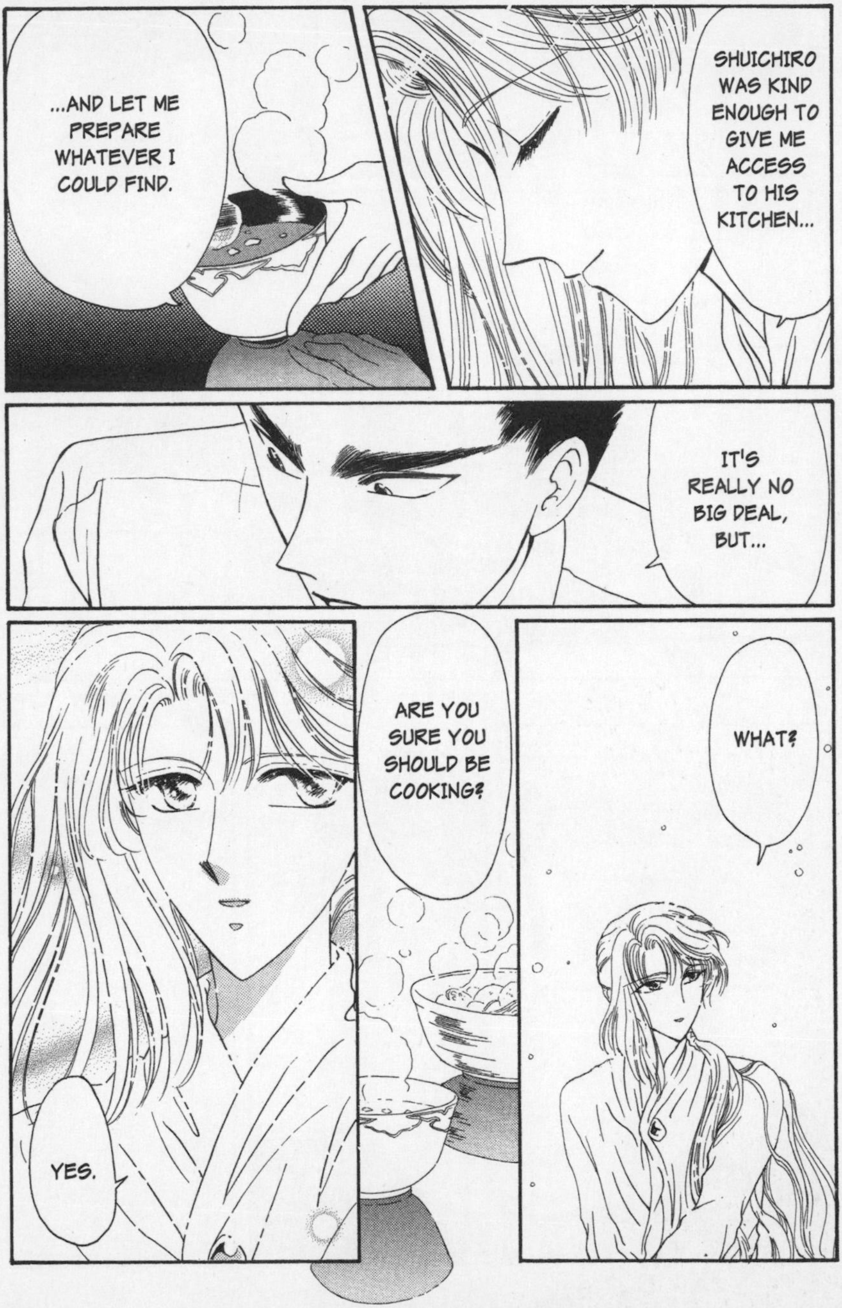
SHUICHIRO WAS KIND ENOUGH TO GIVE ME ACCESS TO HIS KITCHEN...
...AND LET ME PREPARE WHATEVER I COULD FIND.
IT'S REALLY NO BIG DEAL, BUT...
WHAT?
ARE YOU SURE YOU SHOULD BE COOKING?
YES.

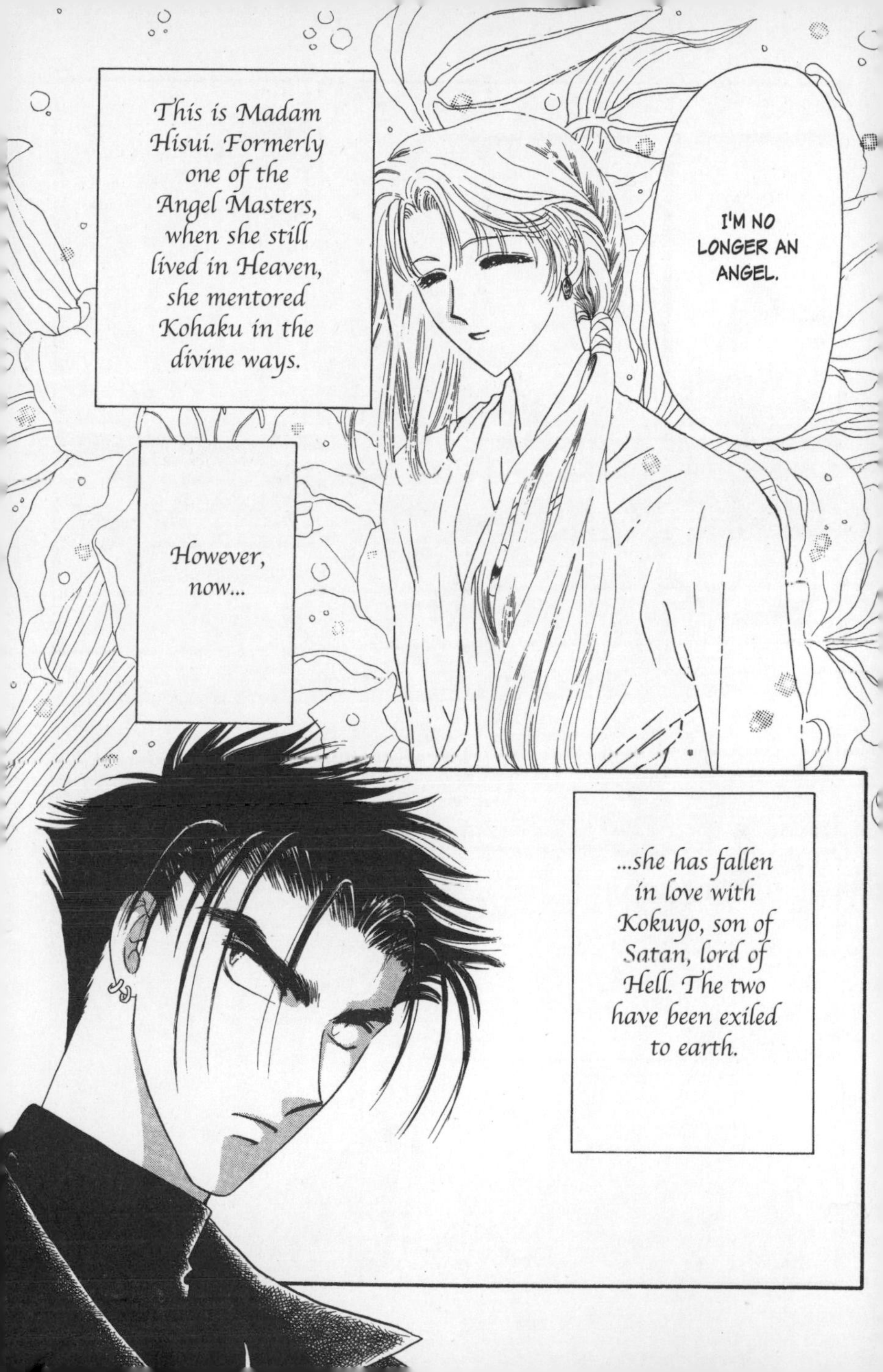
I'M NO LONGER AN ANGEL.
This is Madam Hisui. Formerly one of the Angel Masters, when she still lived in Heaven, she mentored Kohaku in the divine ways.
However, now...
...she has fallen in love with Kokuyo, son of Satan, lord of Hell. The two have been exiled to earth.

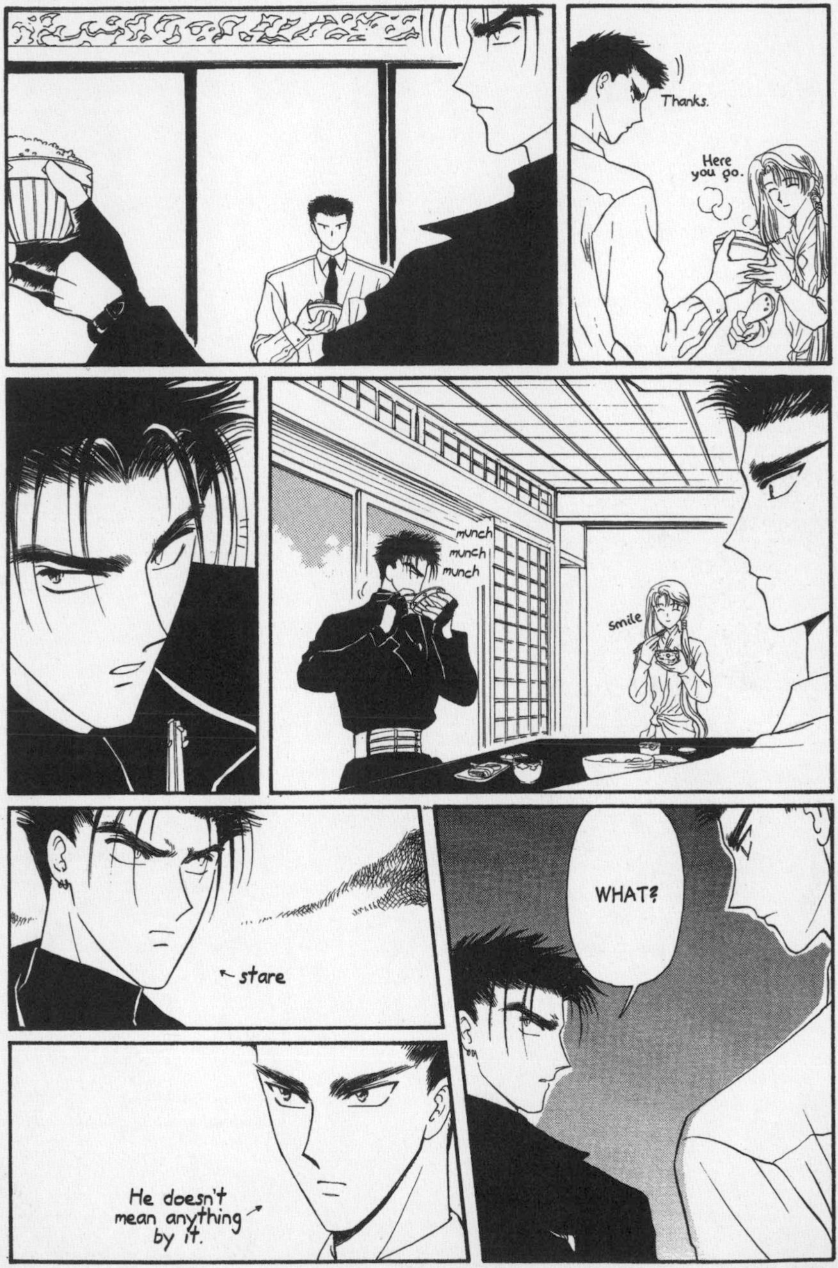

Thanks.
Here you go.
munch munch munch
smile
WHAT?
stare
He doesn't mean anything by it.

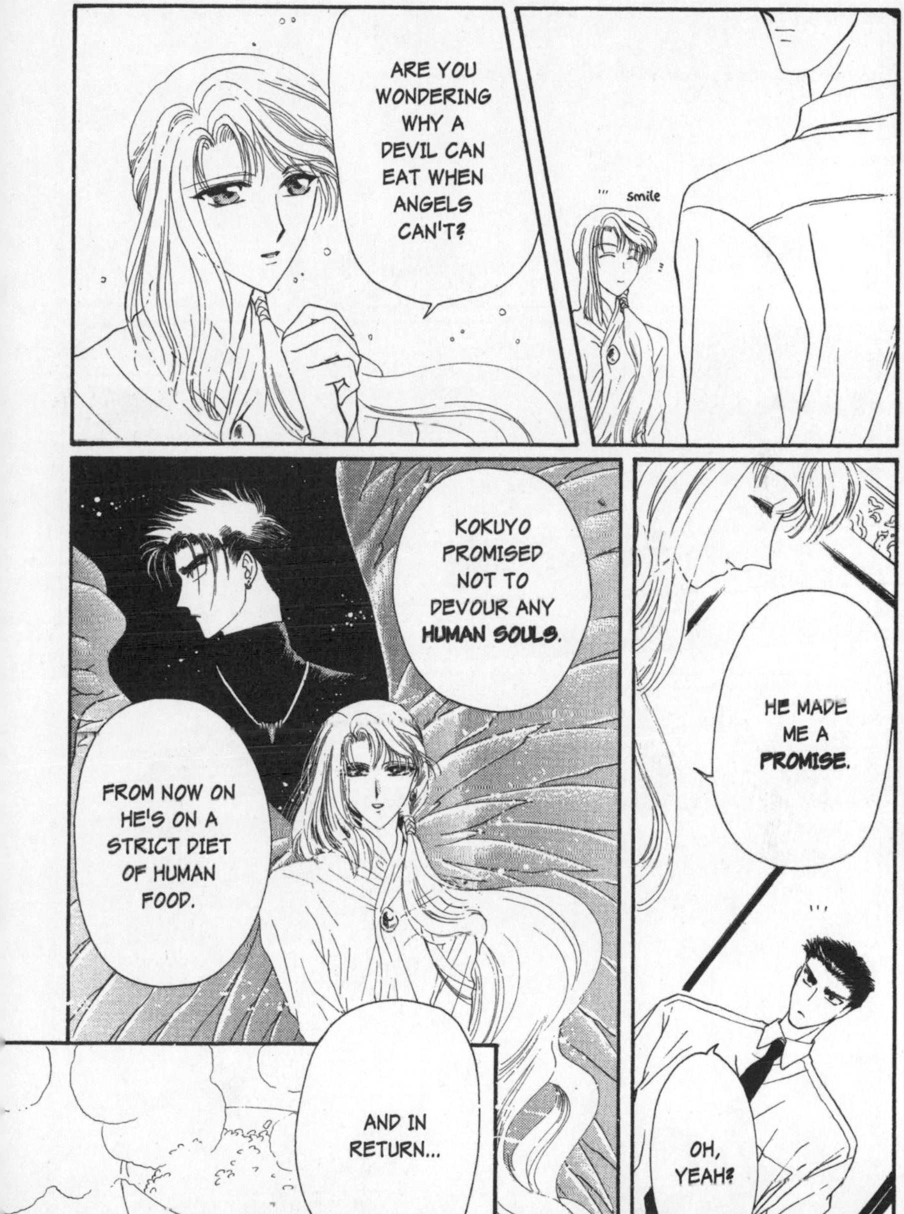

smile
ARE YOU WONDERING WHY A DEVIL CAN EAT WHEN ANGELS CAN'T?
HE MADE ME A PROMISE.
OH, YEAH?
KOKUYO PROMISED NOT TO DEVOUR ANY HUMAN SOULS.
FROM NOW ON HE'S ON A STRICT DIET OF HUMAN FOOD.
AND IN RETURN...

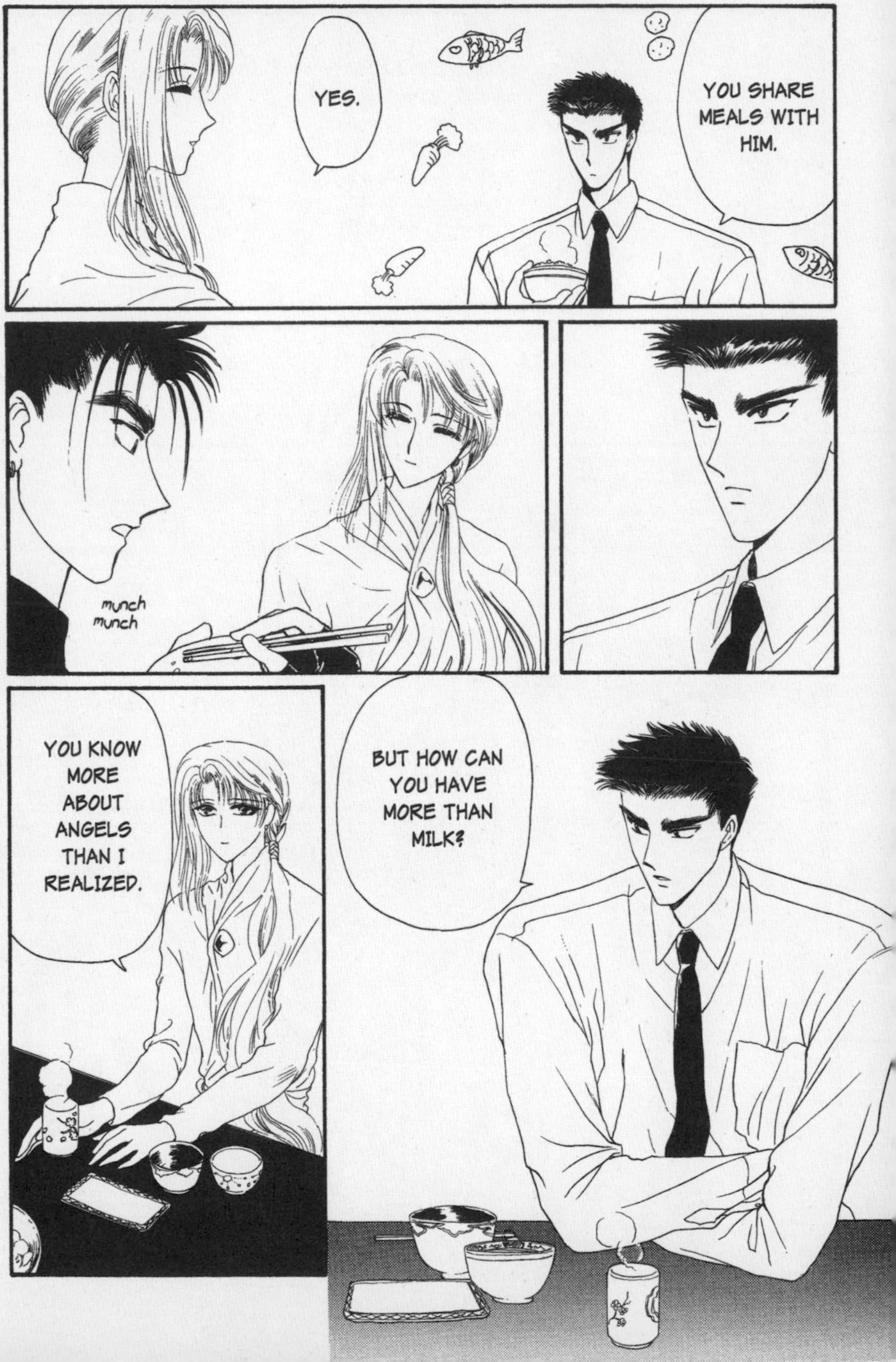
YOU SHARE MEALS WITH HIM.
YES.
munch munch
BUT HOW CAN YOU HAVE MORE THAN MILK?
YOU KNOW MORE ABOUT ANGELS THAN I REALIZED.

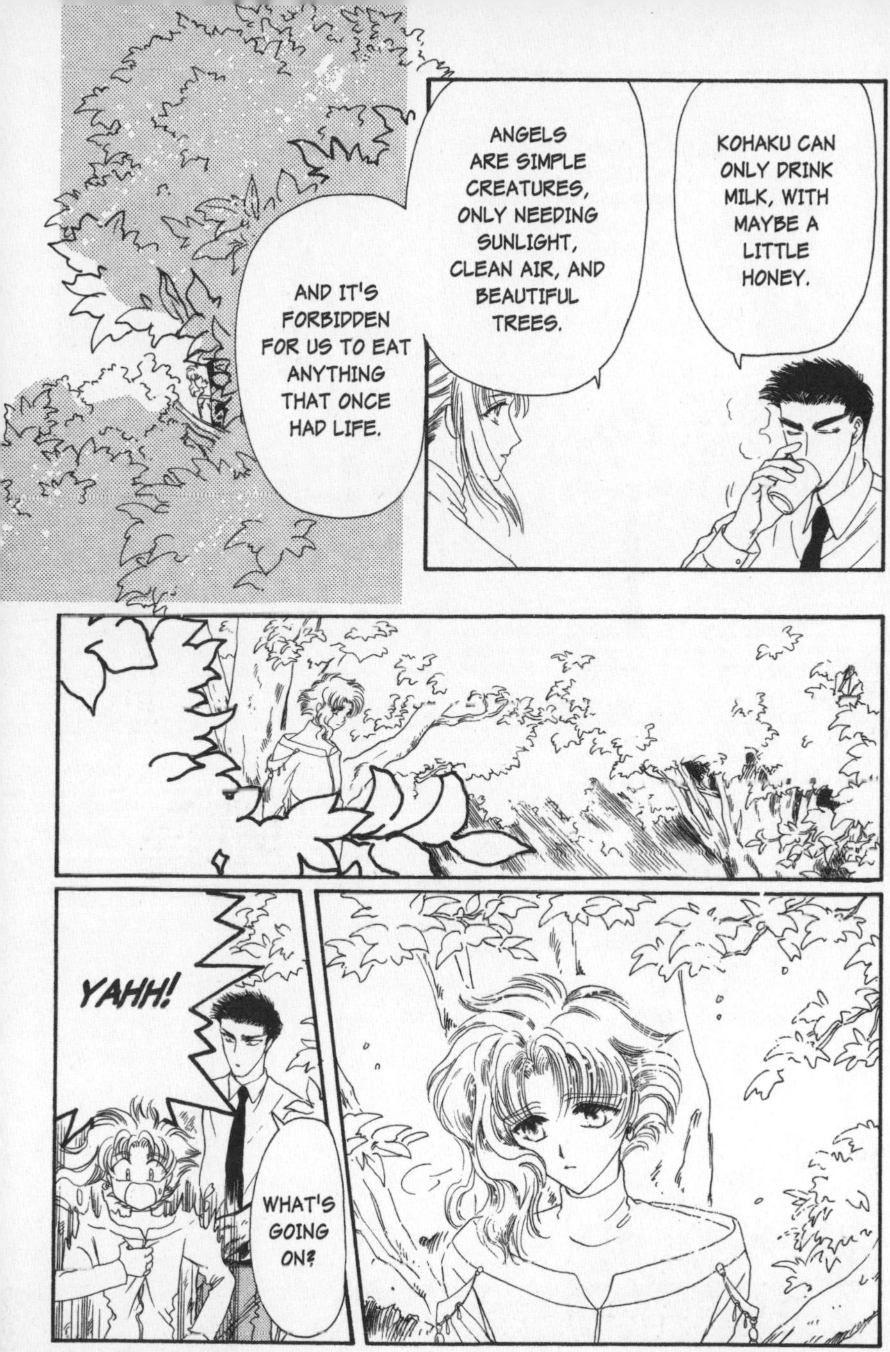
KOHAKU CAN ONLY DRINK MILK, WITH MAYBE A LITTLE HONEY.
ANGELS ARE SIMPLE CREATURES, ONLY NEEDING SUNLIGHT, CLEAN AIR, AND BEAUTIFUL TREES.
AND IT'S FORBIDDEN FOR US TO EAT ANYTHING THAT ONCE HAD LIFE.
YAHH!
WHAT'S GOING ON?

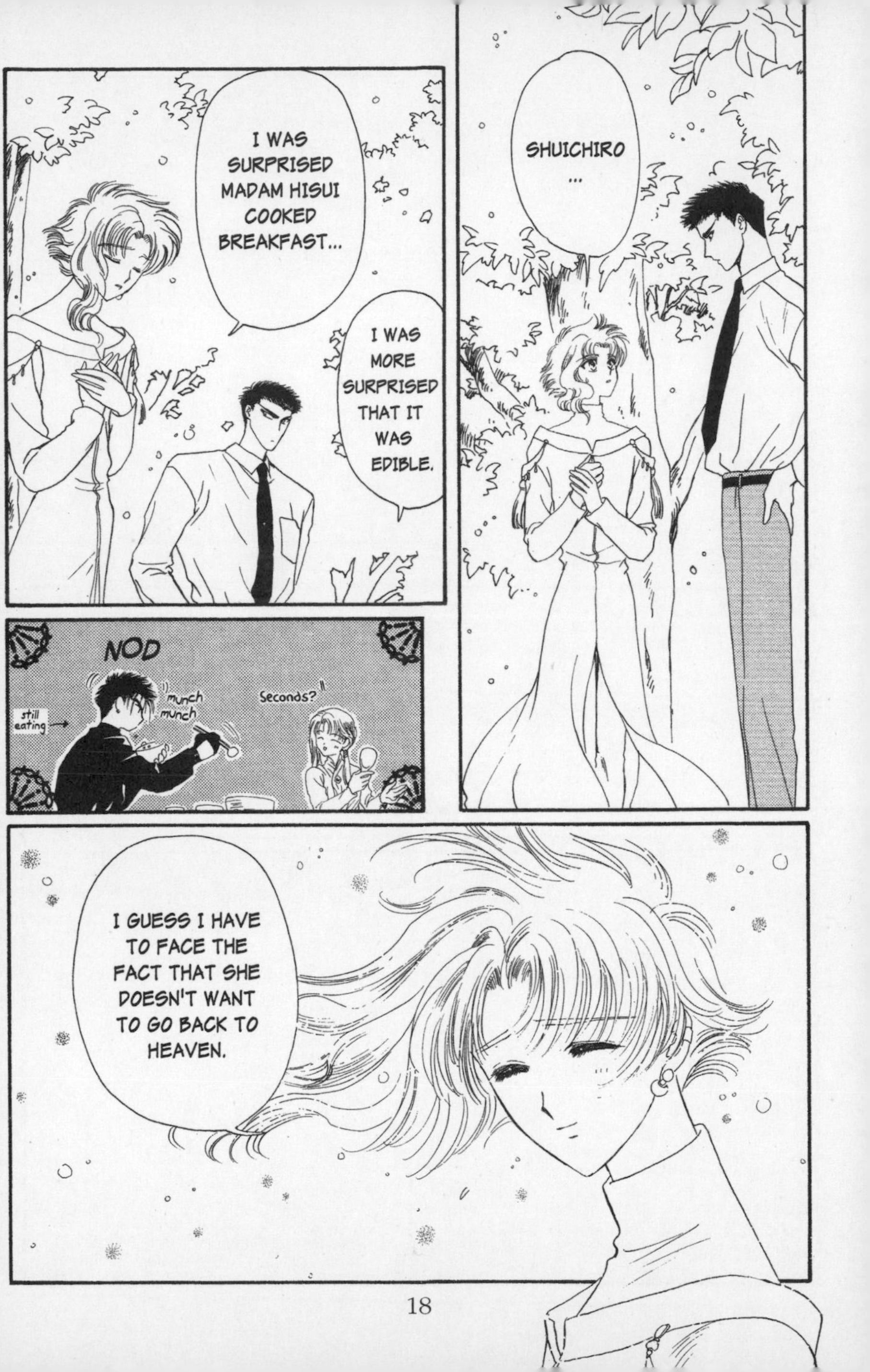
SHUICHIRO ...
I WAS SURPRISED MADAM HISUI COOKED BREAKFAST...
I WAS MORE SURPRISED THAT IT WAS EDIBLE.
Seconds?
NOD
munch munch
still eating
I GUESS I HAVE TO FACE THE FACT THAT SHE DOESN'T WANT TO GO BACK TO HEAVEN.

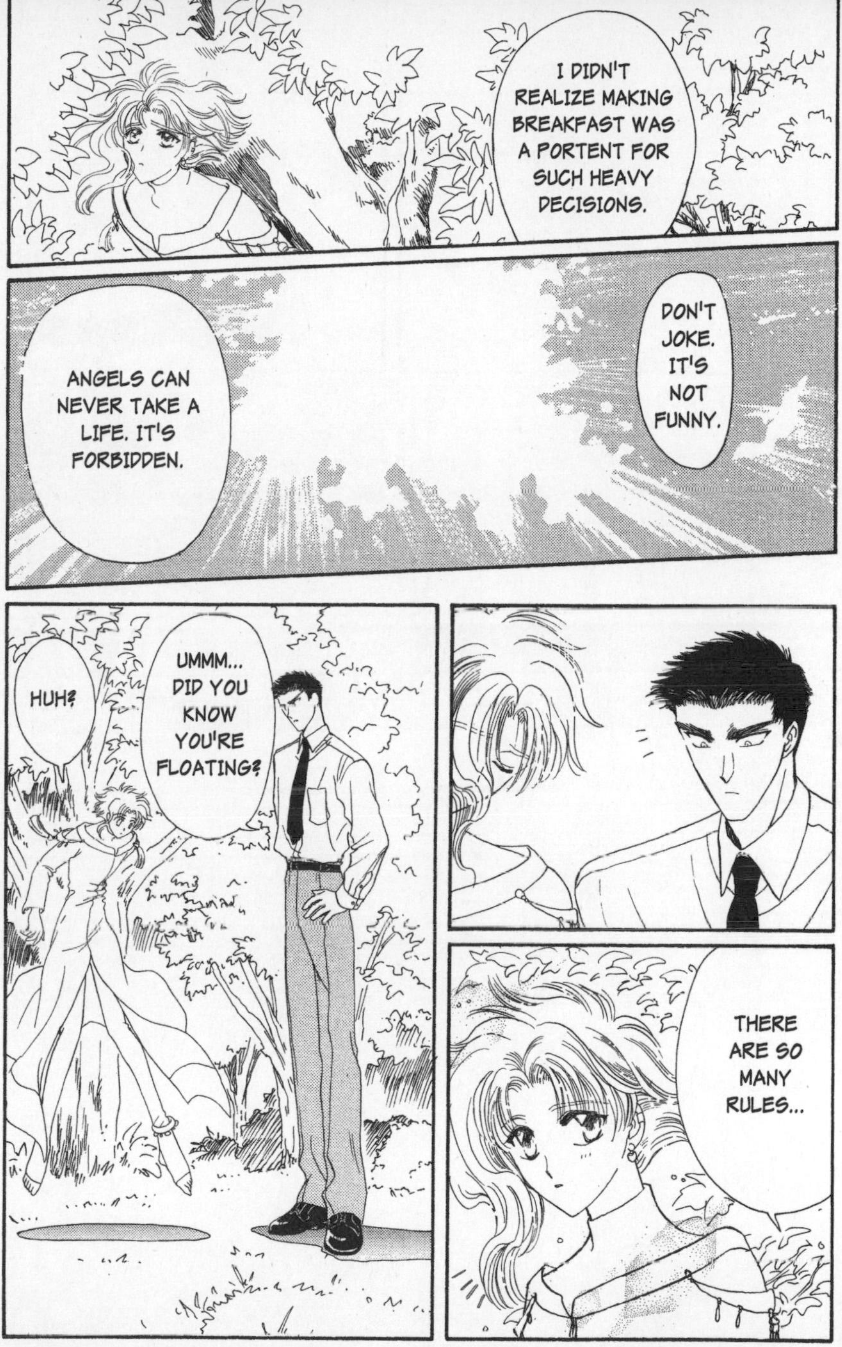
I DIDN'T REALIZE MAKING BREAKFAST WAS A PORTENT FOR SUCH HEAVY DECISIONS.
DON'T JOKE. IT'S NOT FUNNY.
ANGELS CAN NEVER TAKE A LIFE. IT'S FORBIDDEN.
THERE ARE SO MANY RULES...
UMMM... DID YOU KNOW YOU'RE FLOATING?
HUH?

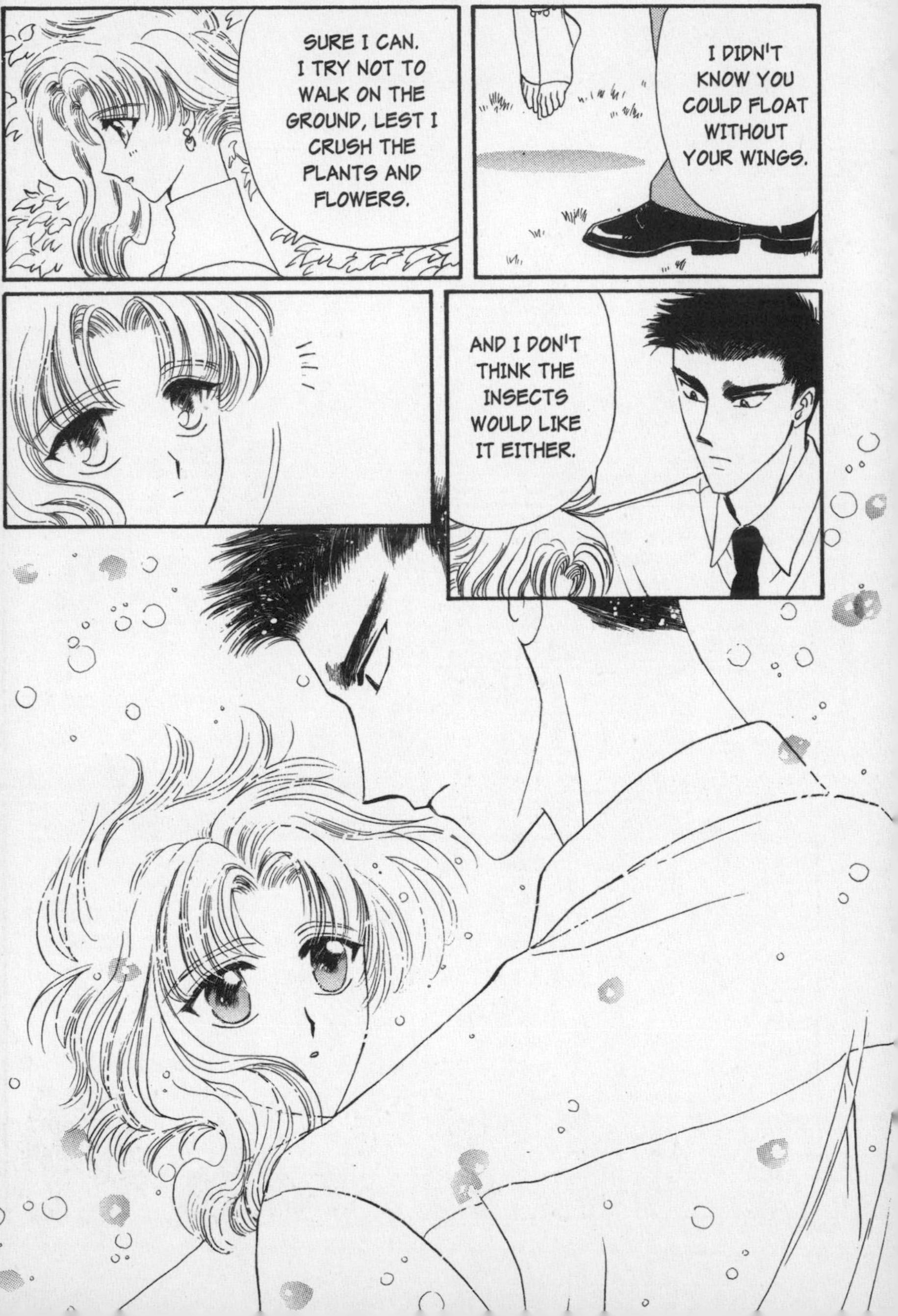
I DIDN'T KNOW YOU COULD FLOAT WITHOUT YOUR WINGS.
SURE I CAN. I TRY NOT TO WALK ON THE GROUND, LEST I CRUSH THE PLANTS AND FLOWERS.
AND I DON'T THINK THE INSECTS WOULD LIKE IT EITHER.

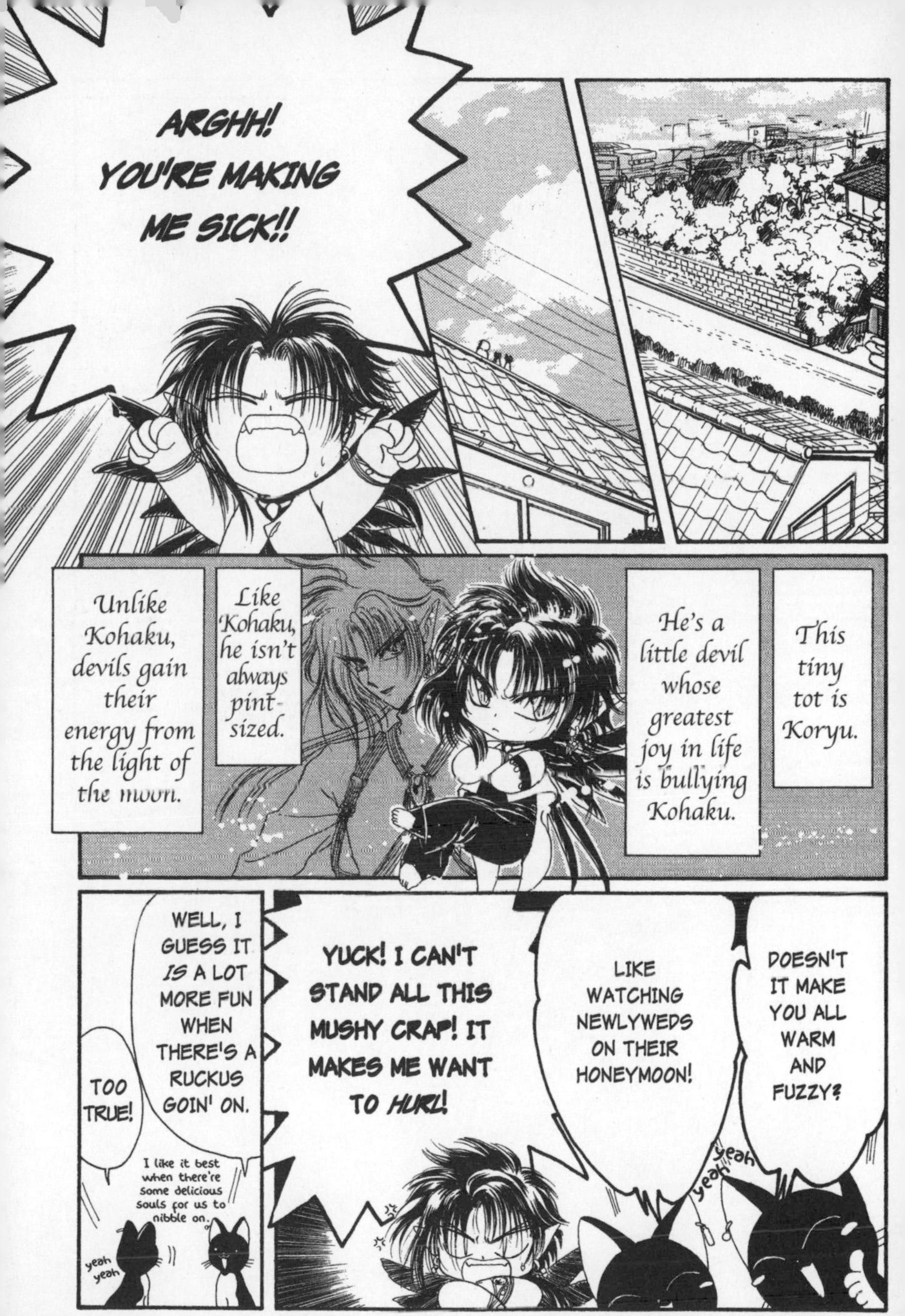
ARGHH! YOU'RE MAKING ME SICK!!
This tiny tot is Koryu.
He's a little devil whose greatest joy in life is bullying Kohaku.
Like Kohaku, he isn't always pint-sized.
Unlike Kohaku, devils gain their energy from the light of the moon.
DOESN'T IT MAKE YOU ALL WARM AND FUZZY?
LIKE WATCHING NEWLYWEDS ON THEIR HONEYMOON!
yeah yeah
YUCK! I CAN'T STAND ALL THIS MUSHY CRAP! IT MAKES ME WANT TO *HURL*!
WELL, I GUESS IT *IS* A LOT MORE FUN WHEN THERE'S A RUCKUS GOIN' ON.
TOO TRUE!
I like it best when there're some delicious souls for us to nibble on.
yeah yeah

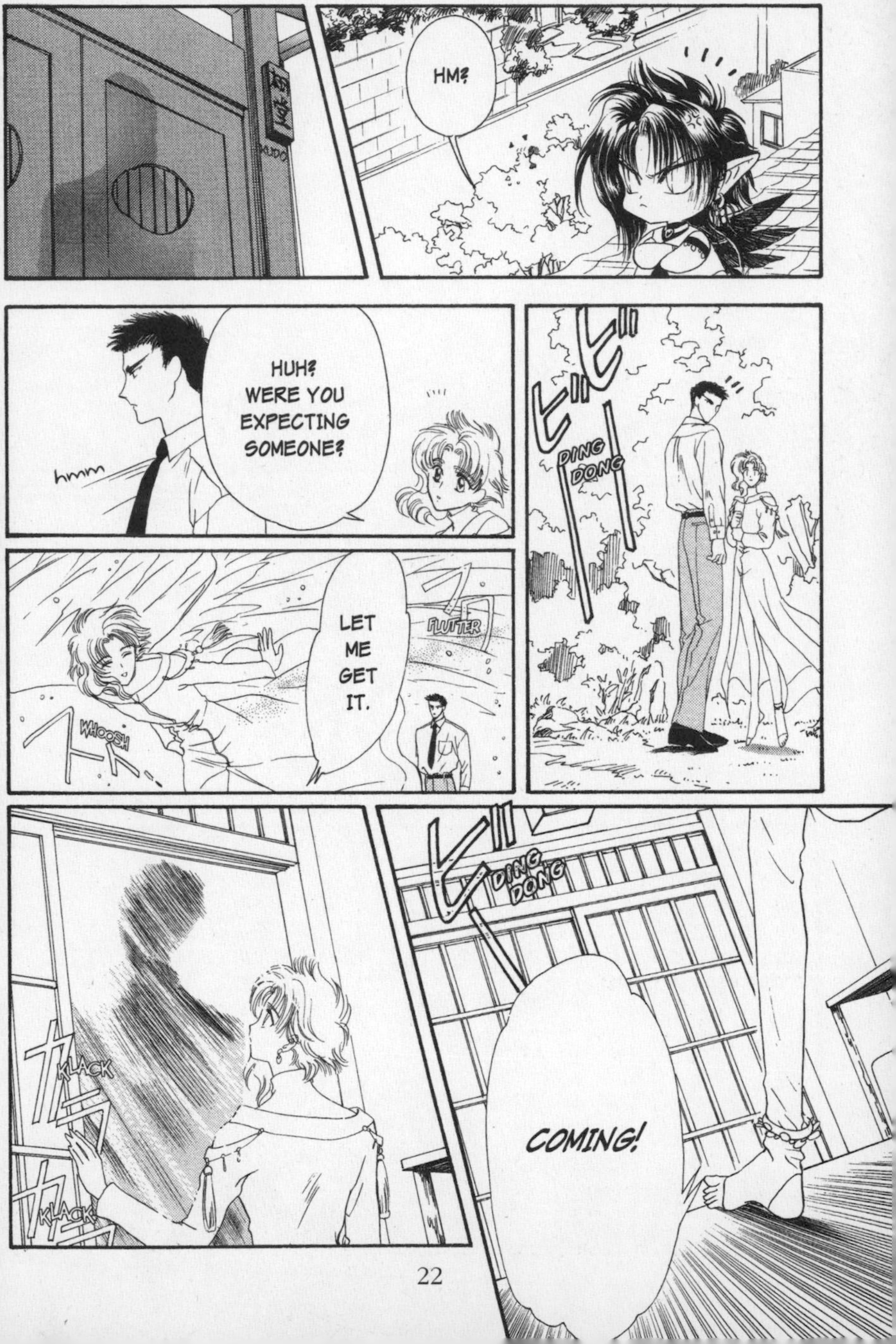
HM?
KUDO
DING DONG
HUH? WERE YOU EXPECTING SOMEONE?
hmm
LET ME GET IT.
FLUTTER
WHOOSH
DING DONG
COMING!
KLACK
KLACK

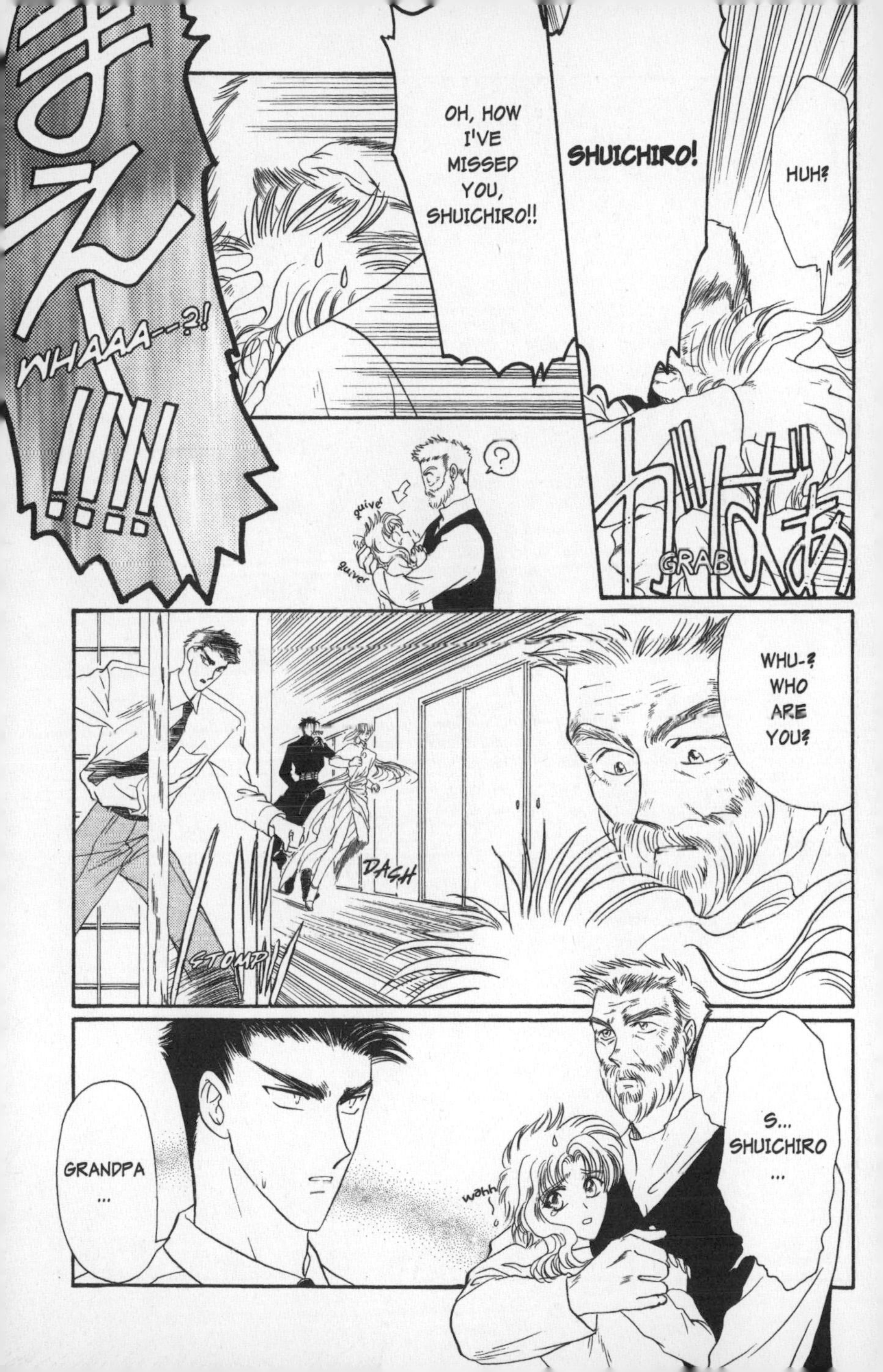
HUH?
SHUICHIRO!
GRAB
OH, HOW I'VE MISSED YOU, SHUICHIRO!!
WHAAA--?!
!!!!!
?
quiver
quiver
WHU-? WHO ARE YOU?
DASH
STOMP
S... SHUICHIRO ...
wahh
GRANDPA ...

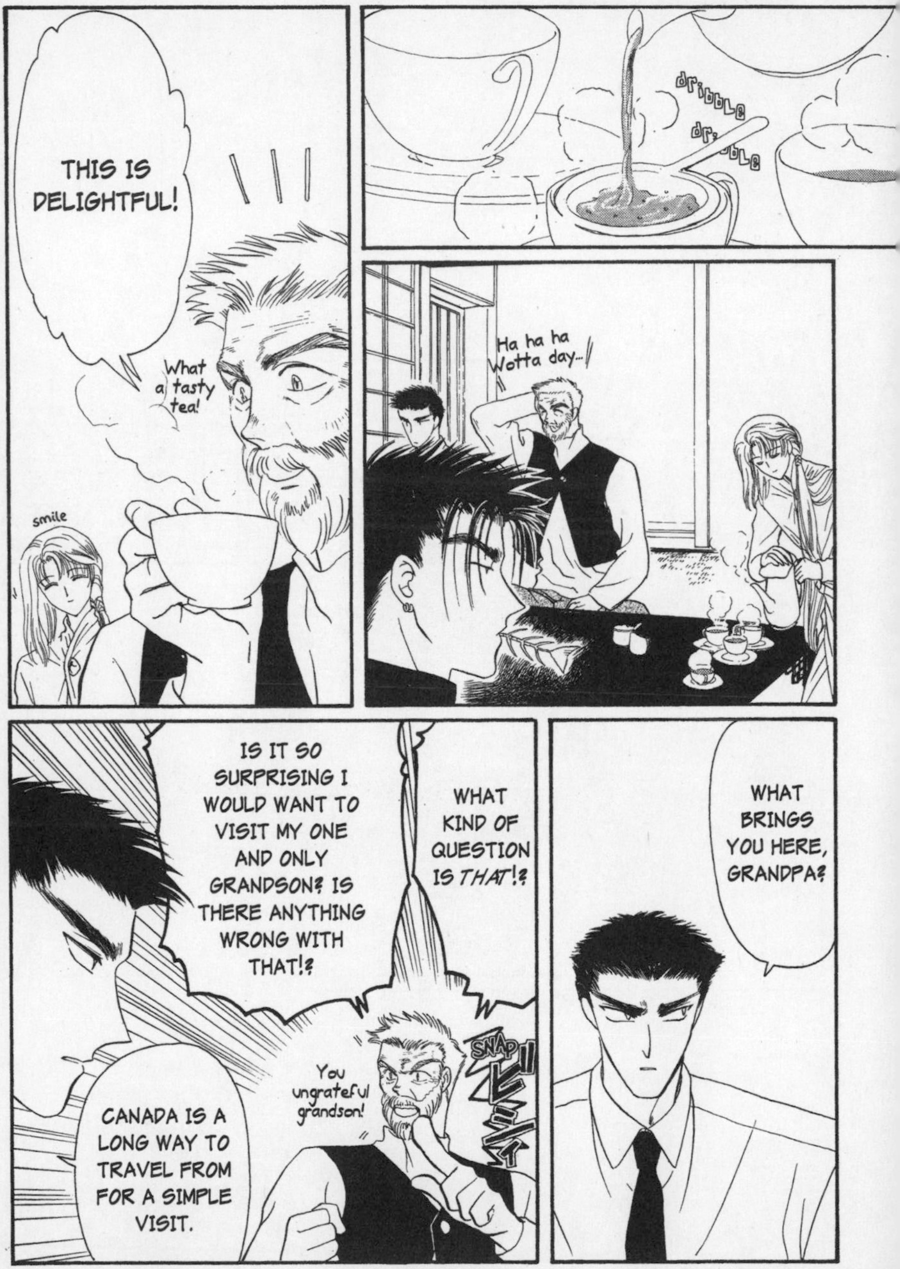
dribble
Ha ha ha Wotta day...
THIS IS DELIGHTFUL!
What a tasty tea!
smile
WHAT BRINGS YOU HERE, GRANDPA?
WHAT KIND OF QUESTION IS *THAT*!?
IS IT SO SURPRISING I WOULD WANT TO VISIT MY ONE AND ONLY GRANDSON? IS THERE ANYTHING WRONG WITH THAT!?
SNAP
You ungrateful grandson!
CANADA IS A LONG WAY TO TRAVEL FROM FOR A SIMPLE VISIT.

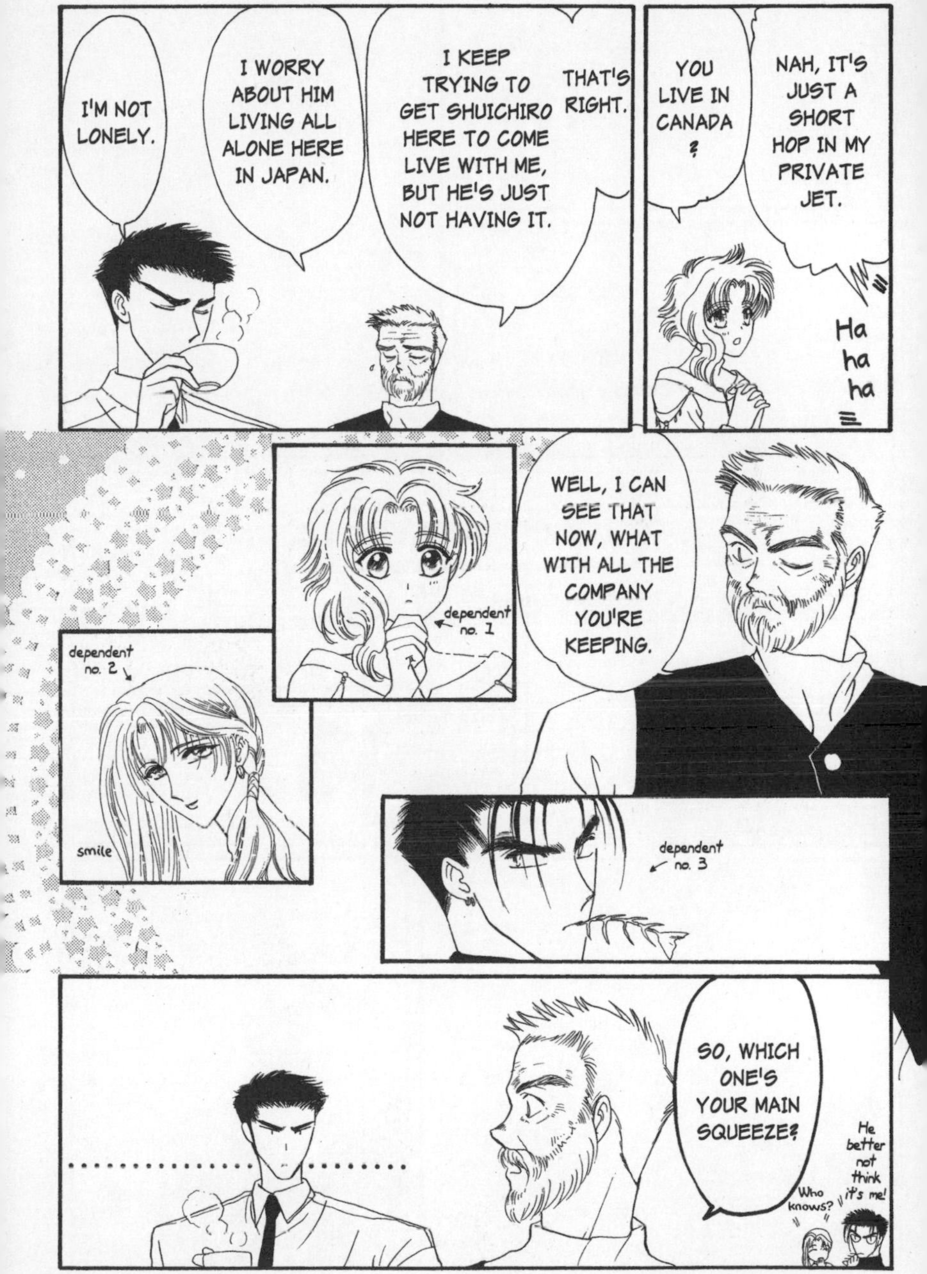
YOU LIVE IN CANADA?
NAH, IT'S JUST A SHORT HOP IN MY PRIVATE JET.
Ha ha ha
THAT'S RIGHT.
I KEEP TRYING TO GET SHUICHIRO HERE TO COME LIVE WITH ME, BUT HE'S JUST NOT HAVING IT.
I WORRY ABOUT HIM LIVING ALL ALONE HERE IN JAPAN.
I'M NOT LONELY.
WELL, I CAN SEE THAT NOW, WHAT WITH ALL THE COMPANY YOU'RE KEEPING.
dependent no. 1
dependent no. 2
smile
dependent no. 3
SO, WHICH ONE'S YOUR MAIN SQUEEZE?
He better not think it's me!
Who knows?
....

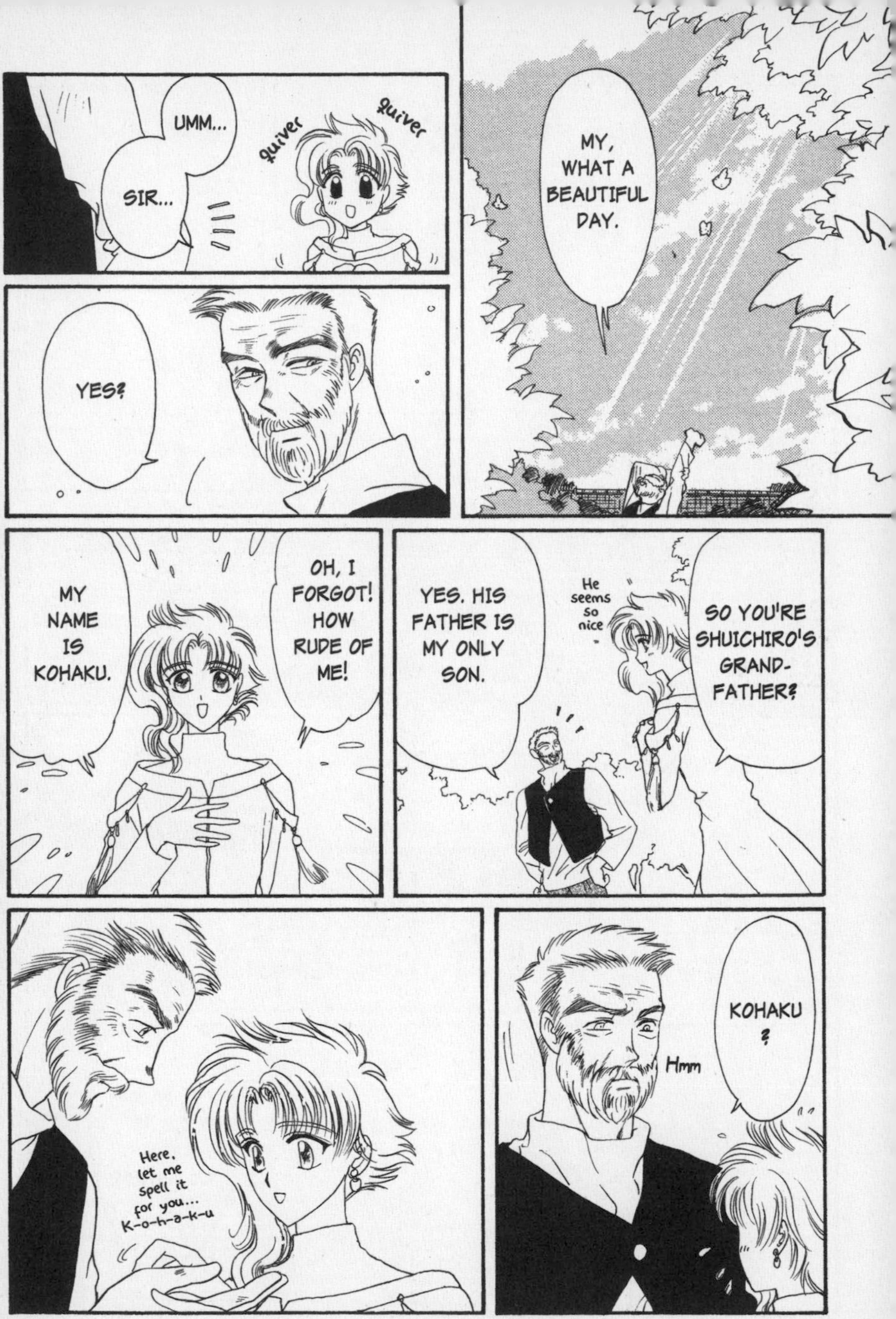
MY, WHAT A BEAUTIFUL DAY.
UMM...
SIR...
quiver
quiver
YES?
SO YOU'RE SHUICHIRO'S GRAND-FATHER?
He seems so nice
YES. HIS FATHER IS MY ONLY SON.
OH, I FORGOT! HOW RUDE OF ME!
MY NAME IS KOHAKU.
KOHAKU?
Hmm
Here, let me spell it for you... K-o-h-a-k-u

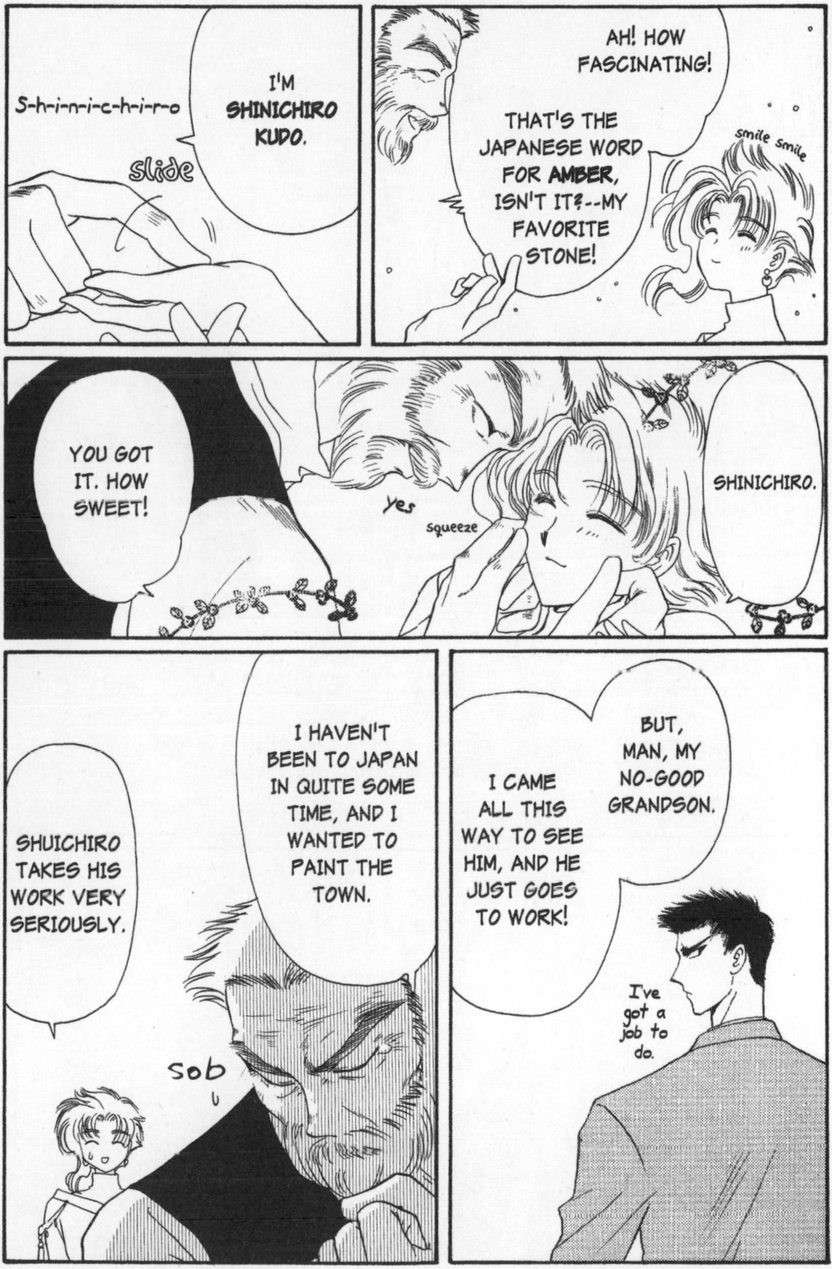

AH! HOW FASCINATING!
THAT'S THE JAPANESE WORD FOR AMBER, ISN'T IT?--MY FAVORITE STONE!
smile smile
I'M SHINICHIRO KUDO.
S-h-i-n-i-c-h-i-r-o
slide
SHINICHIRO.
yes
squeeze
YOU GOT IT. HOW SWEET!
BUT, MAN, MY NO-GOOD GRANDSON.
I CAME ALL THIS WAY TO SEE HIM, AND HE JUST GOES TO WORK!
I've got a job to do.
I HAVEN'T BEEN TO JAPAN IN QUITE SOME TIME, AND I WANTED TO PAINT THE TOWN.
SHUICHIRO TAKES HIS WORK VERY SERIOUSLY.
sob

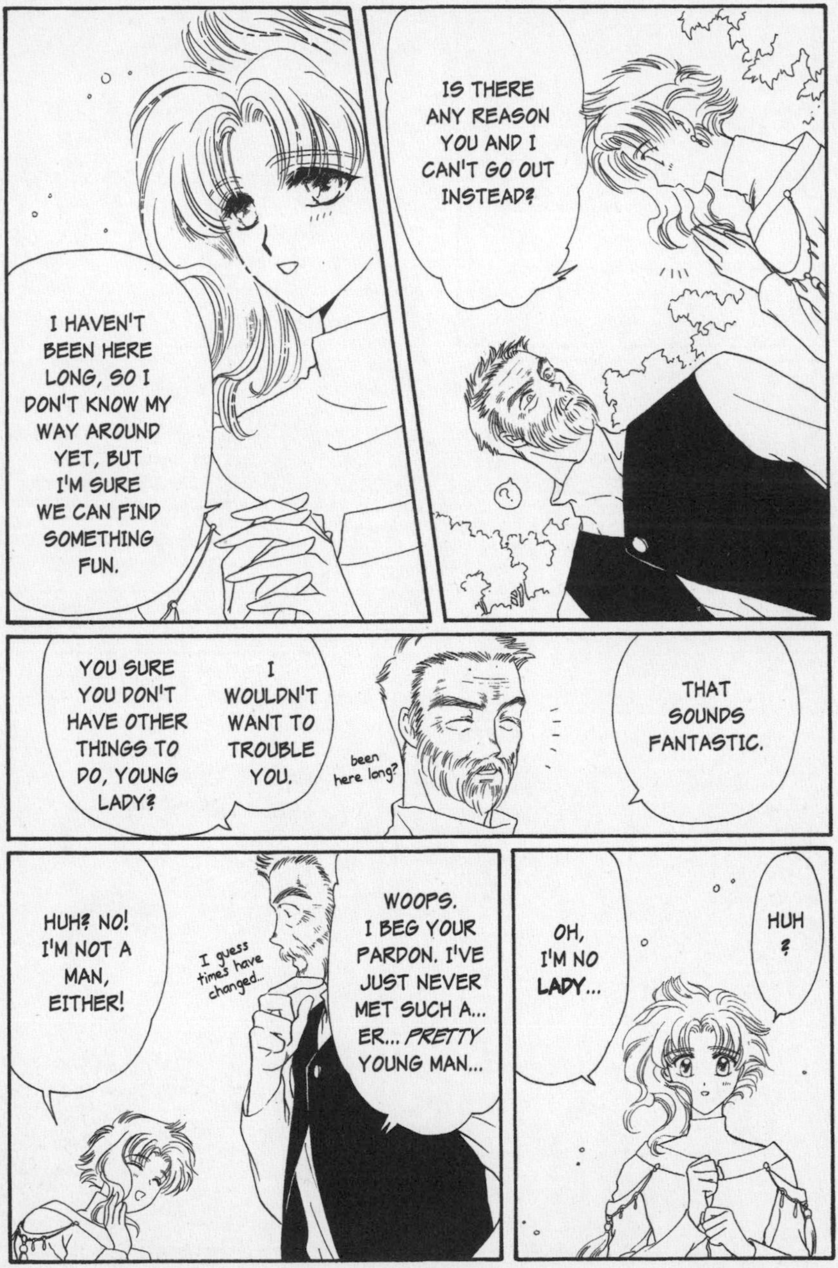
IS THERE ANY REASON YOU AND I CAN'T GO OUT INSTEAD?
?
I HAVEN'T BEEN HERE LONG, SO I DON'T KNOW MY WAY AROUND YET, BUT I'M SURE WE CAN FIND SOMETHING FUN.
THAT SOUNDS FANTASTIC.
been here long?
I WOULDN'T WANT TO TROUBLE YOU.
YOU SURE YOU DON'T HAVE OTHER THINGS TO DO, YOUNG LADY?
HUH?
OH, I'M NO **LADY**...
WOOPS. I BEG YOUR PARDON. I'VE JUST NEVER MET SUCH A... ER... *PRETTY* YOUNG MAN...
I guess times have changed...
HUH? NO! I'M NOT A MAN, EITHER!

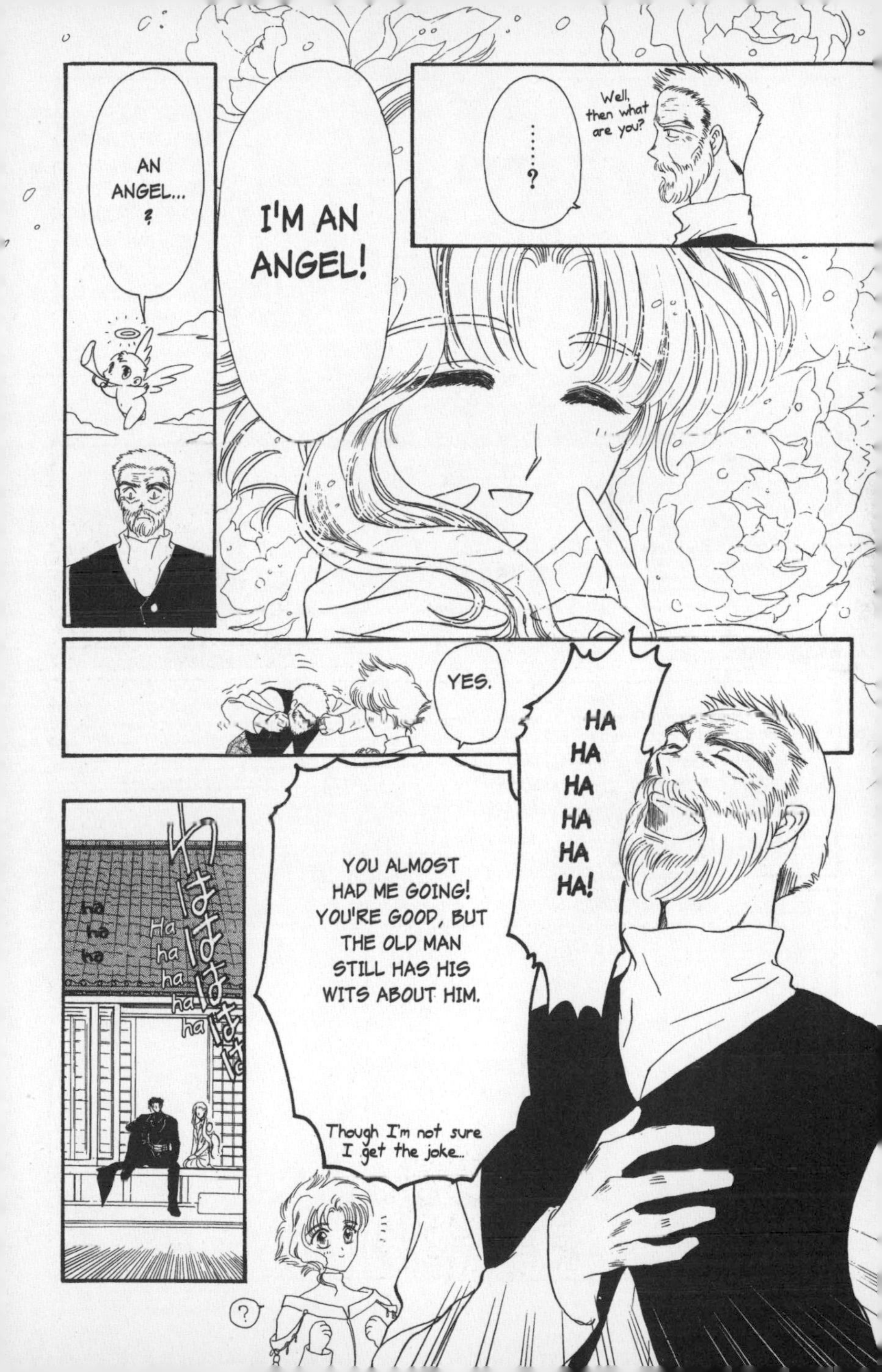
Well, then what are you?
......?
I'M AN ANGEL!
AN ANGEL...?
YES.
HA HA HA HA HA HA!
YOU ALMOST HAD ME GOING! YOU'RE GOOD, BUT THE OLD MAN STILL HAS HIS WITS ABOUT HIM.
Though I'm not sure I get the joke...
?
わははは
Ha ha ha ha ha
ha ha ha

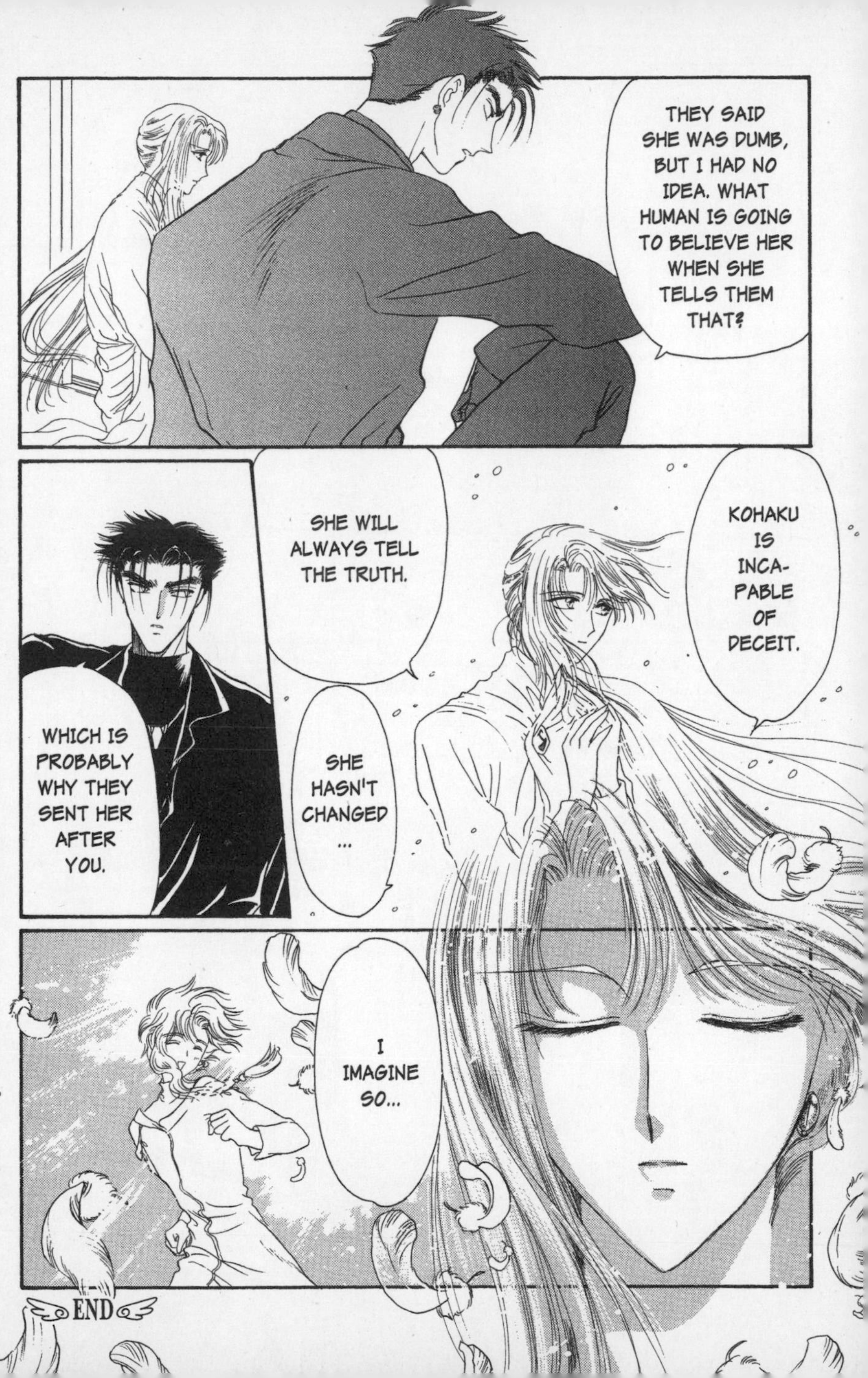
THEY SAID SHE WAS DUMB, BUT I HAD NO IDEA. WHAT HUMAN IS GOING TO BELIEVE HER WHEN SHE TELLS THEM THAT?
KOHAKU IS INCA-PABLE OF DECEIT.
SHE WILL ALWAYS TELL THE TRUTH.
SHE HASN'T CHANGED ...
WHICH IS PROBABLY WHY THEY SENT HER AFTER YOU.
I IMAGINE SO...
END

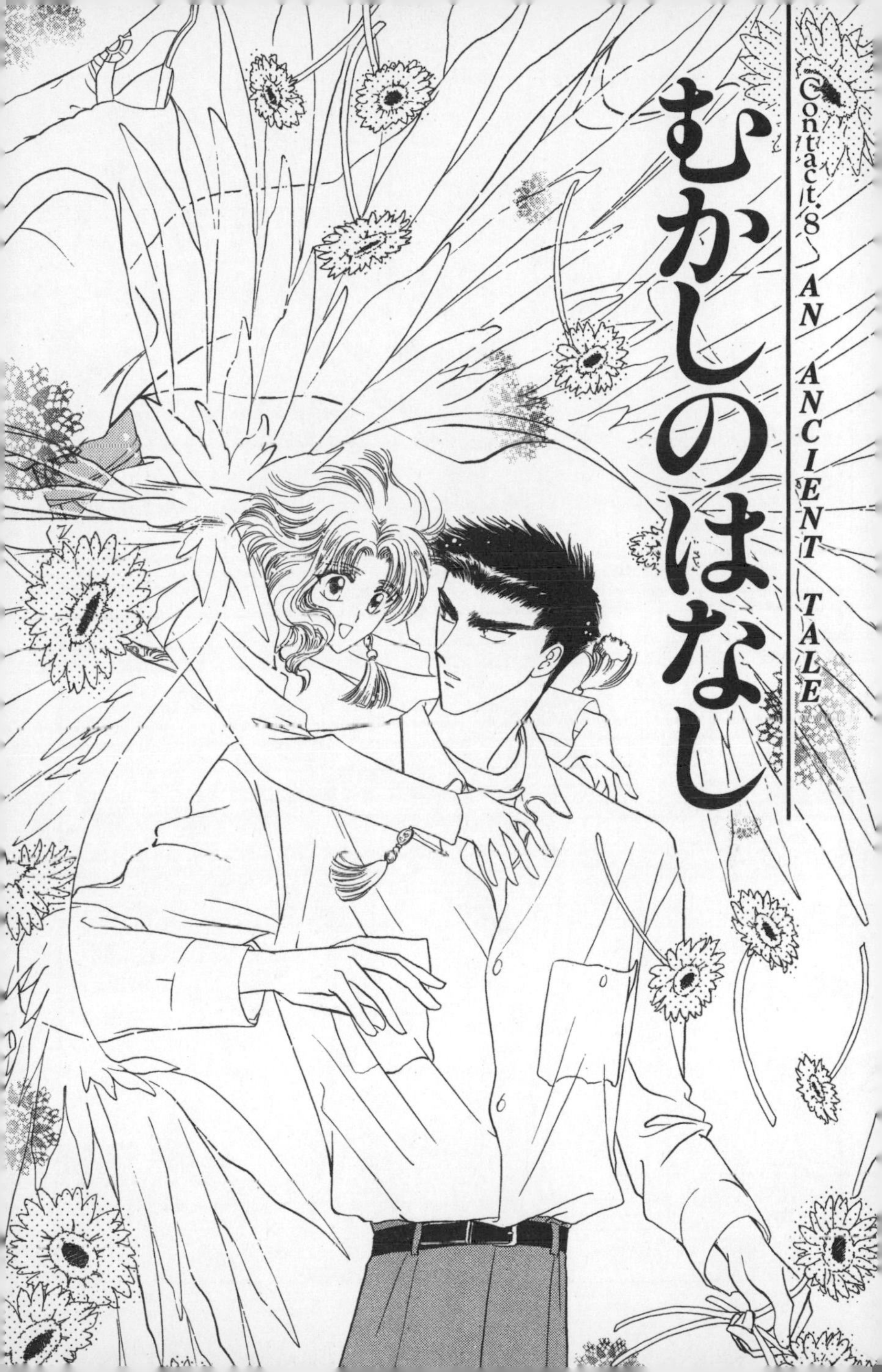
むかしのはなし
Contact.8
AN ANCIENT TALE

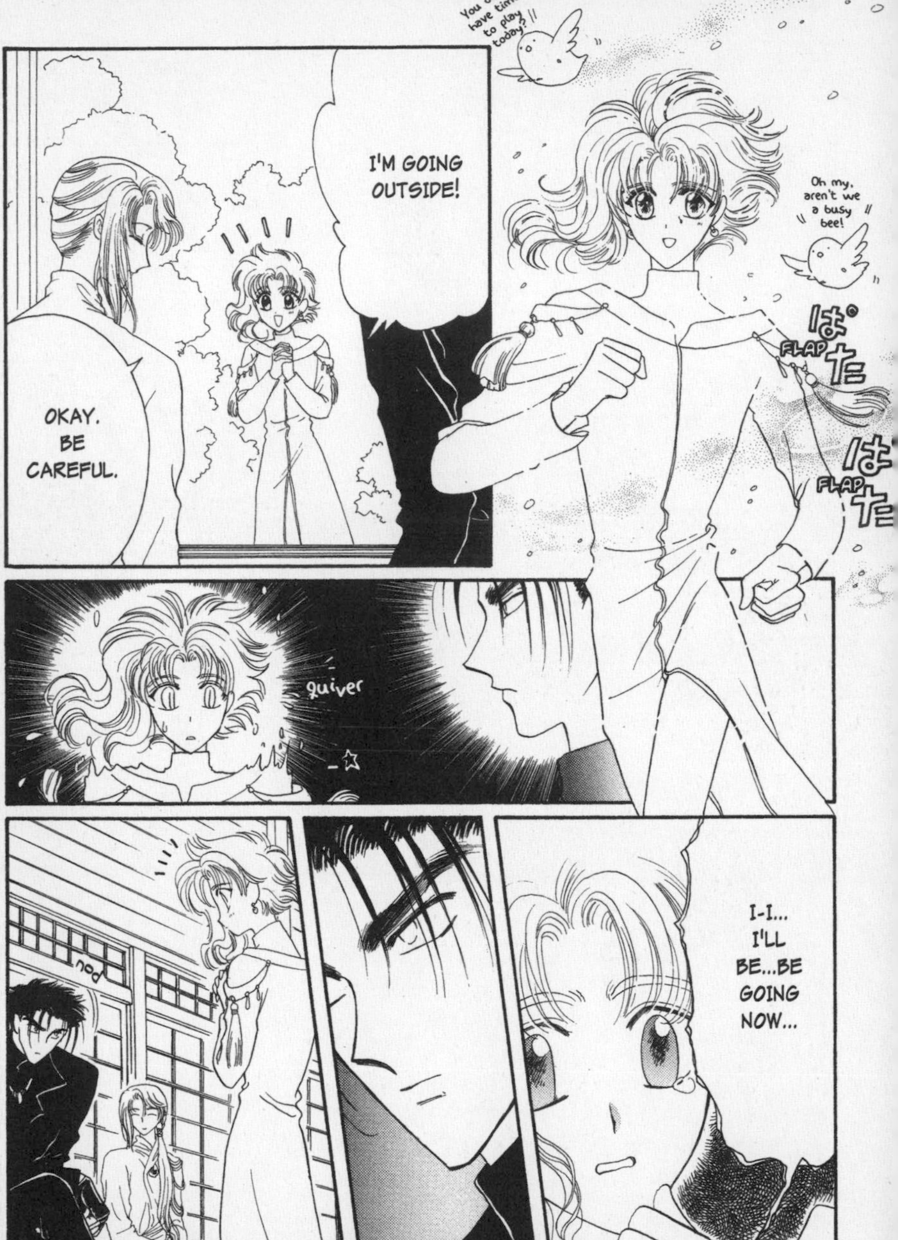

You don't have time to play today?
Oh my, aren't we a busy bee!
ぱた
FLAP
ぱた
FLAP
I'M GOING OUTSIDE!
OKAY. BE CAREFUL.
quiver
I-I... I'LL BE...BE GOING NOW...
nod

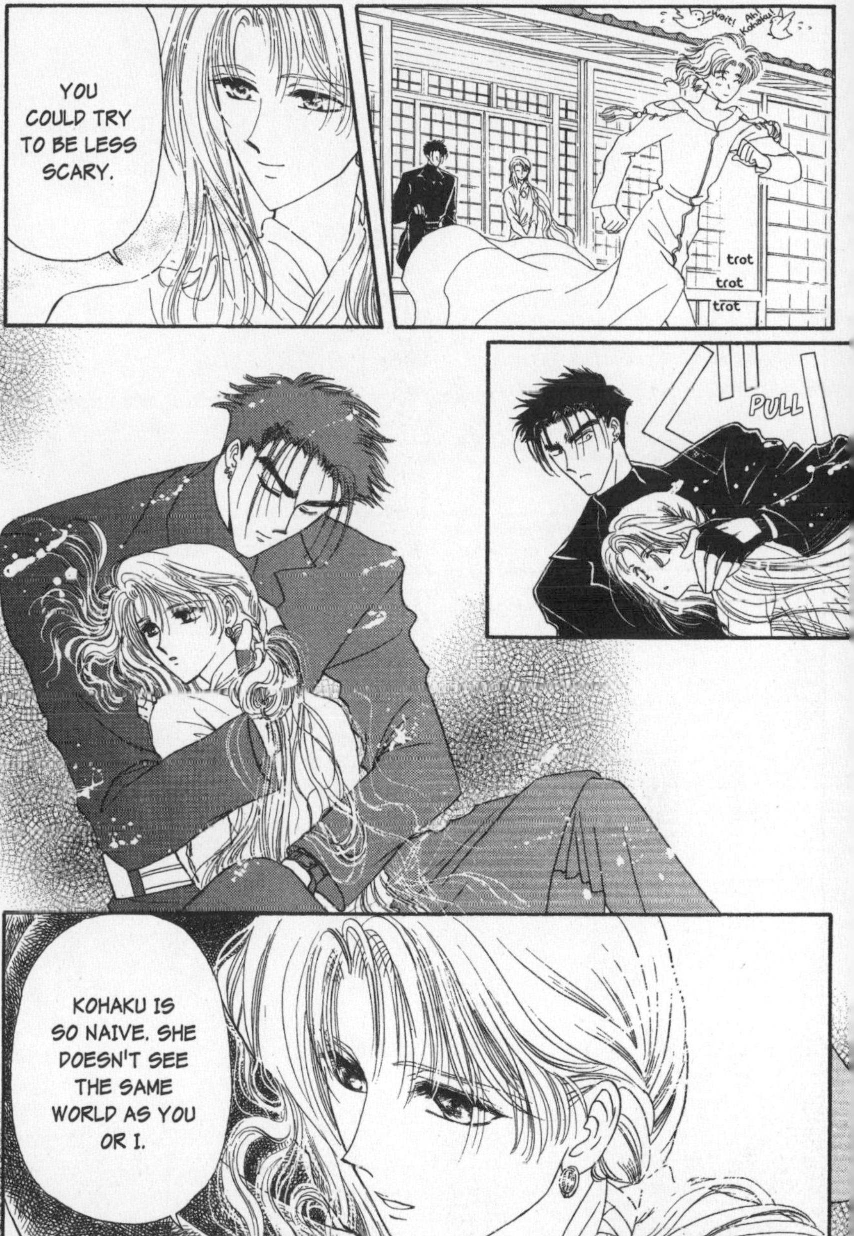
Wait!
Ah! Kohaku!
trot
trot
trot
YOU COULD TRY TO BE LESS SCARY.
PULL
KOHAKU IS SO NAIVE. SHE DOESN'T SEE THE SAME WORLD AS YOU OR I.

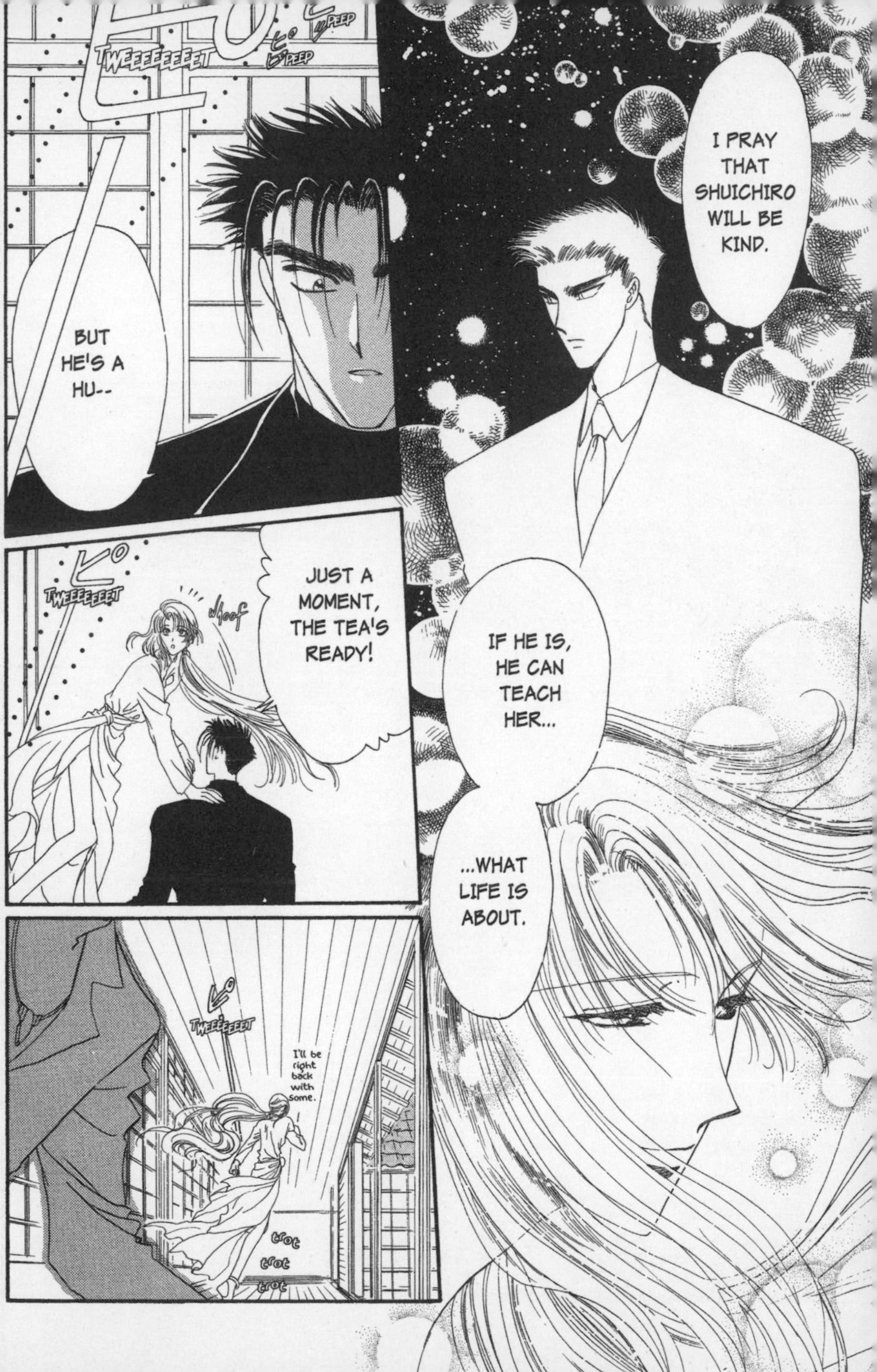

I PRAY THAT SHUICHIRO WILL BE KIND.
IF HE IS, HE CAN TEACH HER...
...WHAT LIFE IS ABOUT.
TWEEEEEEEEET
PEEP
PEEP
BUT HE'S A HU--
TWEEEEEEEET
whoof
JUST A MOMENT, THE TEA'S READY!
TWEEEEEEEET
I'll be right back with some.
trot
trot
trot

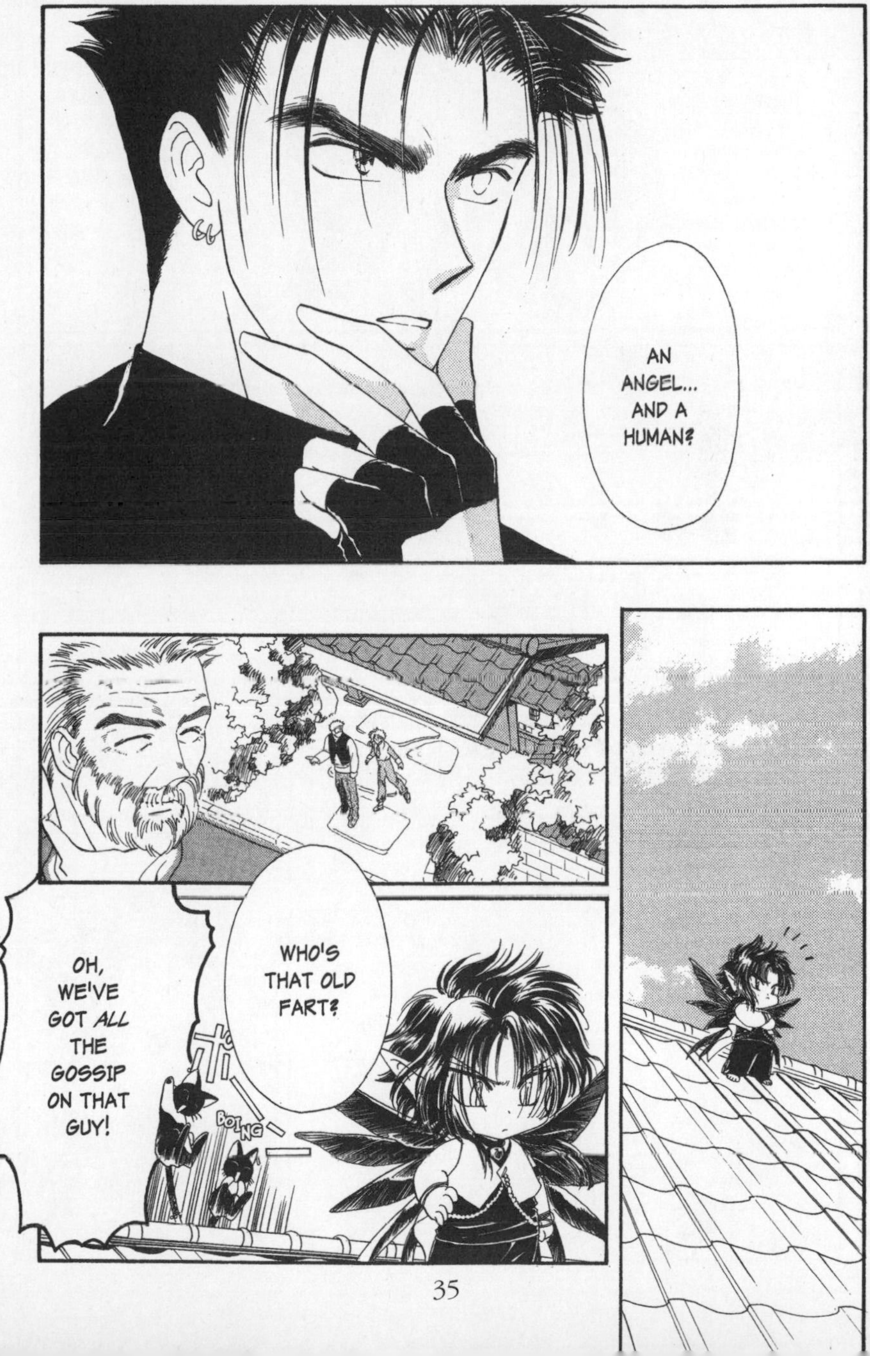
AN ANGEL... AND A HUMAN?
WHO'S THAT OLD FART?
BOING
OH, WE'VE GOT *ALL* THE GOSSIP ON THAT GUY!

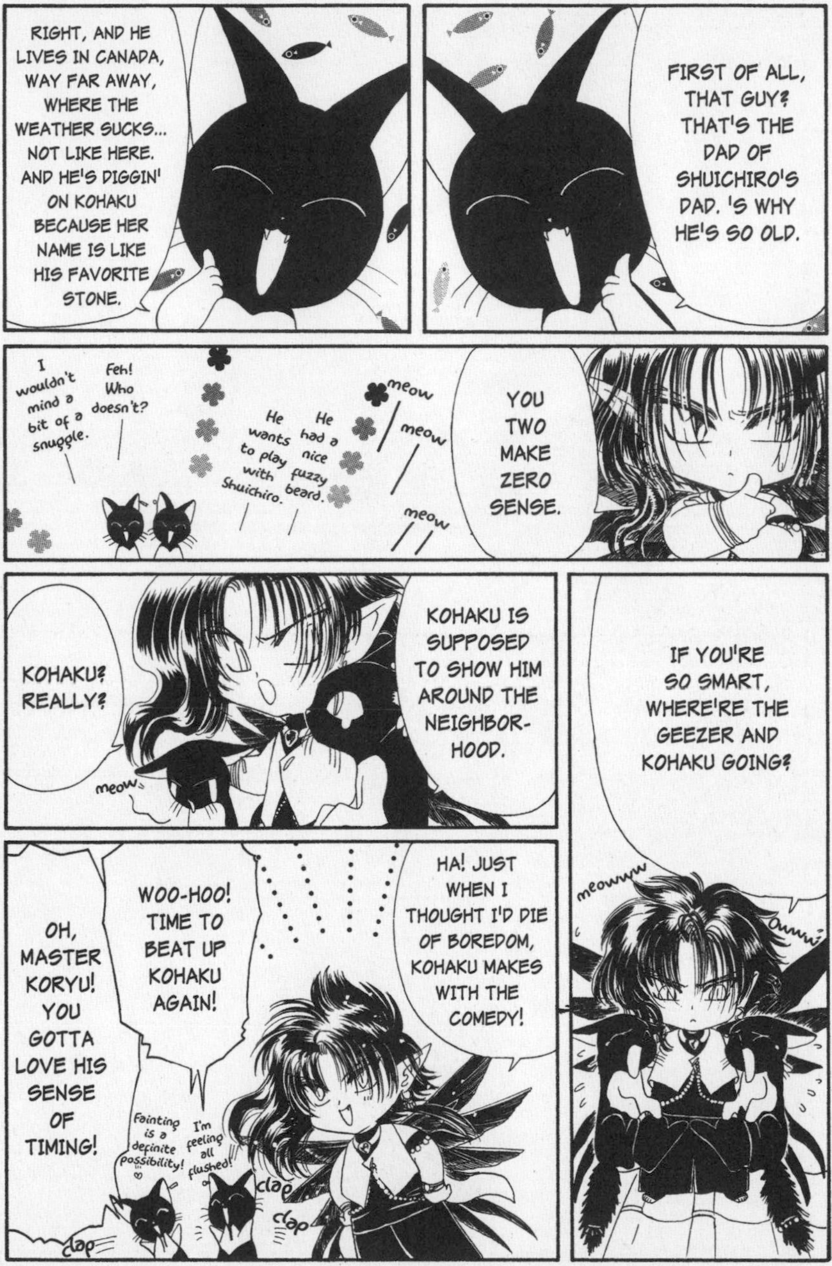
FIRST OF ALL, THAT GUY? THAT'S THE DAD OF SHUICHIRO'S DAD. 'S WHY HE'S SO OLD.
RIGHT, AND HE LIVES IN CANADA, WAY FAR AWAY, WHERE THE WEATHER SUCKS... NOT LIKE HERE. AND HE'S DIGGIN' ON KOHAKU BECAUSE HER NAME IS LIKE HIS FAVORITE STONE.
YOU TWO MAKE ZERO SENSE.
meow
meow
meow
He had a nice fuzzy beard.
He wants to play with Shuichiro.
Feh! Who doesn't?
I wouldn't mind a bit of a snuggle.
IF YOU'RE SO SMART, WHERE'RE THE GEEZER AND KOHAKU GOING?
KOHAKU IS SUPPOSED TO SHOW HIM AROUND THE NEIGHBOR-HOOD.
KOHAKU? REALLY?
meow
meowww
HA! JUST WHEN I THOUGHT I'D DIE OF BOREDOM, KOHAKU MAKES WITH THE COMEDY!
WOO-HOO! TIME TO BEAT UP KOHAKU AGAIN!
OH, MASTER KORYU! YOU GOTTA LOVE HIS SENSE OF TIMING!
I'm feeling all flushed!
Fainting is a definite possibility!
clap
clap
clap

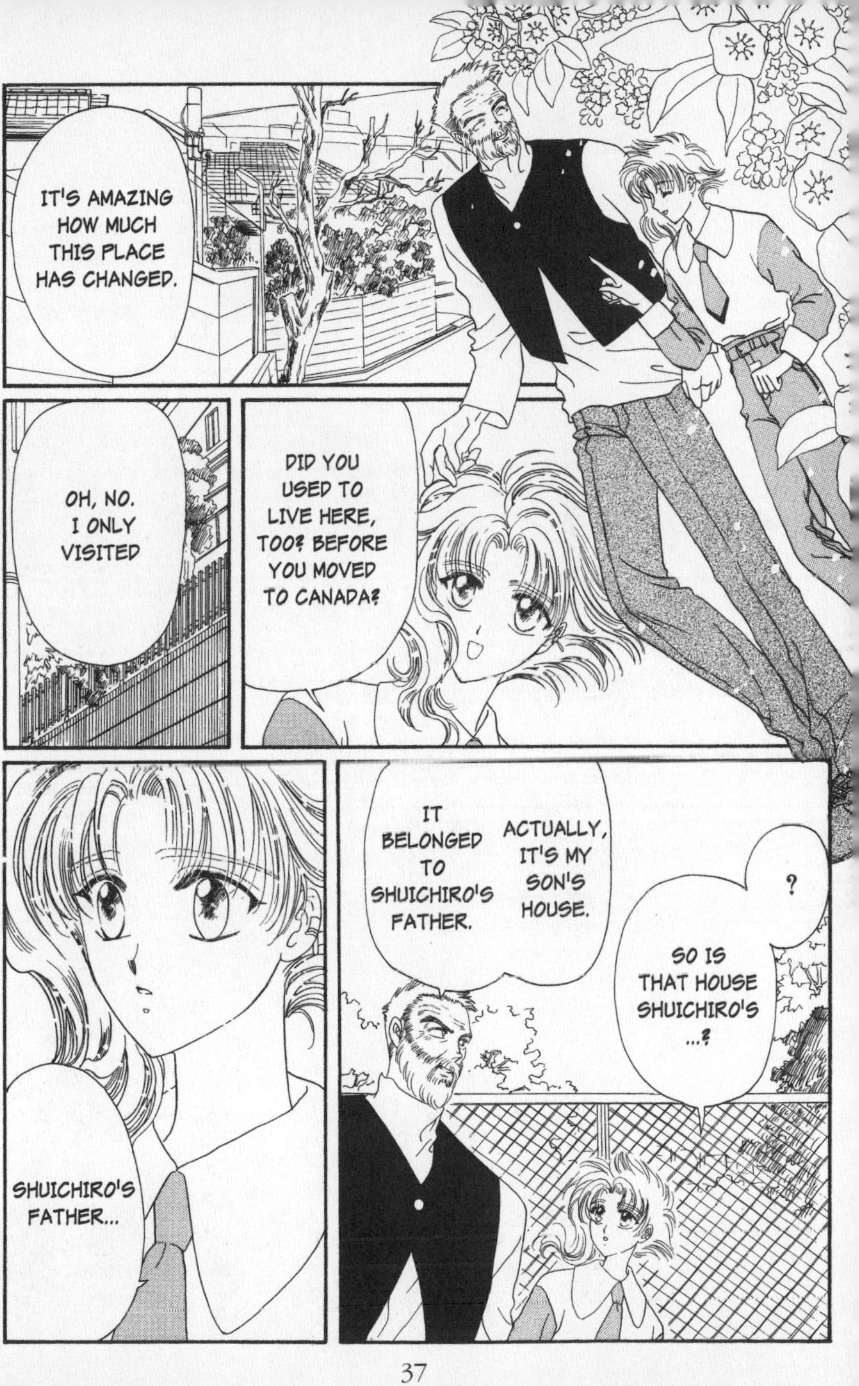
IT'S AMAZING HOW MUCH THIS PLACE HAS CHANGED.
DID YOU USED TO LIVE HERE, TOO? BEFORE YOU MOVED TO CANADA?
OH, NO. I ONLY VISITED
ACTUALLY, IT'S MY SON'S HOUSE.
IT BELONGED TO SHUICHIRO'S FATHER.
?
SO IS THAT HOUSE SHUICHIRO'S ...?
SHUICHIRO'S FATHER...

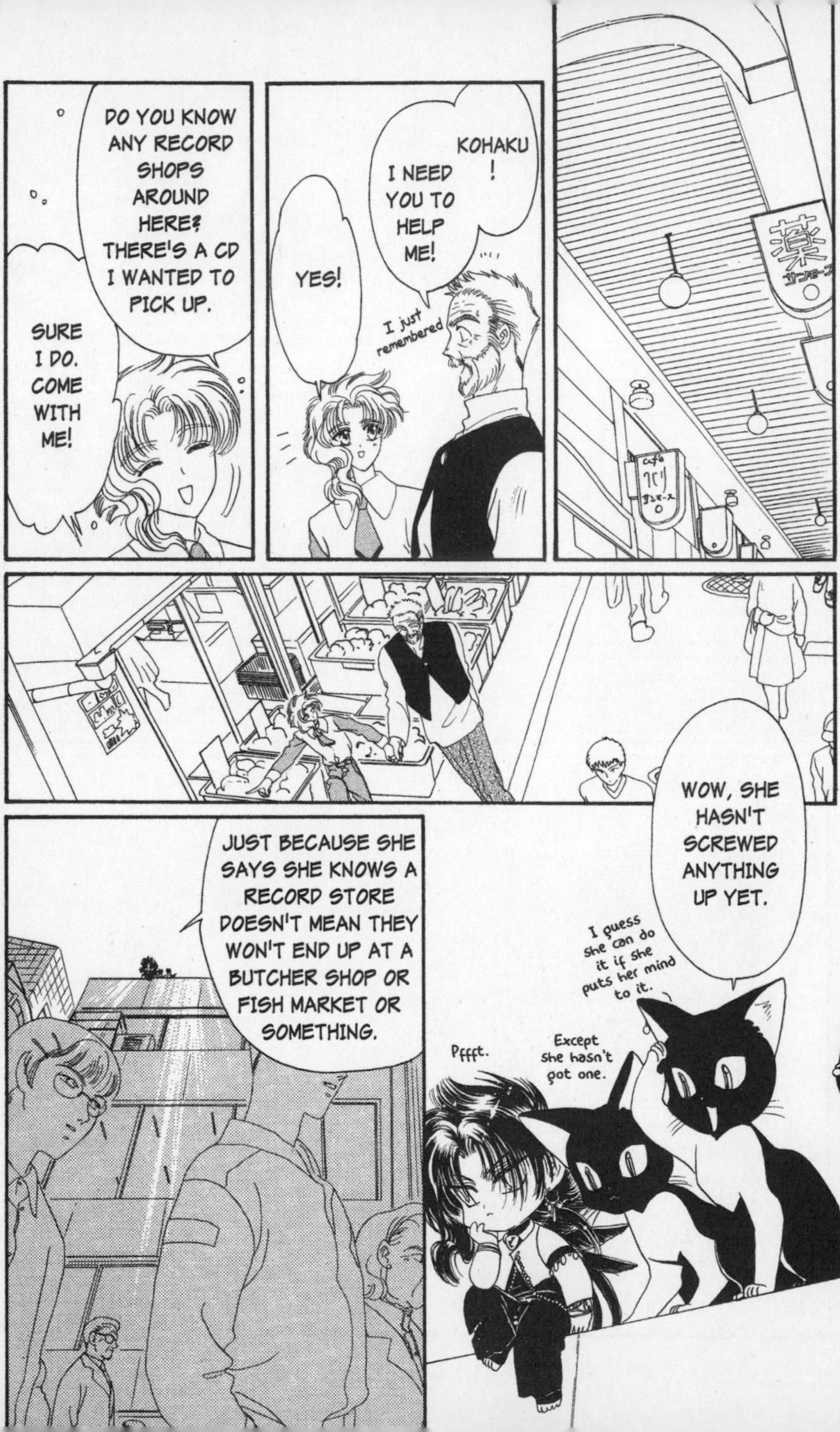
薬
KOHAKU!
I NEED YOU TO HELP ME!
I just remembered
YES!
DO YOU KNOW ANY RECORD SHOPS AROUND HERE? THERE'S A CD I WANTED TO PICK UP.
SURE I DO. COME WITH ME!
WOW, SHE HASN'T SCREWED ANYTHING UP YET.
I guess she can do it if she puts her mind to it.
Except she hasn't got one.
Pffft.
JUST BECAUSE SHE SAYS SHE KNOWS A RECORD STORE DOESN'T MEAN THEY WON'T END UP AT A BUTCHER SHOP OR FISH MARKET OR SOMETHING.

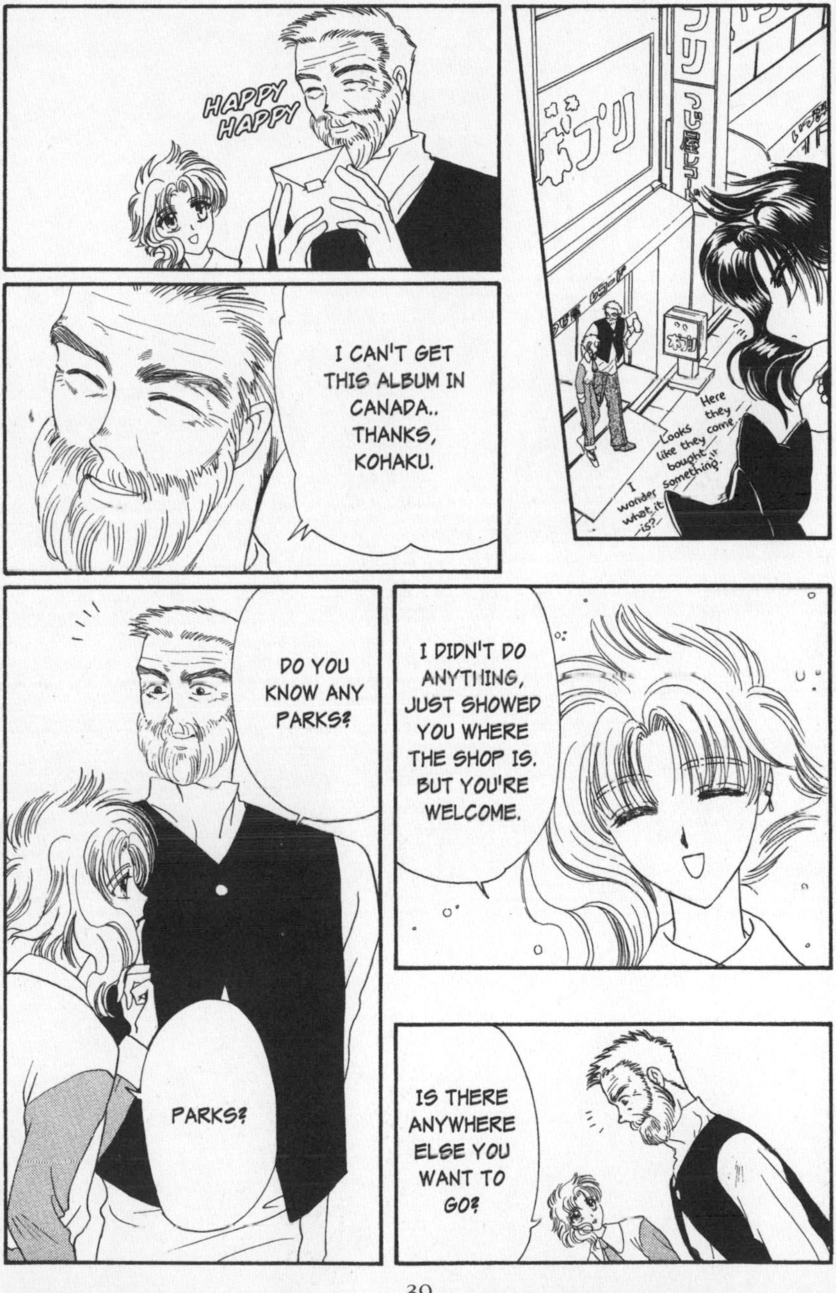

つじ屋レコード
Here they come.
Looks like they bought something.
I wonder what it is?
HAPPY HAPPY
I CAN'T GET THIS ALBUM IN CANADA.. THANKS, KOHAKU.
I DIDN'T DO ANYTHING, JUST SHOWED YOU WHERE THE SHOP IS. BUT YOU'RE WELCOME.
IS THERE ANYWHERE ELSE YOU WANT TO GO?
DO YOU KNOW ANY PARKS?
PARKS?

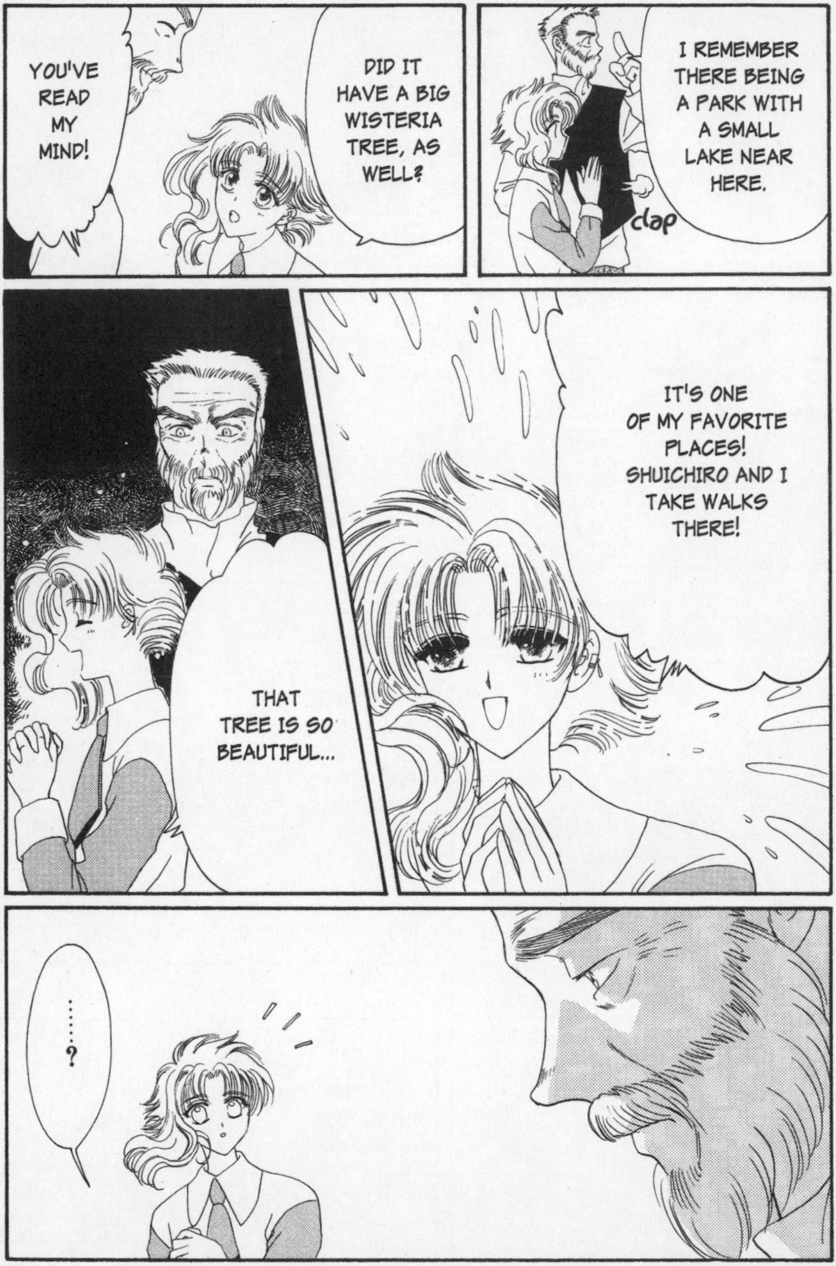
I REMEMBER THERE BEING A PARK WITH A SMALL LAKE NEAR HERE.
clap
DID IT HAVE A BIG WISTERIA TREE, AS WELL?
YOU'VE READ MY MIND!
IT'S ONE OF MY FAVORITE PLACES! SHUICHIRO AND I TAKE WALKS THERE!
THAT TREE IS SO BEAUTIFUL...
......?

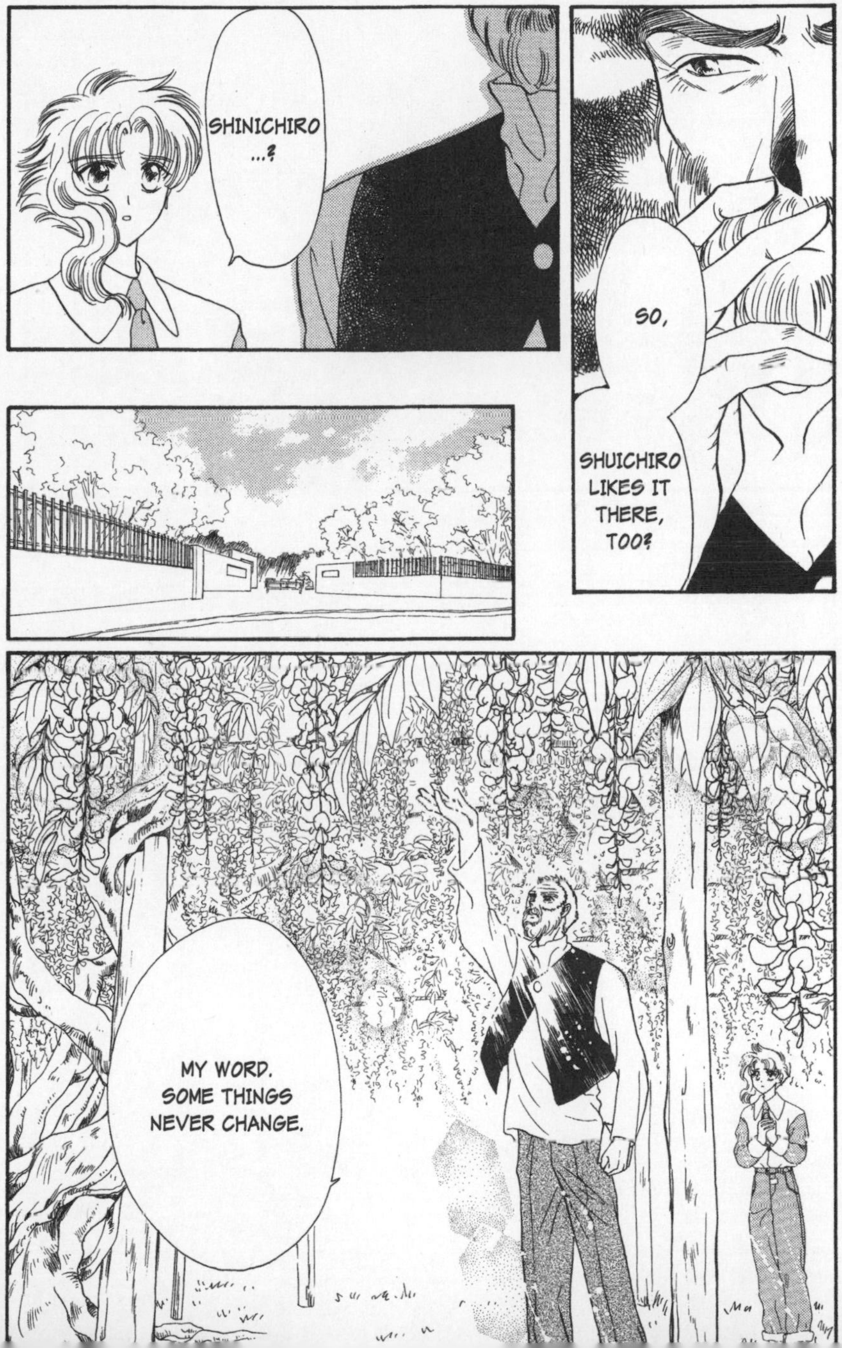
SO,
SHUICHIRO LIKES IT THERE, TOO?
SHINICHIRO ...?
MY WORD. SOME THINGS NEVER CHANGE.

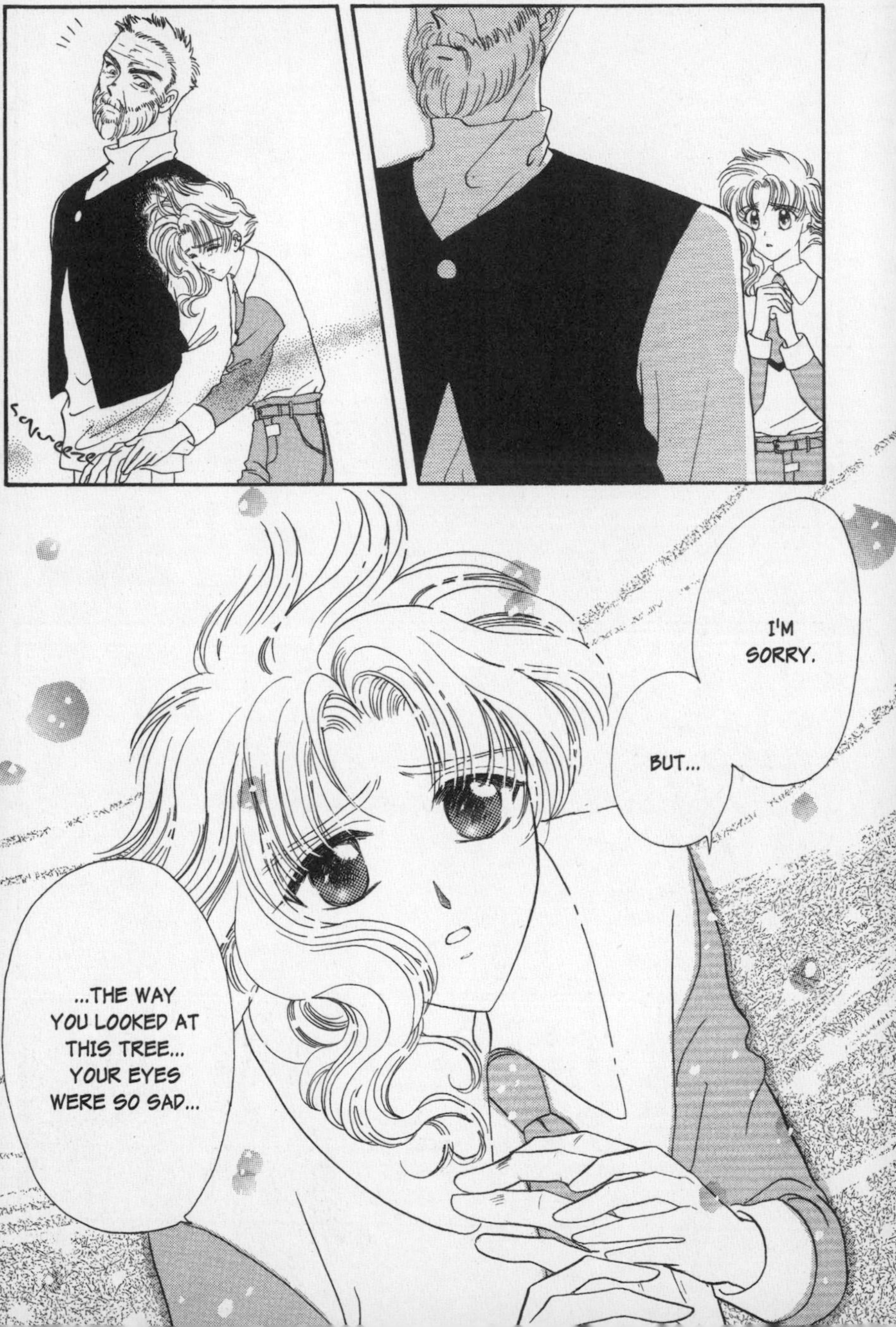

SQUEEZE
I'M SORRY.
BUT...
...THE WAY YOU LOOKED AT THIS TREE... YOUR EYES WERE SO SAD...

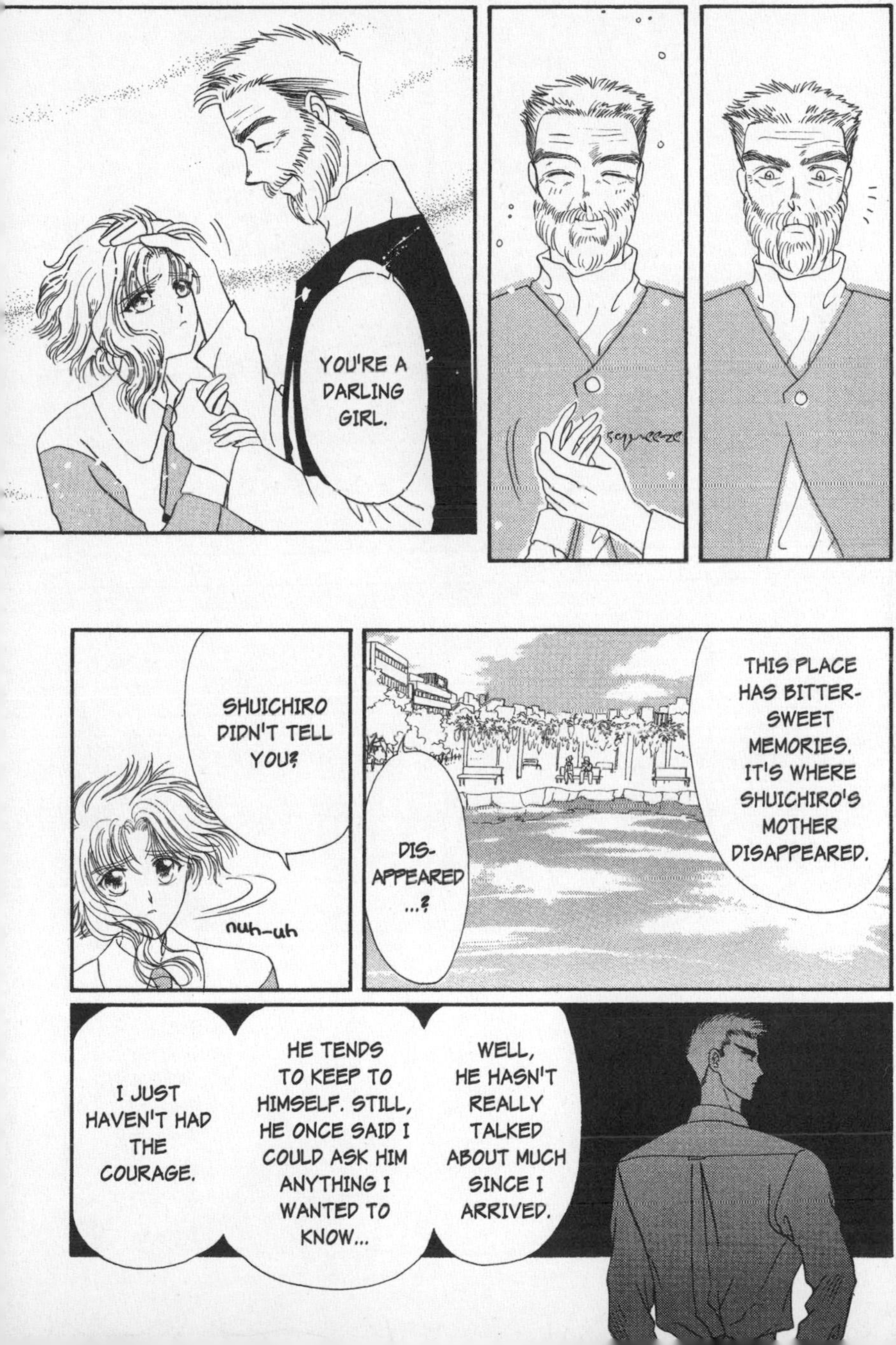
squeeze
YOU'RE A DARLING GIRL.
THIS PLACE HAS BITTER-SWEET MEMORIES. IT'S WHERE SHUICHIRO'S MOTHER DISAPPEARED.
DIS-APPEARED ...?
SHUICHIRO DIDN'T TELL YOU?
nuh-uh
WELL, HE HASN'T REALLY TALKED ABOUT MUCH SINCE I ARRIVED.
HE TENDS TO KEEP TO HIMSELF. STILL, HE ONCE SAID I COULD ASK HIM ANYTHING I WANTED TO KNOW...
I JUST HAVEN'T HAD THE COURAGE.

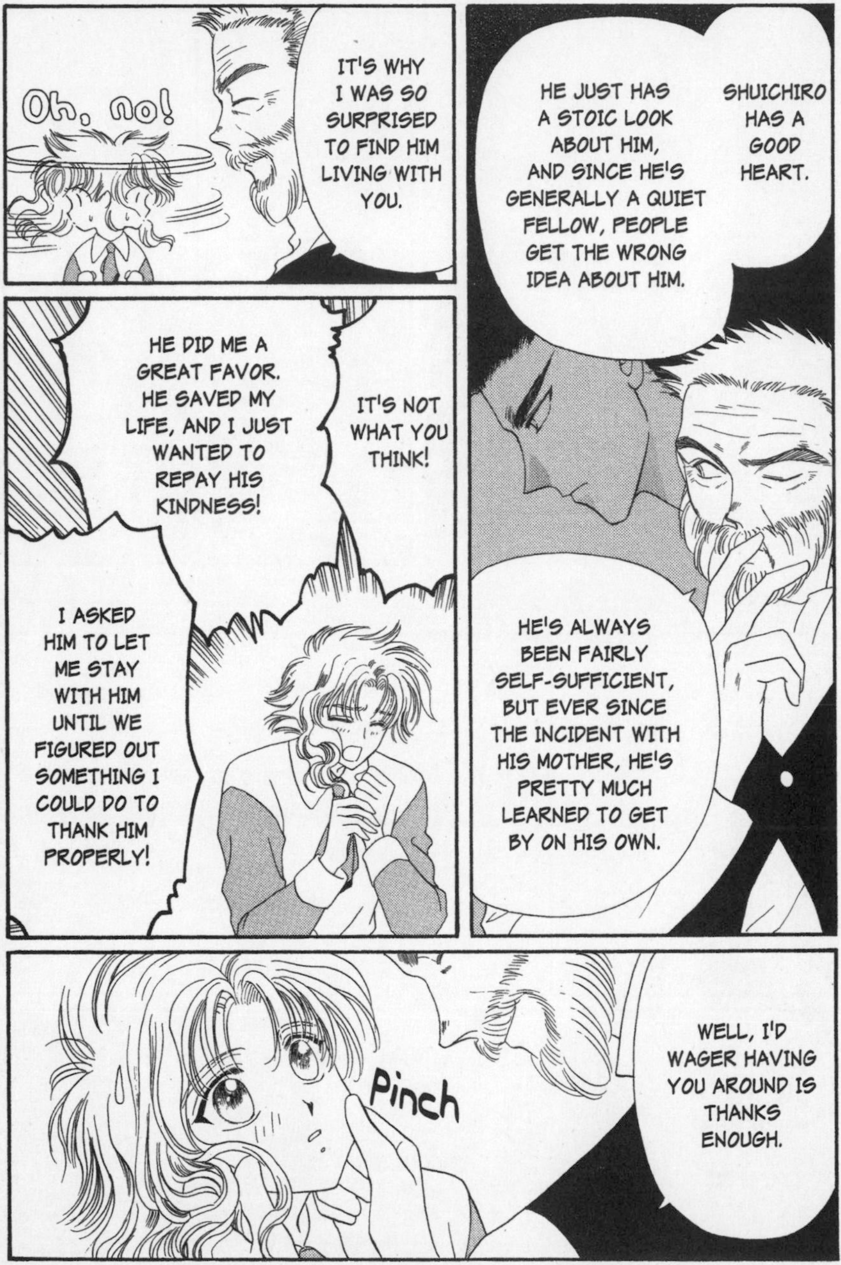
SHUICHIRO HAS A GOOD HEART.
HE JUST HAS A STOIC LOOK ABOUT HIM, AND SINCE HE'S GENERALLY A QUIET FELLOW, PEOPLE GET THE WRONG IDEA ABOUT HIM.
HE'S ALWAYS BEEN FAIRLY SELF-SUFFICIENT, BUT EVER SINCE THE INCIDENT WITH HIS MOTHER, HE'S PRETTY MUCH LEARNED TO GET BY ON HIS OWN.
IT'S WHY I WAS SO SURPRISED TO FIND HIM LIVING WITH YOU.
Oh, no!
IT'S NOT WHAT YOU THINK!
HE DID ME A GREAT FAVOR. HE SAVED MY LIFE, AND I JUST WANTED TO REPAY HIS KINDNESS!
I ASKED HIM TO LET ME STAY WITH HIM UNTIL WE FIGURED OUT SOMETHING I COULD DO TO THANK HIM PROPERLY!
WELL, I'D WAGER HAVING YOU AROUND IS THANKS ENOUGH.
Pinch

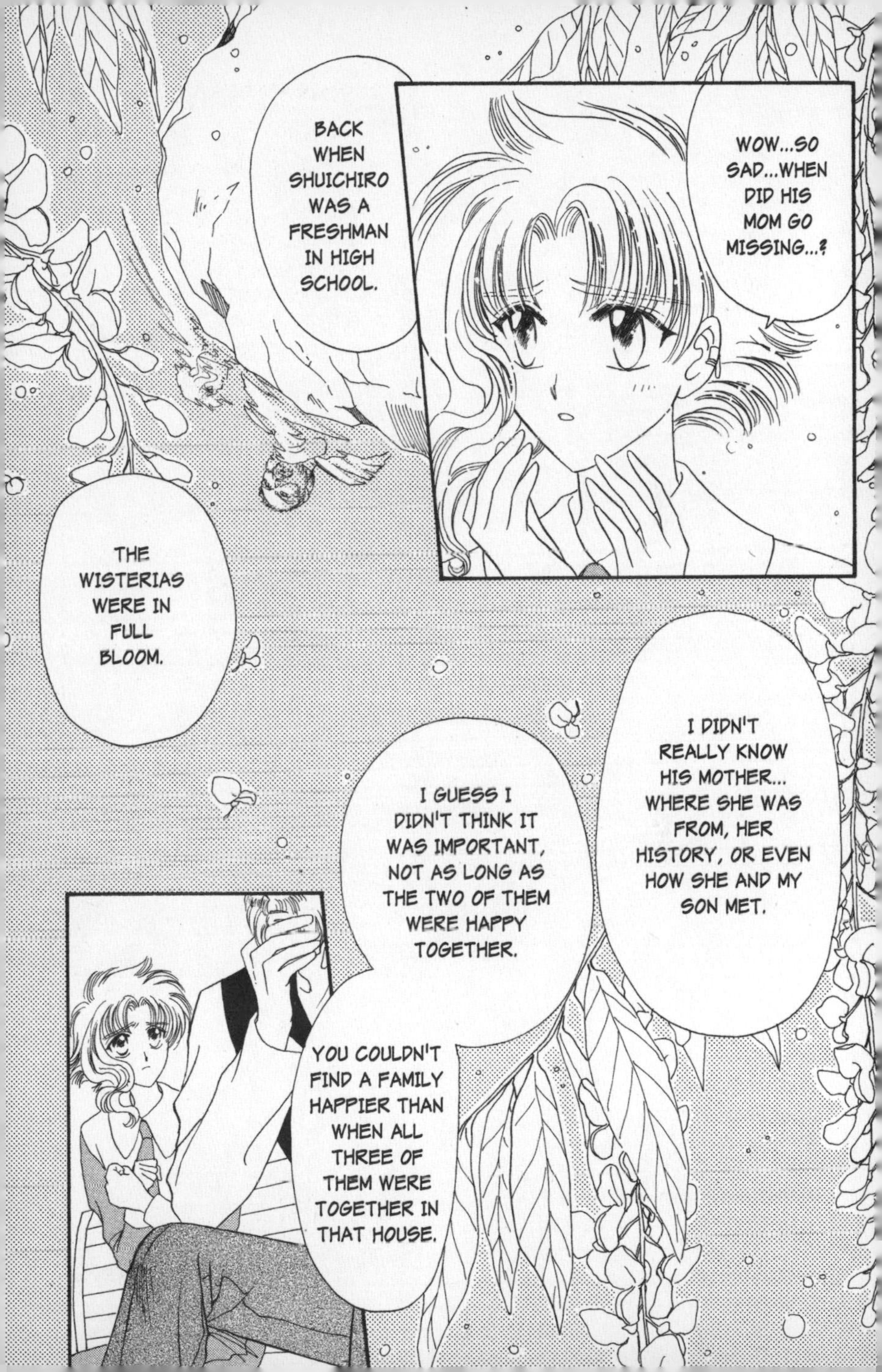
WOW...SO SAD...WHEN DID HIS MOM GO MISSING...?
BACK WHEN SHUICHIRO WAS A FRESHMAN IN HIGH SCHOOL.
THE WISTERIAS WERE IN FULL BLOOM.
I DIDN'T REALLY KNOW HIS MOTHER... WHERE SHE WAS FROM, HER HISTORY, OR EVEN HOW SHE AND MY SON MET.
I GUESS I DIDN'T THINK IT WAS IMPORTANT, NOT AS LONG AS THE TWO OF THEM WERE HAPPY TOGETHER.
YOU COULDN'T FIND A FAMILY HAPPIER THAN WHEN ALL THREE OF THEM WERE TOGETHER IN THAT HOUSE.

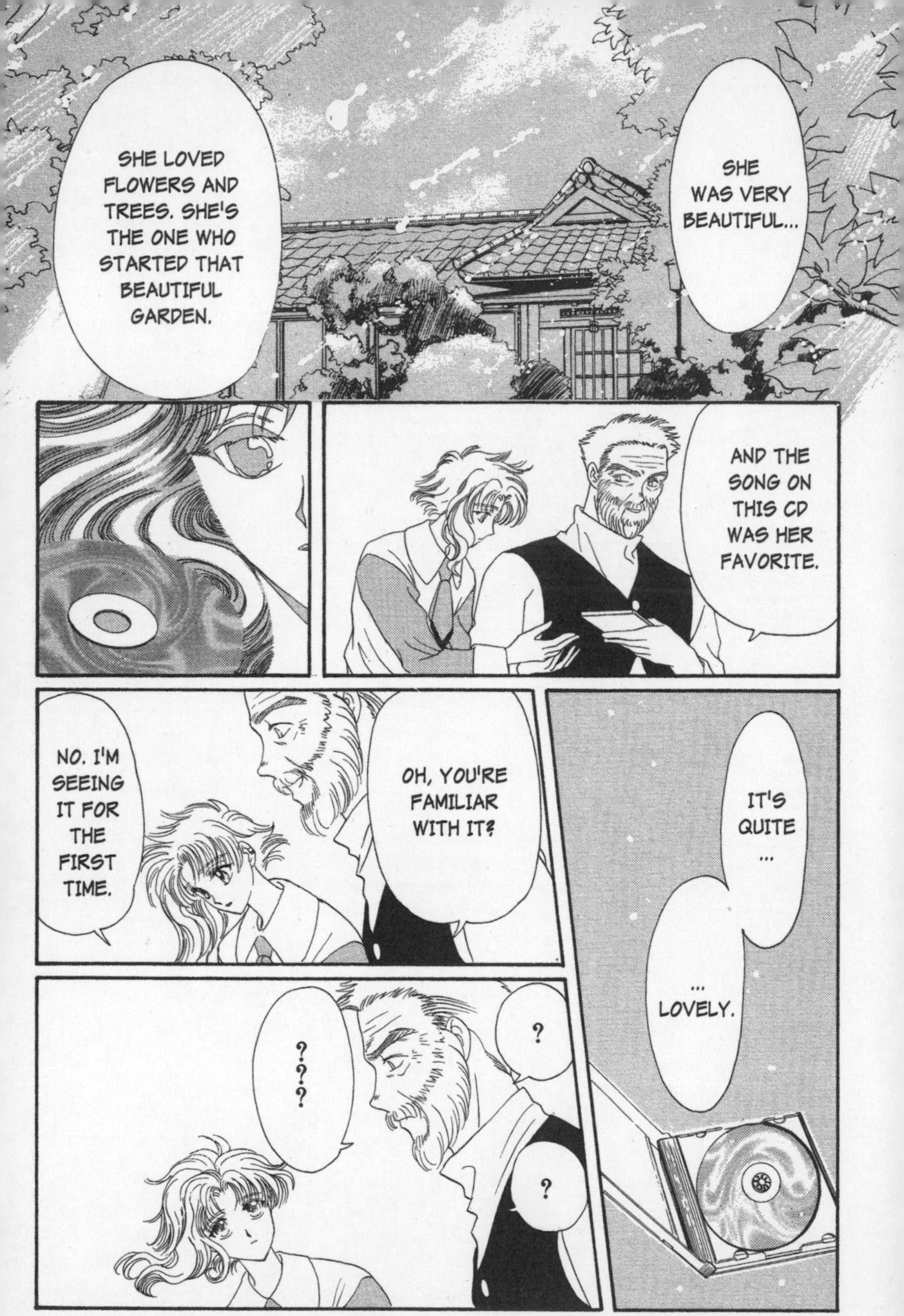
SHE WAS VERY BEAUTIFUL...
SHE LOVED FLOWERS AND TREES. SHE'S THE ONE WHO STARTED THAT BEAUTIFUL GARDEN.
AND THE SONG ON THIS CD WAS HER FAVORITE.
IT'S QUITE ...
... LOVELY.
OH, YOU'RE FAMILIAR WITH IT?
NO. I'M SEEING IT FOR THE FIRST TIME.
?
???
?

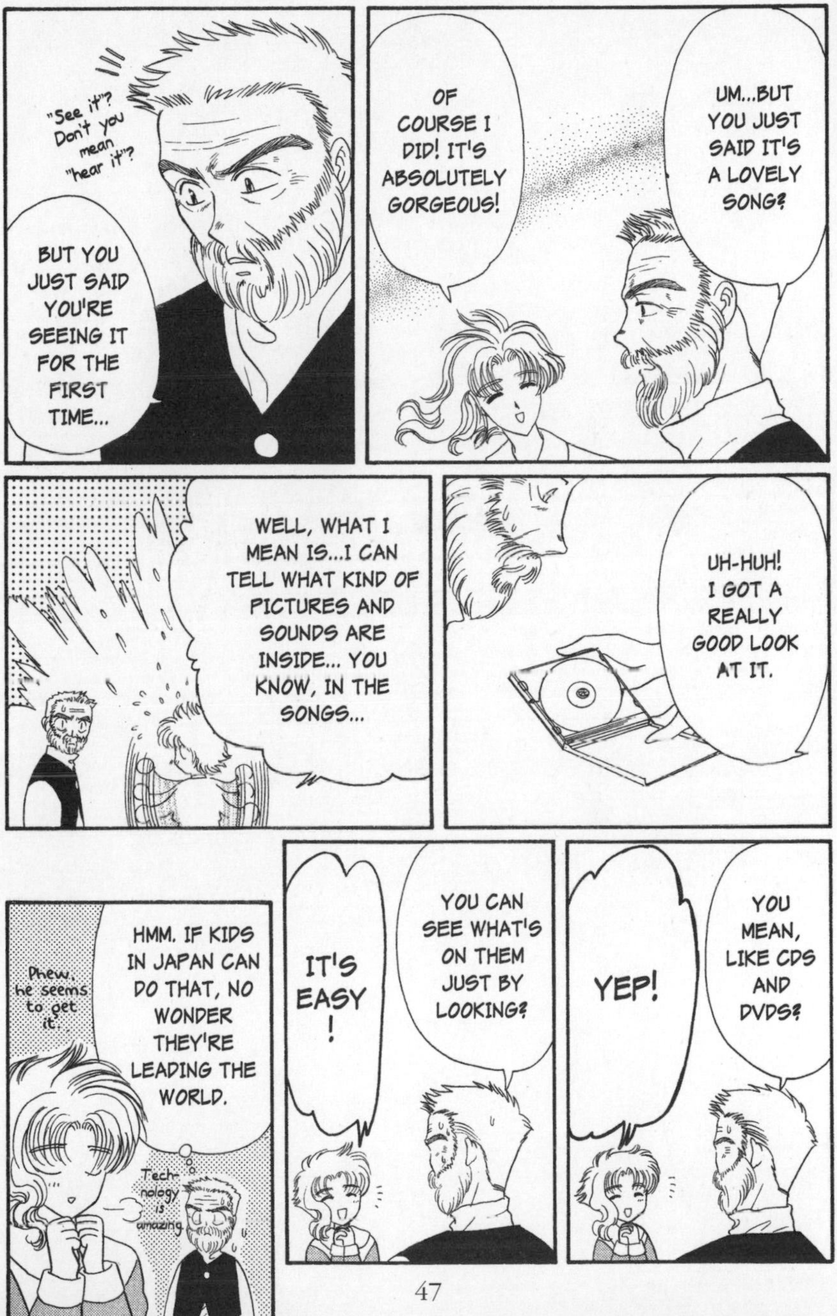
UM...BUT YOU JUST SAID IT'S A LOVELY SONG?
OF COURSE I DID! IT'S ABSOLUTELY GORGEOUS!
"See it"? Don't you mean "hear it"?
BUT YOU JUST SAID YOU'RE SEEING IT FOR THE FIRST TIME...
UH-HUH! I GOT A REALLY GOOD LOOK AT IT.
WELL, WHAT I MEAN IS...I CAN TELL WHAT KIND OF PICTURES AND SOUNDS ARE INSIDE... YOU KNOW, IN THE SONGS...
YOU MEAN, LIKE CDS AND DVDS?
YEP!
YOU CAN SEE WHAT'S ON THEM JUST BY LOOKING?
IT'S EASY!
HMM. IF KIDS IN JAPAN CAN DO THAT, NO WONDER THEY'RE LEADING THE WORLD.
Phew, he seems to get it.
Technology is amazing.

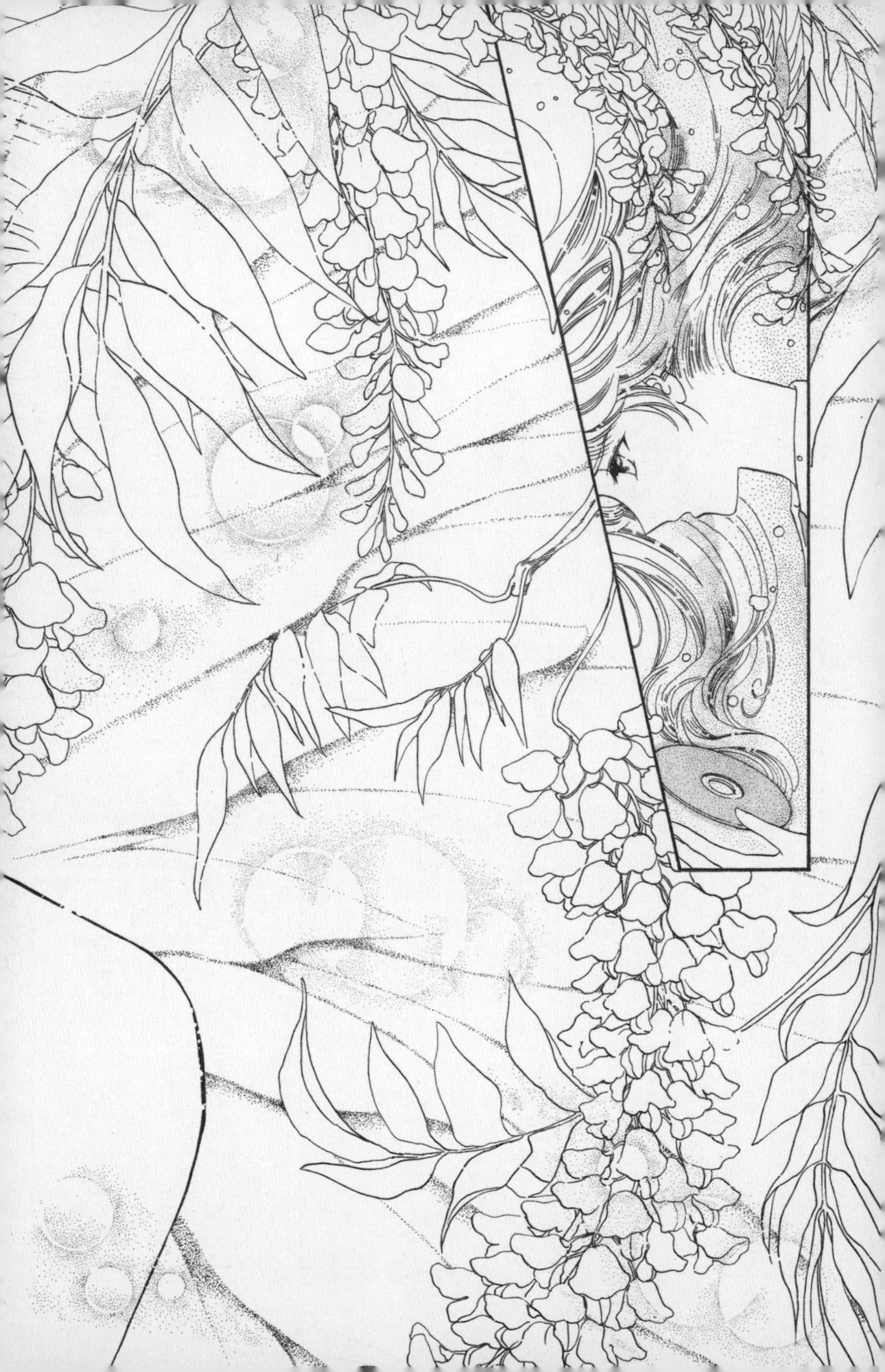

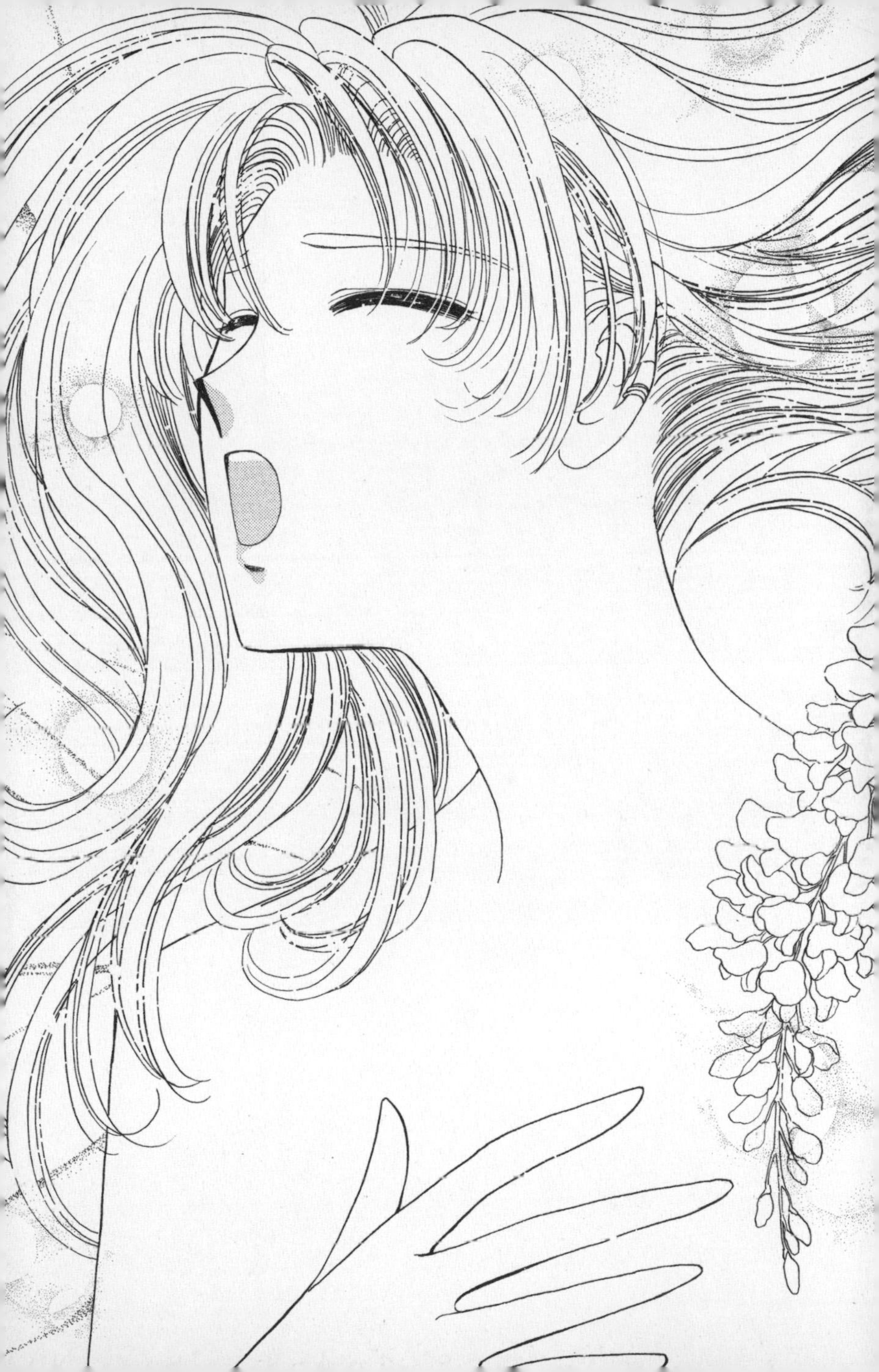

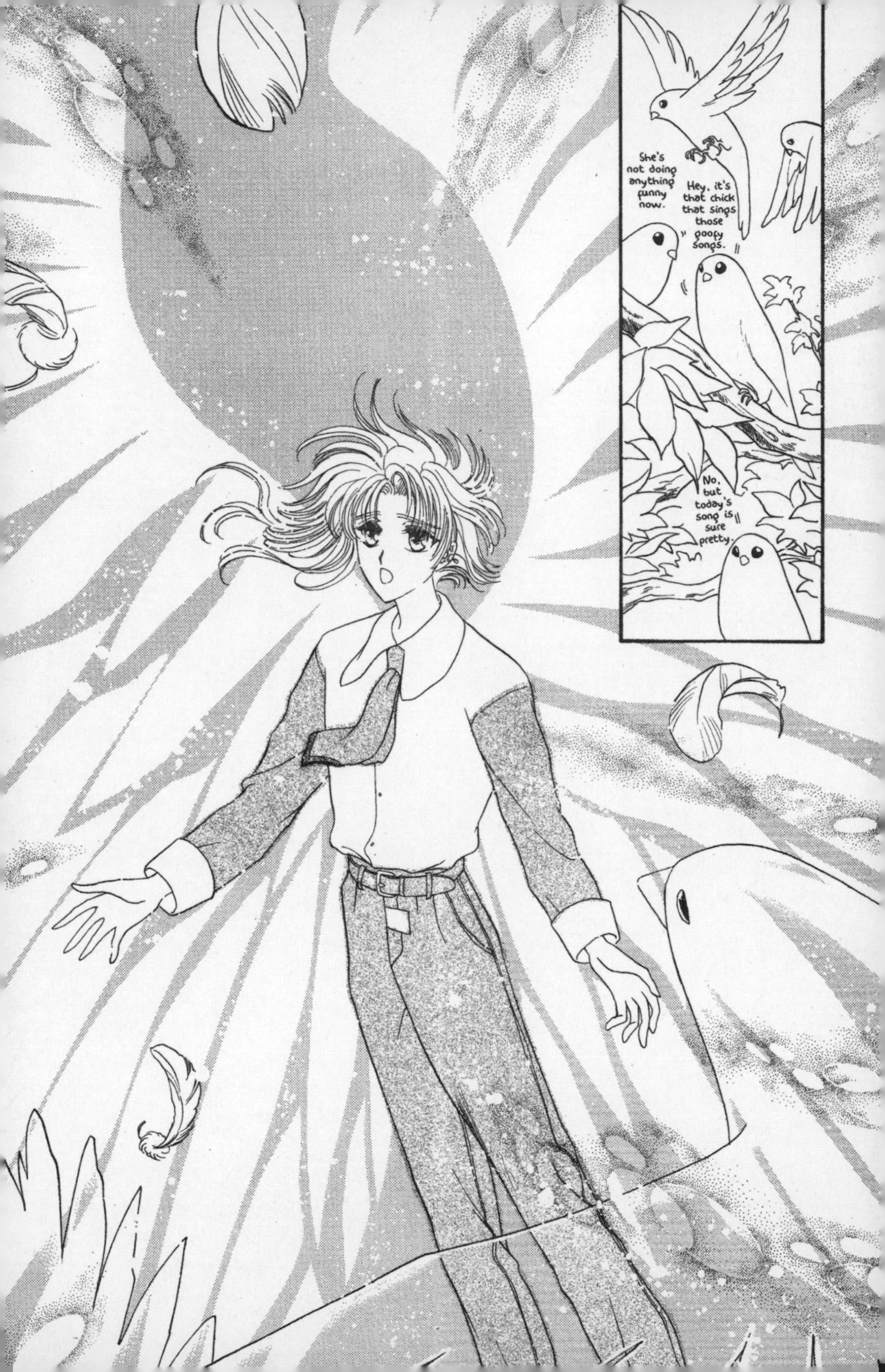
Hey, it's that chick that sings those goofy songs.
She's not doing anything funny now.
No, but today's song is sure pretty.

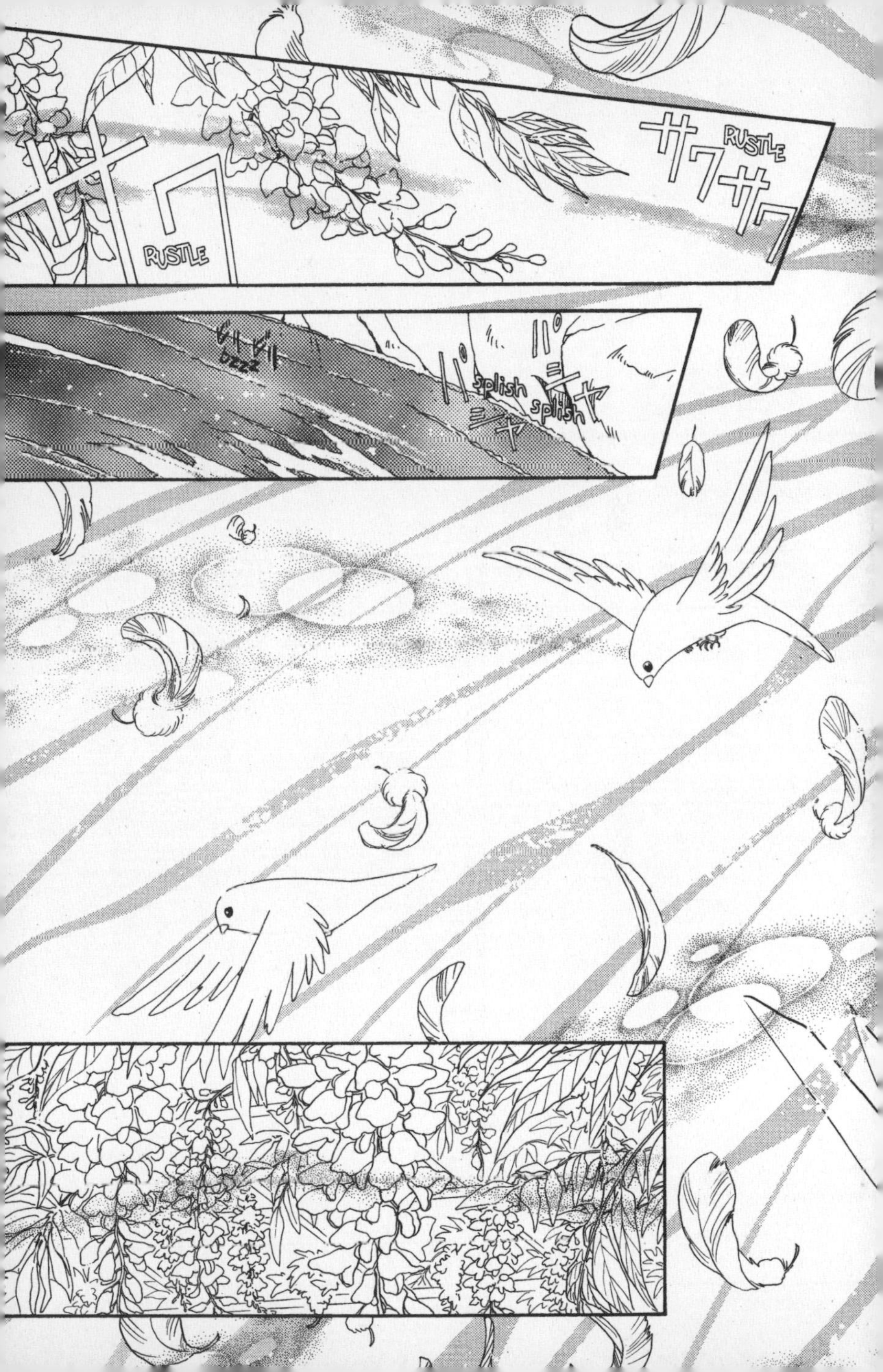
サワサワ
RUSTLE
サワ
RUSTLE
パシャ
splish
パシャ
splish
bzzz

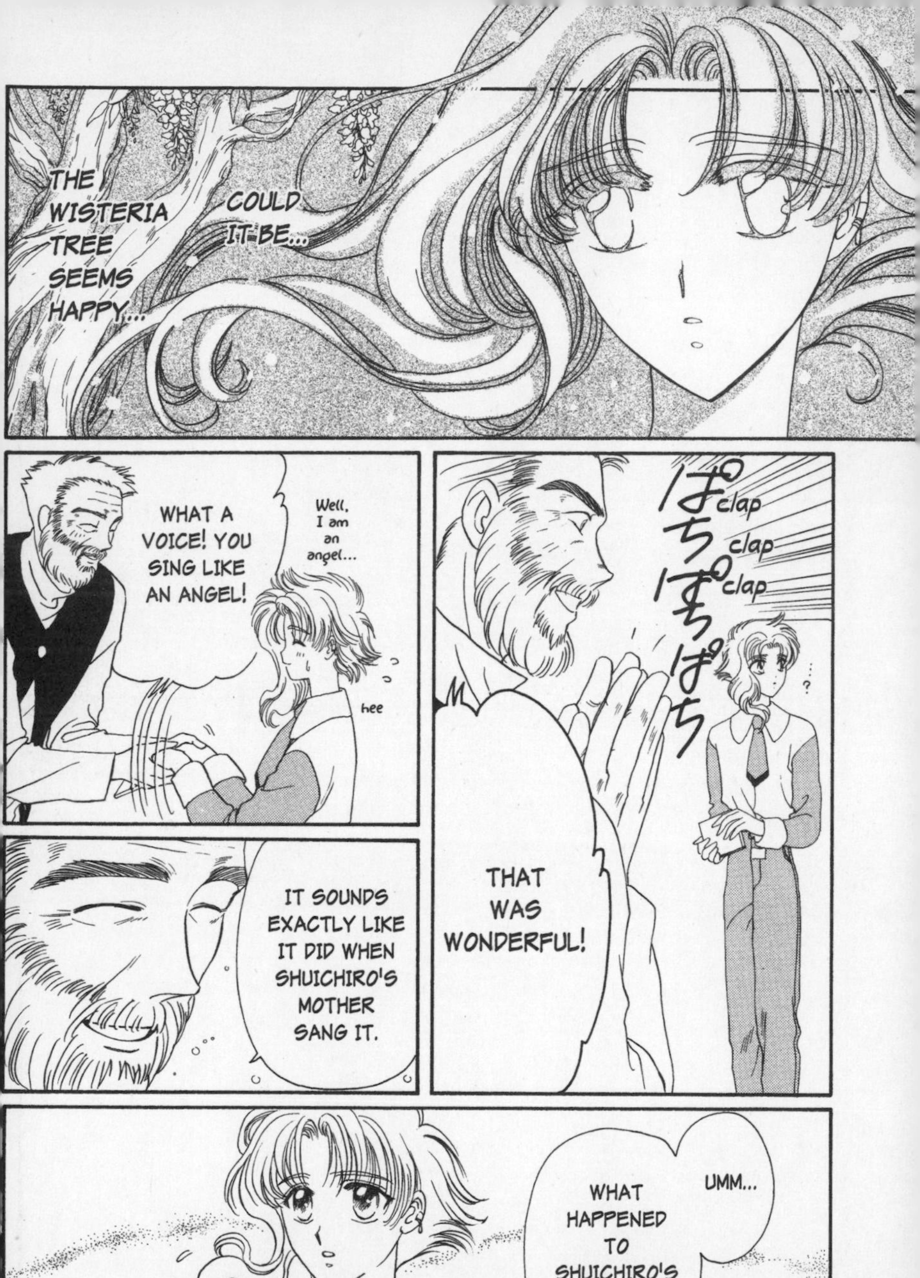
COULD IT BE...
THE WISTERIA TREE SEEMS HAPPY...
ぱちぱちぱちぱち
clap clap clap
THAT WAS WONDERFUL!
...?
WHAT A VOICE! YOU SING LIKE AN ANGEL!
Well, I am an angel...
hee
IT SOUNDS EXACTLY LIKE IT DID WHEN SHUICHIRO'S MOTHER SANG IT.
UMM...
WHAT HAPPENED TO SHUICHIRO'S FATHER...?

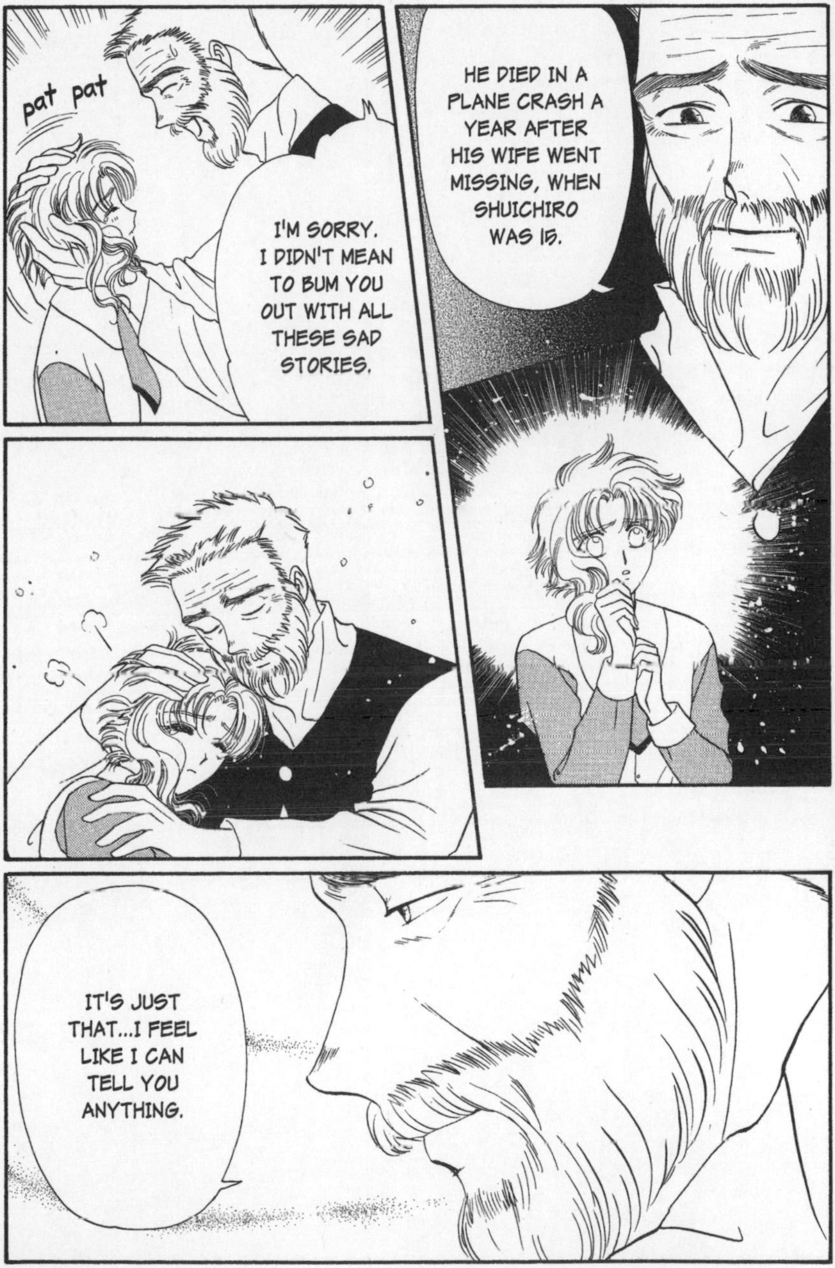
HE DIED IN A PLANE CRASH A YEAR AFTER HIS WIFE WENT MISSING, WHEN SHUICHIRO WAS 15.
pat pat
I'M SORRY. I DIDN'T MEAN TO BUM YOU OUT WITH ALL THESE SAD STORIES.
IT'S JUST THAT...I FEEL LIKE I CAN TELL YOU ANYTHING.

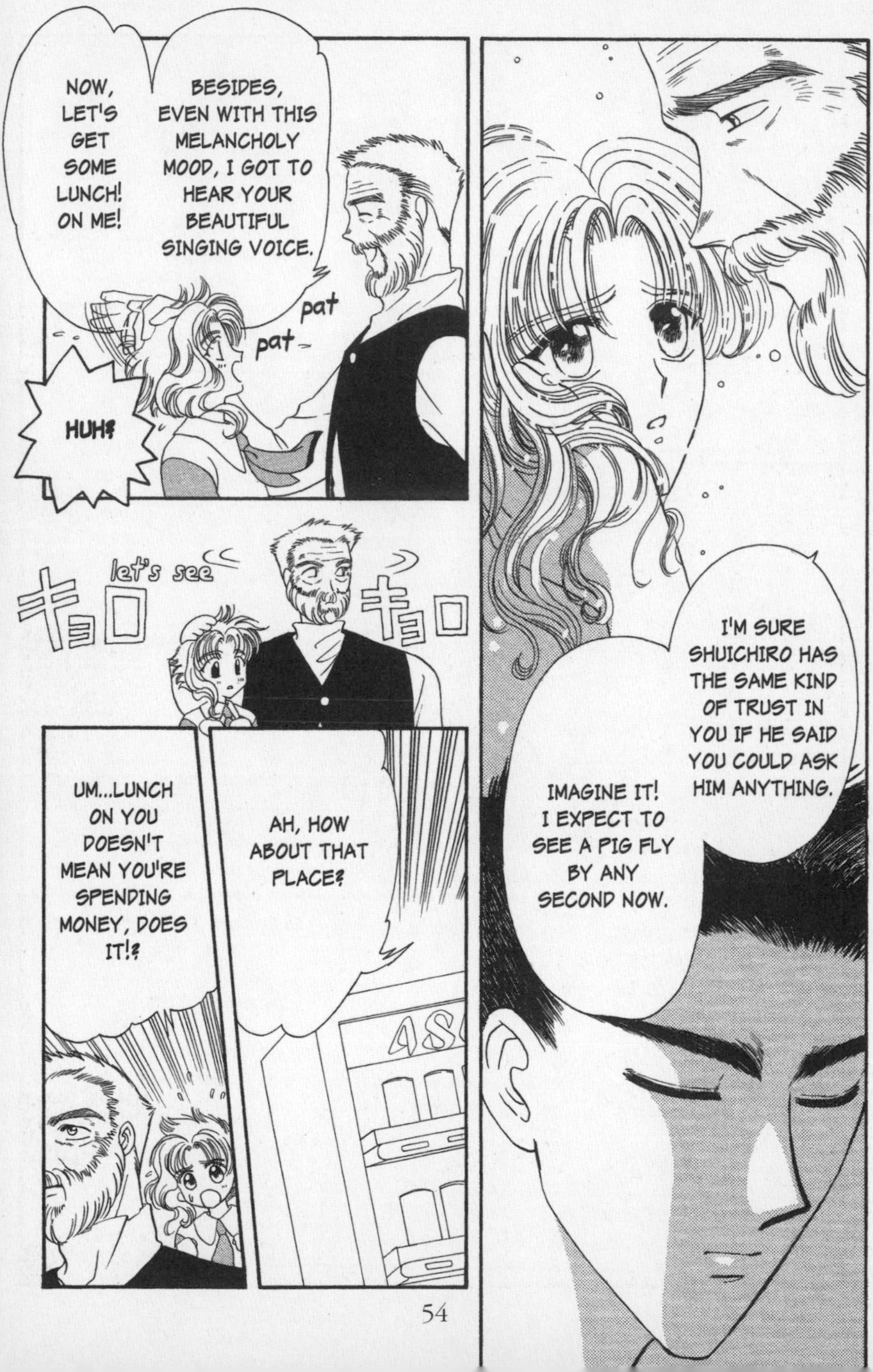
I'M SURE SHUICHIRO HAS THE SAME KIND OF TRUST IN YOU IF HE SAID YOU COULD ASK HIM ANYTHING.
IMAGINE IT! I EXPECT TO SEE A PIG FLY BY ANY SECOND NOW.
BESIDES, EVEN WITH THIS MELANCHOLY MOOD, I GOT TO HEAR YOUR BEAUTIFUL SINGING VOICE.
NOW, LET'S GET SOME LUNCH! ON ME!
pat
pat
HUH?
キョロ
let's see
キョロ
AH, HOW ABOUT THAT PLACE?
UM...LUNCH ON YOU DOESN'T MEAN YOU'RE SPENDING MONEY, DOES IT!?

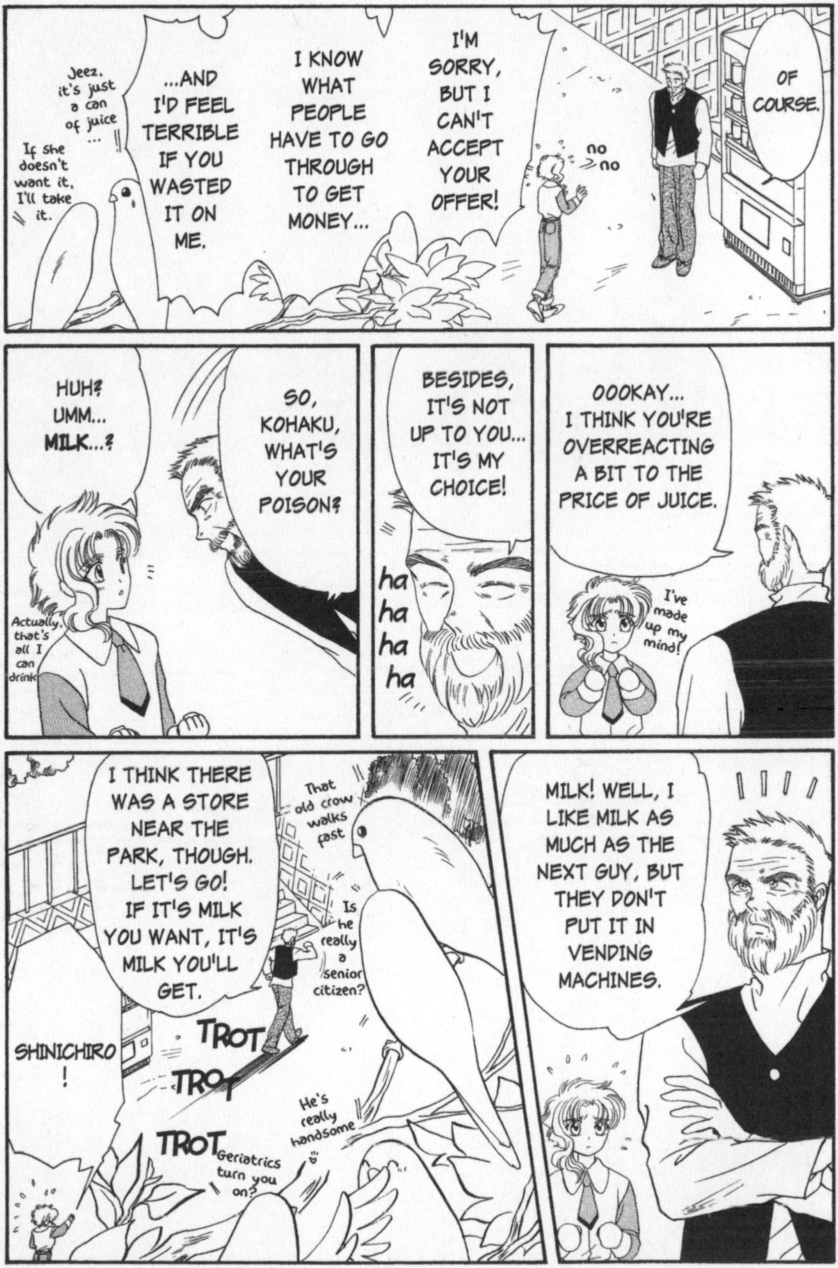
OF COURSE.
no no
I'M SORRY, BUT I CAN'T ACCEPT YOUR OFFER!
I KNOW WHAT PEOPLE HAVE TO GO THROUGH TO GET MONEY...
...AND I'D FEEL TERRIBLE IF YOU WASTED IT ON ME.
Jeez, it's just a can of juice ...
If she doesn't want it, I'll take it.
OOOKAY... I THINK YOU'RE OVERREACTING A BIT TO THE PRICE OF JUICE.
I've made up my mind!
BESIDES, IT'S NOT UP TO YOU... IT'S MY CHOICE!
ha ha ha ha
SO, KOHAKU, WHAT'S YOUR POISON?
HUH? UMM... MILK...?
Actually, that's all I can drink
MILK! WELL, I LIKE MILK AS MUCH AS THE NEXT GUY, BUT THEY DON'T PUT IT IN VENDING MACHINES.
That old crow walks fast
I THINK THERE WAS A STORE NEAR THE PARK, THOUGH. LET'S GO! IF IT'S MILK YOU WANT, IT'S MILK YOU'LL GET.
Is he really a senior citizen?
TROT
TROT
TROT
He's really handsome
Geriatrics turn you on?
SHINICHIRO!

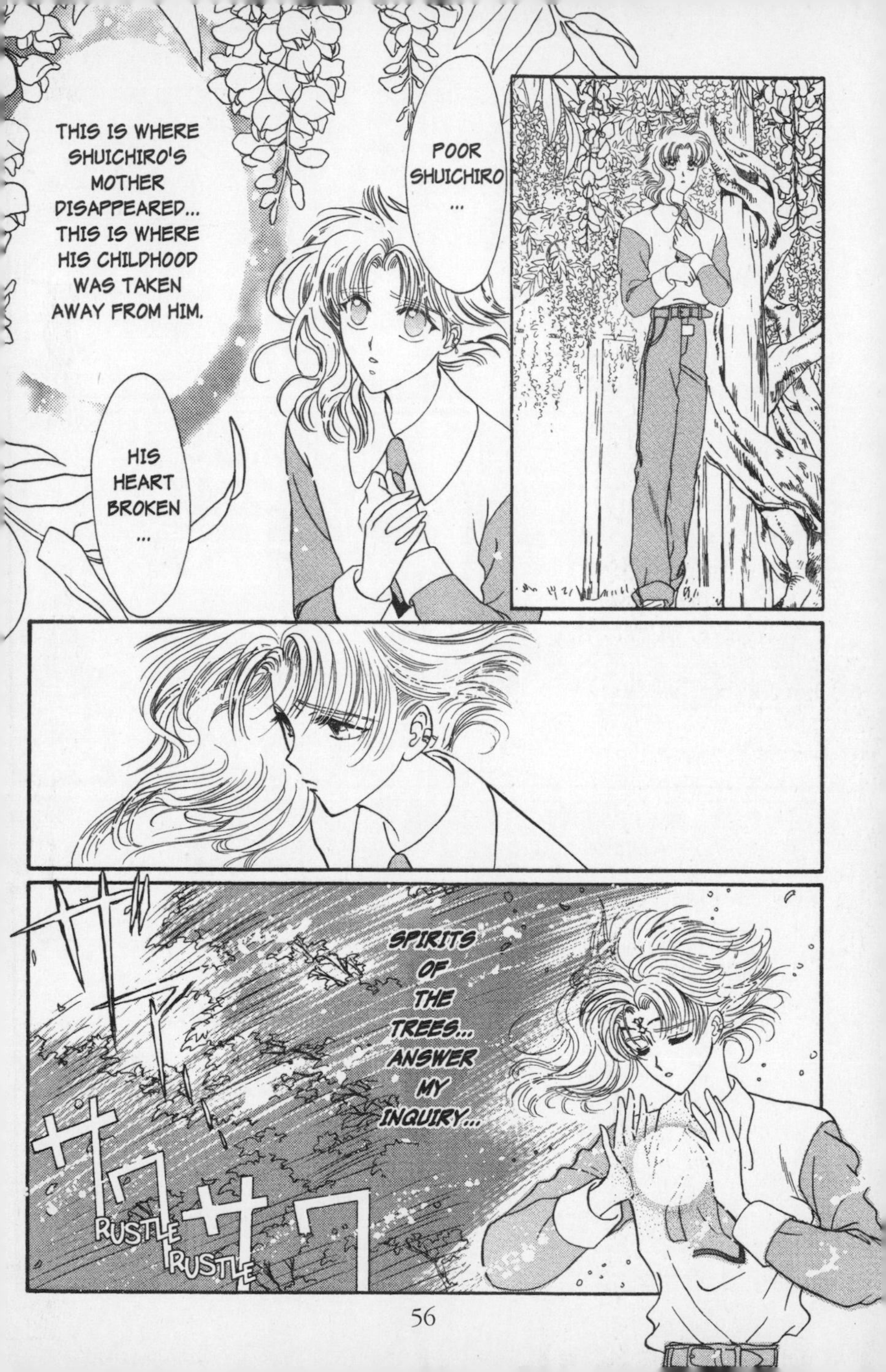
POOR SHUICHIRO ...
THIS IS WHERE SHUICHIRO'S MOTHER DISAPPEARED... THIS IS WHERE HIS CHILDHOOD WAS TAKEN AWAY FROM HIM.
HIS HEART BROKEN ...
SPIRITS OF THE TREES... ANSWER MY INQUIRY...
RUSTLE
RUSTLE

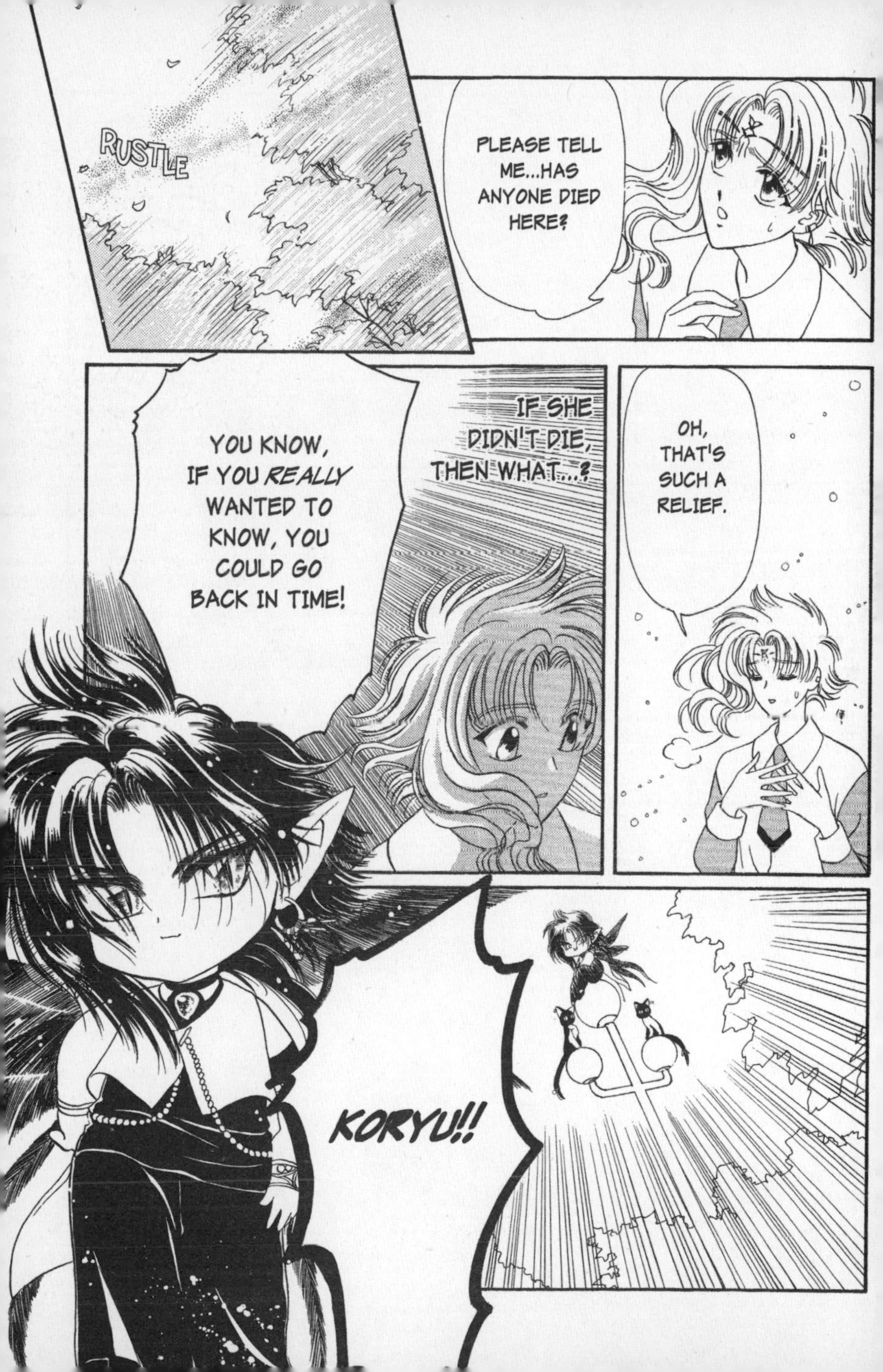
PLEASE TELL ME...HAS ANYONE DIED HERE?
RUSTLE
OH, THAT'S SUCH A RELIEF.
IF SHE DIDN'T DIE, THEN WHAT...?
YOU KNOW, IF YOU *REALLY* WANTED TO KNOW, YOU COULD GO BACK IN TIME!
KORYU!!

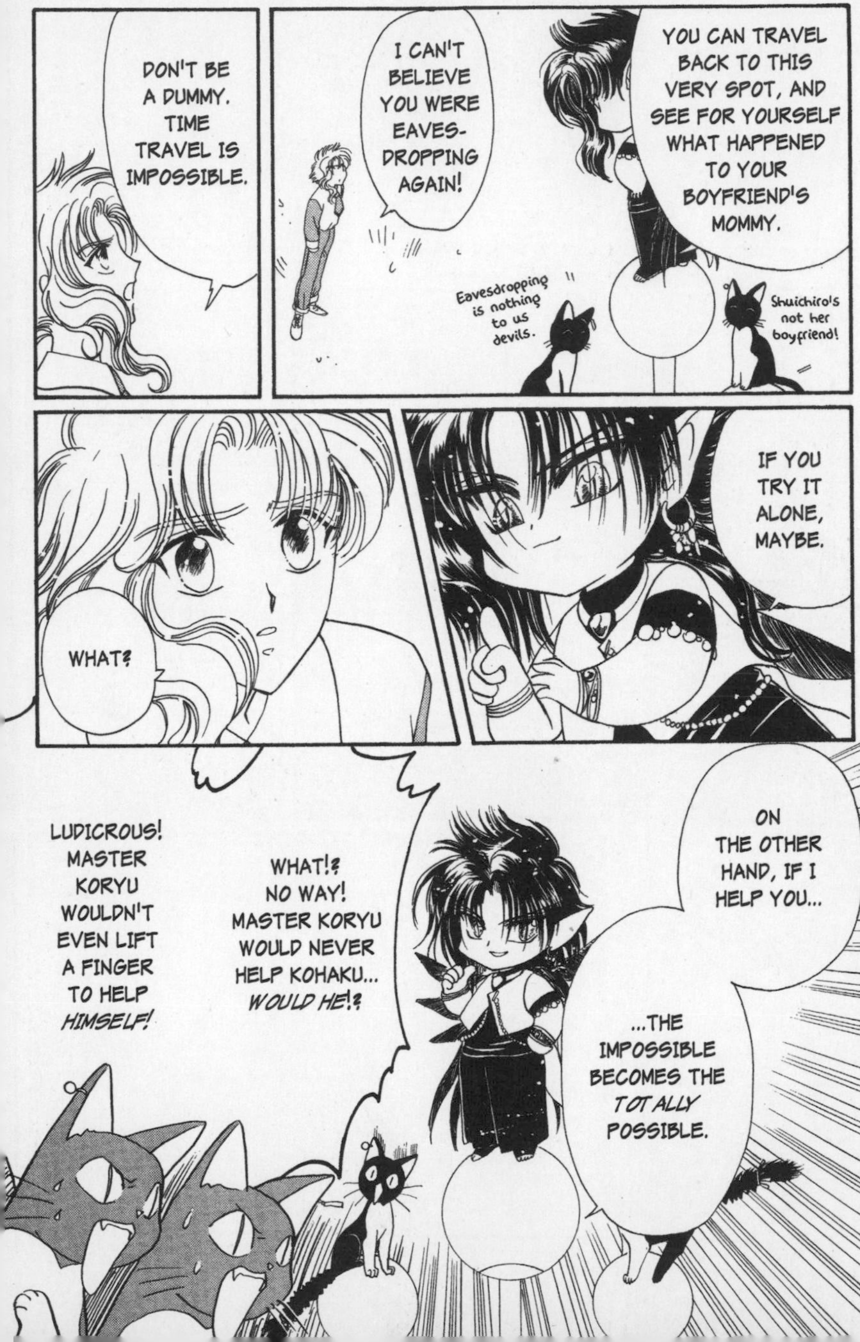
YOU CAN TRAVEL BACK TO THIS VERY SPOT, AND SEE FOR YOURSELF WHAT HAPPENED TO YOUR BOYFRIEND'S MOMMY.
I CAN'T BELIEVE YOU WERE EAVES-DROPPING AGAIN!
Shuichiro's not her boyfriend!
Eavesdropping is nothing to us devils.
DON'T BE A DUMMY. TIME TRAVEL IS IMPOSSIBLE.
IF YOU TRY IT ALONE, MAYBE.
WHAT?
ON THE OTHER HAND, IF I HELP YOU...
...THE IMPOSSIBLE BECOMES THE *TOTALLY* POSSIBLE.
WHAT!? NO WAY! MASTER KORYU WOULD NEVER HELP KOHAKU... *WOULD HE!?*
LUDICROUS! MASTER KORYU WOULDN'T EVEN LIFT A FINGER TO HELP *HIMSELF!*

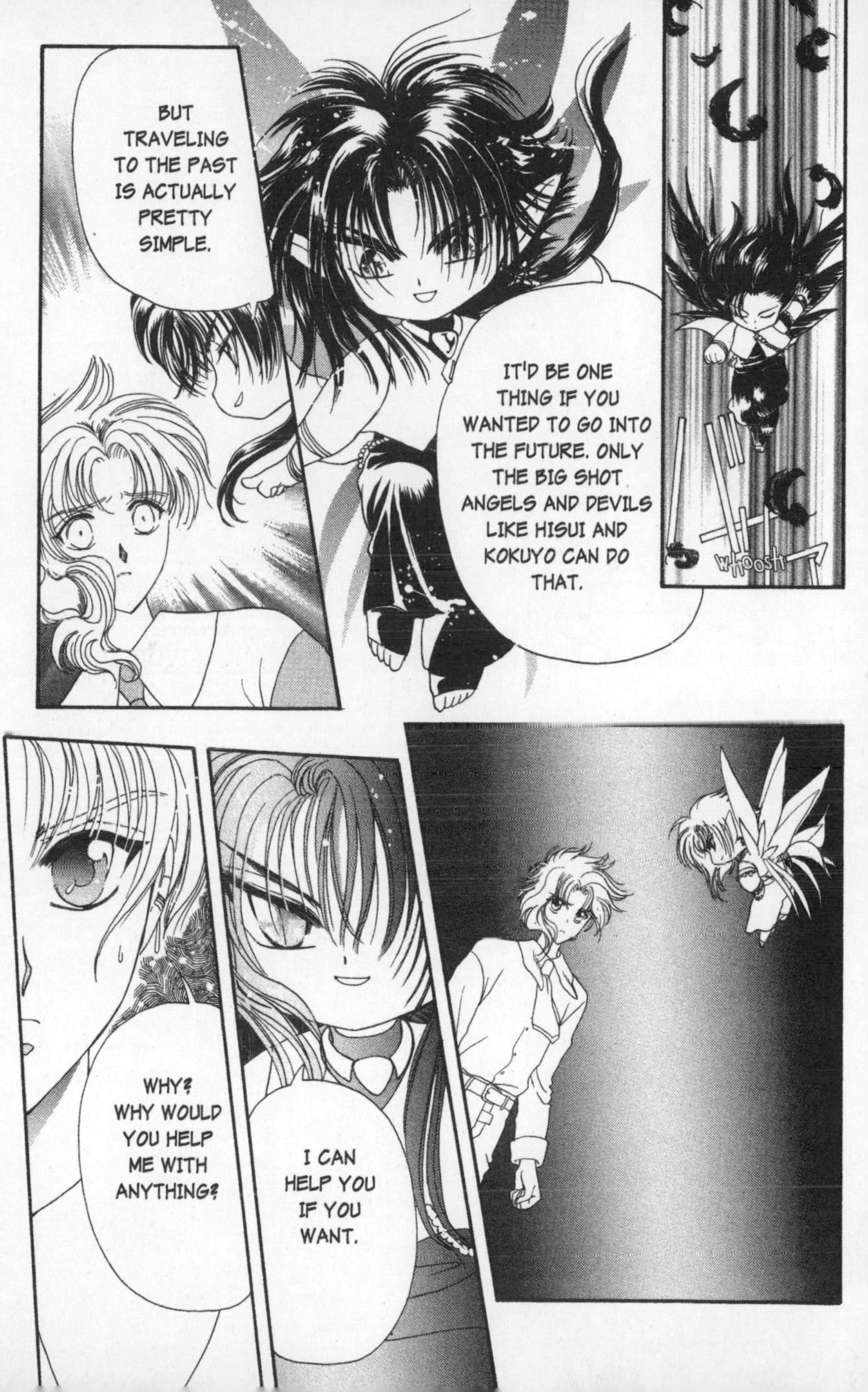
WHOOSH!
BUT TRAVELING TO THE PAST IS ACTUALLY PRETTY SIMPLE.
IT'D BE ONE THING IF YOU WANTED TO GO INTO THE FUTURE. ONLY THE BIG SHOT ANGELS AND DEVILS LIKE HISUI AND KOKUYO CAN DO THAT.
I CAN HELP YOU IF YOU WANT.
WHY? WHY WOULD YOU HELP ME WITH ANYTHING?

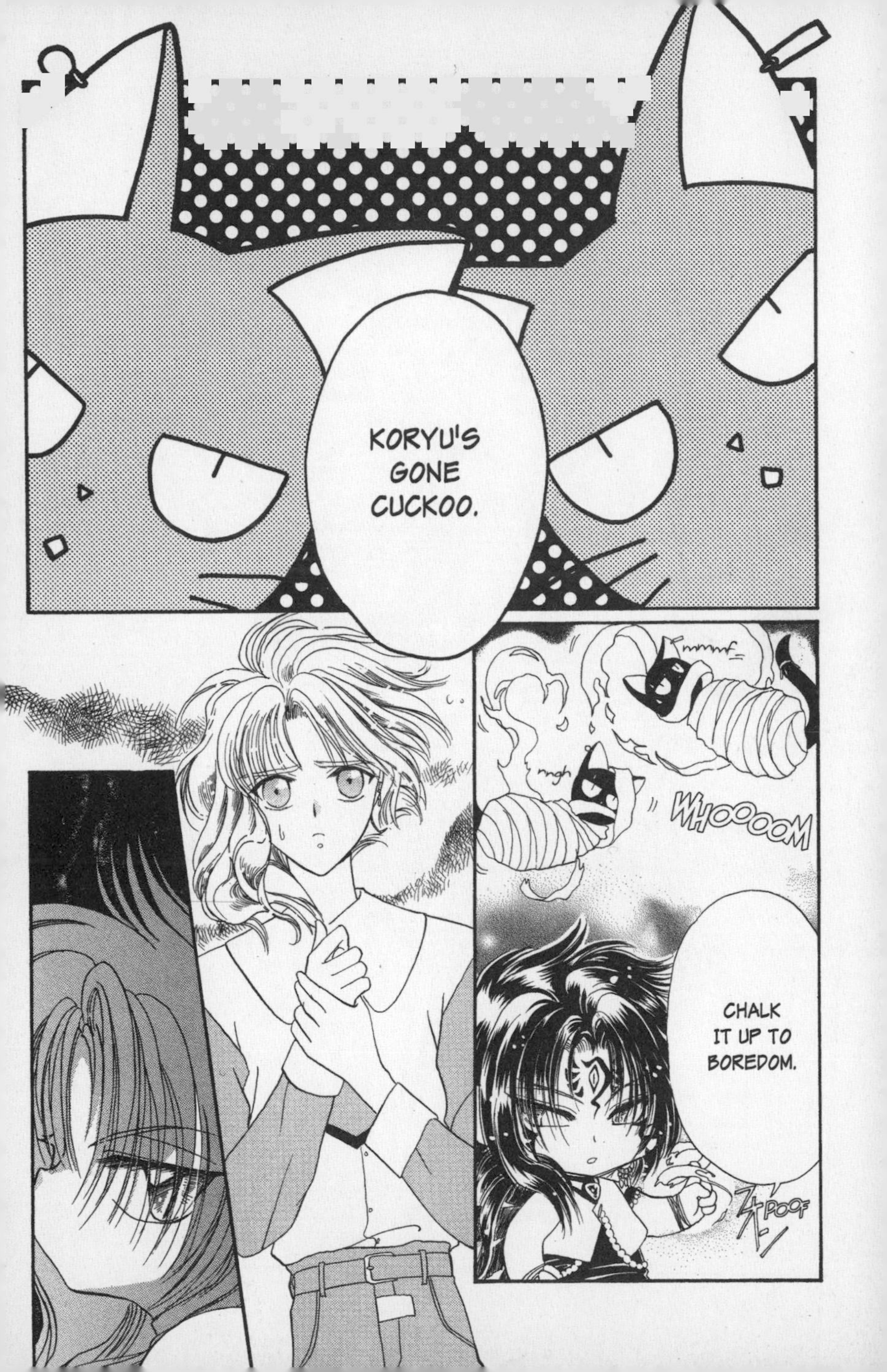
KORYU'S GONE CUCKOO.
mmmf
WHOOOOM
CHALK IT UP TO BOREDOM.
POOF

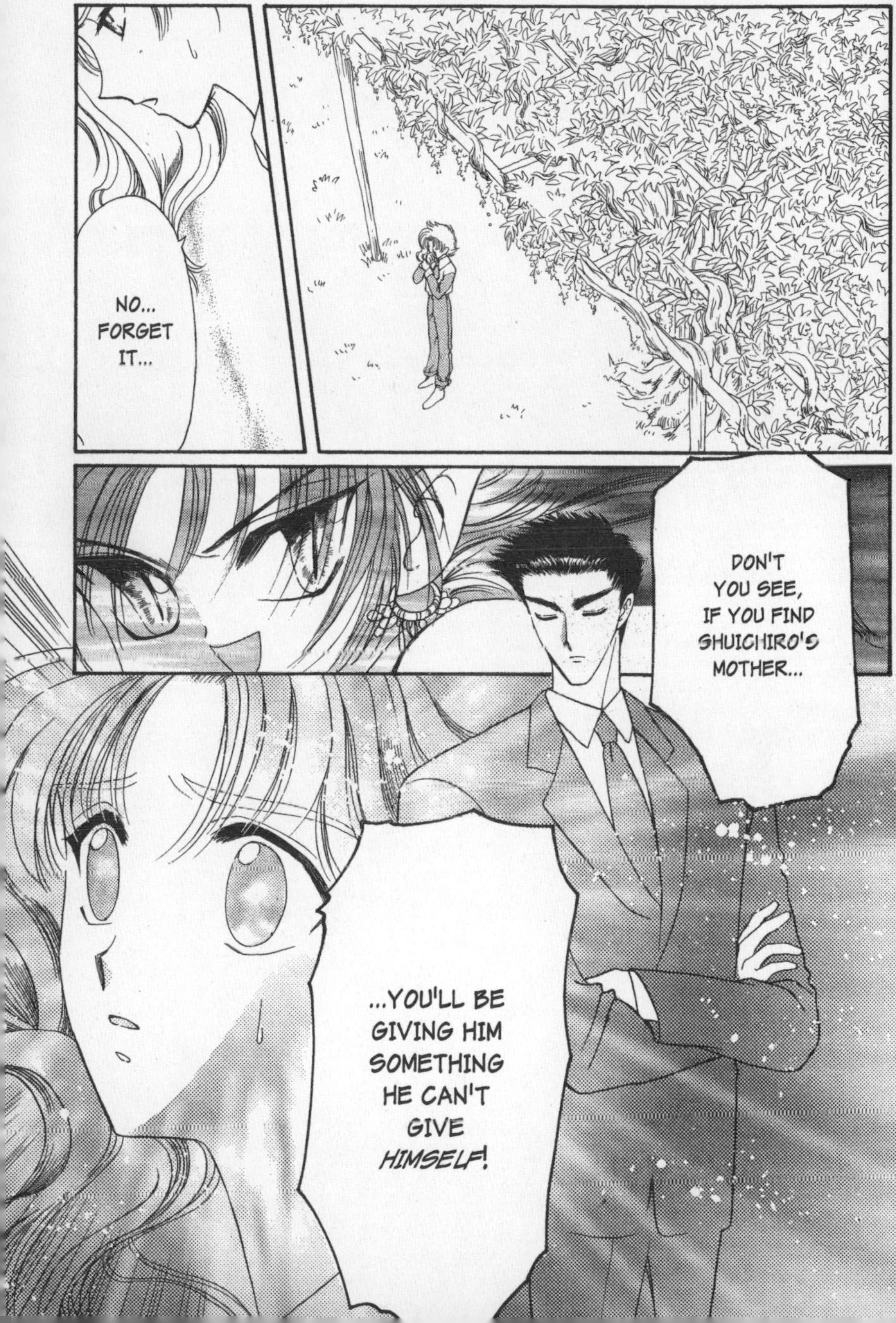
NO... FORGET IT...
DON'T YOU SEE, IF YOU FIND SHUICHIRO'S MOTHER...
...YOU'LL BE GIVING HIM SOMETHING HE CAN'T GIVE *HIMSELF*!

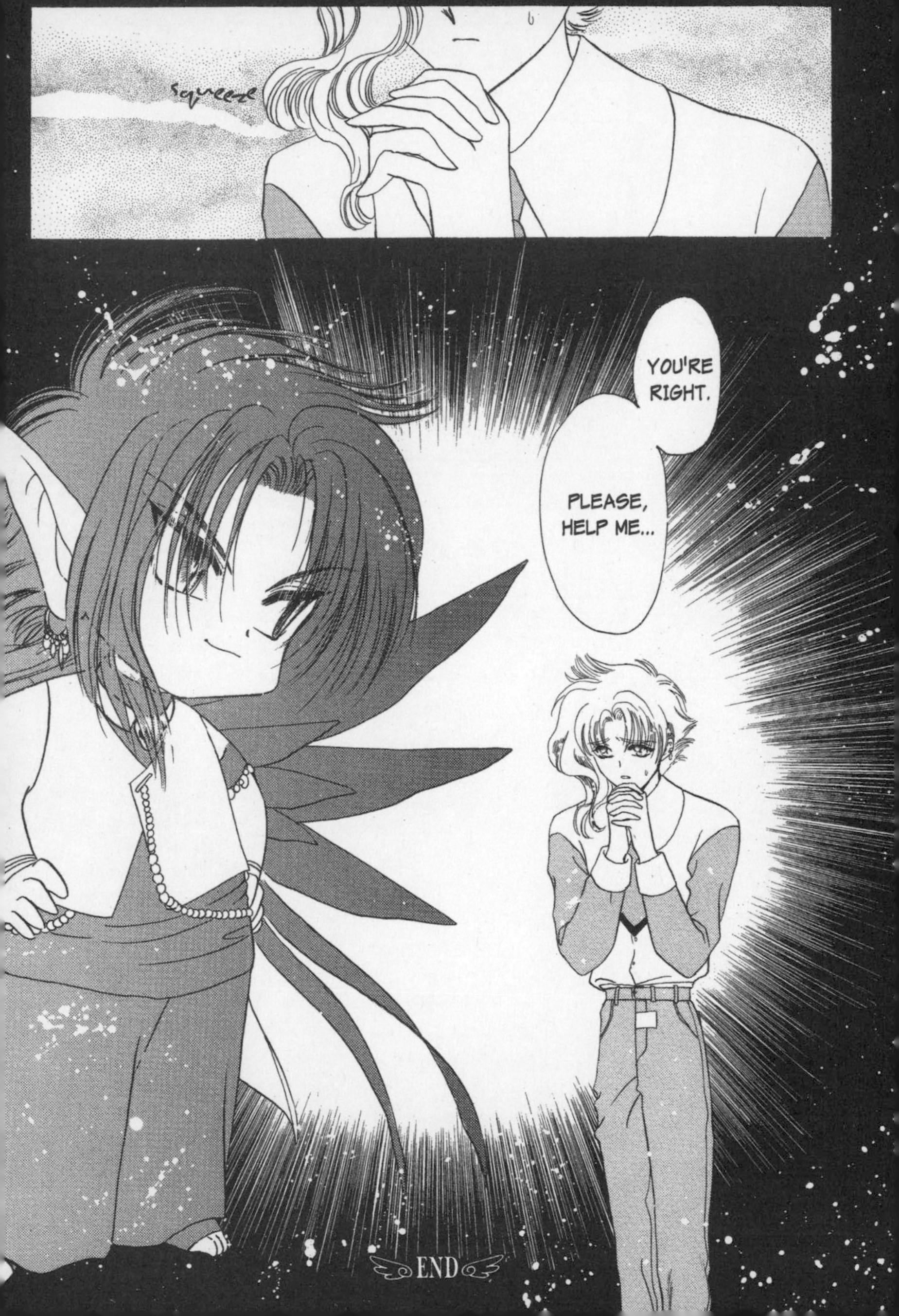
squeeze
YOU'RE RIGHT.
PLEASE, HELP ME...
END

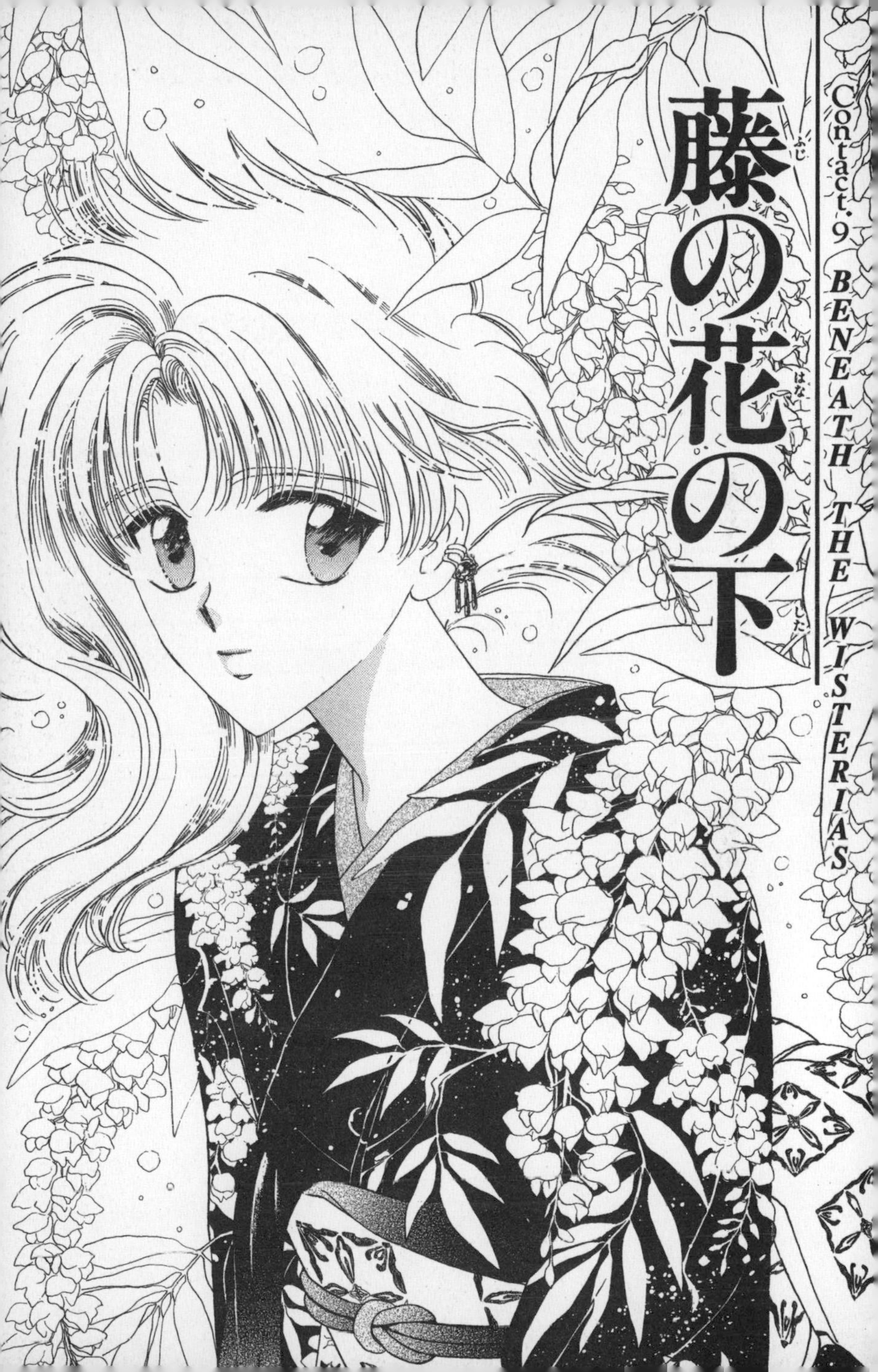
Contact.9
藤の花の下
BENEATH THE WISTERIAS

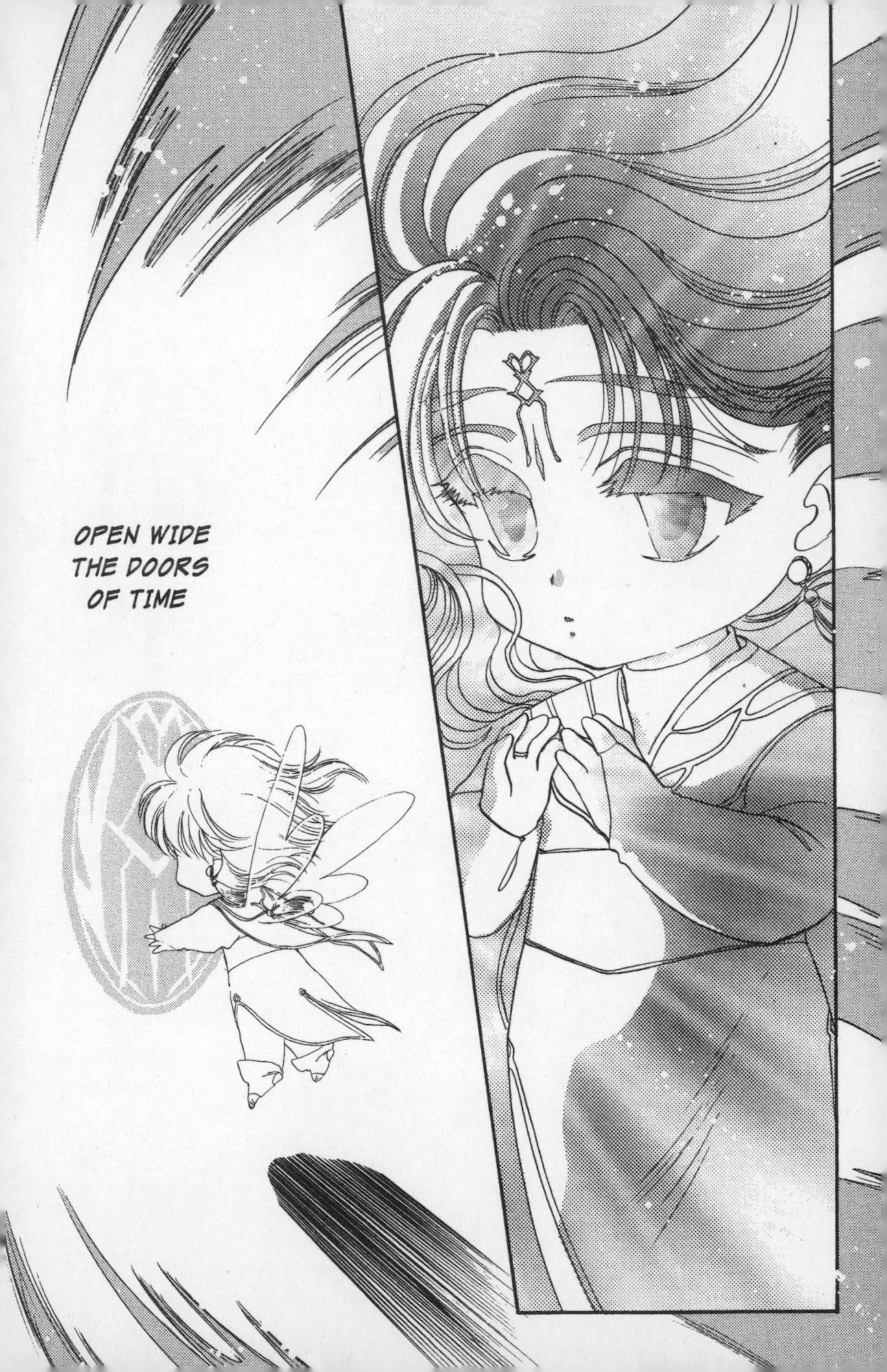
OPEN WIDE
THE DOORS
OF TIME

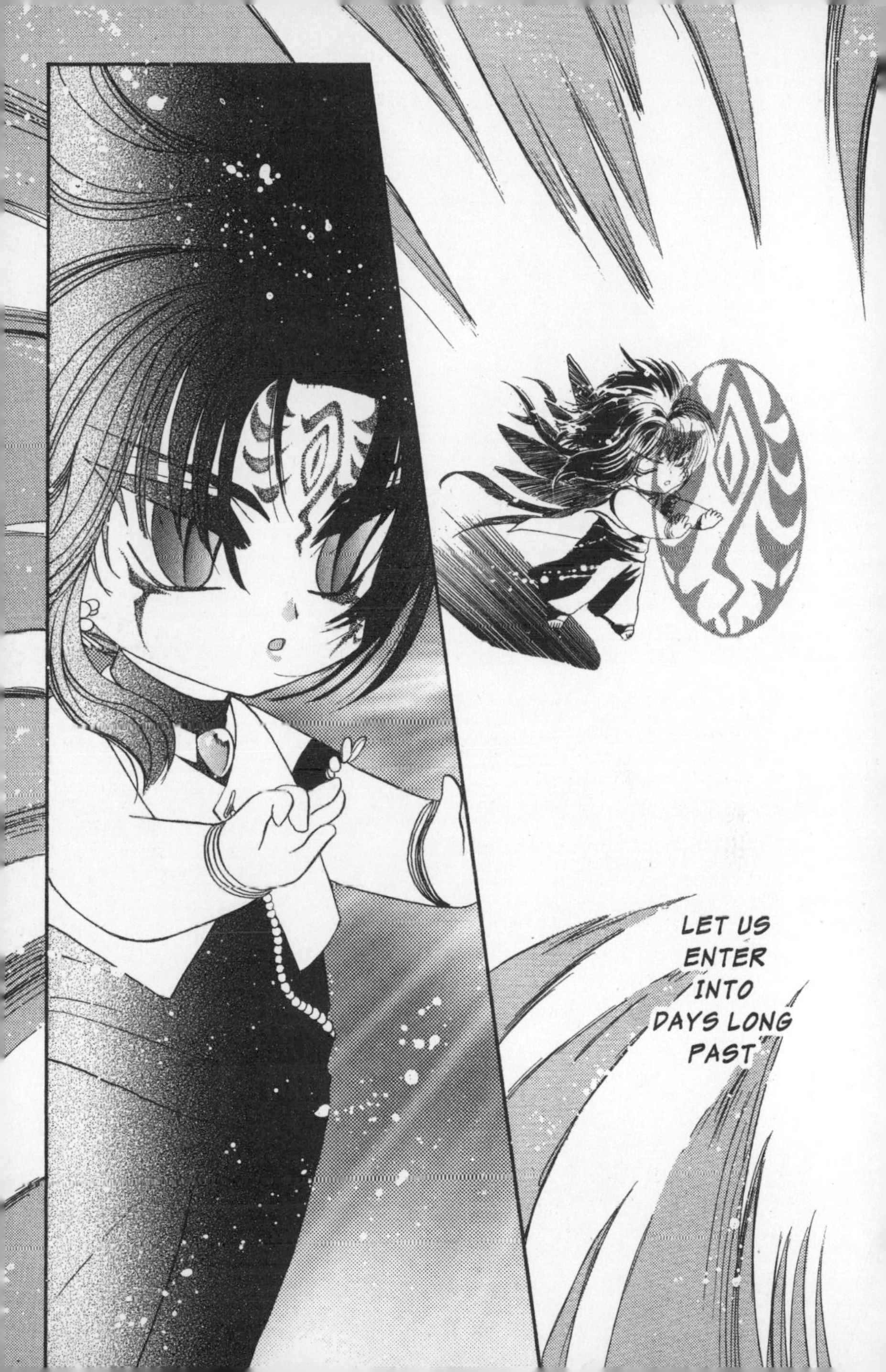
LET US ENTER INTO DAYS LONG PAST"

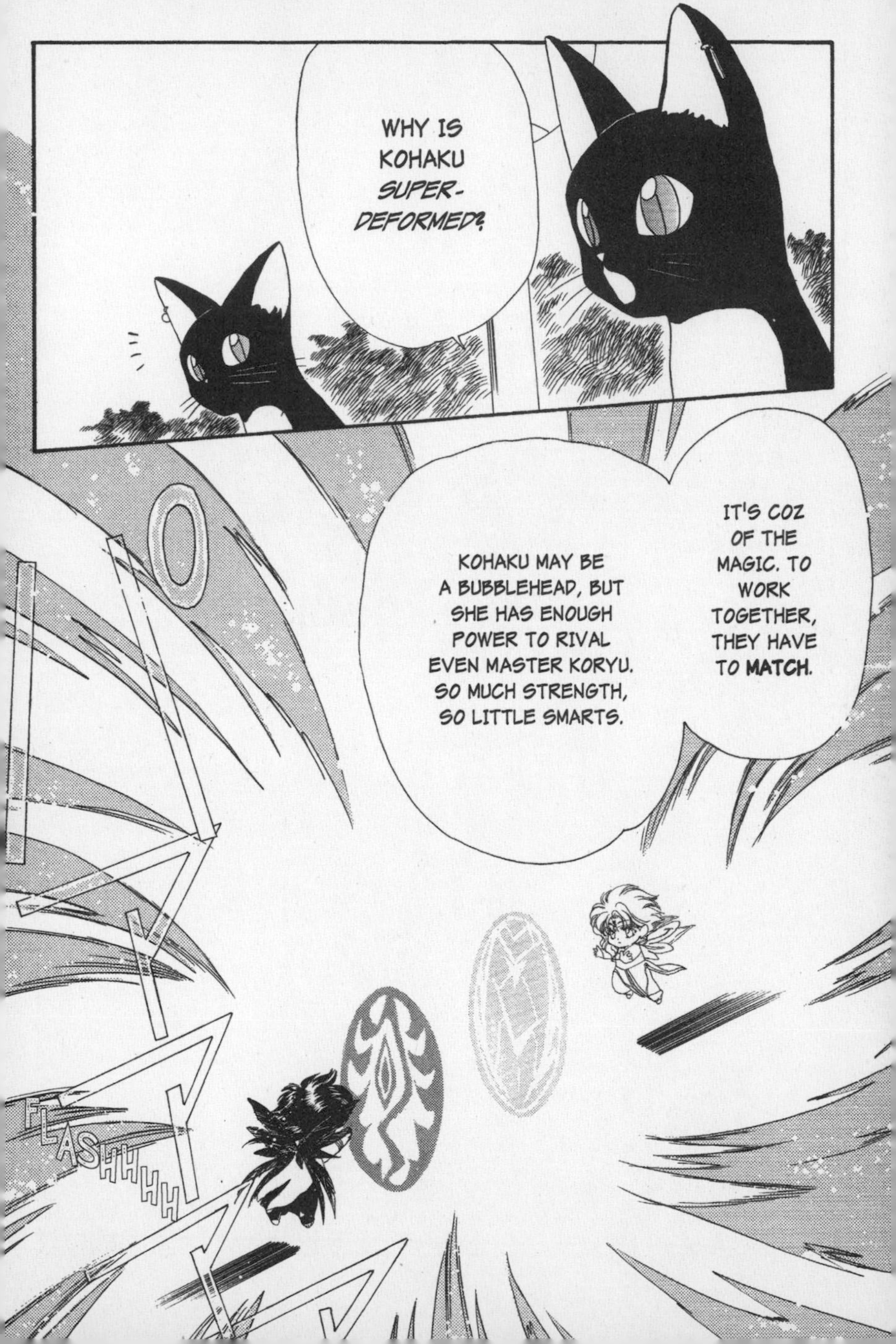
WHY IS KOHAKU SUPER-DEFORMED?
IT'S COZ OF THE MAGIC. TO WORK TOGETHER, THEY HAVE TO MATCH.
KOHAKU MAY BE A BUBBLEHEAD, BUT SHE HAS ENOUGH POWER TO RIVAL EVEN MASTER KORYU. SO MUCH STRENGTH, SO LITTLE SMARTS.
FLASHHHHH

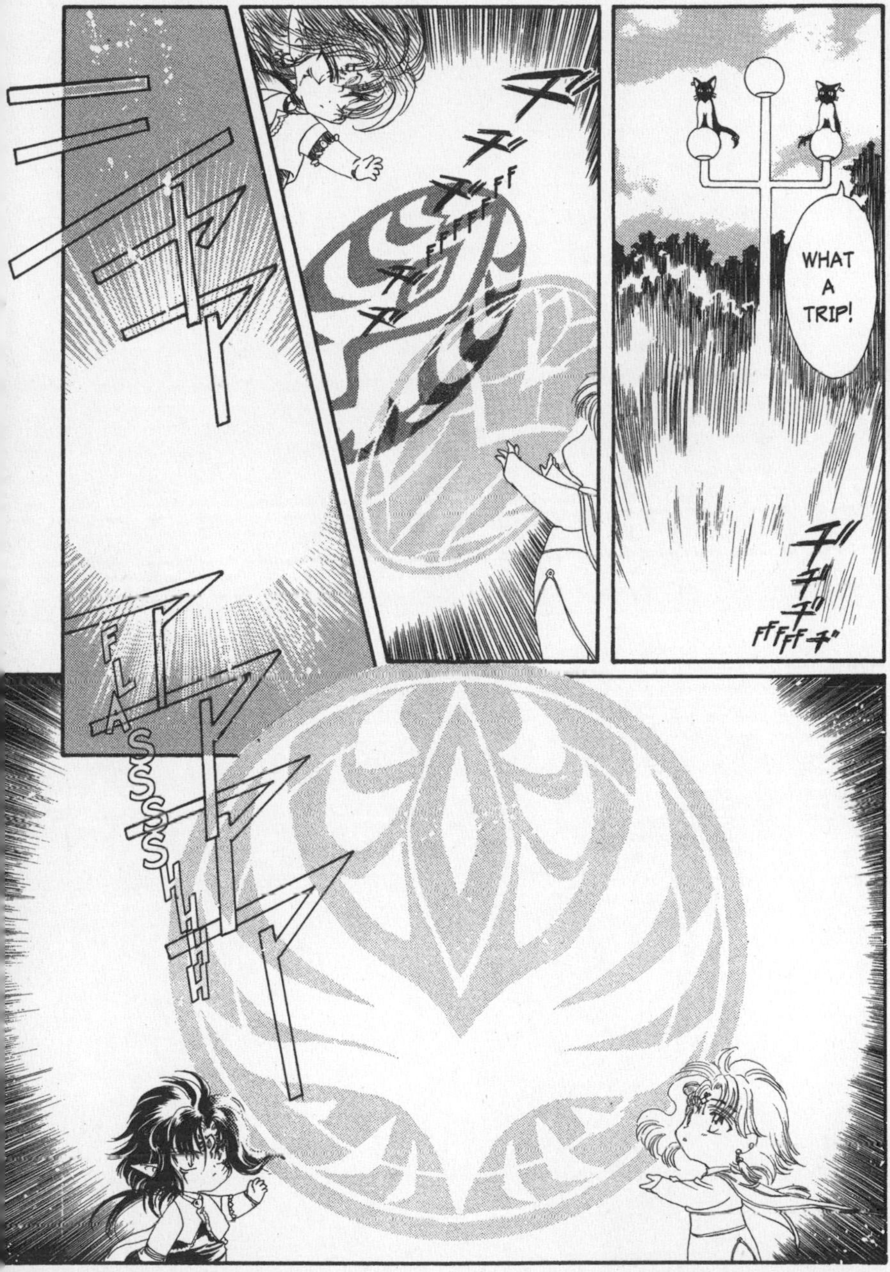
WHAT A TRIP!
FFFFF
FF
FFFFF
FLASSSHHHH

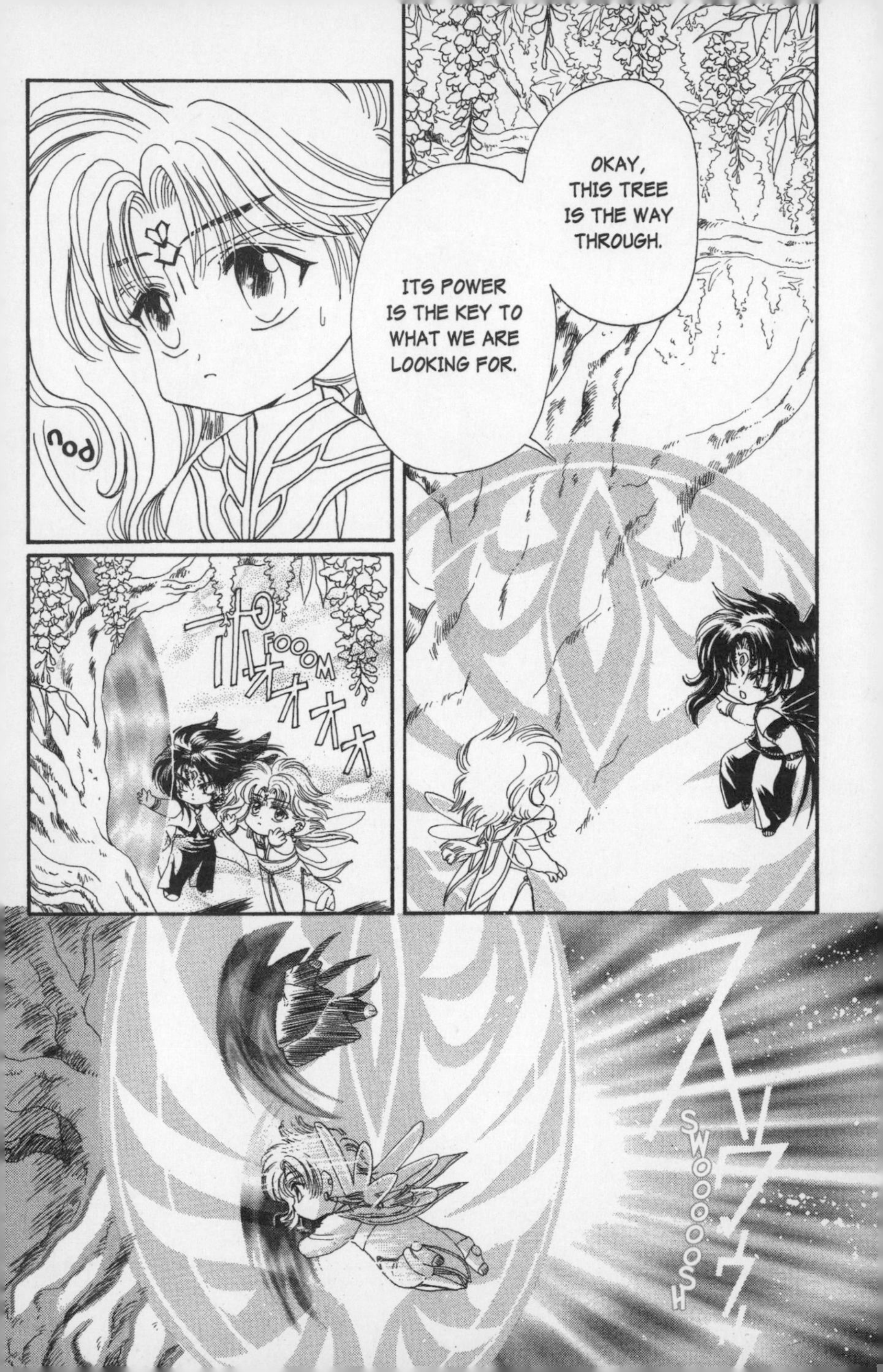
OKAY, THIS TREE IS THE WAY THROUGH.
ITS POWER IS THE KEY TO WHAT WE ARE LOOKING FOR.
nod
FOOOM
SWOOOOOSH

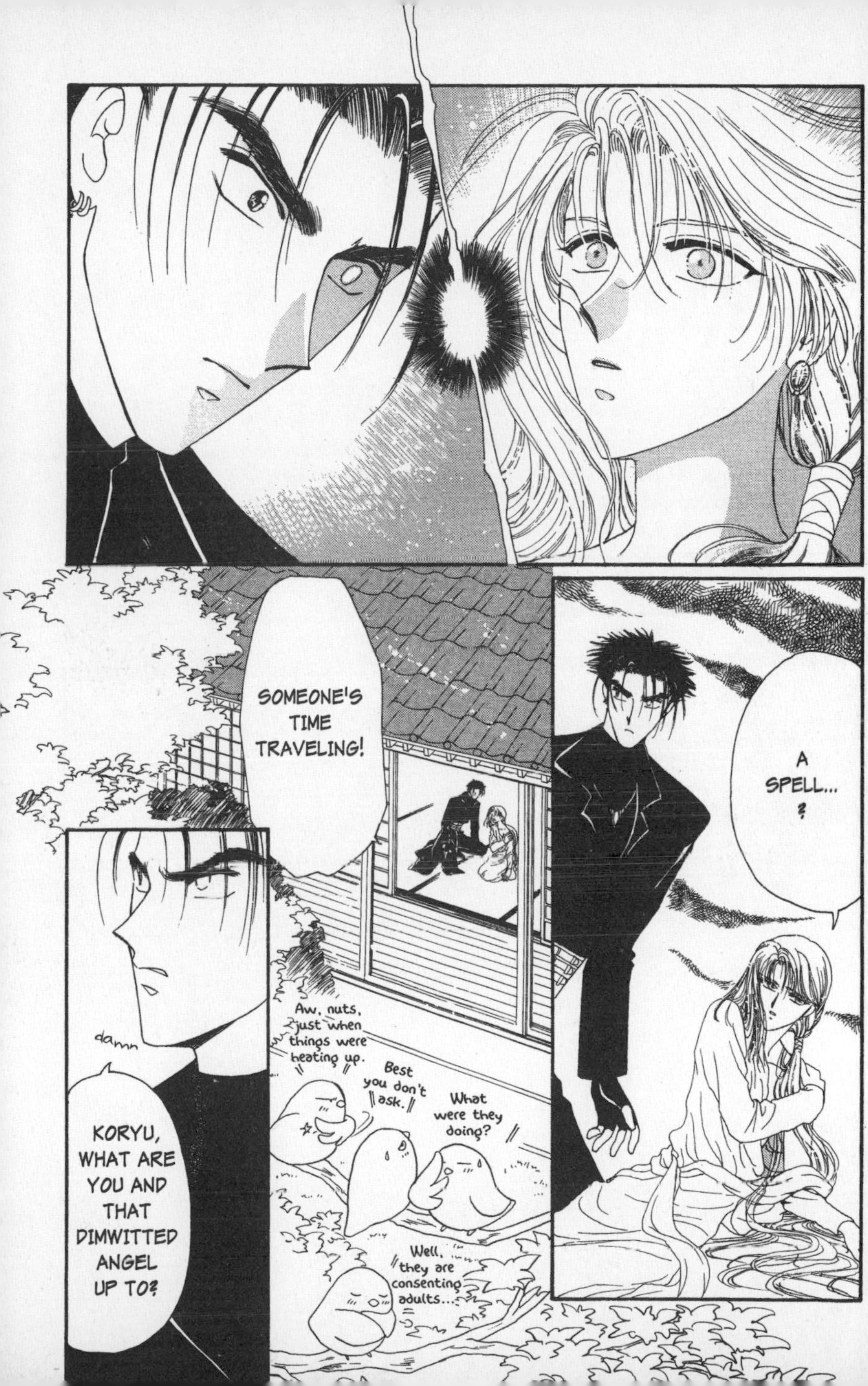
A SPELL...?
SOMEONE'S TIME TRAVELING!
Aw, nuts, just when things were heating up.
What were they doing?
Best you don't ask.
Well, they are consenting adults...
damn
KORYU, WHAT ARE YOU AND THAT DIMWITTED ANGEL UP TO?

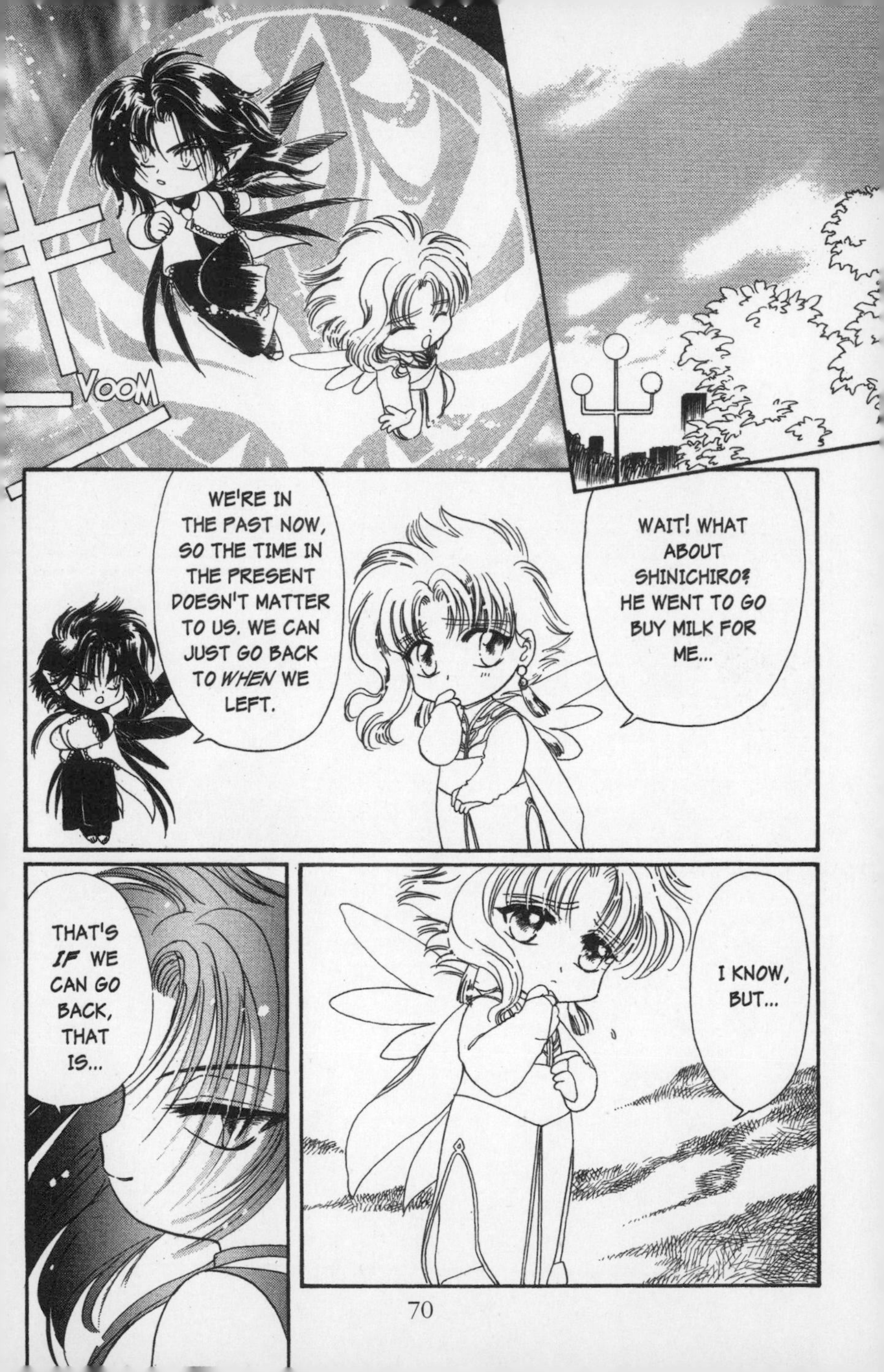
VOOM
WAIT! WHAT ABOUT SHINICHIRO? HE WENT TO GO BUY MILK FOR ME...
WE'RE IN THE PAST NOW, SO THE TIME IN THE PRESENT DOESN'T MATTER TO US. WE CAN JUST GO BACK TO *WHEN* WE LEFT.
I KNOW, BUT...
THAT'S *IF* WE CAN GO BACK, THAT IS...

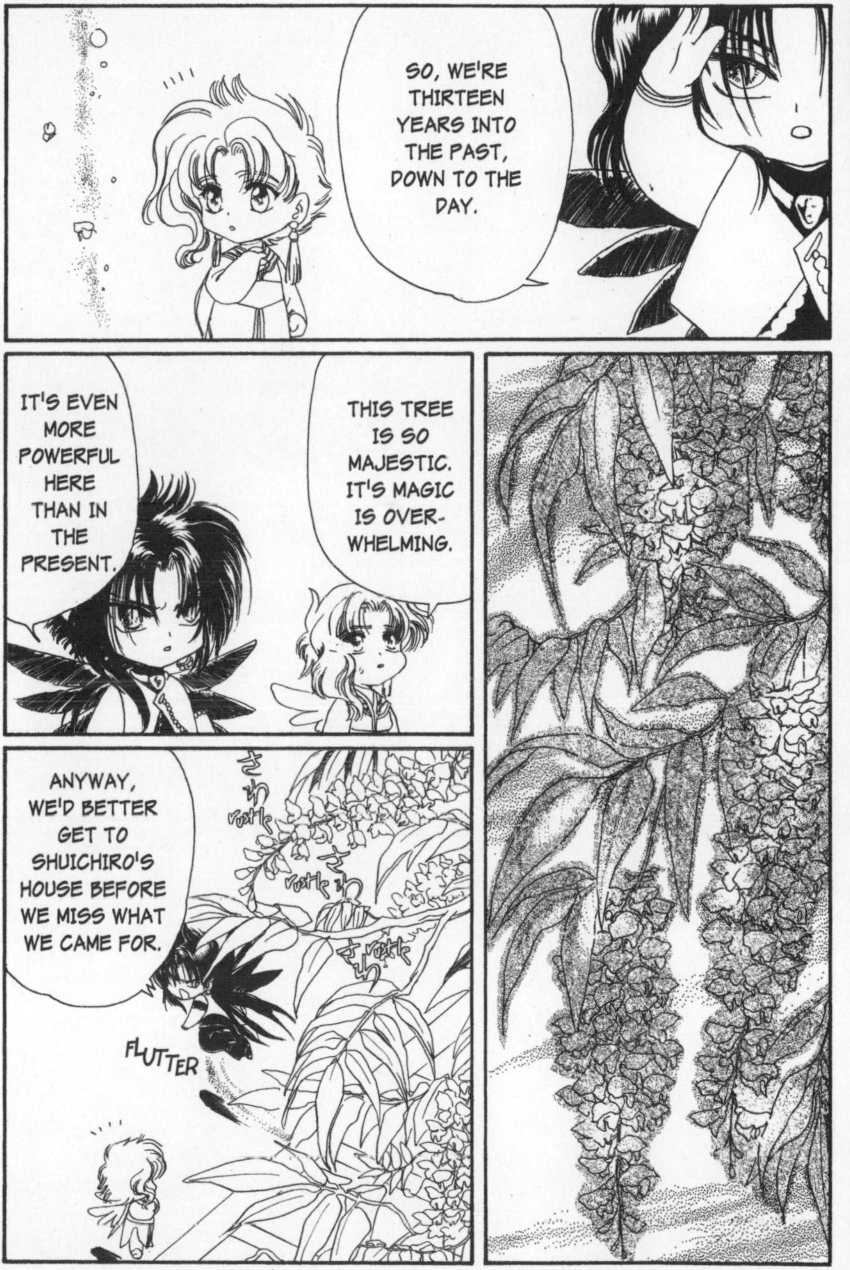
SO, WE'RE THIRTEEN YEARS INTO THE PAST, DOWN TO THE DAY.
THIS TREE IS SO MAJESTIC. IT'S MAGIC IS OVER-WHELMING.
IT'S EVEN MORE POWERFUL HERE THAN IN THE PRESENT.
さわ
rustle
さわ
rustle
さわ
rustle
ANYWAY, WE'D BETTER GET TO SHUICHIRO'S HOUSE BEFORE WE MISS WHAT WE CAME FOR.
FLUTTER

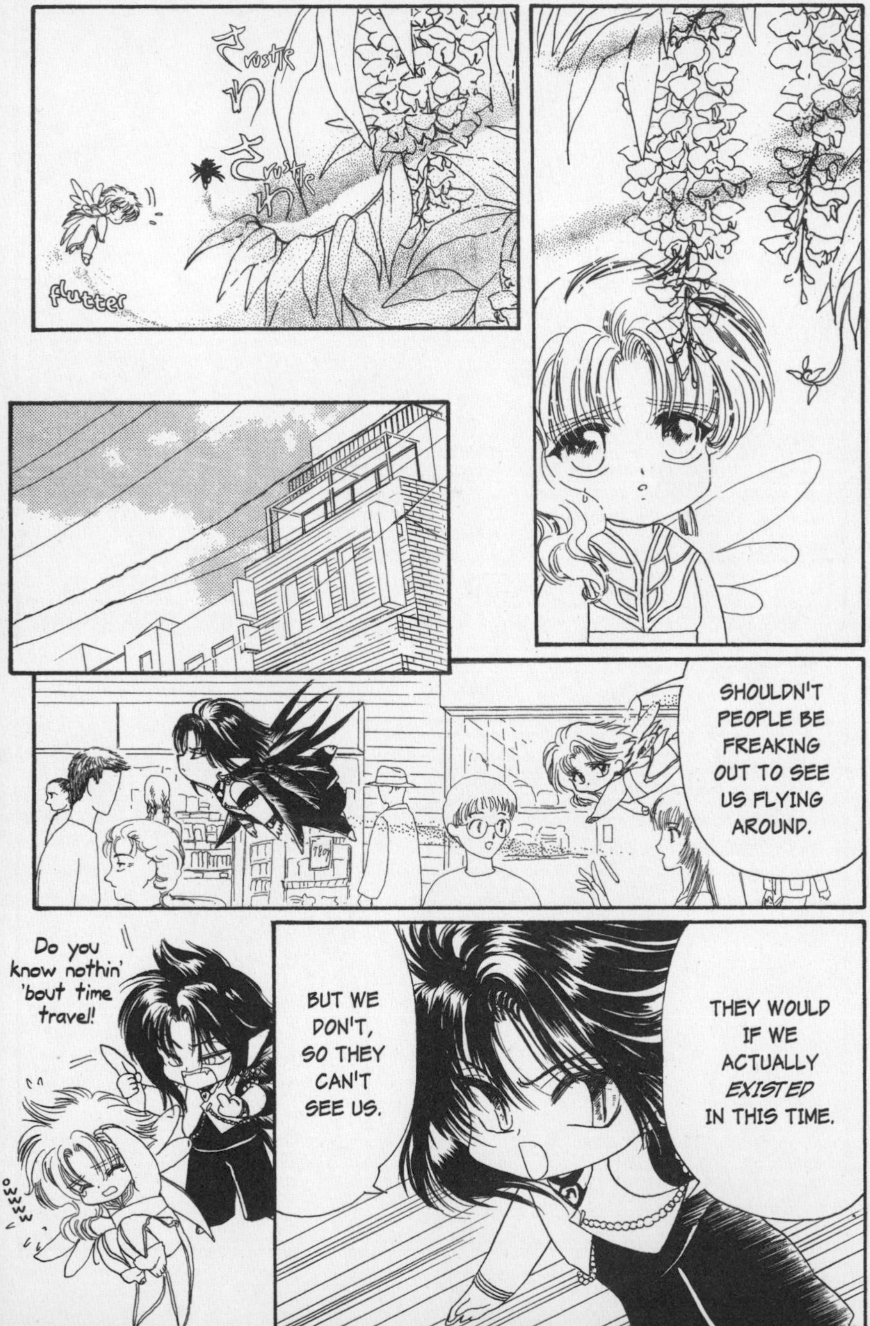

さわ rustle
さわ rustle
flutter
SHOULDN'T PEOPLE BE FREAKING OUT TO SEE US FLYING AROUND.
THEY WOULD IF WE ACTUALLY *EXISTED* IN THIS TIME.
BUT WE DON'T, SO THEY CAN'T SEE US.
Do you know nothin' 'bout time travel!
owww

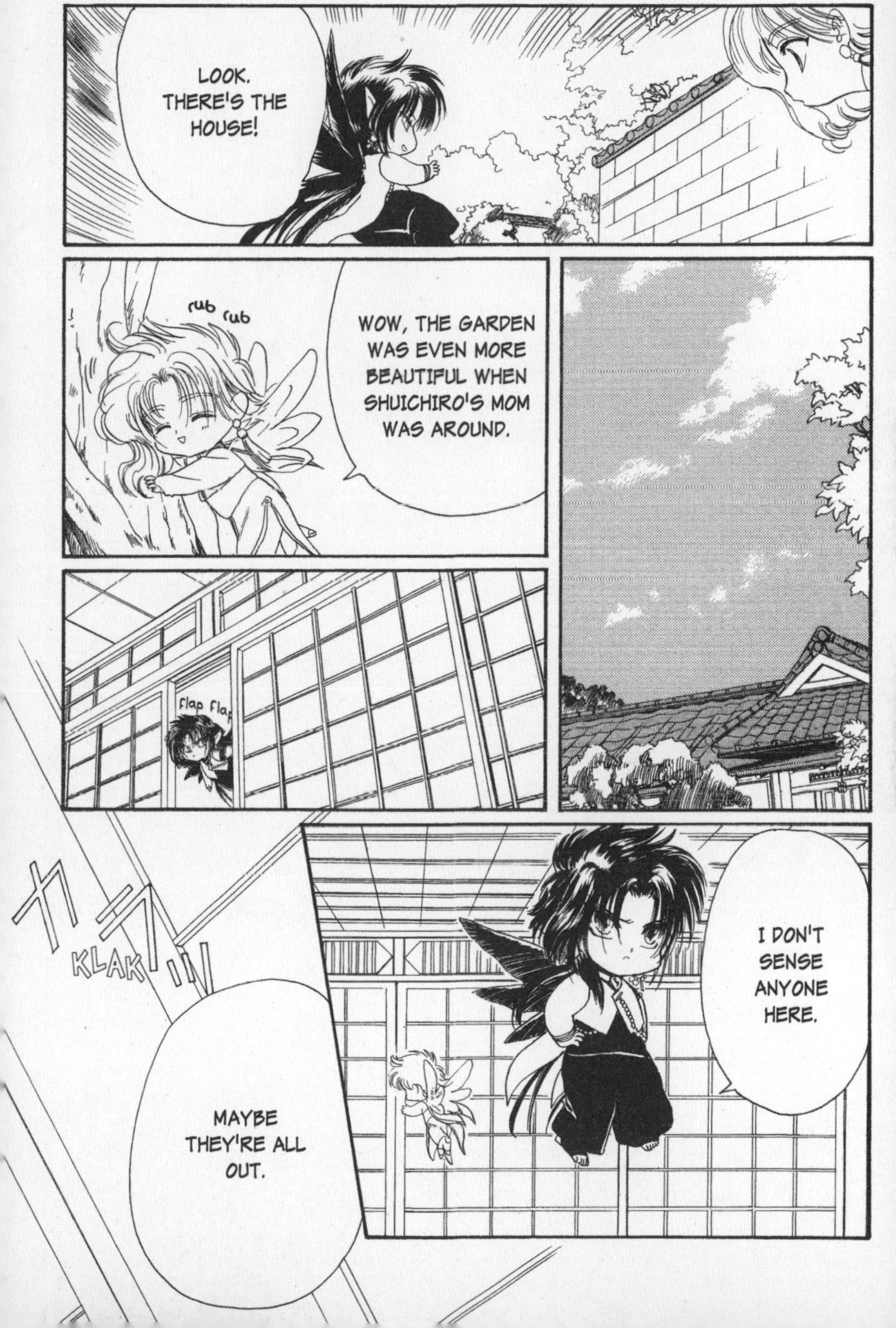
LOOK. THERE'S THE HOUSE!
rub rub
WOW, THE GARDEN WAS EVEN MORE BEAUTIFUL WHEN SHUICHIRO'S MOM WAS AROUND.
flap flap
I DON'T SENSE ANYONE HERE.
KLAK
MAYBE THEY'RE ALL OUT.

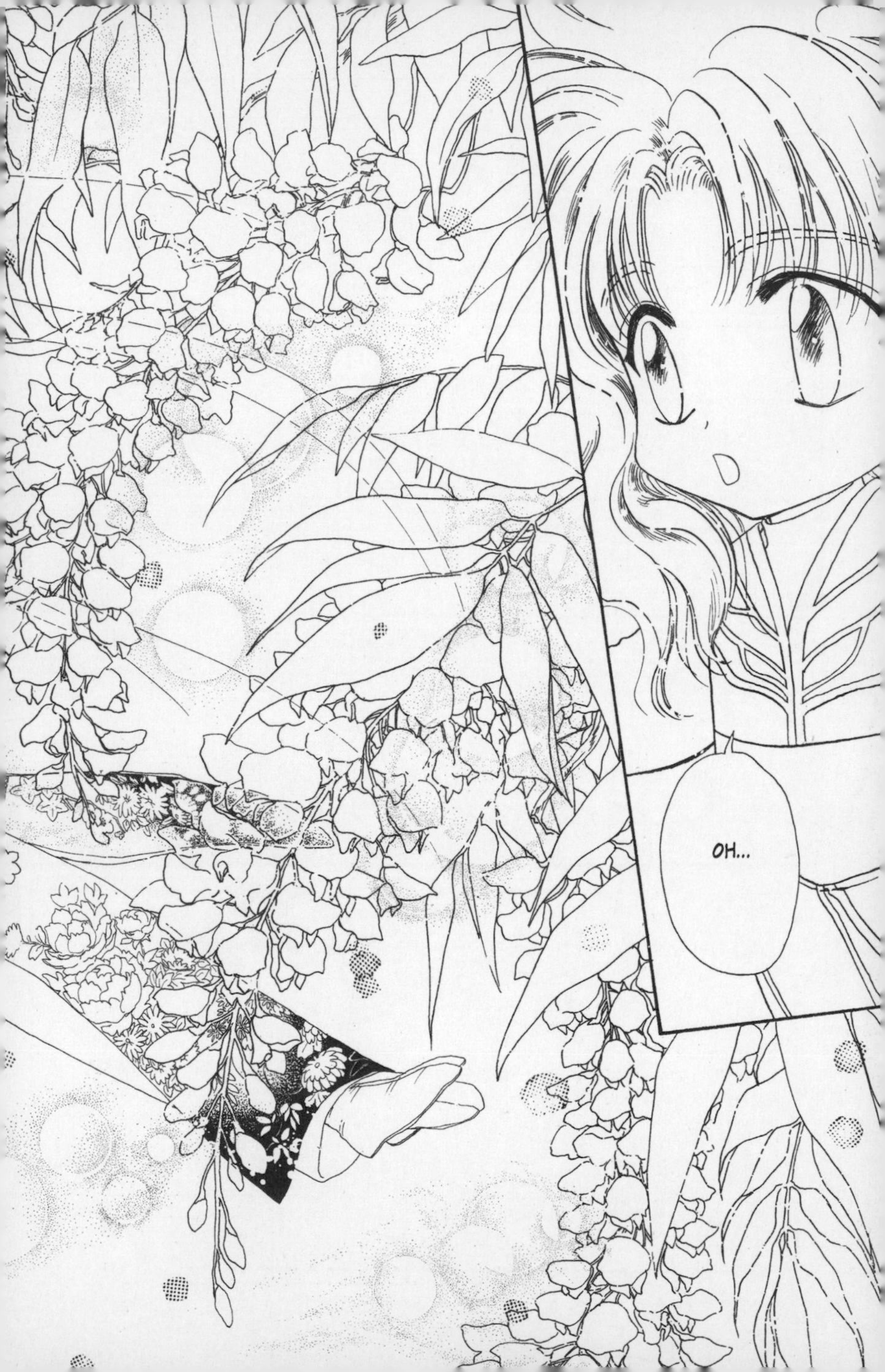
OH...

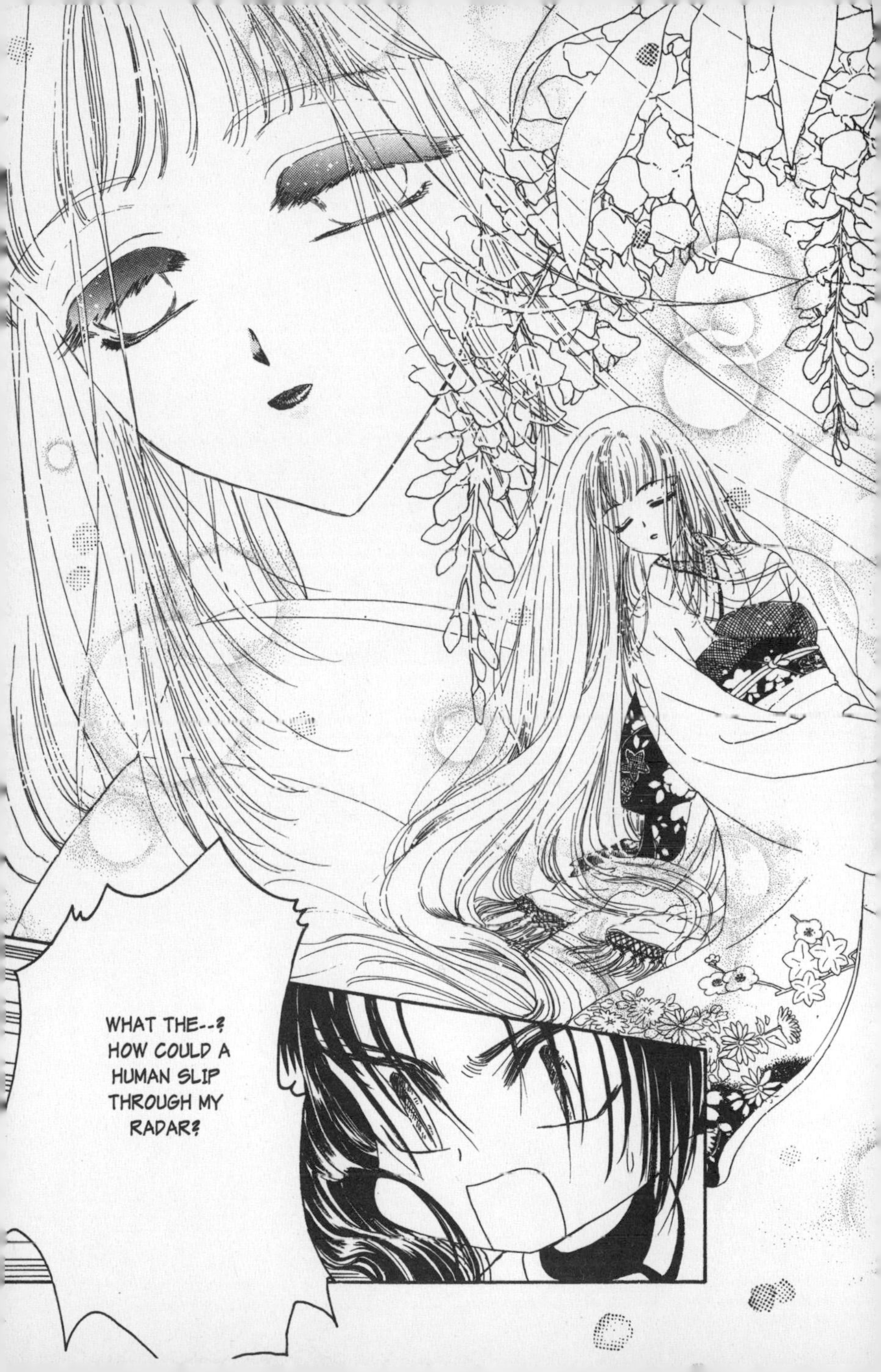
WHAT THE--? HOW COULD A HUMAN SLIP THROUGH MY RADAR?

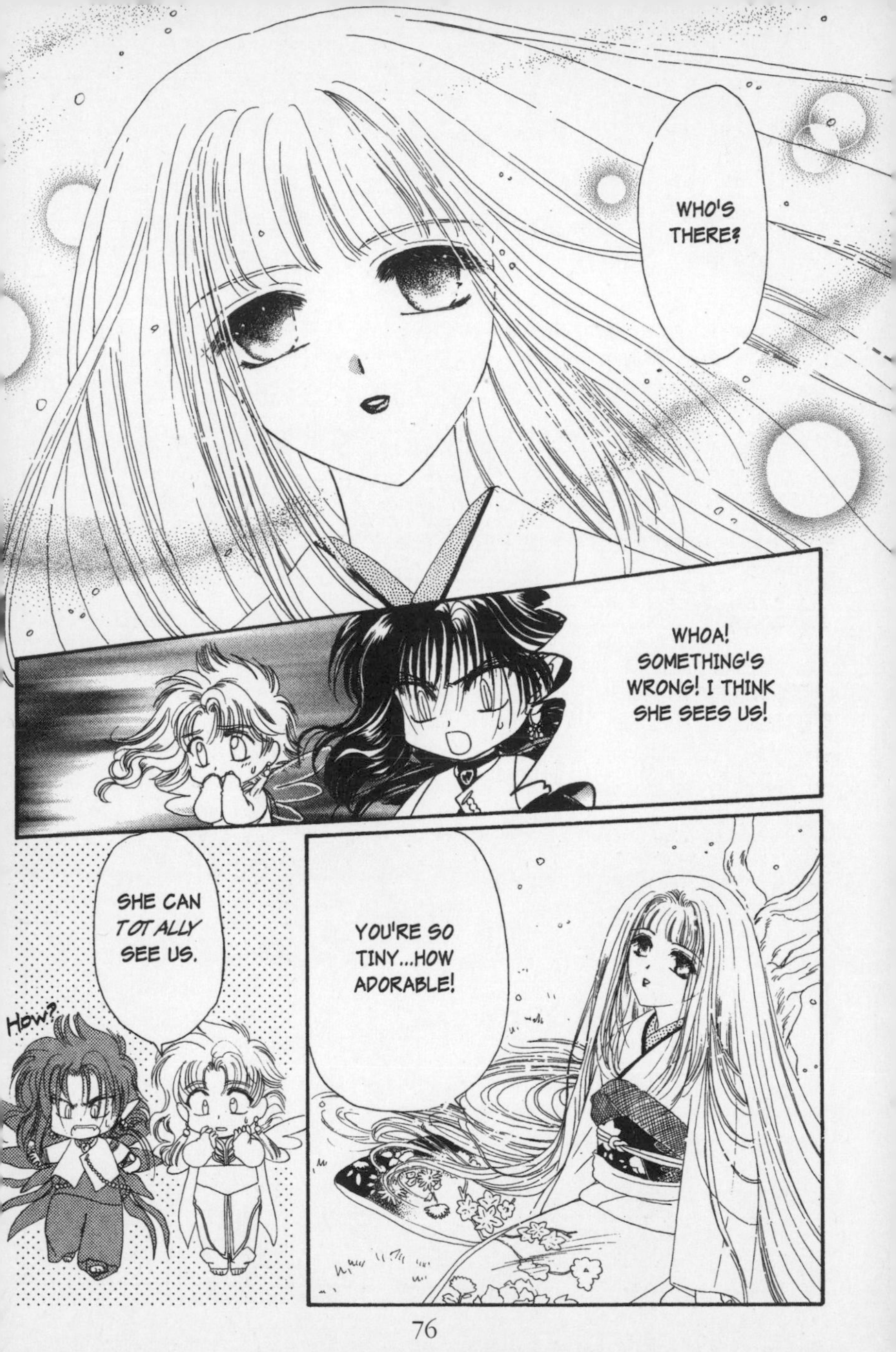
WHO'S THERE?
WHOA! SOMETHING'S WRONG! I THINK SHE SEES US!
YOU'RE SO TINY...HOW ADORABLE!
SHE CAN *TOTALLY* SEE US.
How?

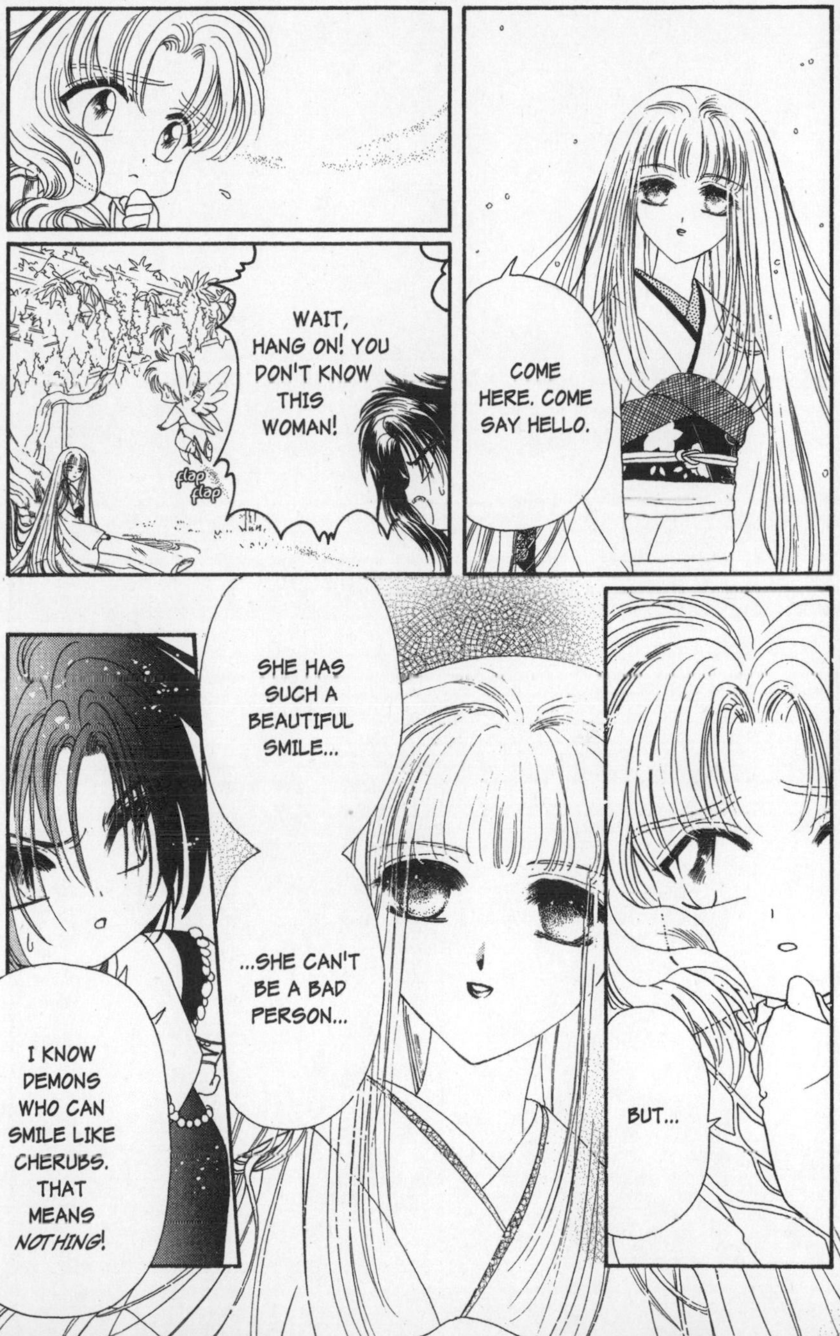
COME HERE. COME SAY HELLO.
WAIT, HANG ON! YOU DON'T KNOW THIS WOMAN!
flap flap
BUT...
SHE HAS SUCH A BEAUTIFUL SMILE...
...SHE CAN'T BE A BAD PERSON...
I KNOW DEMONS WHO CAN SMILE LIKE CHERUBS. THAT MEANS *NOTHING*!

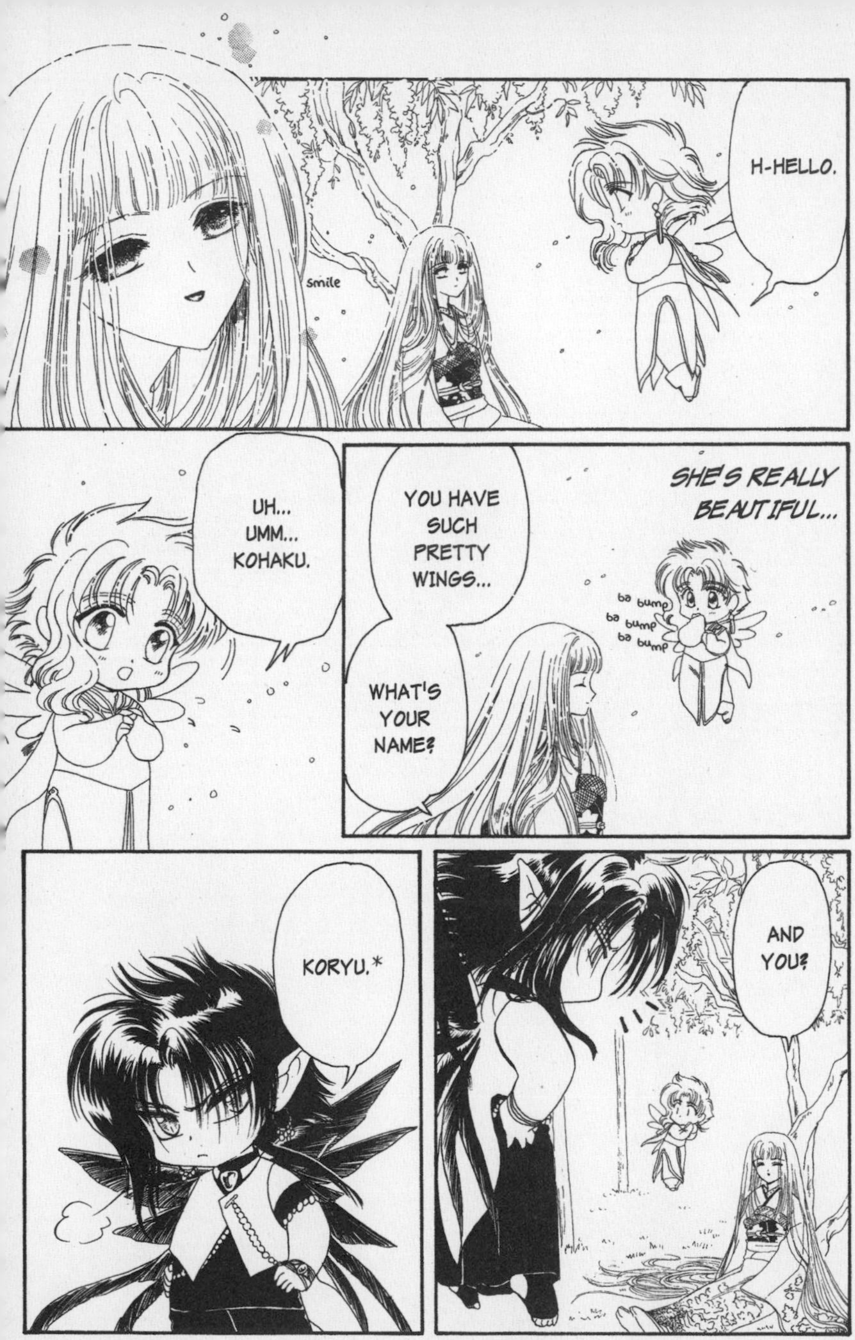
H-HELLO.
smile
SHE'S REALLY BEAUTIFUL...
YOU HAVE SUCH PRETTY WINGS...
ba bump ba bump ba bump
WHAT'S YOUR NAME?
UH... UMM... KOHAKU.
AND YOU?
KORYU.*

*Koryu- His name means "Garnet"

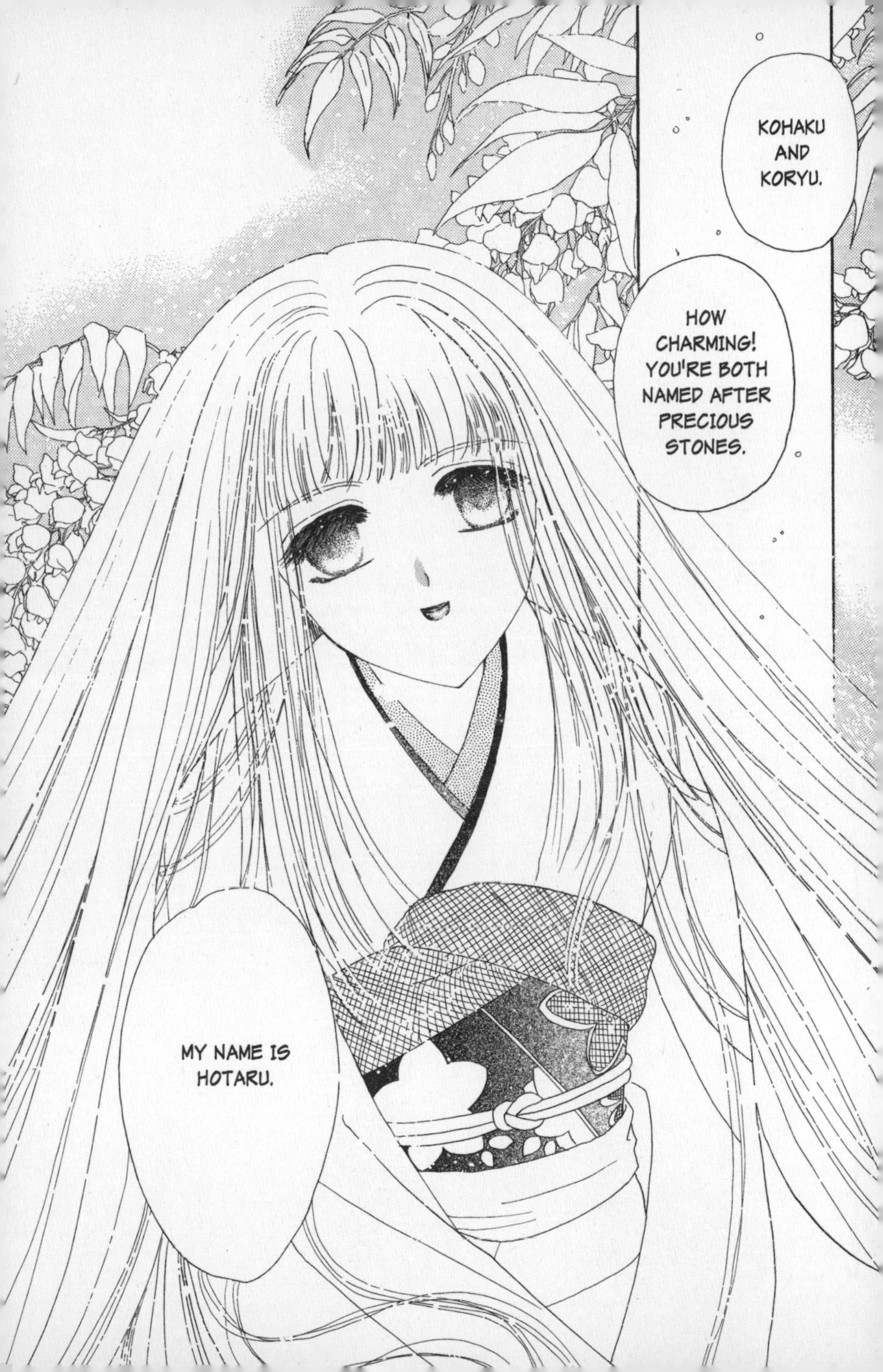
KOHAKU AND KORYU.
HOW CHARMING! YOU'RE BOTH NAMED AFTER PRECIOUS STONES.
MY NAME IS HOTARU.

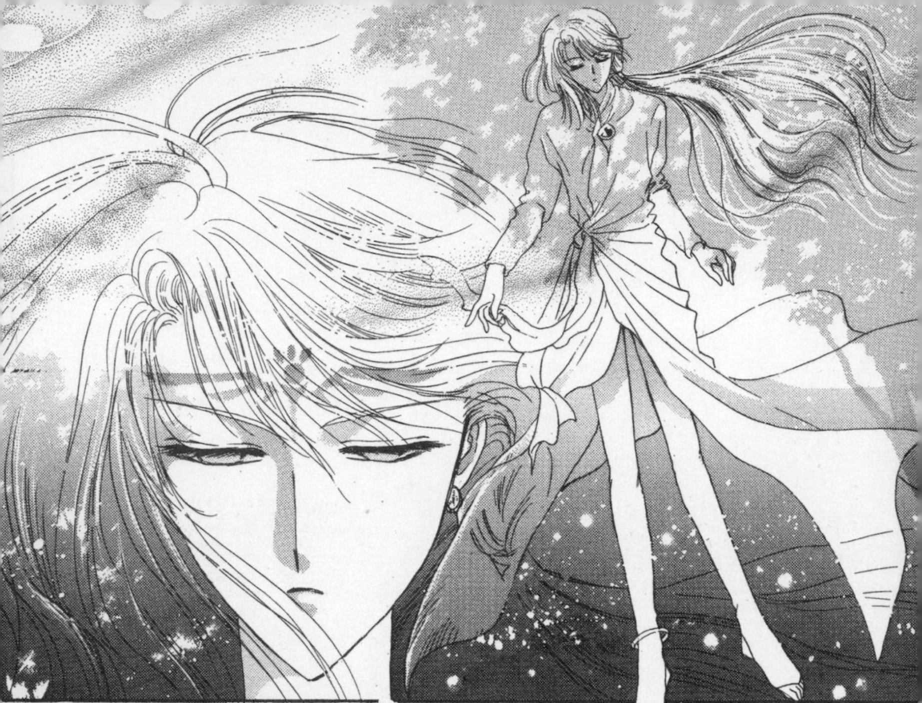

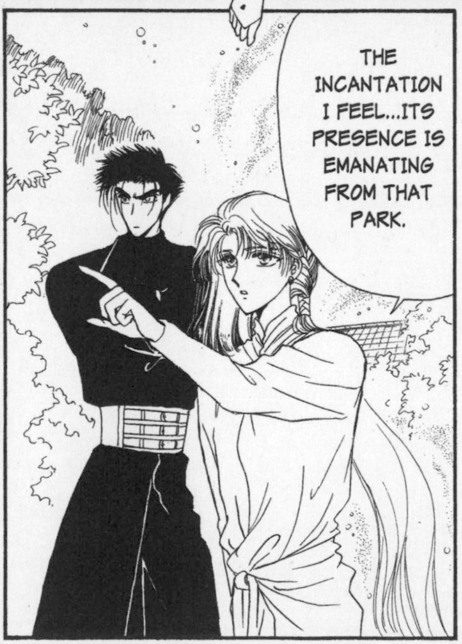
THE INCANTATION I FEEL...ITS PRESENCE IS EMANATING FROM THAT PARK.

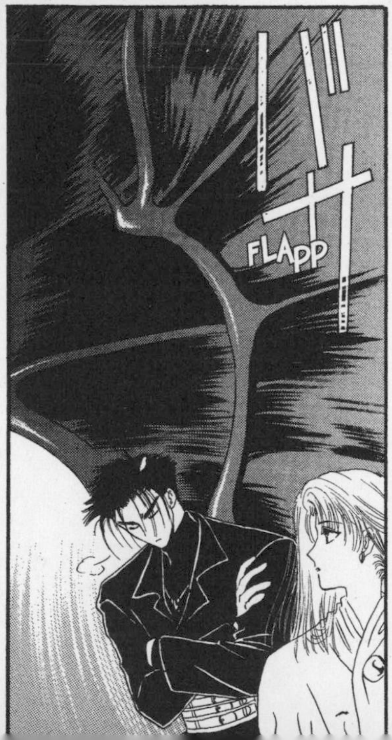
FLAPP

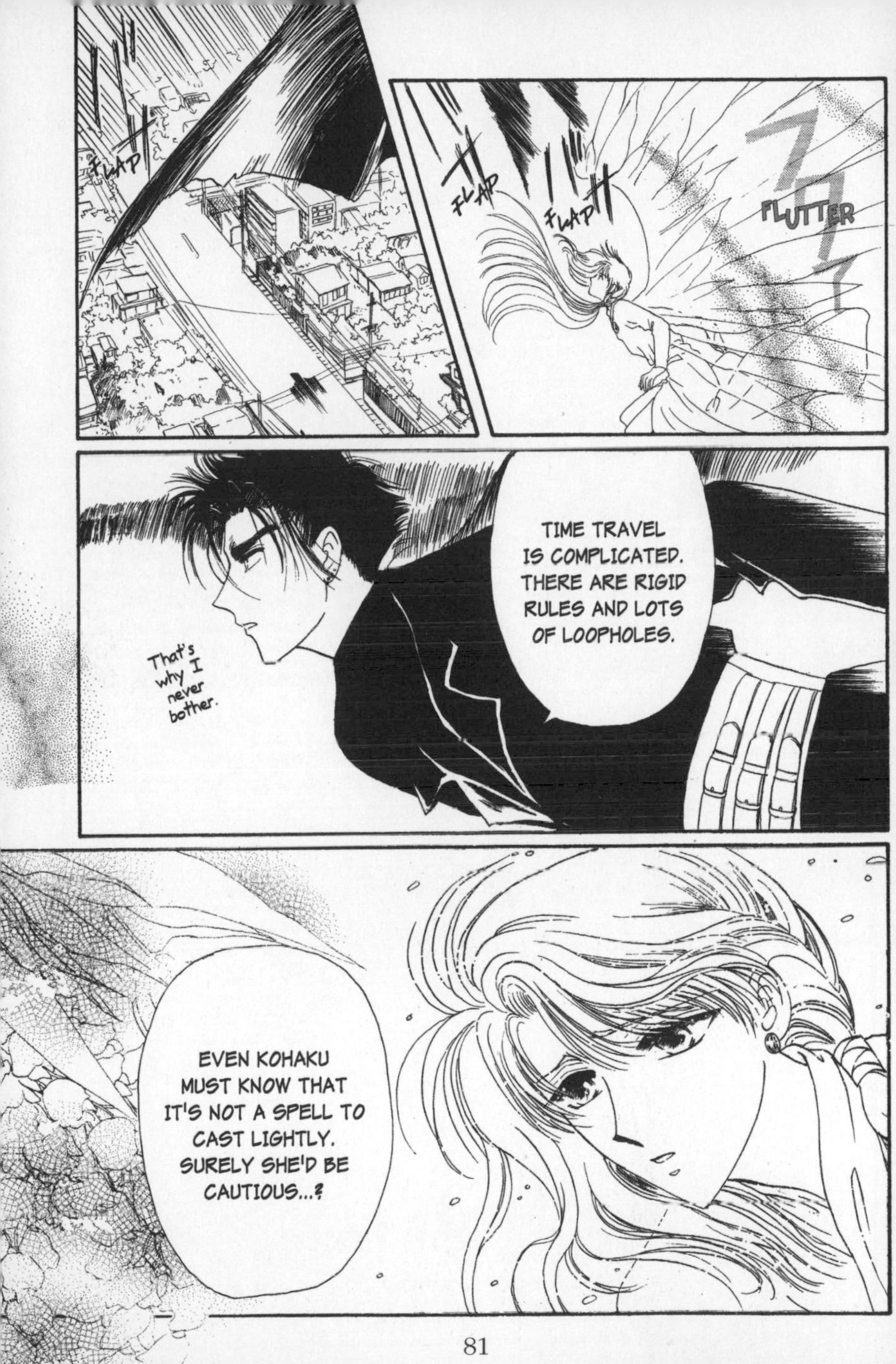
FLAP
FLAP
FLUTTER
FLAP
TIME TRAVEL IS COMPLICATED. THERE ARE RIGID RULES AND LOTS OF LOOPHOLES.
That's why I never bother.
EVEN KOHAKU MUST KNOW THAT IT'S NOT A SPELL TO CAST LIGHTLY. SURELY SHE'D BE CAUTIOUS...?

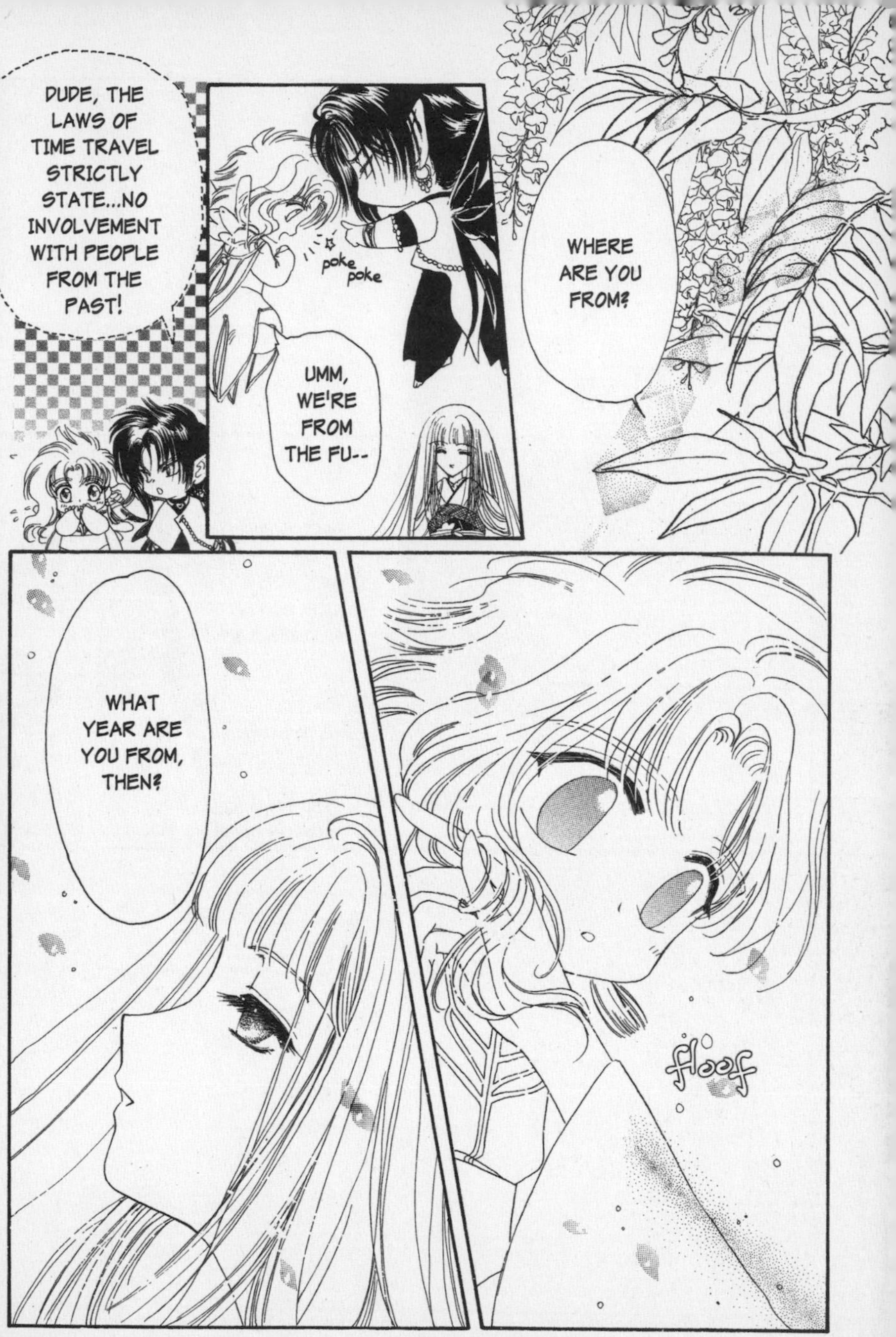
WHERE ARE YOU FROM?
UMM, WE'RE FROM THE FU--
poke poke
DUDE, THE LAWS OF TIME TRAVEL STRICTLY STATE...NO INVOLVEMENT WITH PEOPLE FROM THE PAST!
floof
WHAT YEAR ARE YOU FROM, THEN?

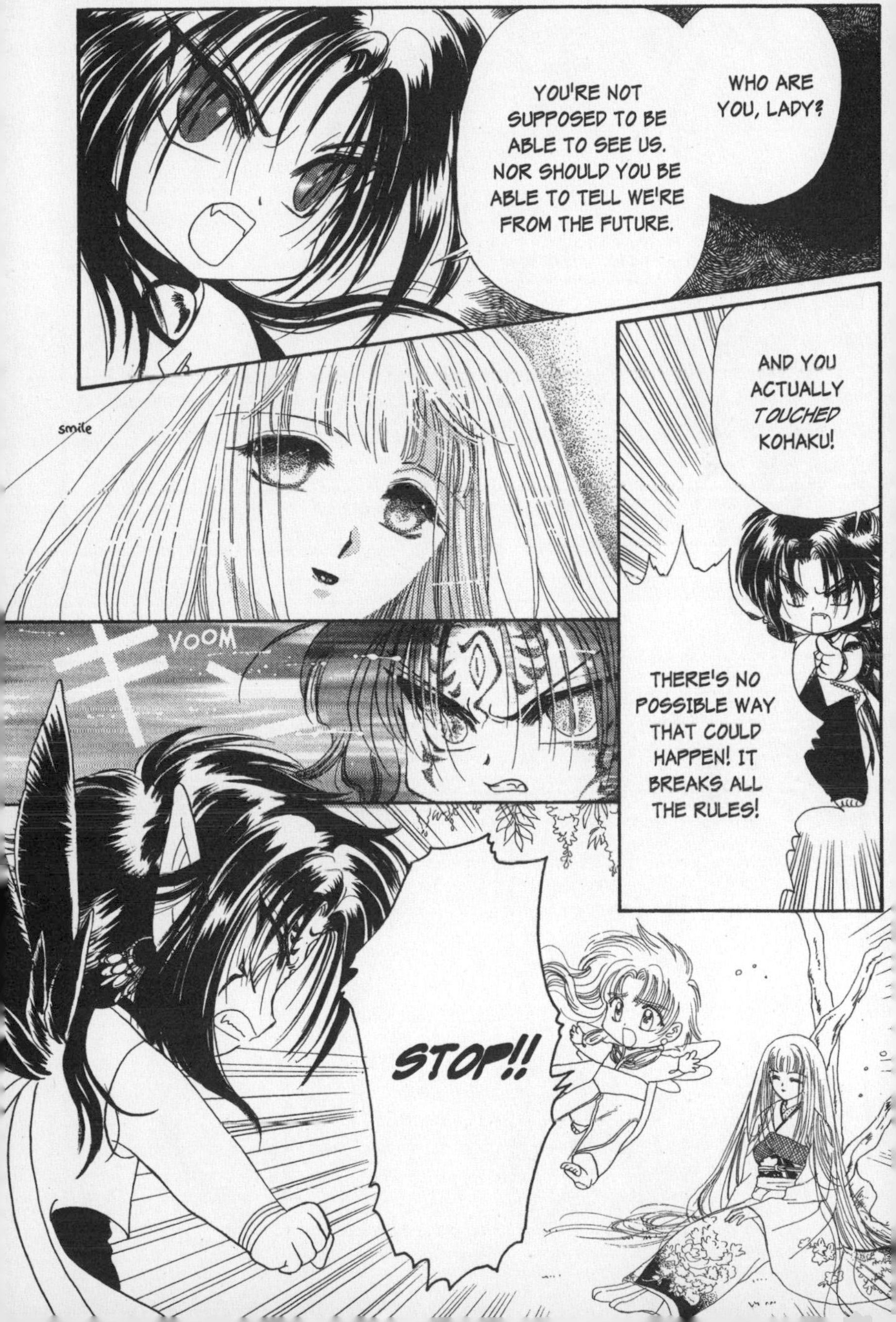
WHO ARE YOU, LADY?
YOU'RE NOT SUPPOSED TO BE ABLE TO SEE US. NOR SHOULD YOU BE ABLE TO TELL WE'RE FROM THE FUTURE.
AND YOU ACTUALLY *TOUCHED* KOHAKU!
THERE'S NO POSSIBLE WAY THAT COULD HAPPEN! IT BREAKS ALL THE RULES!
smile
VOOM
STOP!!

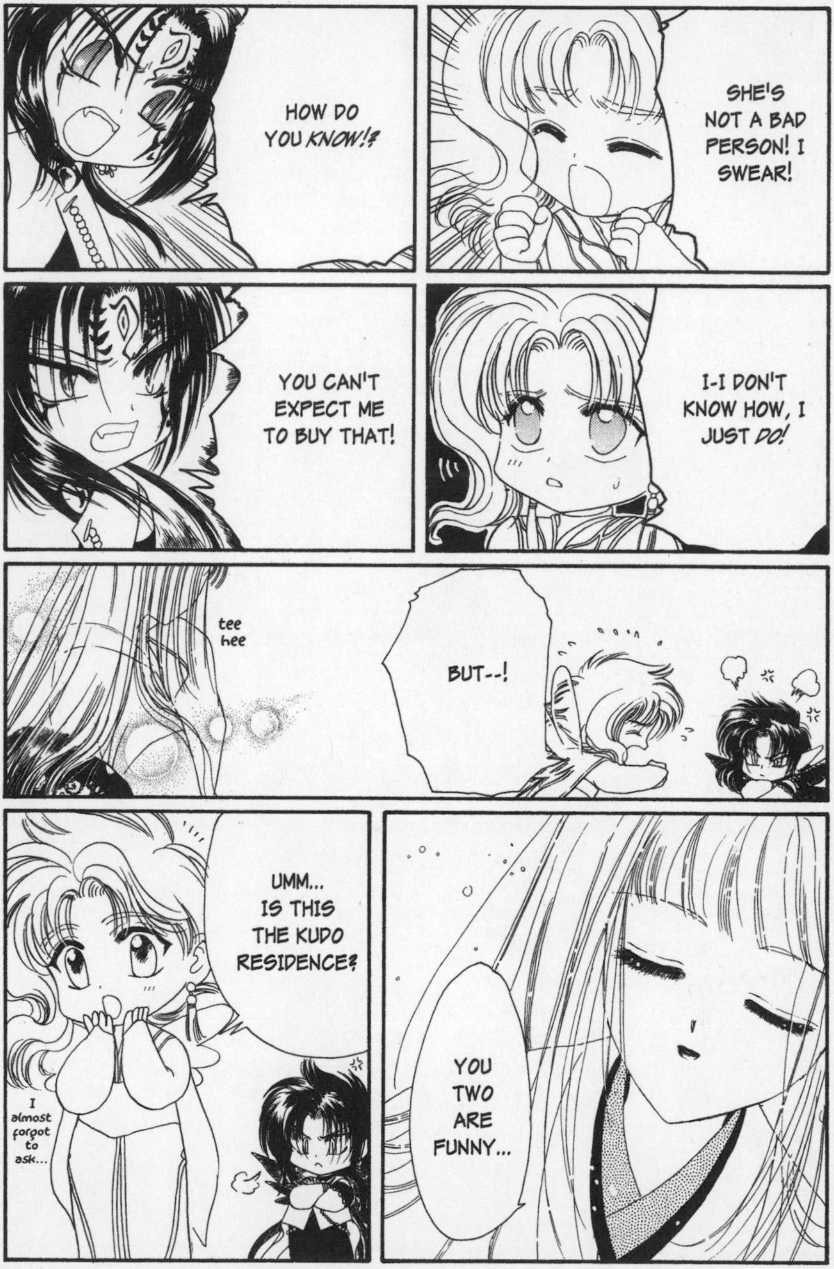
SHE'S NOT A BAD PERSON! I SWEAR!
HOW DO YOU KNOW!?
I-I DON'T KNOW HOW, I JUST DO!
YOU CAN'T EXPECT ME TO BUY THAT!
BUT--!
tee hee
YOU TWO ARE FUNNY...
UMM... IS THIS THE KUDO RESIDENCE?
I almost forgot to ask...

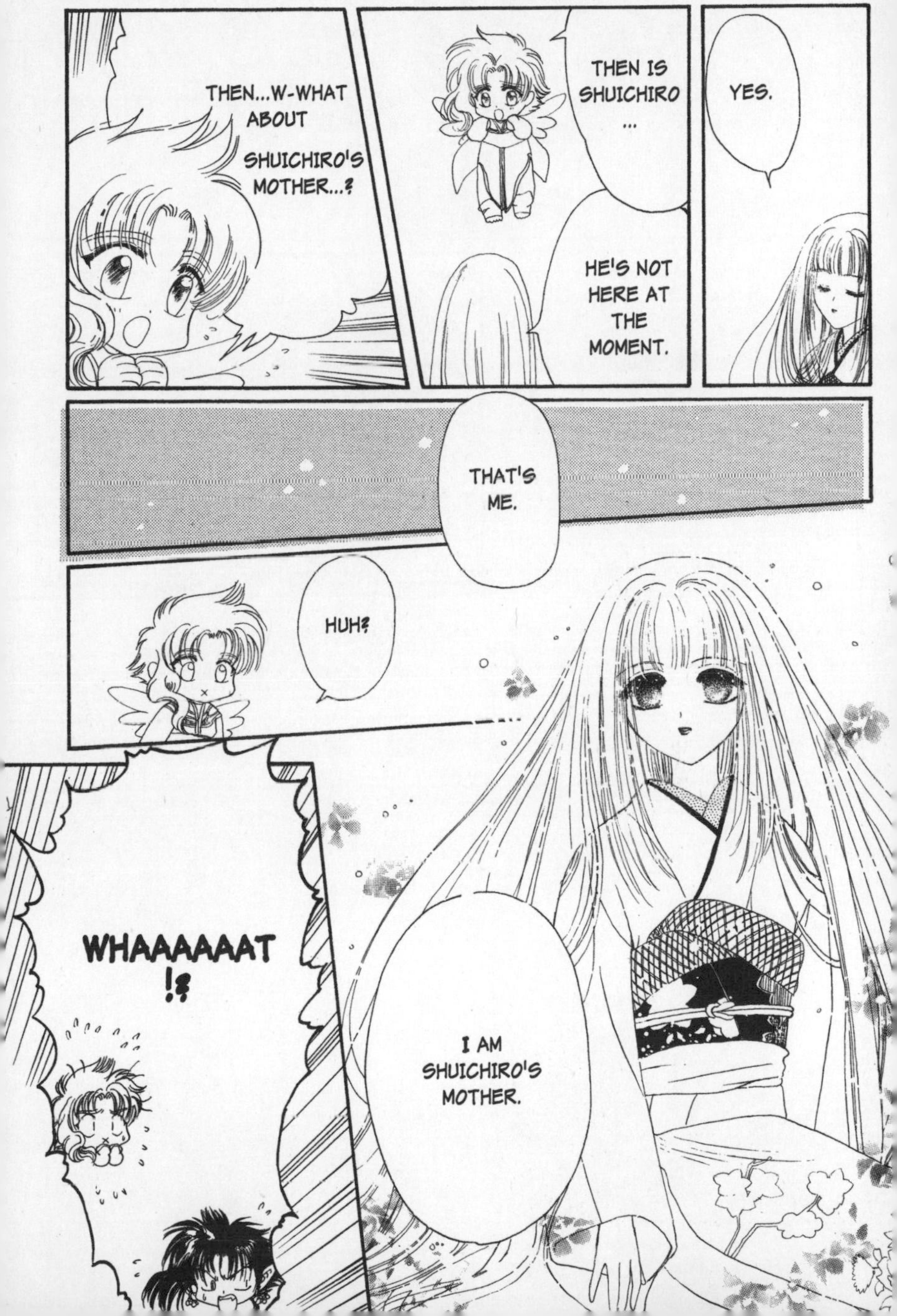
YES.
THEN IS SHUICHIRO ...
HE'S NOT HERE AT THE MOMENT.
THEN...W-WHAT ABOUT SHUICHIRO'S MOTHER...?
THAT'S ME.
HUH?
I AM SHUICHIRO'S MOTHER.
WHAAAAAAT !?

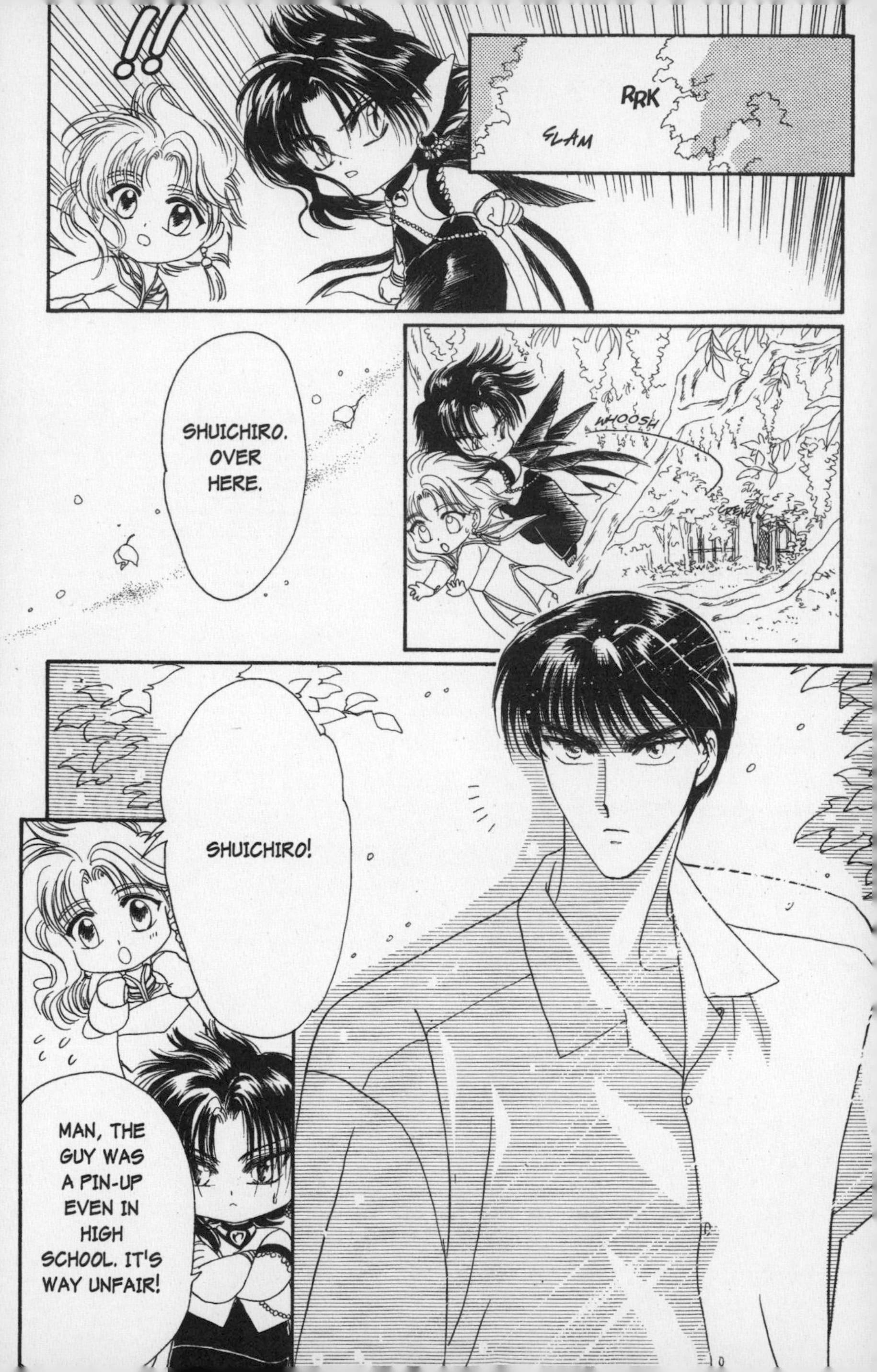
RRK
SLAM
!!
WHOOSH
SHUICHIRO. OVER HERE.
SHUICHIRO!
MAN, THE GUY WAS A PIN-UP EVEN IN HIGH SCHOOL. IT'S WAY UNFAIR!

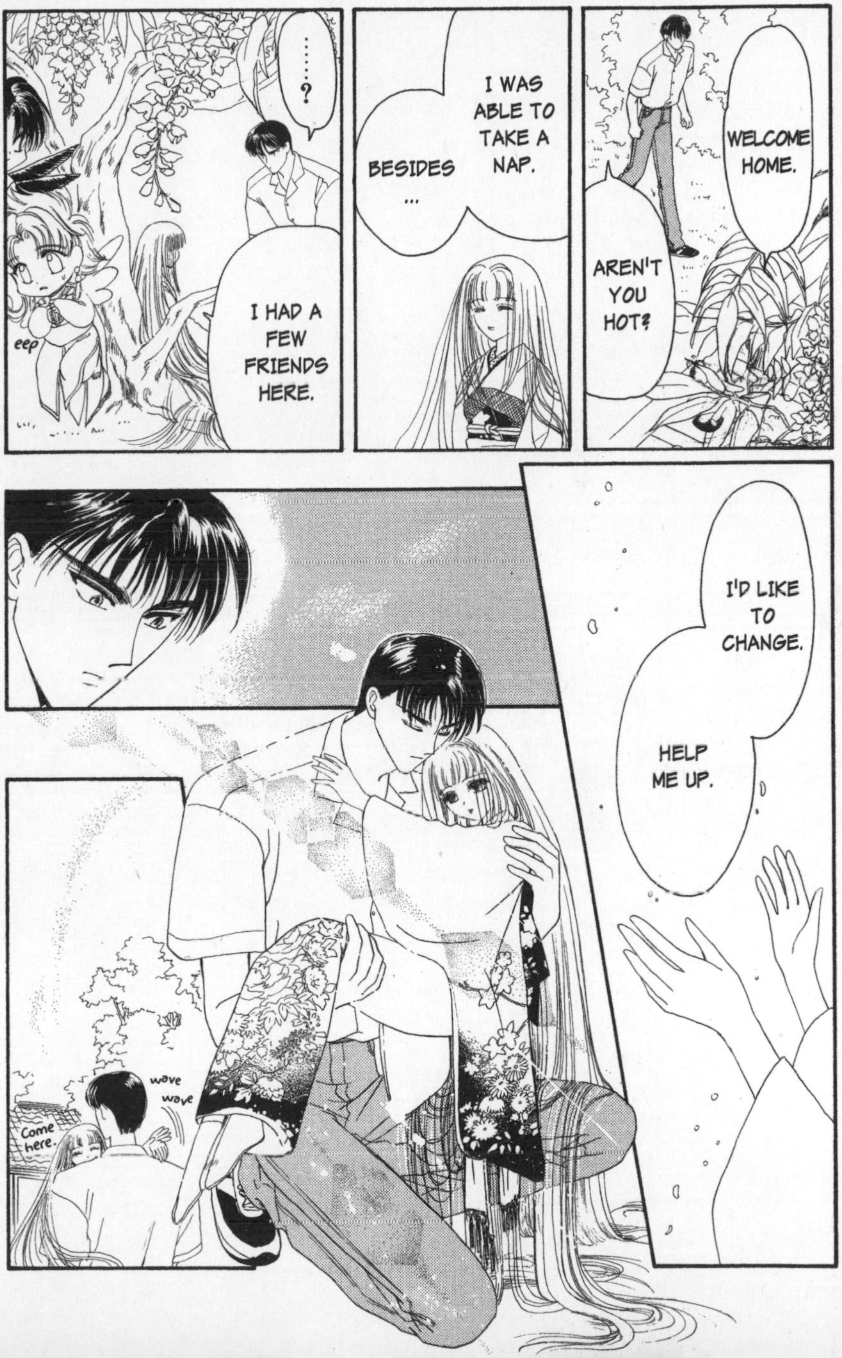
WELCOME HOME.
AREN'T YOU HOT?
I WAS ABLE TO TAKE A NAP.
BESIDES ...
......?
I HAD A FEW FRIENDS HERE.
eep
I'D LIKE TO CHANGE.
HELP ME UP.
wave wave
Come here.

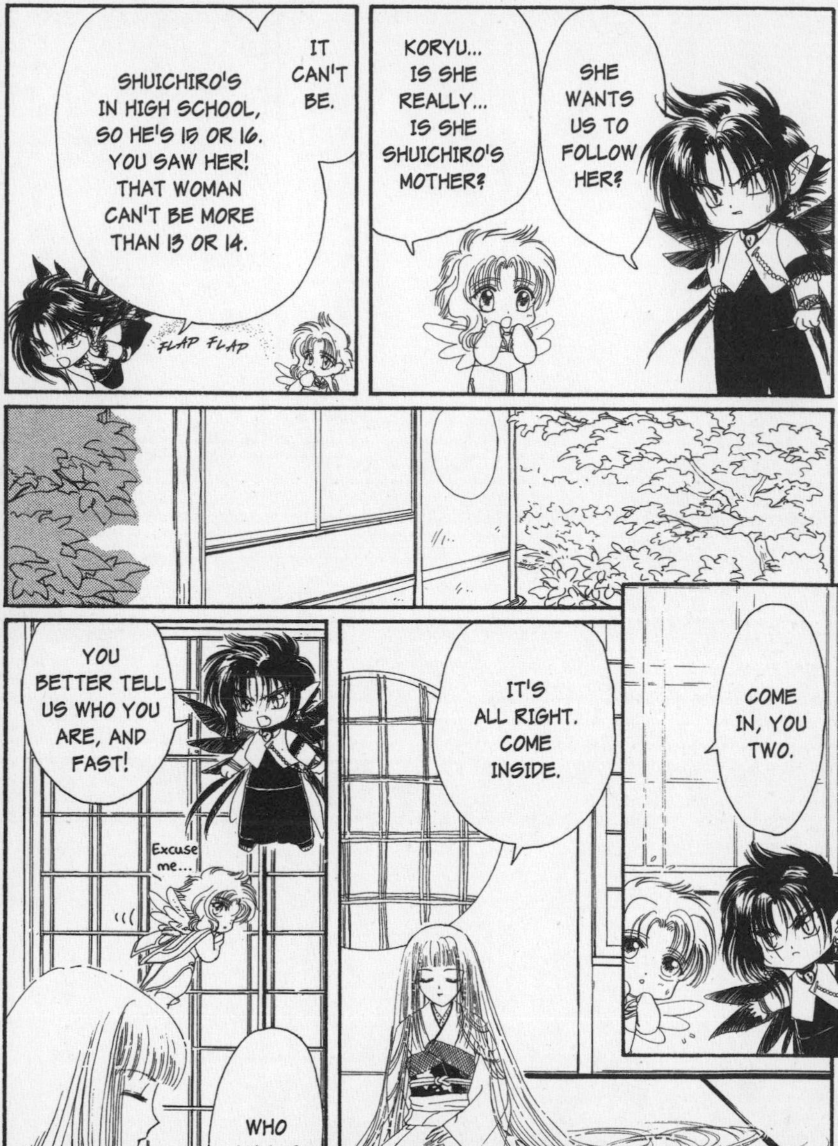
SHE WANTS US TO FOLLOW HER?
KORYU... IS SHE REALLY... IS SHE SHUICHIRO'S MOTHER?
IT CAN'T BE.
SHUICHIRO'S IN HIGH SCHOOL, SO HE'S 15 OR 16. YOU SAW HER! THAT WOMAN CAN'T BE MORE THAN 13 OR 14.
FLAP FLAP
COME IN, YOU TWO.
IT'S ALL RIGHT. COME INSIDE.
YOU BETTER TELL US WHO YOU ARE, AND FAST!
Excuse me...
WHO AM I...?

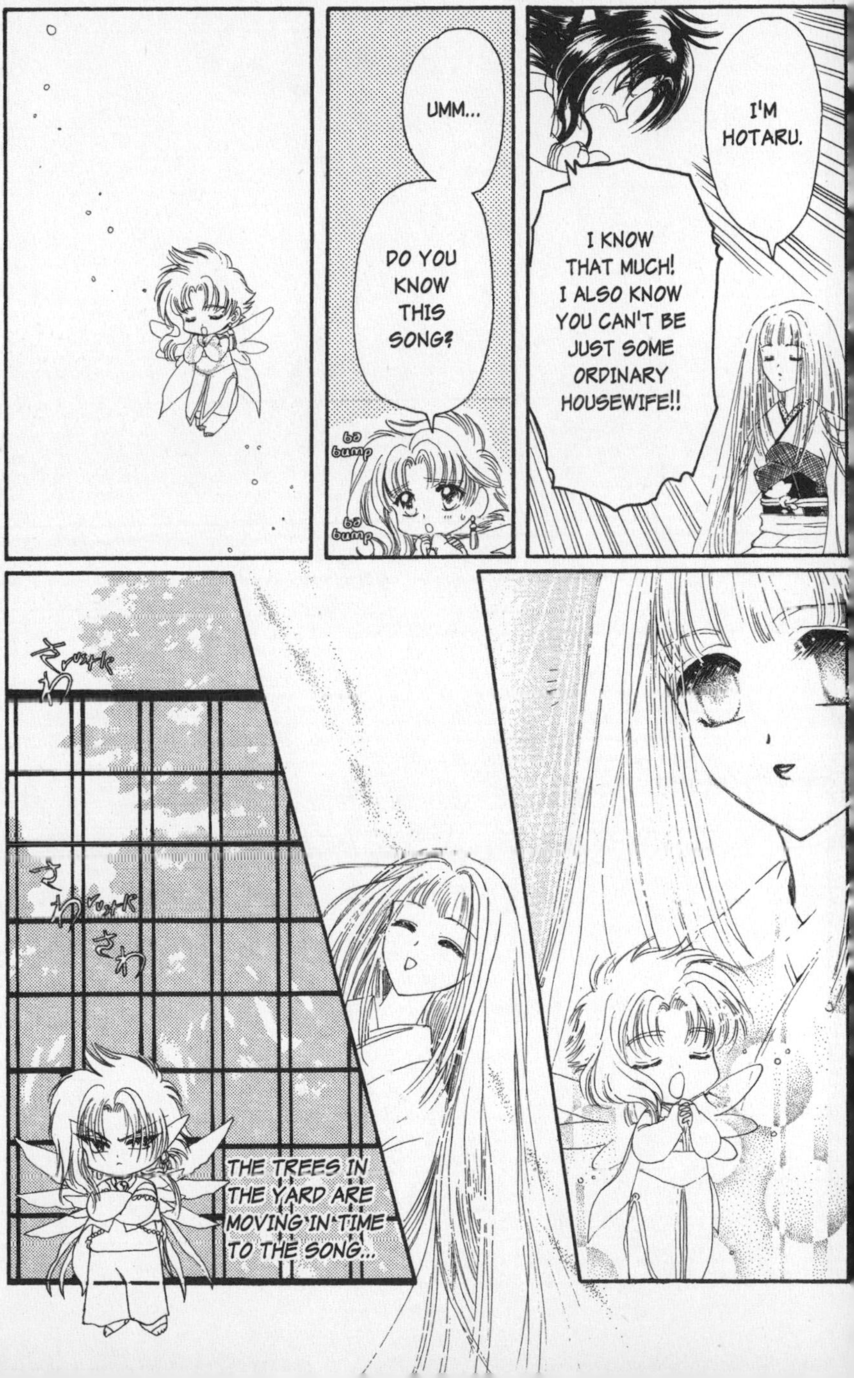
I'M HOTARU.
I KNOW THAT MUCH! I ALSO KNOW YOU CAN'T BE JUST SOME ORDINARY HOUSEWIFE!!
UMM...
DO YOU KNOW THIS SONG?
ba bump
ba bump
さわ
さわ
さわ
THE TREES IN THE YARD ARE MOVING IN TIME TO THE SONG...

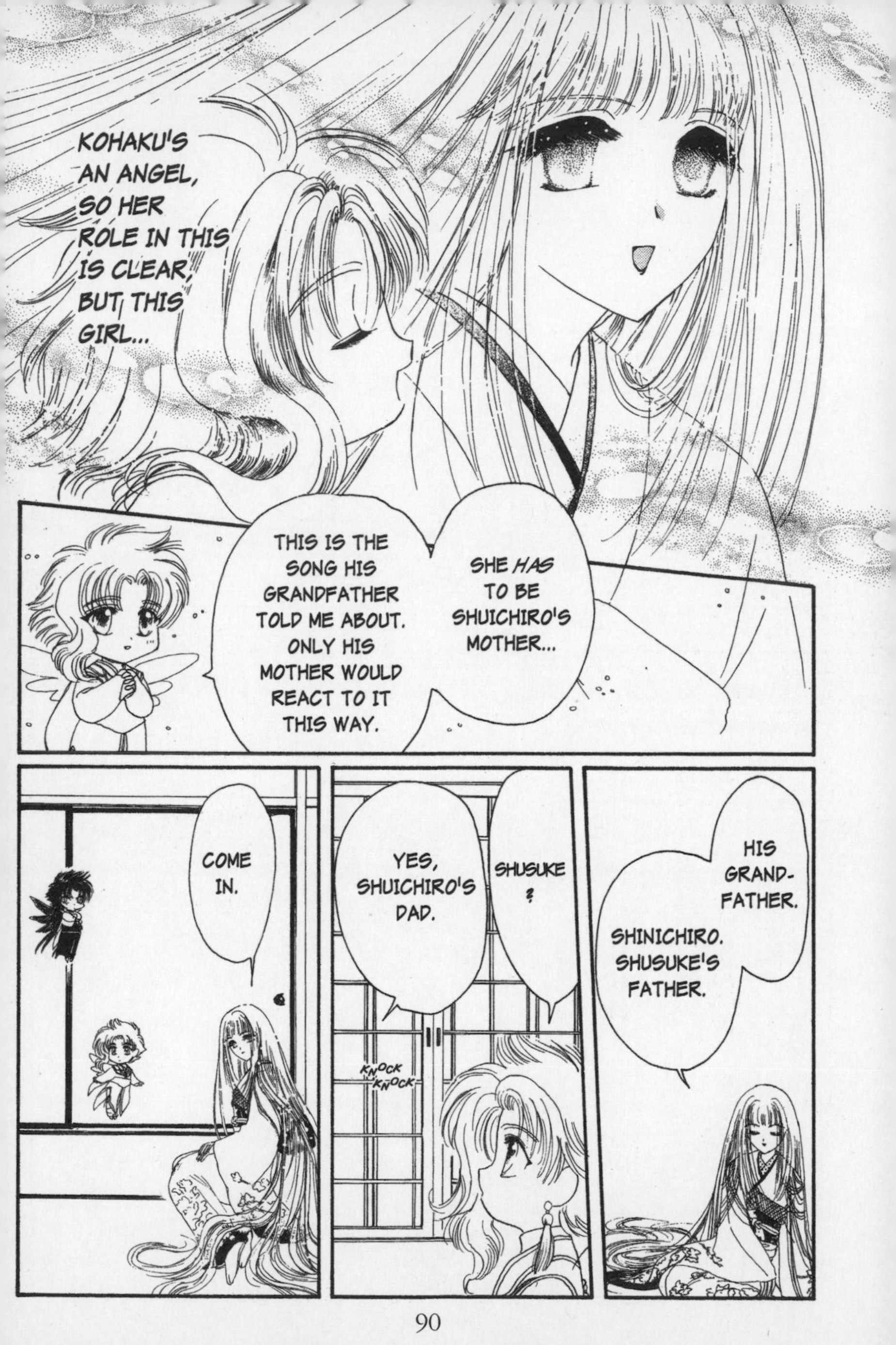

KOHAKU'S AN ANGEL, SO HER ROLE IN THIS IS CLEAR, BUT THIS GIRL...
SHE *HAS* TO BE SHUICHIRO'S MOTHER...
THIS IS THE SONG HIS GRANDFATHER TOLD ME ABOUT. ONLY HIS MOTHER WOULD REACT TO IT THIS WAY.
HIS GRAND-FATHER.
SHINICHIRO. SHUSUKE'S FATHER.
SHUSUKE?
YES, SHUICHIRO'S DAD.
KNOCK KNOCK
COME IN.

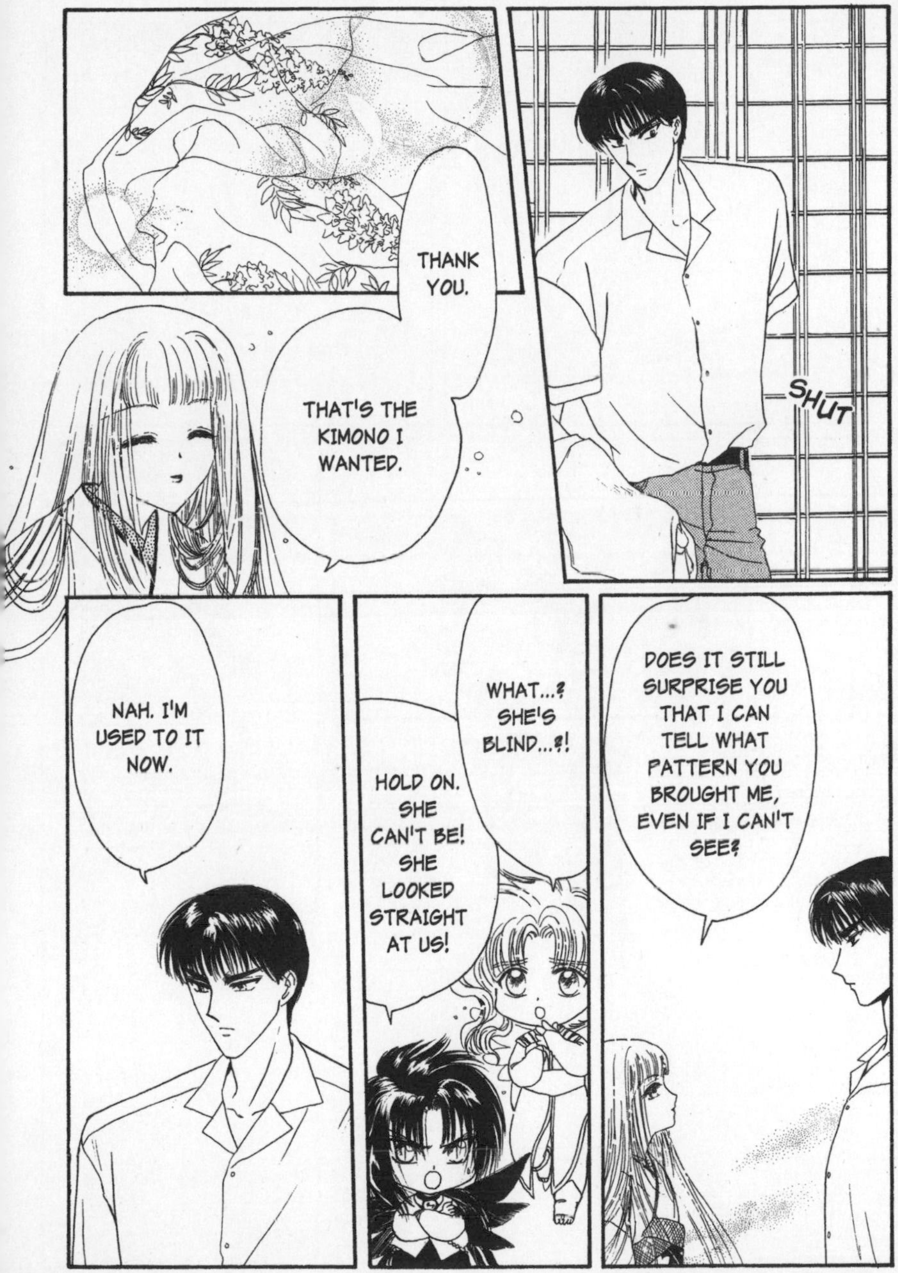
SHUT
THANK YOU.
THAT'S THE KIMONO I WANTED.
DOES IT STILL SURPRISE YOU THAT I CAN TELL WHAT PATTERN YOU BROUGHT ME, EVEN IF I CAN'T SEE?
WHAT...? SHE'S BLIND...?!
HOLD ON. SHE CAN'T BE! SHE LOOKED STRAIGHT AT US!
NAH. I'M USED TO IT NOW.

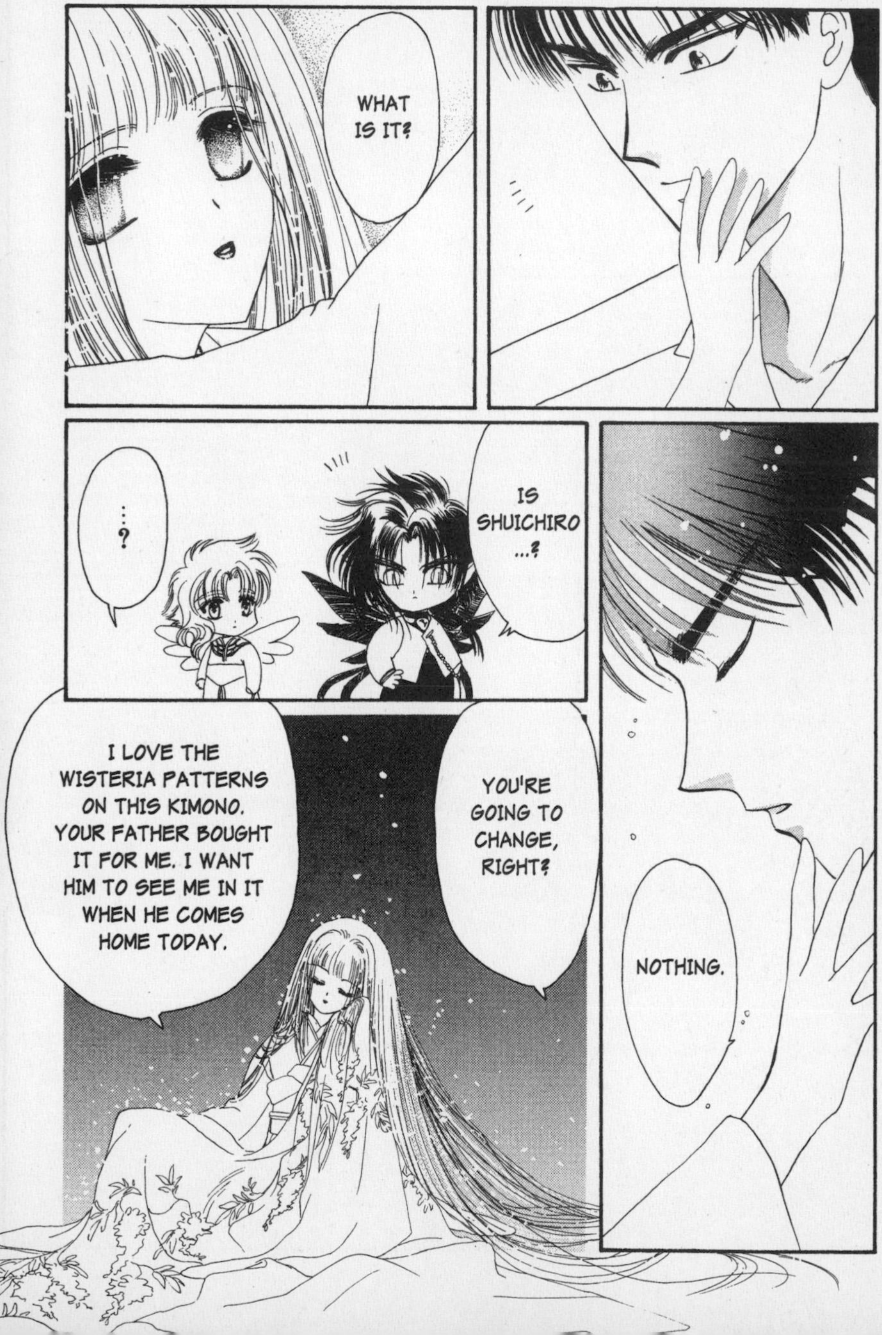
WHAT IS IT?
NOTHING.
IS SHUICHIRO ...?
...?
YOU'RE GOING TO CHANGE, RIGHT?
I LOVE THE WISTERIA PATTERNS ON THIS KIMONO. YOUR FATHER BOUGHT IT FOR ME. I WANT HIM TO SEE ME IN IT WHEN HE COMES HOME TODAY.

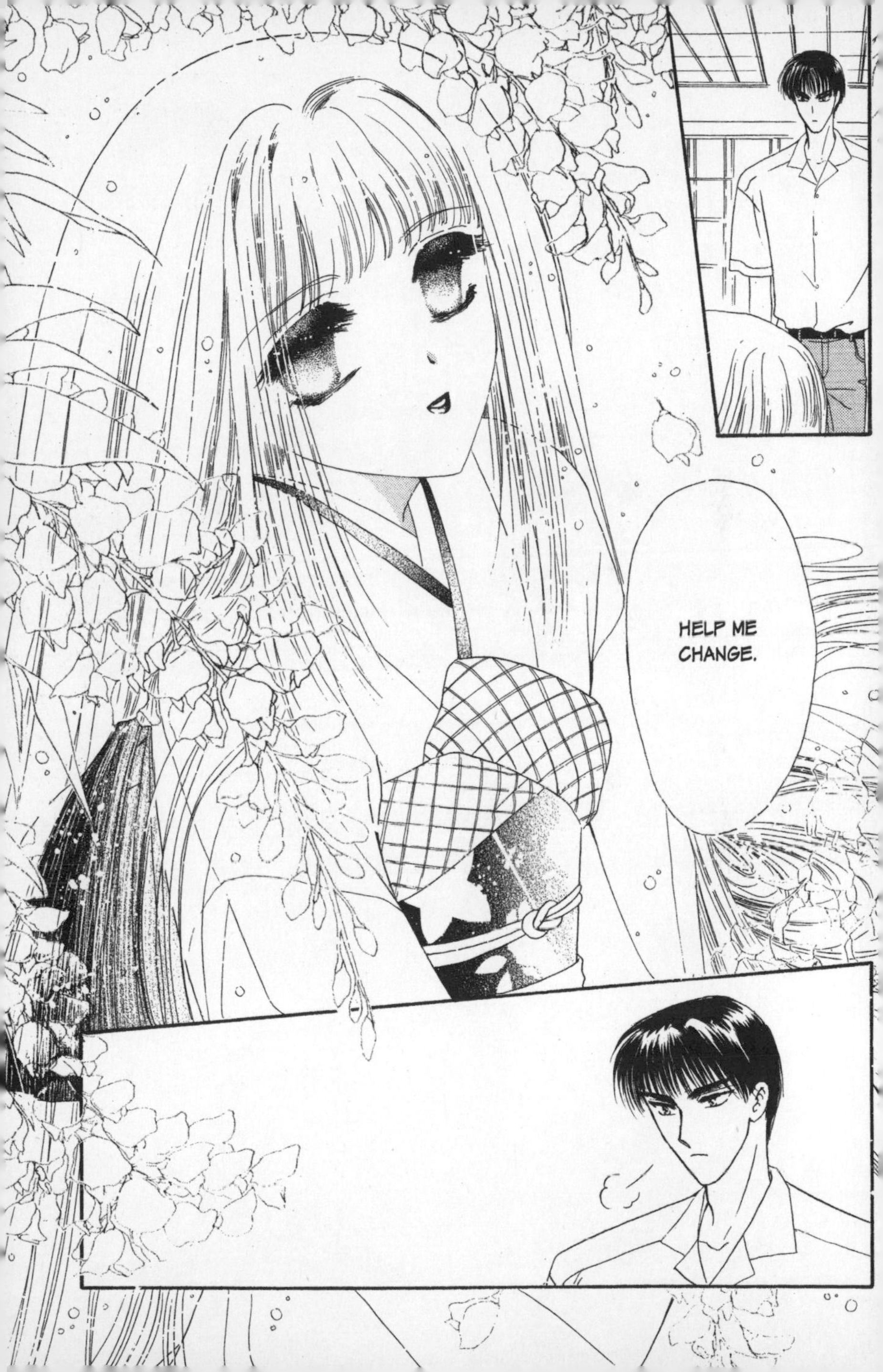
HELP ME CHANGE.

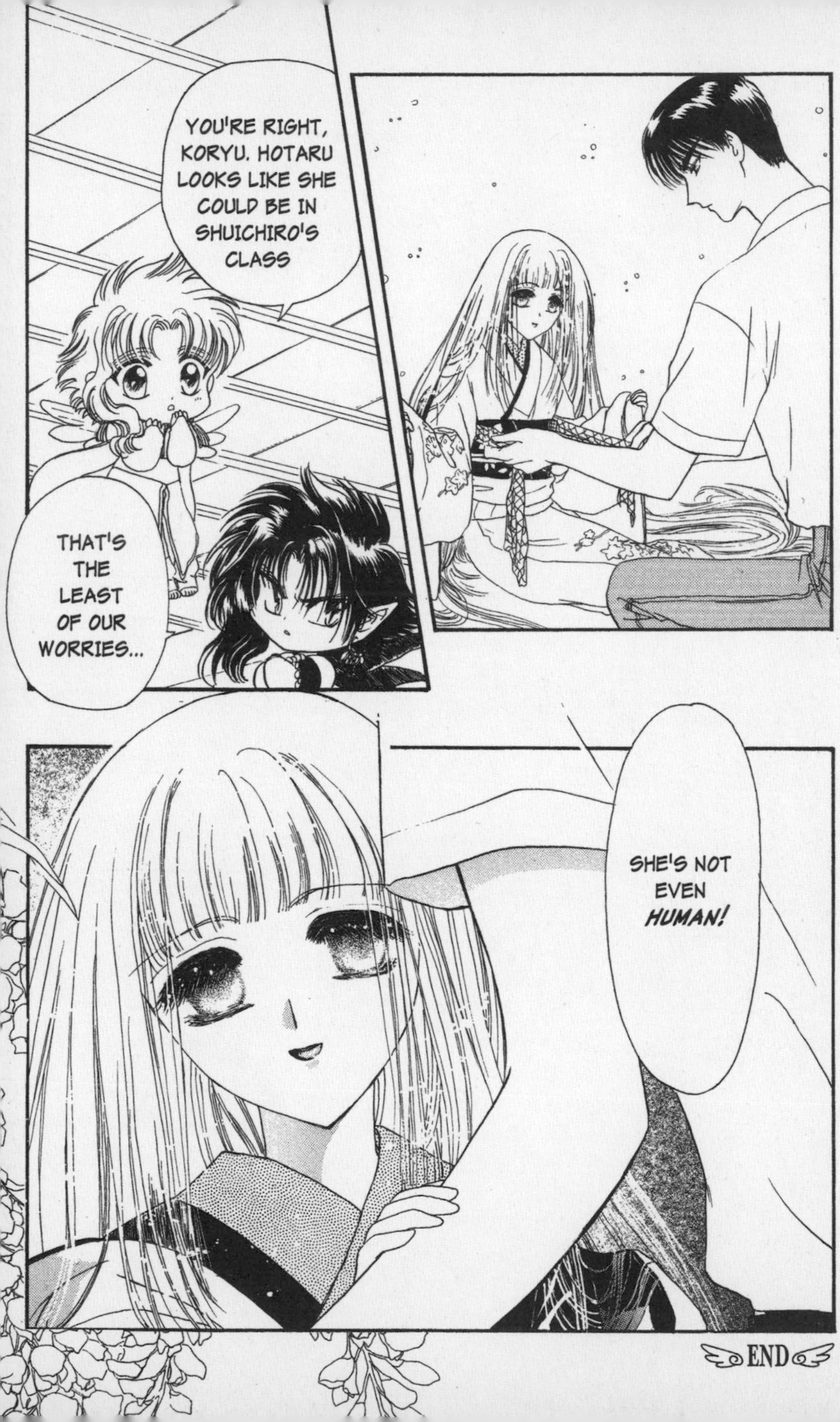
YOU'RE RIGHT, KORYU. HOTARU LOOKS LIKE SHE COULD BE IN SHUICHIRO'S CLASS
THAT'S THE LEAST OF OUR WORRIES...
SHE'S NOT EVEN *HUMAN!*
END

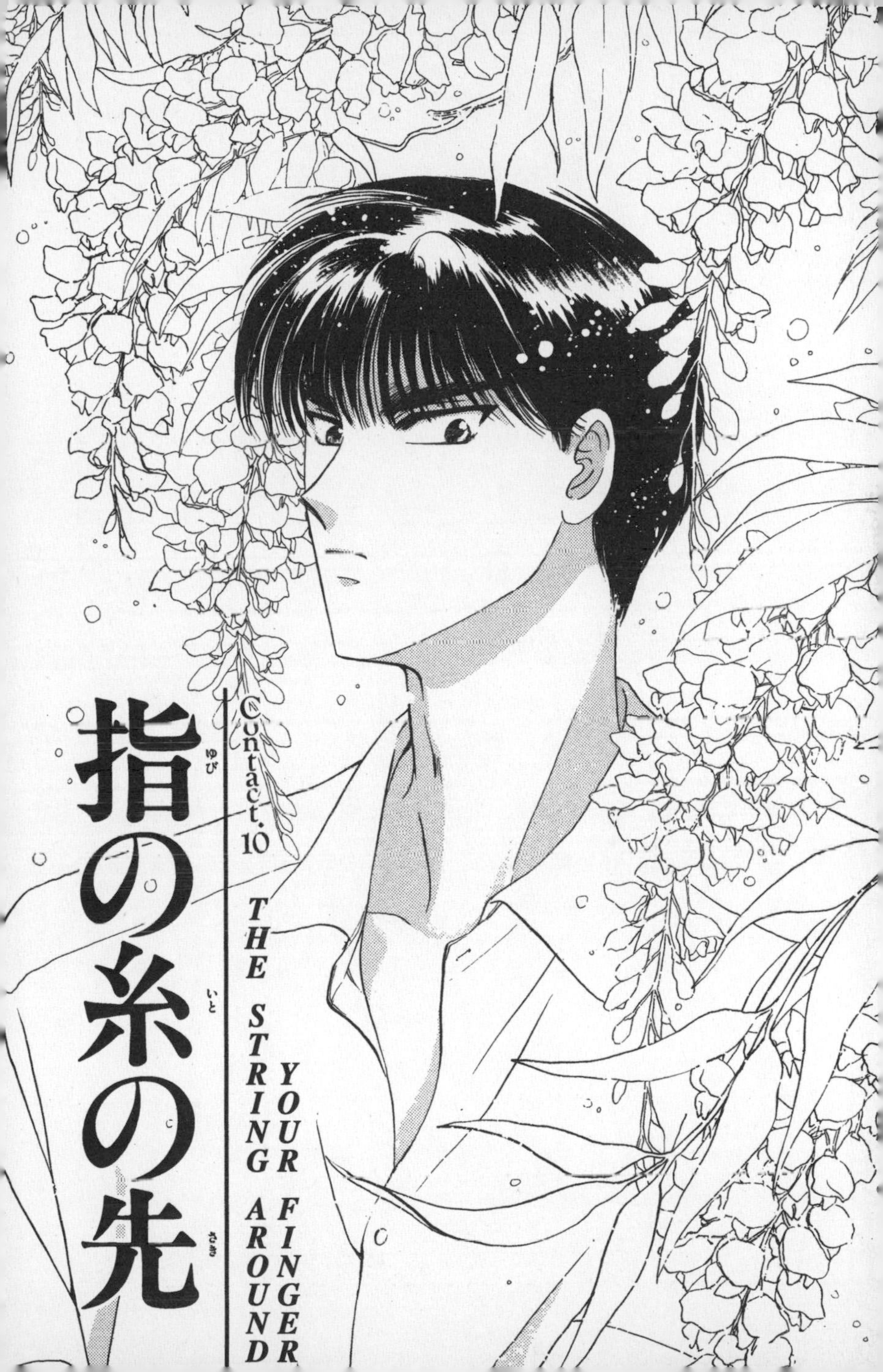
指の糸の先
ゆび いと さき
Contact.10
THE STRING AROUND YOUR FINGER

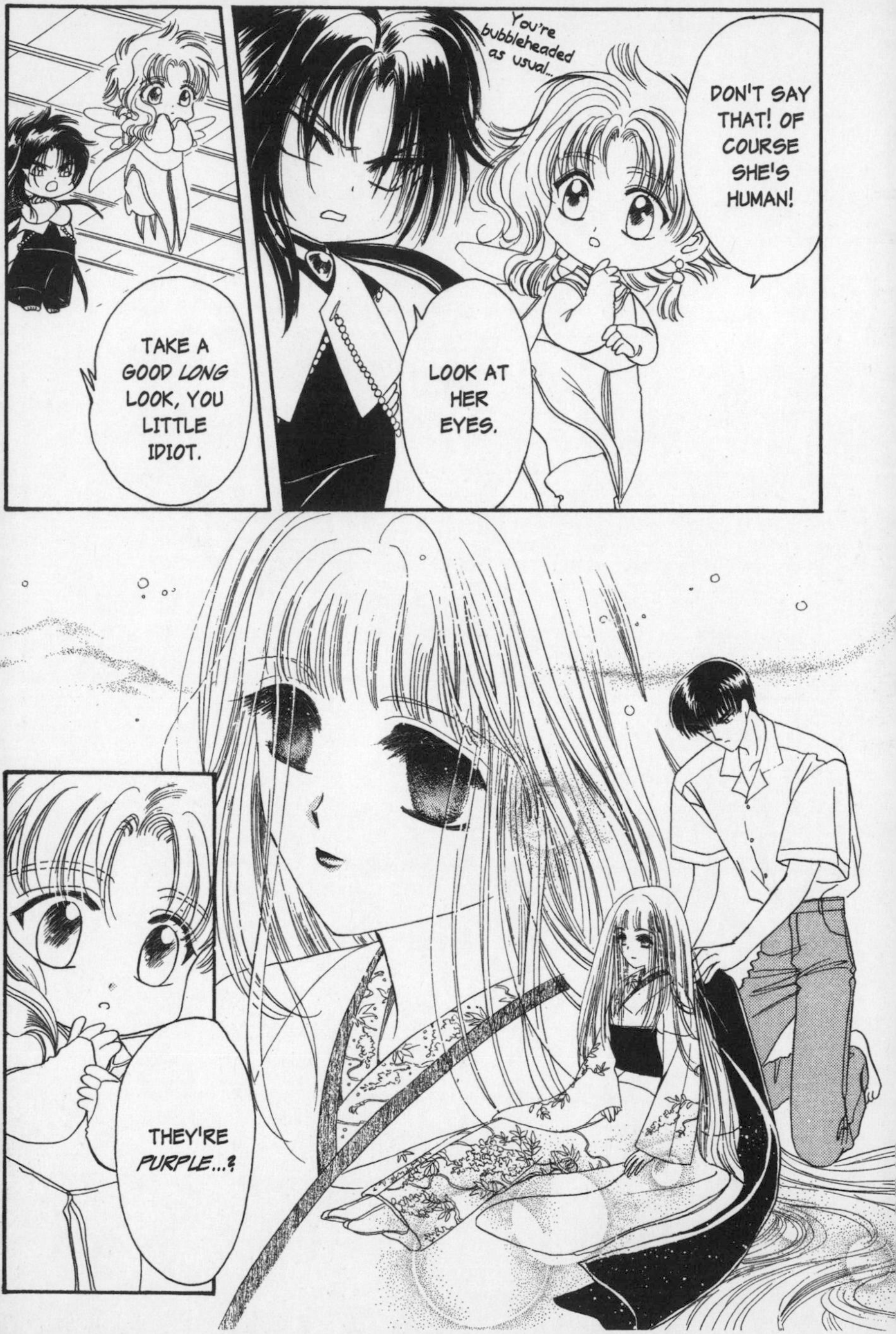
DON'T SAY THAT! OF COURSE SHE'S HUMAN!
You're bubbleheaded as usual...
LOOK AT HER EYES.
TAKE A GOOD *LONG* LOOK, YOU LITTLE IDIOT.
THEY'RE *PURPLE*...?

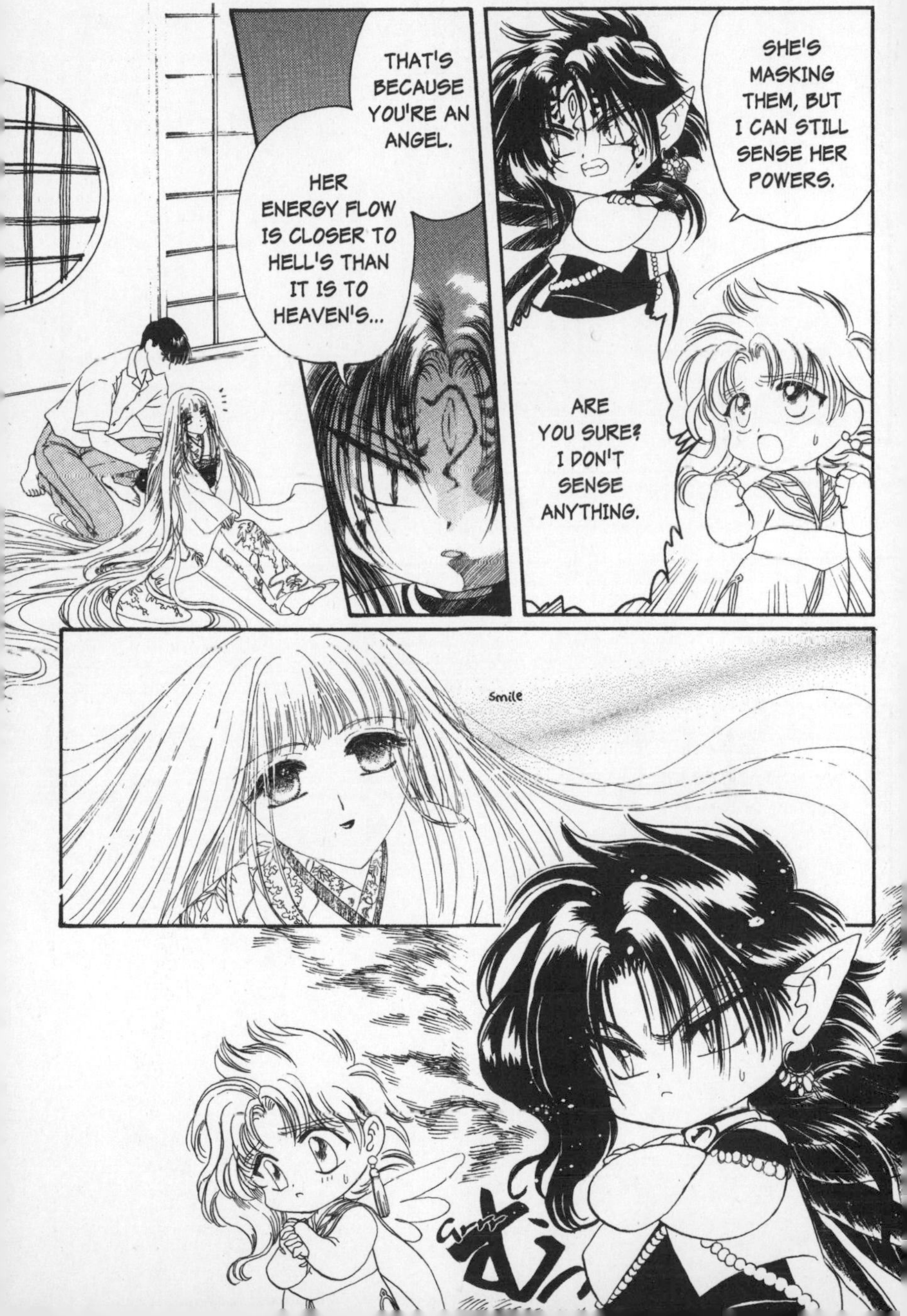
SHE'S MASKING THEM, BUT I CAN STILL SENSE HER POWERS.
ARE YOU SURE? I DON'T SENSE ANYTHING.
THAT'S BECAUSE YOU'RE AN ANGEL.
HER ENERGY FLOW IS CLOSER TO HELL'S THAN IT IS TO HEAVEN'S...
Smile

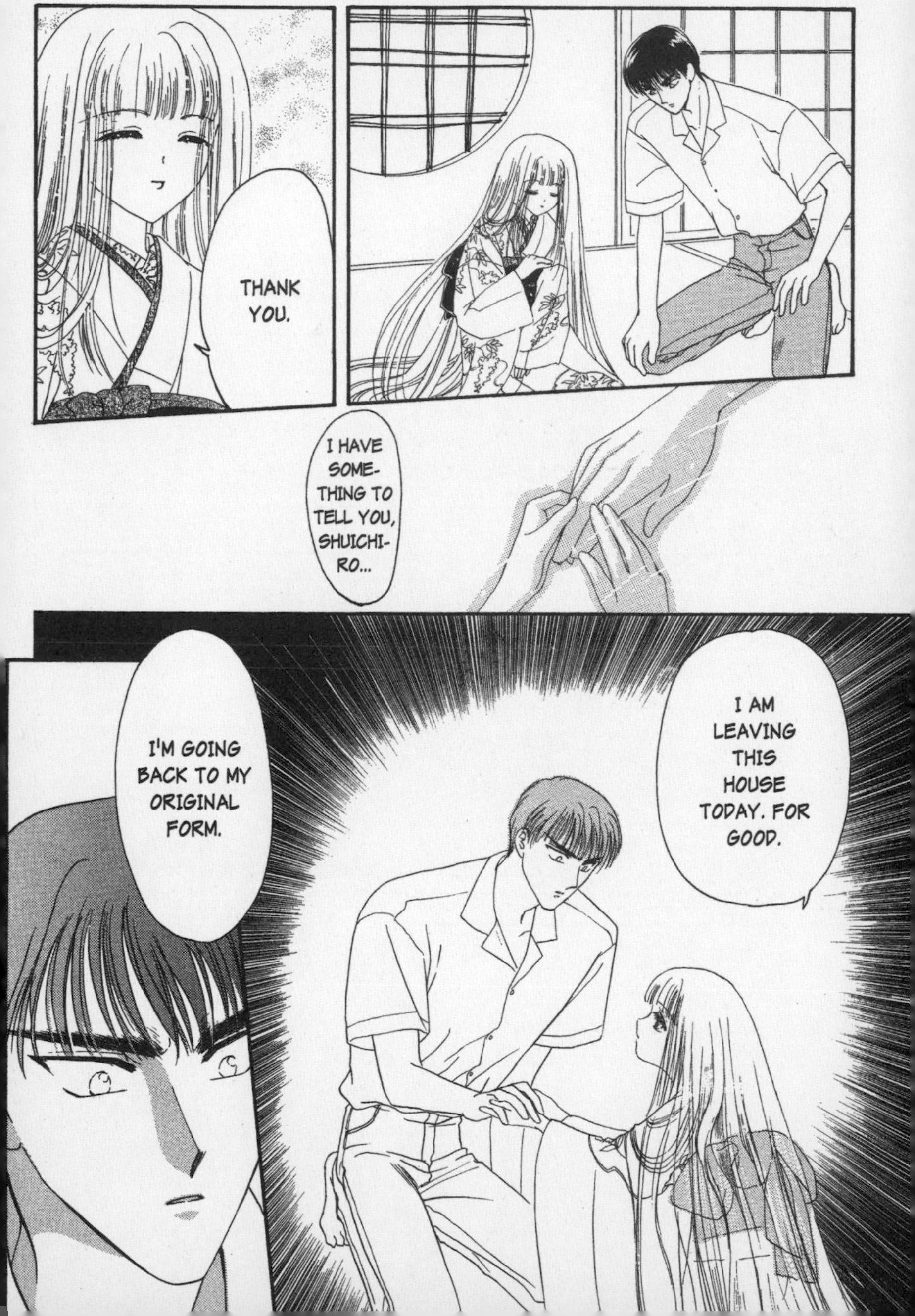
THANK YOU.
I HAVE SOME-THING TO TELL YOU, SHUICHI-RO...
I AM LEAVING THIS HOUSE TODAY. FOR GOOD.
I'M GOING BACK TO MY ORIGINAL FORM.

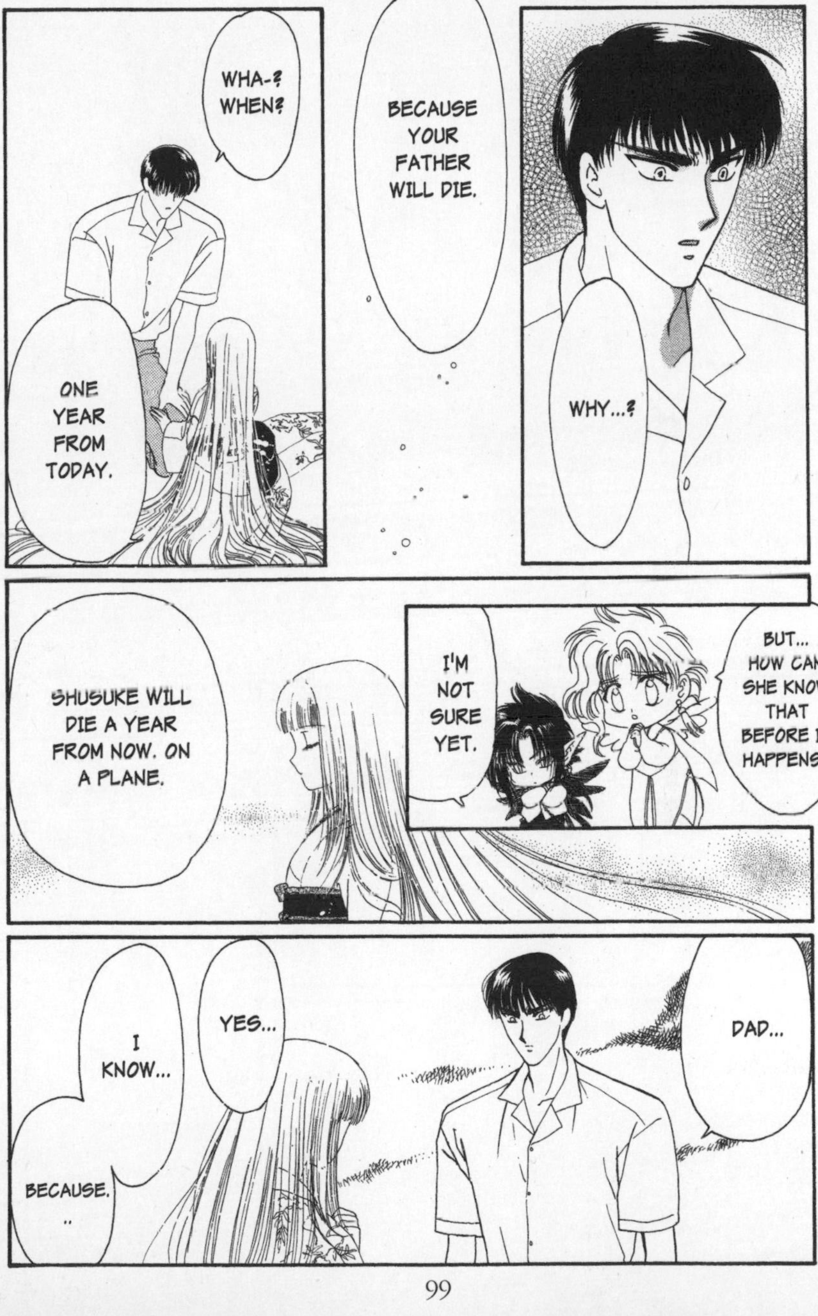
WHY...?
BECAUSE YOUR FATHER WILL DIE.
WHA-? WHEN?
ONE YEAR FROM TODAY.
BUT... HOW CAN SHE KNOW THAT BEFORE IT HAPPENS?
I'M NOT SURE YET.
SHUSUKE WILL DIE A YEAR FROM NOW. ON A PLANE.
DAD...
YES...
I KNOW...
BECAUSE. ..

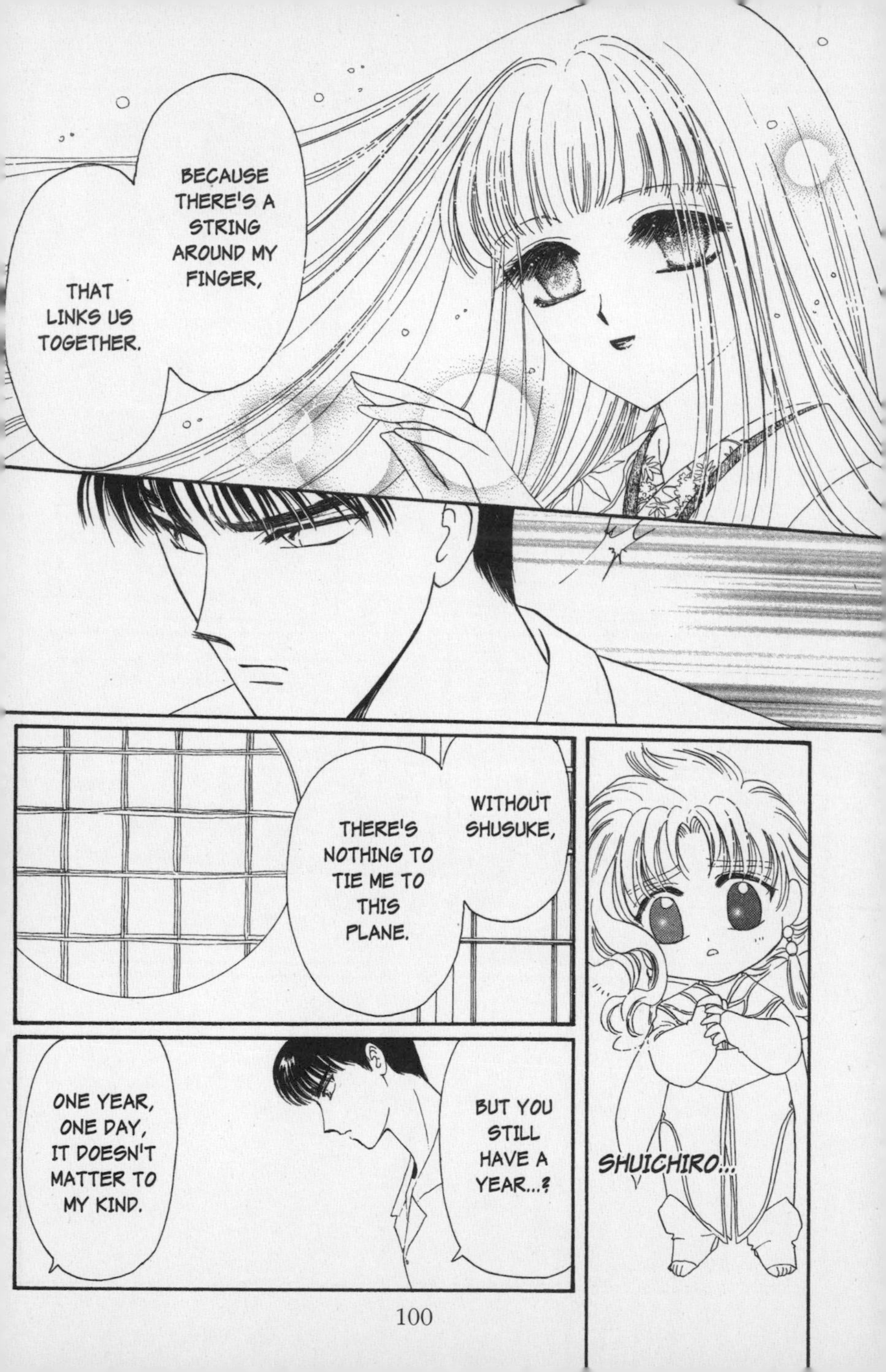
BECAUSE THERE'S A STRING AROUND MY FINGER,
THAT LINKS US TOGETHER.
SHUICHIRO...
WITHOUT SHUSUKE,
THERE'S NOTHING TO TIE ME TO THIS PLANE.
BUT YOU STILL HAVE A YEAR...?
ONE YEAR, ONE DAY, IT DOESN'T MATTER TO MY KIND.

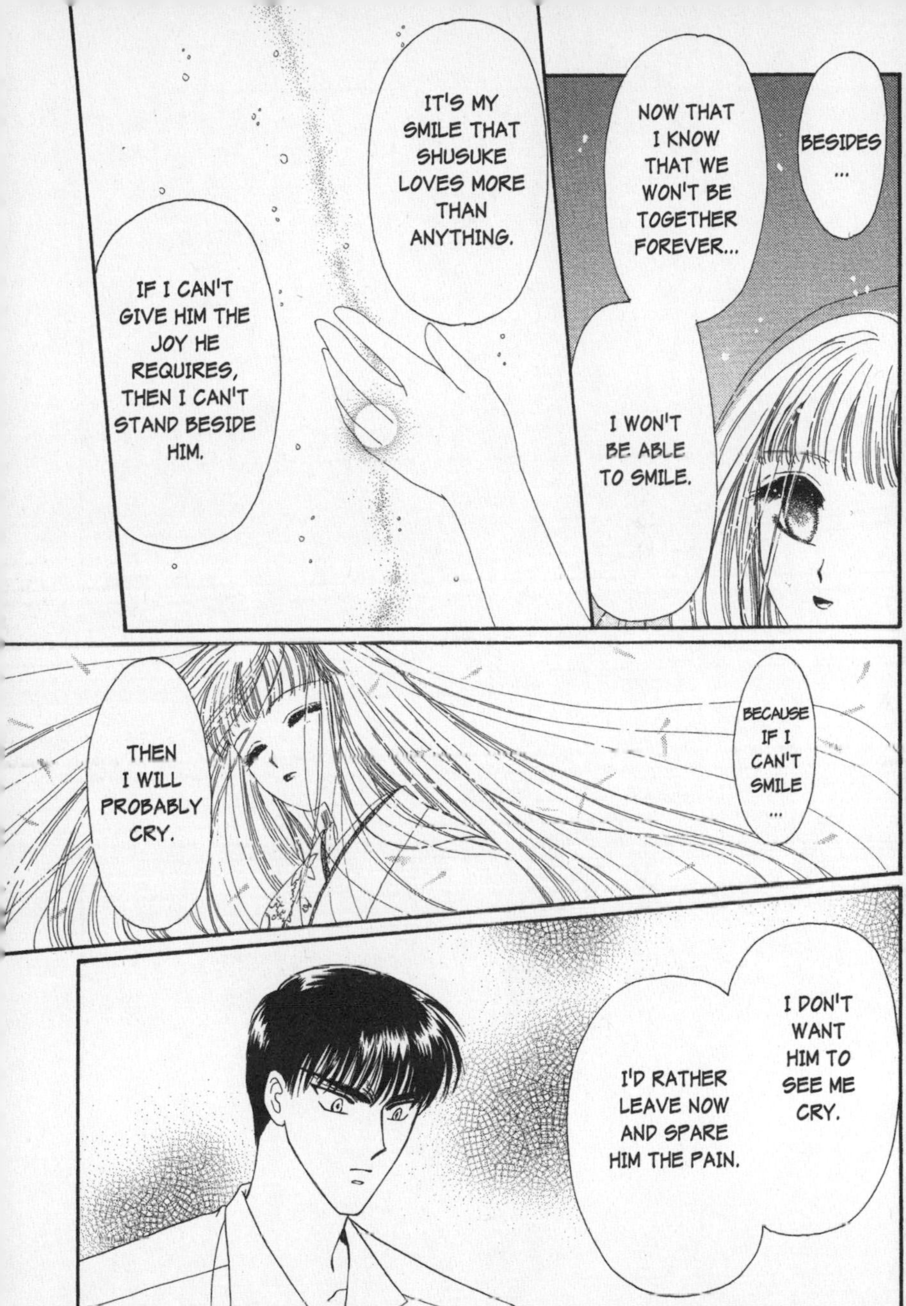
BESIDES...
NOW THAT I KNOW THAT WE WON'T BE TOGETHER FOREVER...
I WON'T BE ABLE TO SMILE.
IT'S MY SMILE THAT SHUSUKE LOVES MORE THAN ANYTHING.
IF I CAN'T GIVE HIM THE JOY HE REQUIRES, THEN I CAN'T STAND BESIDE HIM.
BECAUSE IF I CAN'T SMILE...
THEN I WILL PROBABLY CRY.
I DON'T WANT HIM TO SEE ME CRY.
I'D RATHER LEAVE NOW AND SPARE HIM THE PAIN.

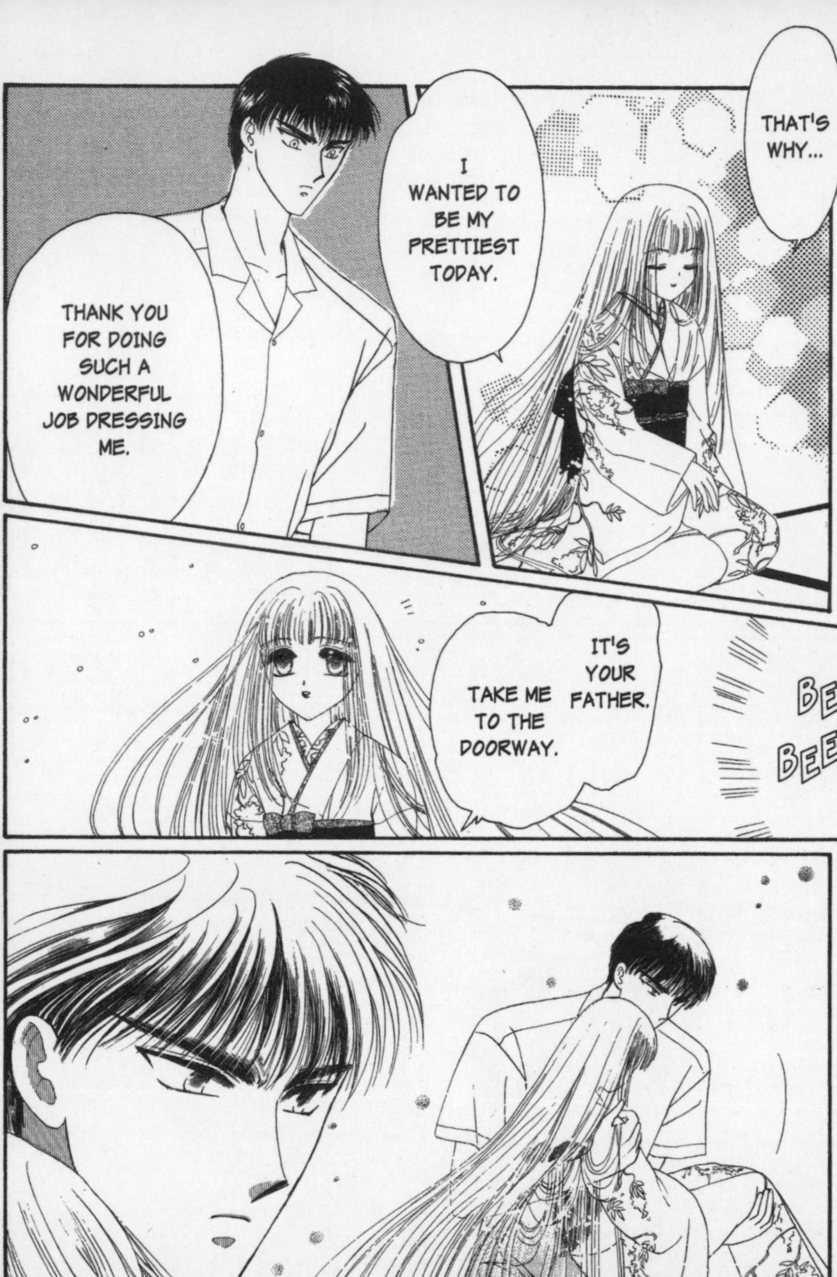
THAT'S WHY...
I WANTED TO BE MY PRETTIEST TODAY.
THANK YOU FOR DOING SUCH A WONDERFUL JOB DRESSING ME.
BEEP BEEP
IT'S YOUR FATHER.
TAKE ME TO THE DOORWAY.

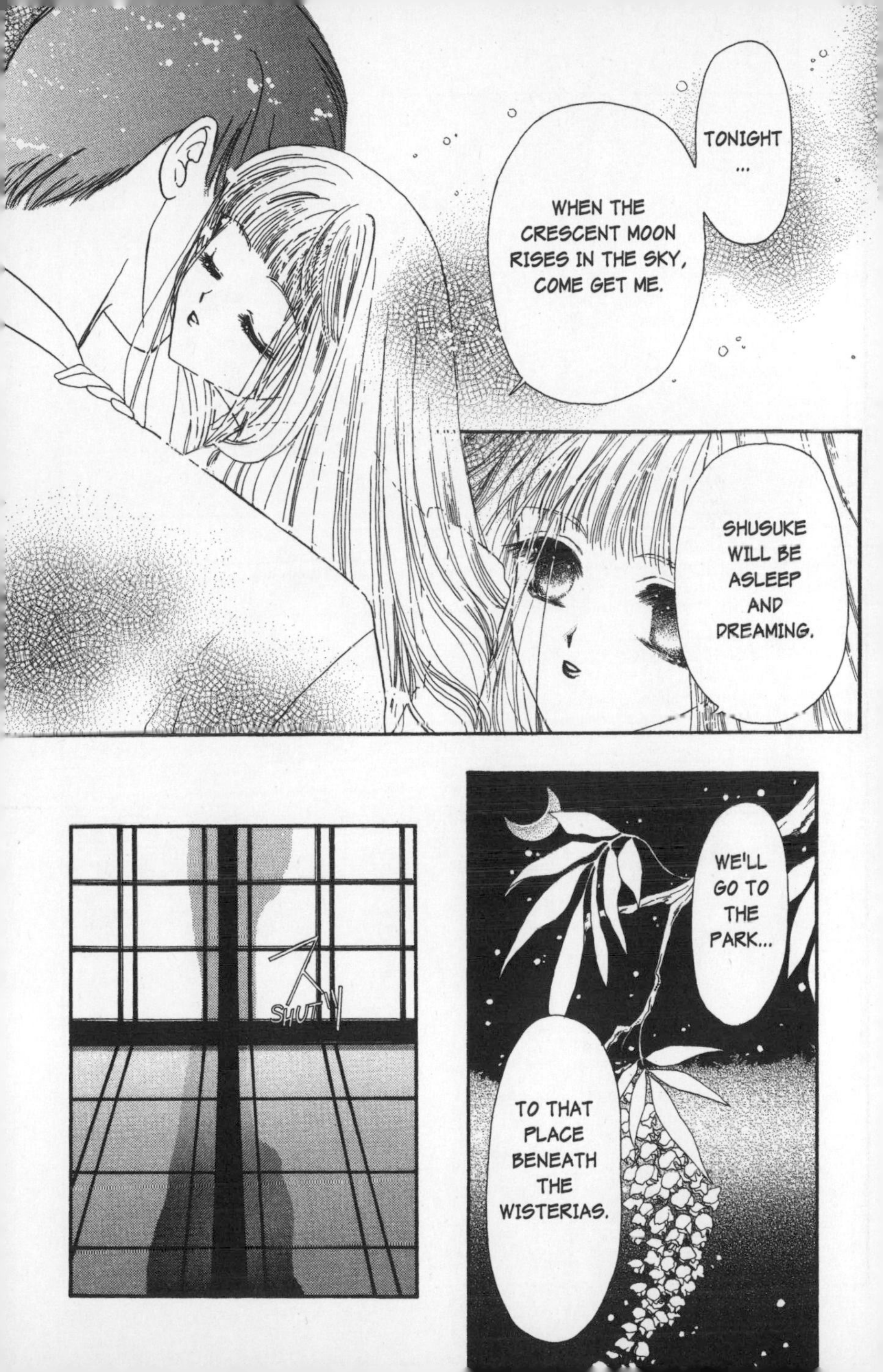
TONIGHT ...
WHEN THE CRESCENT MOON RISES IN THE SKY, COME GET ME.
SHUSUKE WILL BE ASLEEP AND DREAMING.
WE'LL GO TO THE PARK...
TO THAT PLACE BENEATH THE WISTERIAS.
SHUT

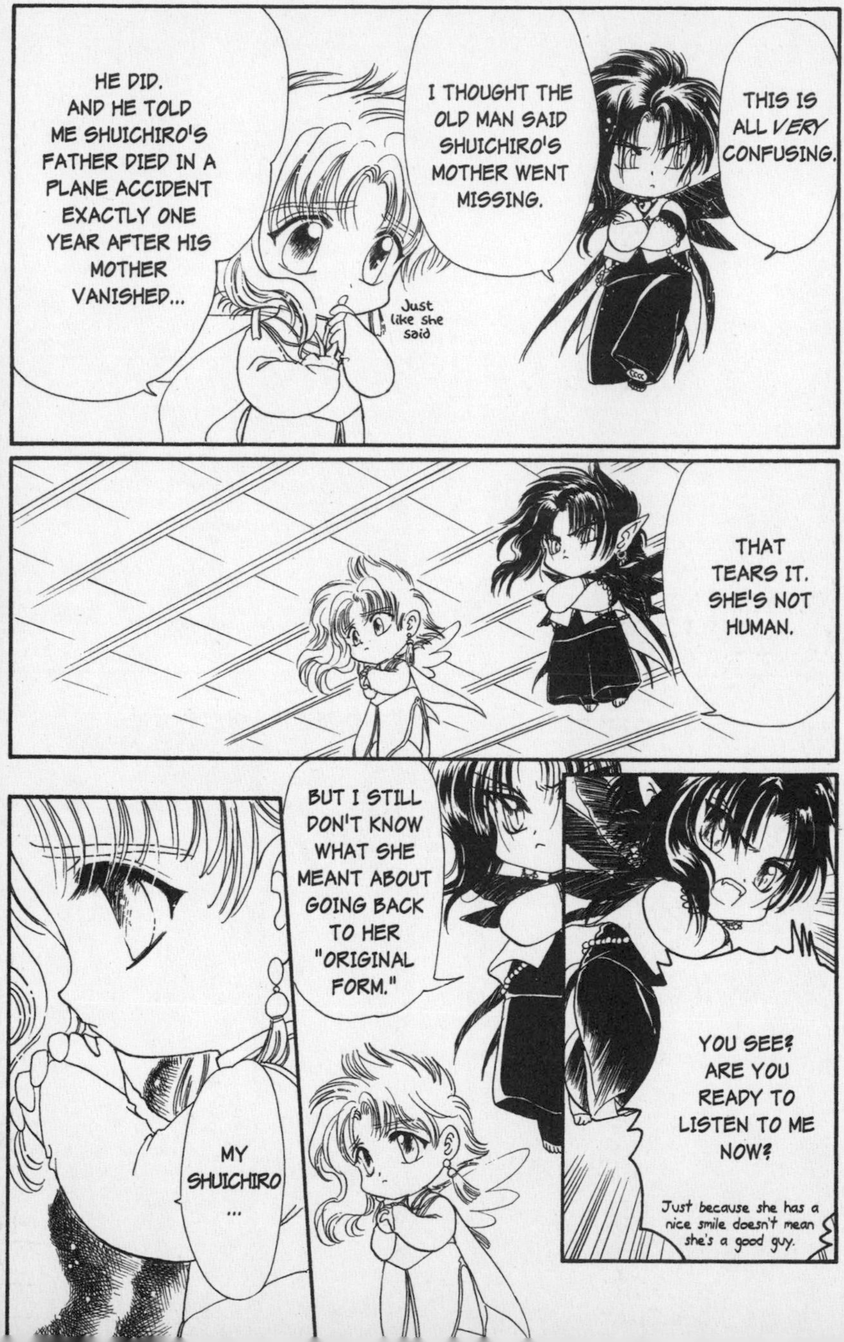
THIS IS ALL *VERY* CONFUSING.
I THOUGHT THE OLD MAN SAID SHUICHIRO'S MOTHER WENT MISSING.
HE DID. AND HE TOLD ME SHUICHIRO'S FATHER DIED IN A PLANE ACCIDENT EXACTLY ONE YEAR AFTER HIS MOTHER VANISHED...
Just like she said
THAT TEARS IT. SHE'S NOT HUMAN.
YOU SEE? ARE YOU READY TO LISTEN TO ME NOW?
Just because she has a nice smile doesn't mean she's a good guy.
BUT I STILL DON'T KNOW WHAT SHE MEANT ABOUT GOING BACK TO HER "ORIGINAL FORM."
MY SHUICHIRO ...

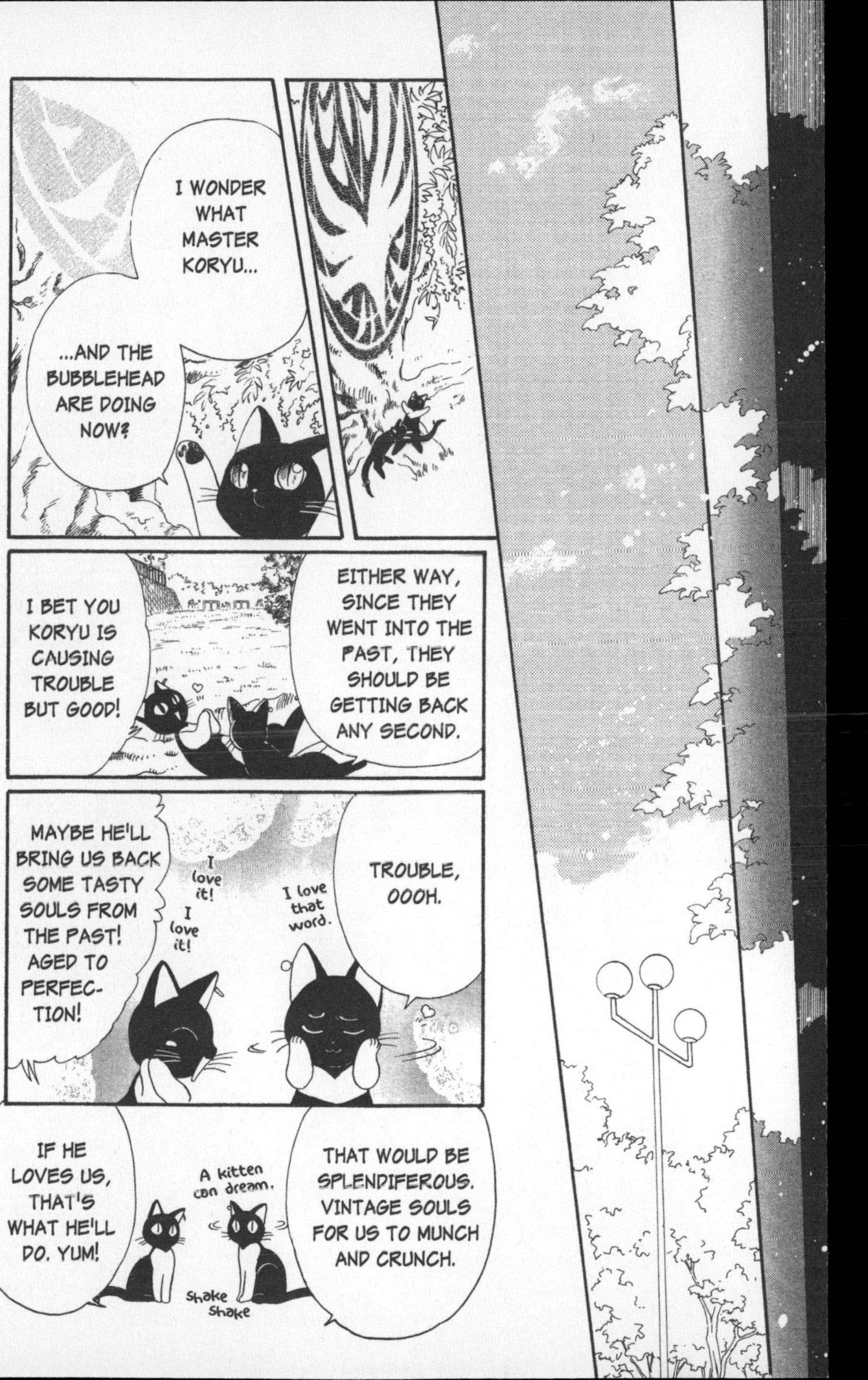
I WONDER WHAT MASTER KORYU...
...AND THE BUBBLEHEAD ARE DOING NOW?
EITHER WAY, SINCE THEY WENT INTO THE PAST, THEY SHOULD BE GETTING BACK ANY SECOND.
I BET YOU KORYU IS CAUSING TROUBLE BUT GOOD!
TROUBLE, OOOH.
I love that word.
MAYBE HE'LL BRING US BACK SOME TASTY SOULS FROM THE PAST! AGED TO PERFEC-TION!
I love it!
I love it!
THAT WOULD BE SPLENDIFEROUS. VINTAGE SOULS FOR US TO MUNCH AND CRUNCH.
A kitten can dream.
Shake Shake
IF HE LOVES US, THAT'S WHAT HE'LL DO. YUM!

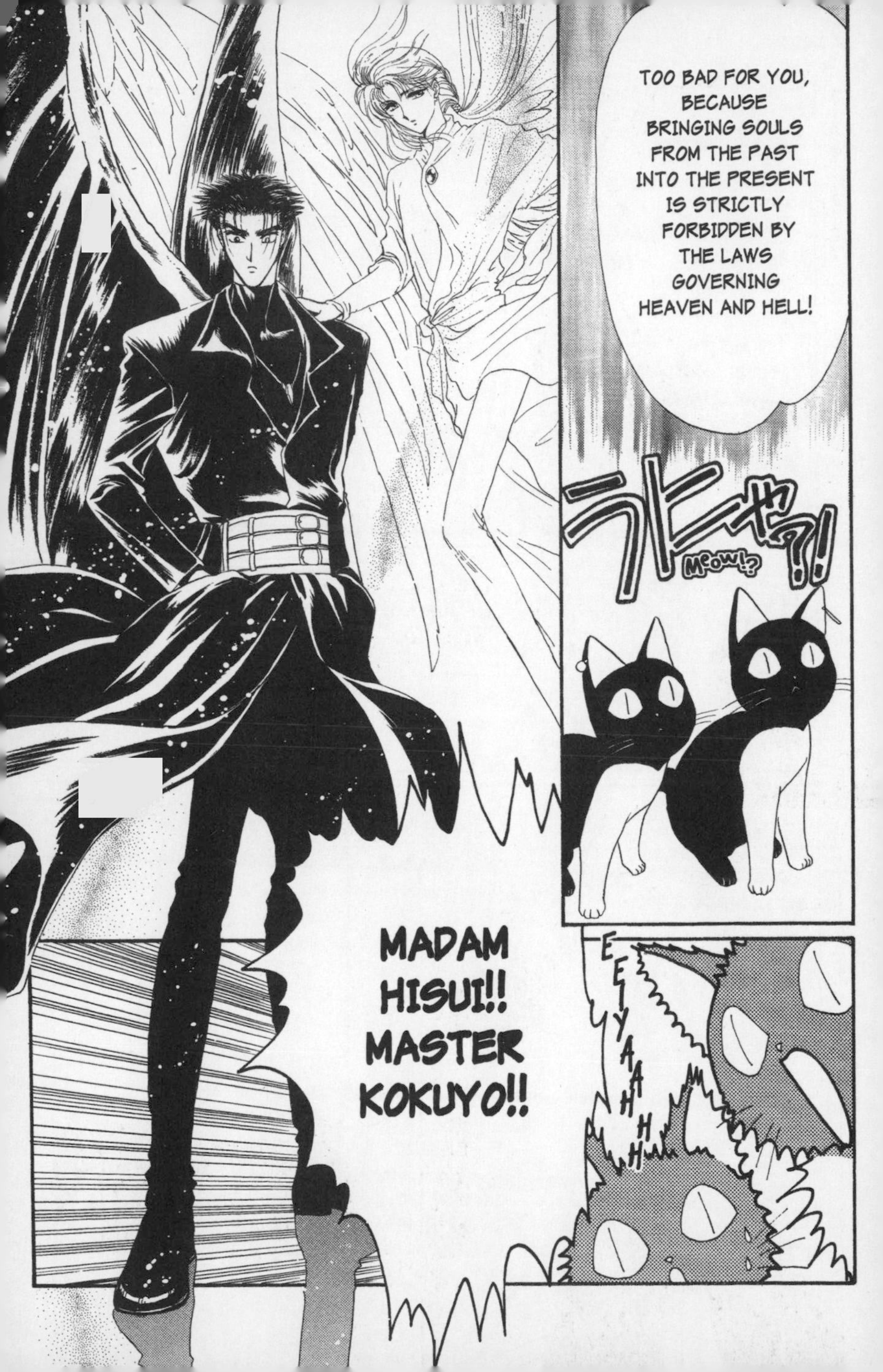
TOO BAD FOR YOU, BECAUSE BRINGING SOULS FROM THE PAST INTO THE PRESENT IS STRICTLY FORBIDDEN BY THE LAWS GOVERNING HEAVEN AND HELL!
MEOW!?
EEIYAAHHH
MADAM HISUI!! MASTER KOKUYO!!

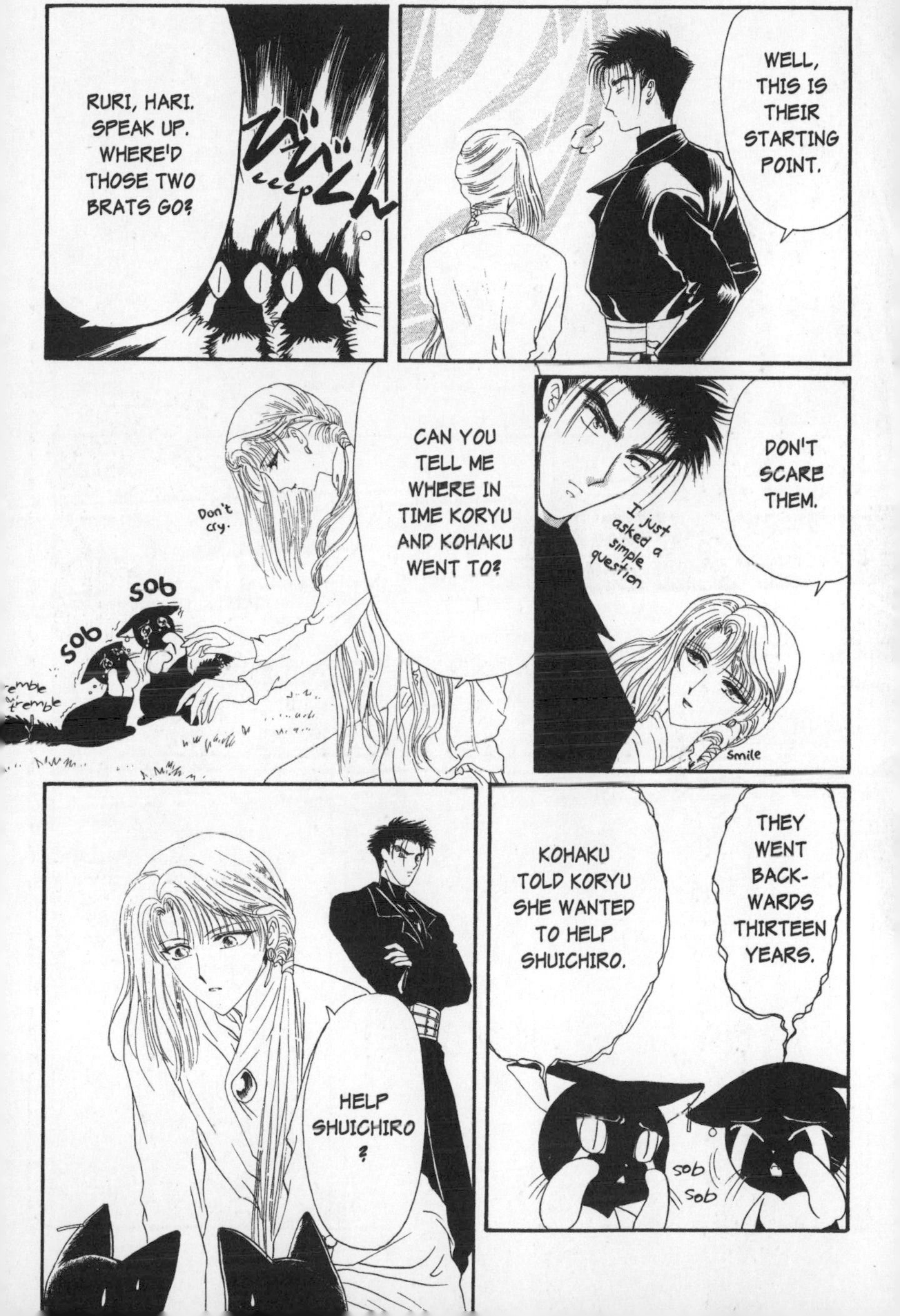
WELL, THIS IS THEIR STARTING POINT.
RURI, HARI. SPEAK UP. WHERE'D THOSE TWO BRATS GO?
びびくん
eeep
DON'T SCARE THEM.
I just asked a simple question
Smile
CAN YOU TELL ME WHERE IN TIME KORYU AND KOHAKU WENT TO?
Don't cry.
sob
sob
tremble tremble
THEY WENT BACK-WARDS THIRTEEN YEARS.
KOHAKU TOLD KORYU SHE WANTED TO HELP SHUICHIRO.
sob sob
HELP SHUICHIRO?

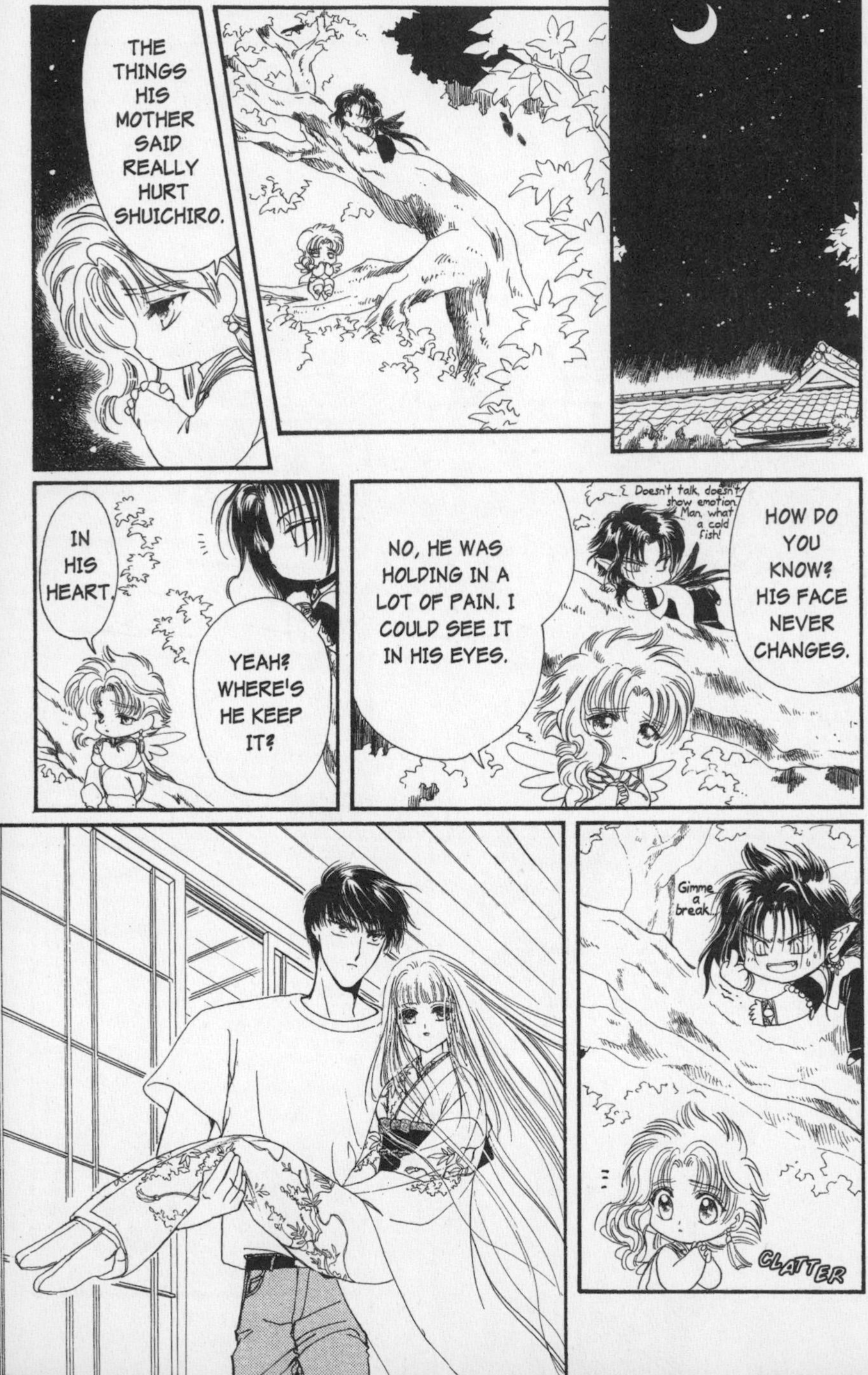
THE THINGS HIS MOTHER SAID REALLY HURT SHUICHIRO.
HOW DO YOU KNOW? HIS FACE NEVER CHANGES.
Doesn't talk, doesn't show emotion. Man, what a cold fish!
NO, HE WAS HOLDING IN A LOT OF PAIN. I COULD SEE IT IN HIS EYES.
YEAH? WHERE'S HE KEEP IT?
IN HIS HEART.
Gimme a break...
CLATTER

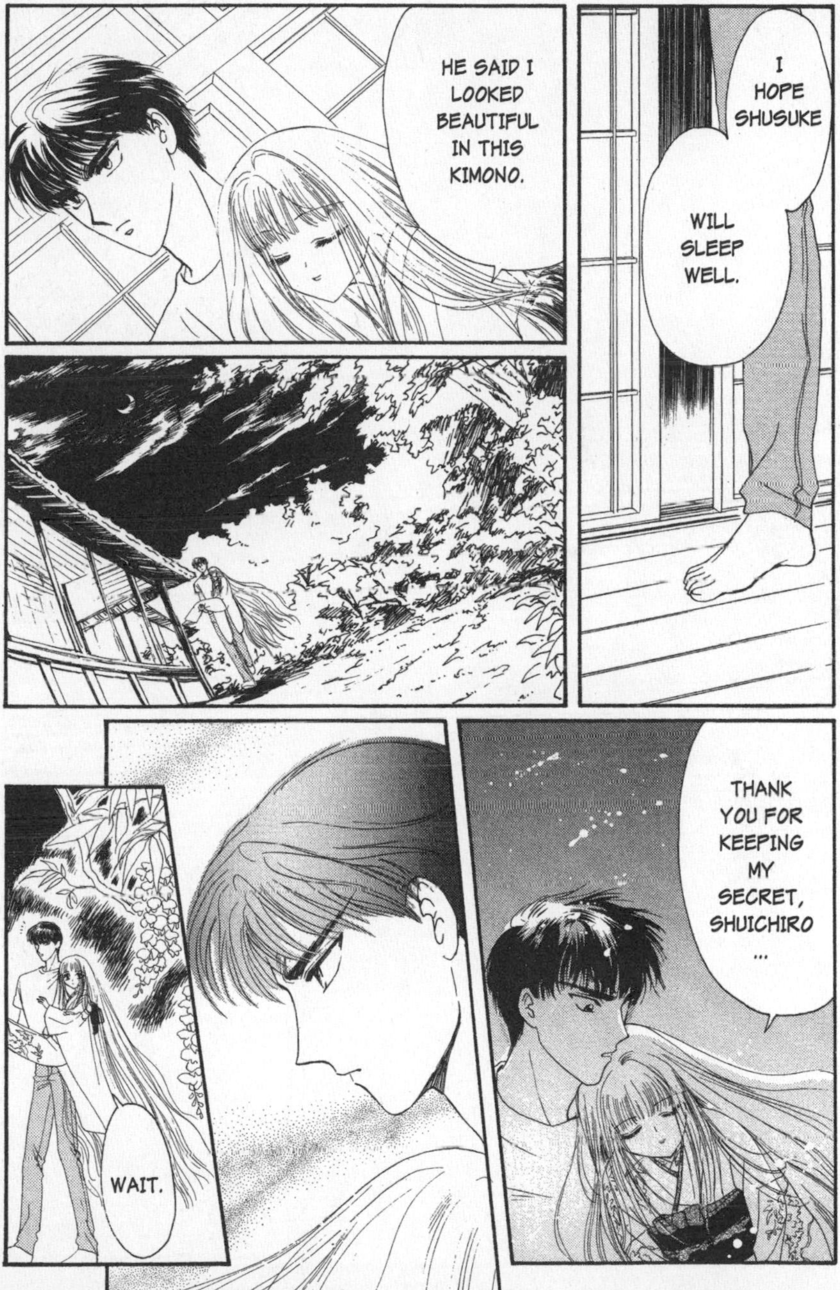
I HOPE SHUSUKE
WILL SLEEP WELL.
HE SAID I LOOKED BEAUTIFUL IN THIS KIMONO.
THANK YOU FOR KEEPING MY SECRET, SHUICHIRO ...
WAIT.

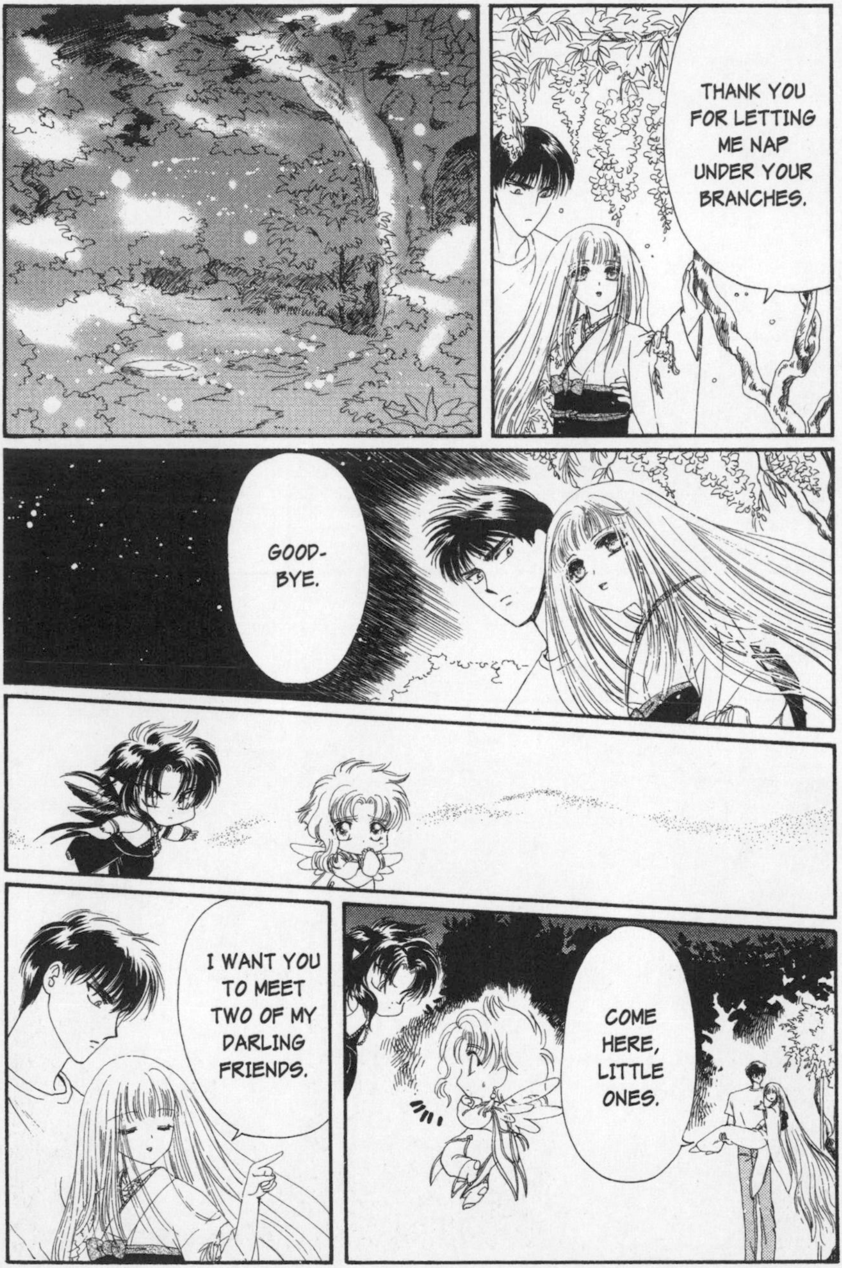
THANK YOU FOR LETTING ME NAP UNDER YOUR BRANCHES.
GOOD-BYE.
COME HERE, LITTLE ONES.
I WANT YOU TO MEET TWO OF MY DARLING FRIENDS.

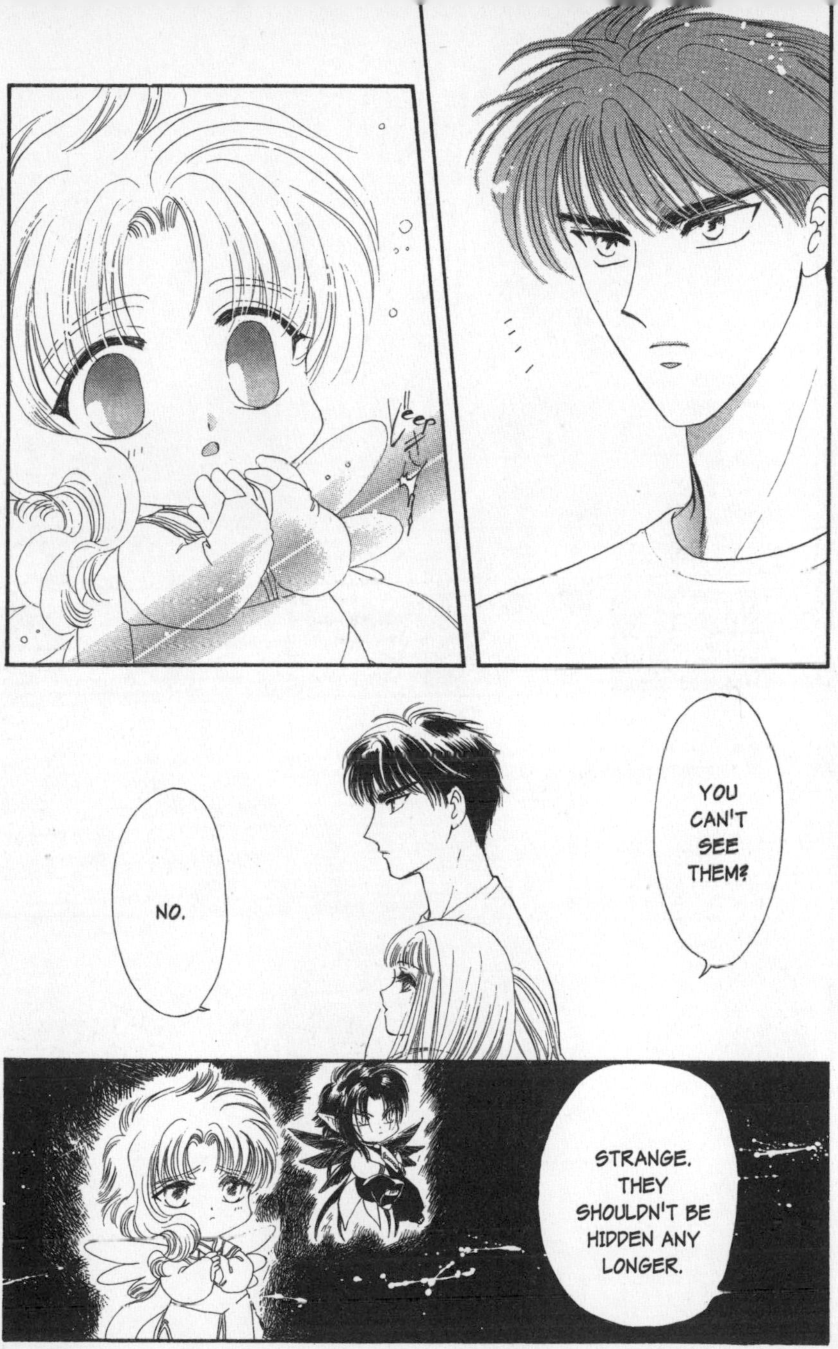
Veep
YOU CAN'T SEE THEM?
NO.
STRANGE. THEY SHOULDN'T BE HIDDEN ANY LONGER.

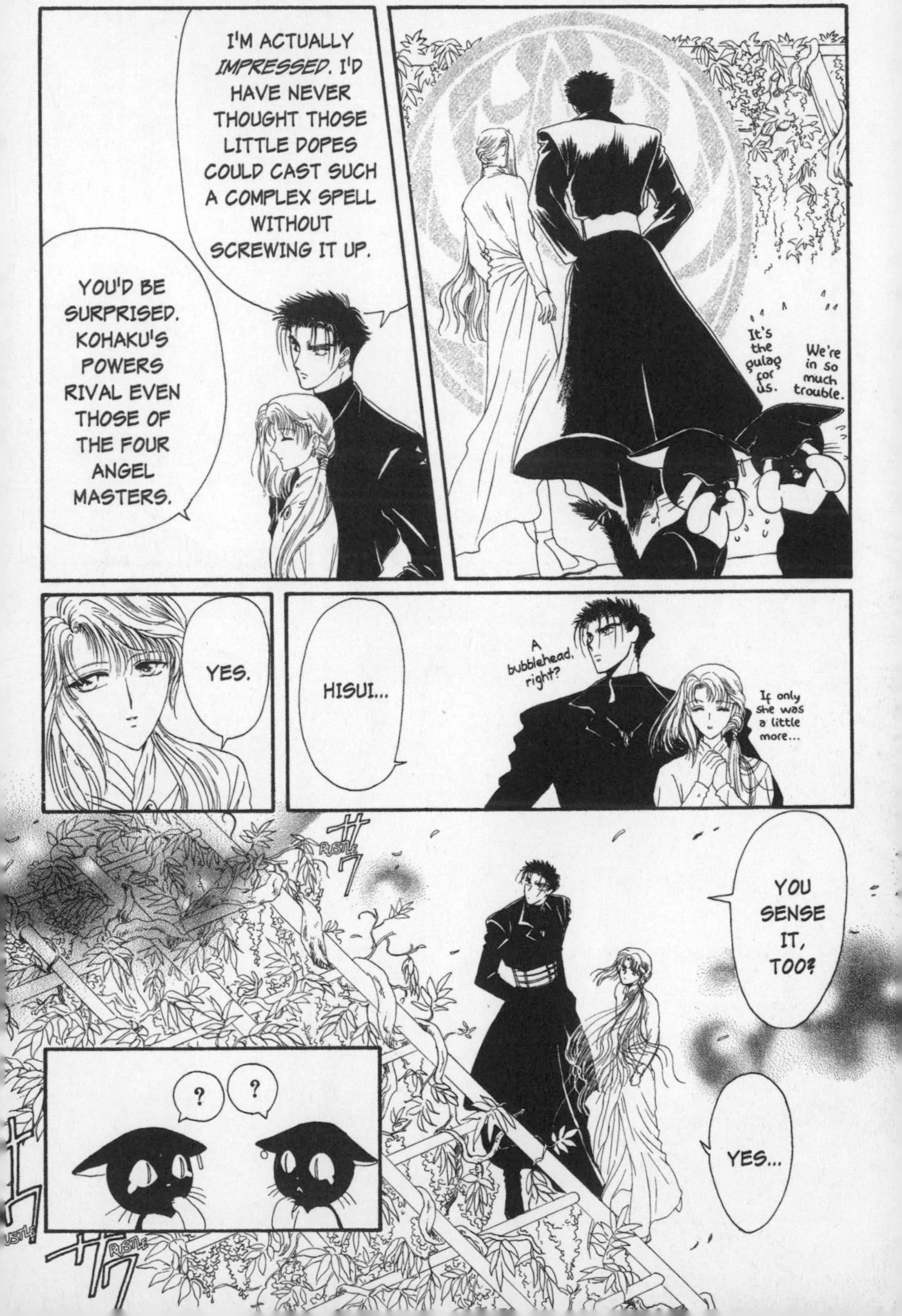
We're in so much trouble.
It's the gulag for us.
I'M ACTUALLY *IMPRESSED*. I'D HAVE NEVER THOUGHT THOSE LITTLE DOPES COULD CAST SUCH A COMPLEX SPELL WITHOUT SCREWING IT UP.
YOU'D BE SURPRISED. KOHAKU'S POWERS RIVAL EVEN THOSE OF THE FOUR ANGEL MASTERS.
A bubblehead, right?
If only she was a little more...
HISUI...
YES.
YOU SENSE IT, TOO?
RUSTLE
YES...
?
?
RUSTLE
RUSTLE

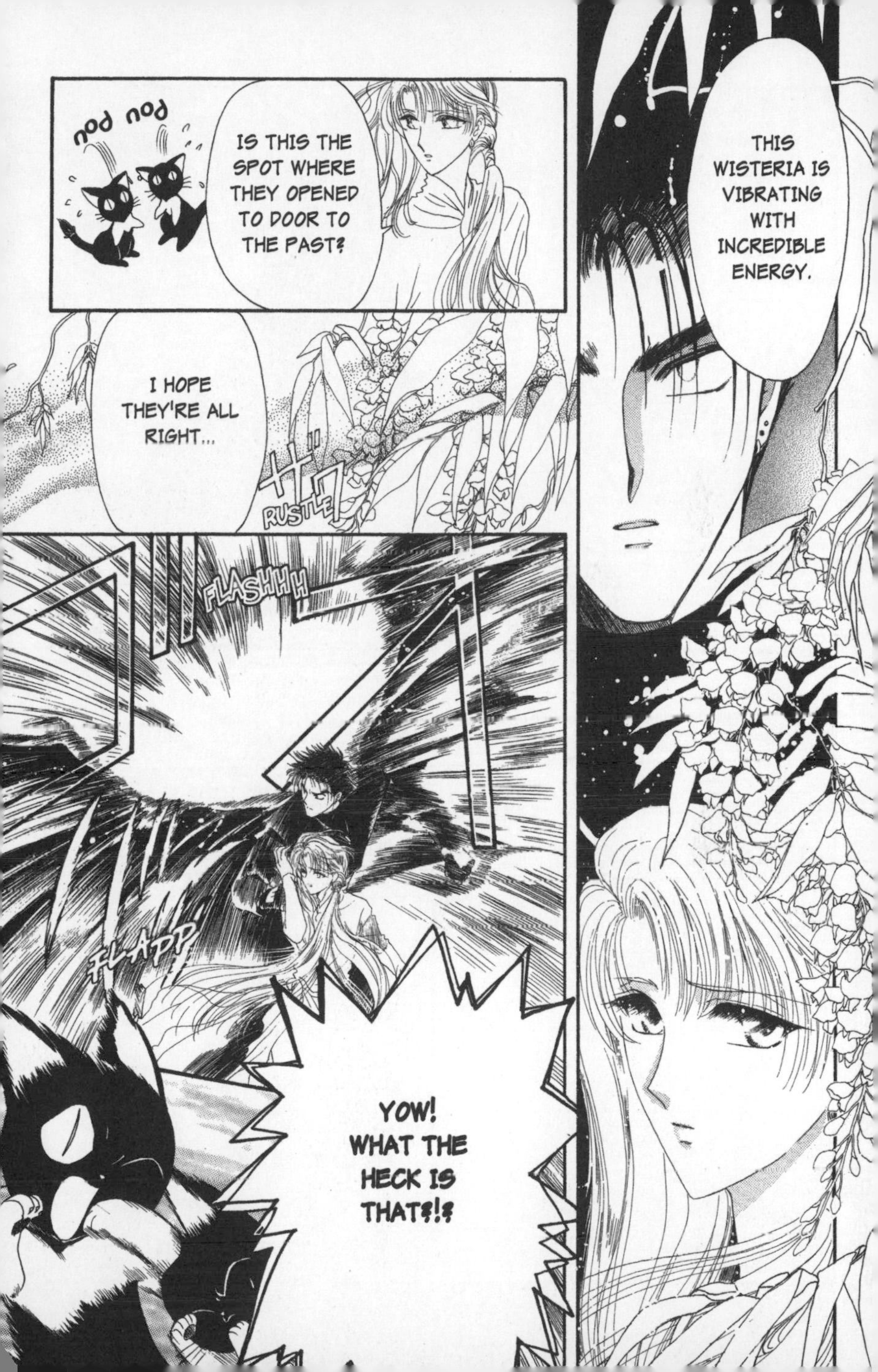
THIS WISTERIA IS VIBRATING WITH INCREDIBLE ENERGY.
IS THIS THE SPOT WHERE THEY OPENED TO DOOR TO THE PAST?
nod nod
I HOPE THEY'RE ALL RIGHT...
RUSTLE
FLASHHH
FLAPP
YOW! WHAT THE HECK IS THAT?!?

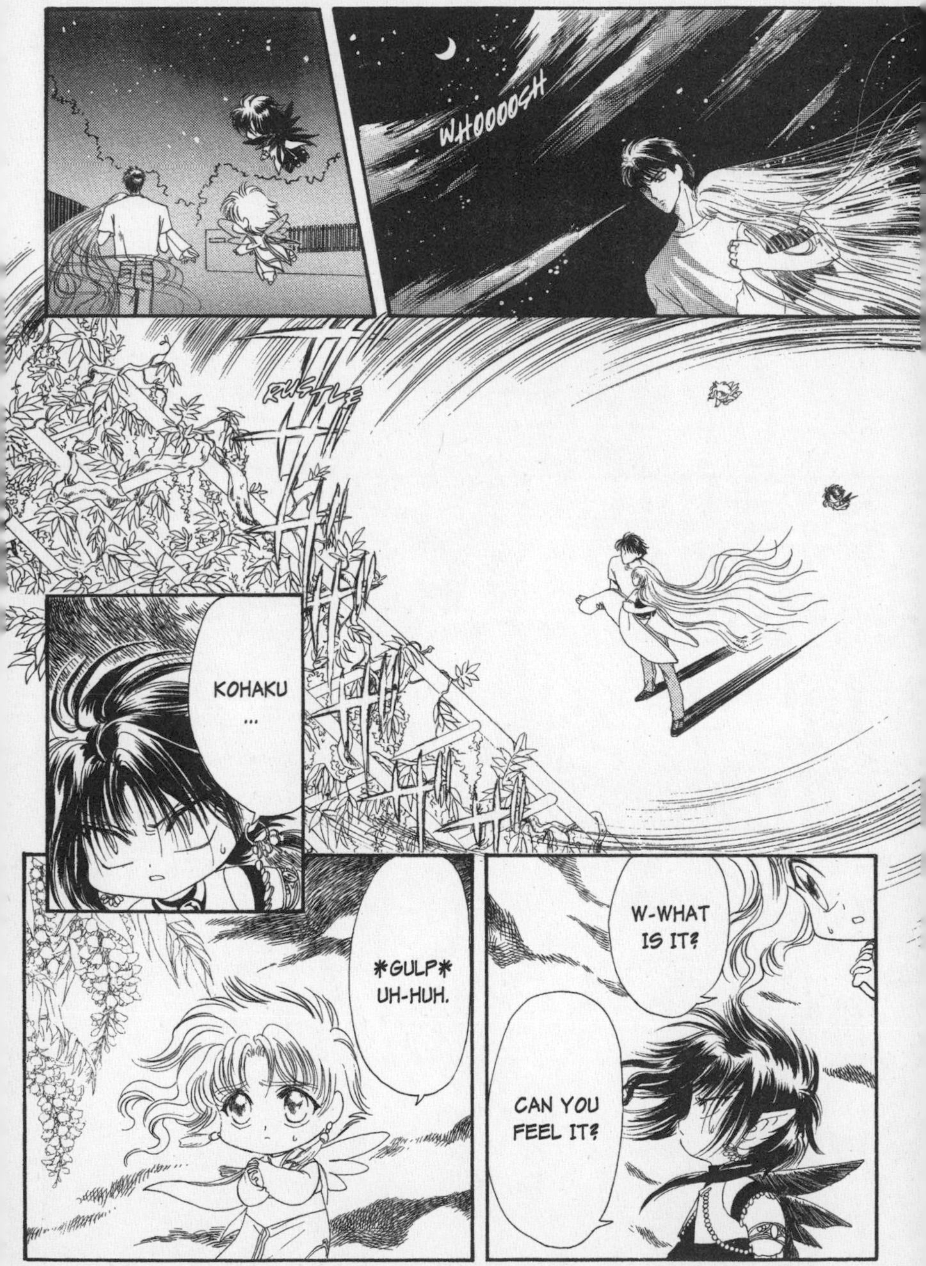
WHOOOOSH
RUSTLE
KOHAKU ...
W-WHAT IS IT?
CAN YOU FEEL IT?
GULP UH-HUH.

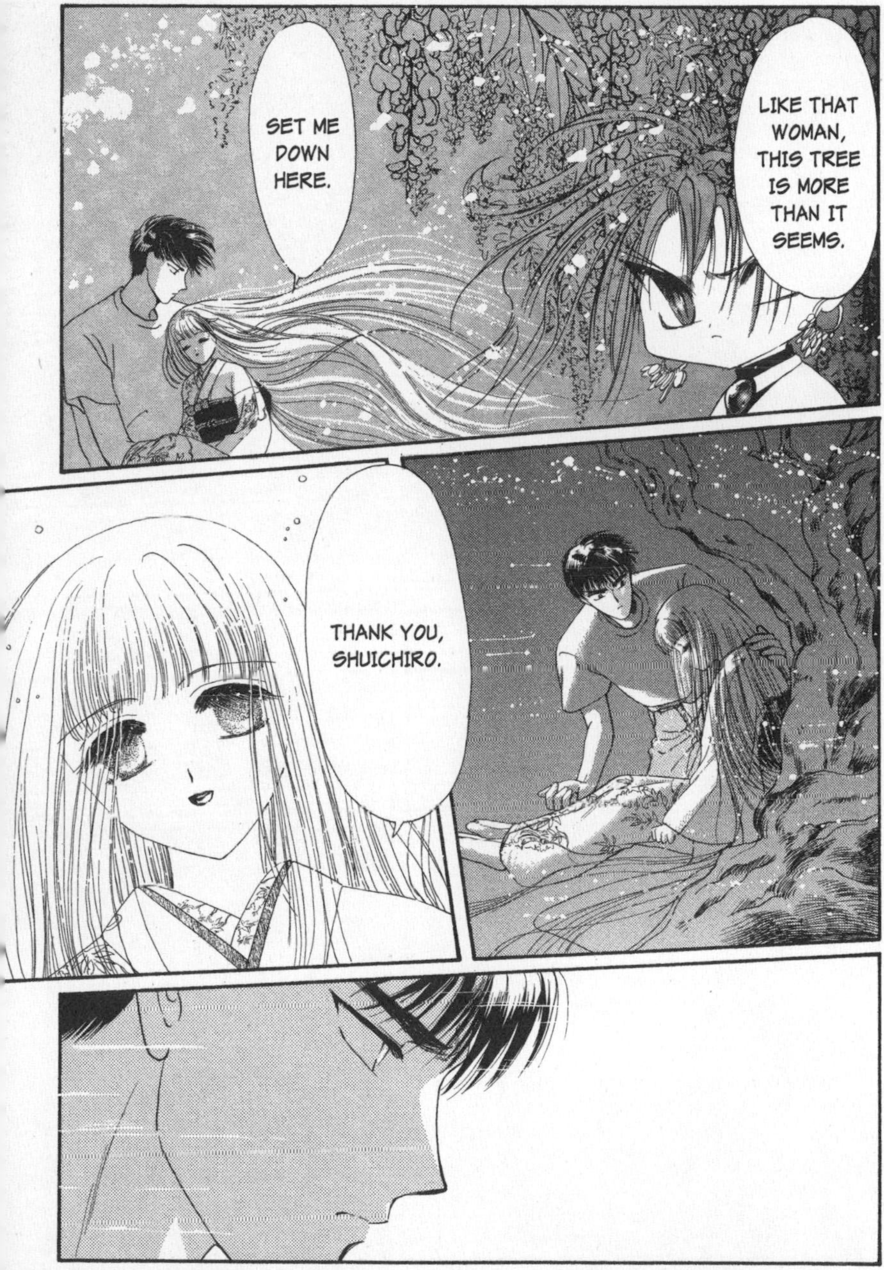
LIKE THAT WOMAN, THIS TREE IS MORE THAN IT SEEMS.
SET ME DOWN HERE.
THANK YOU, SHUICHIRO.

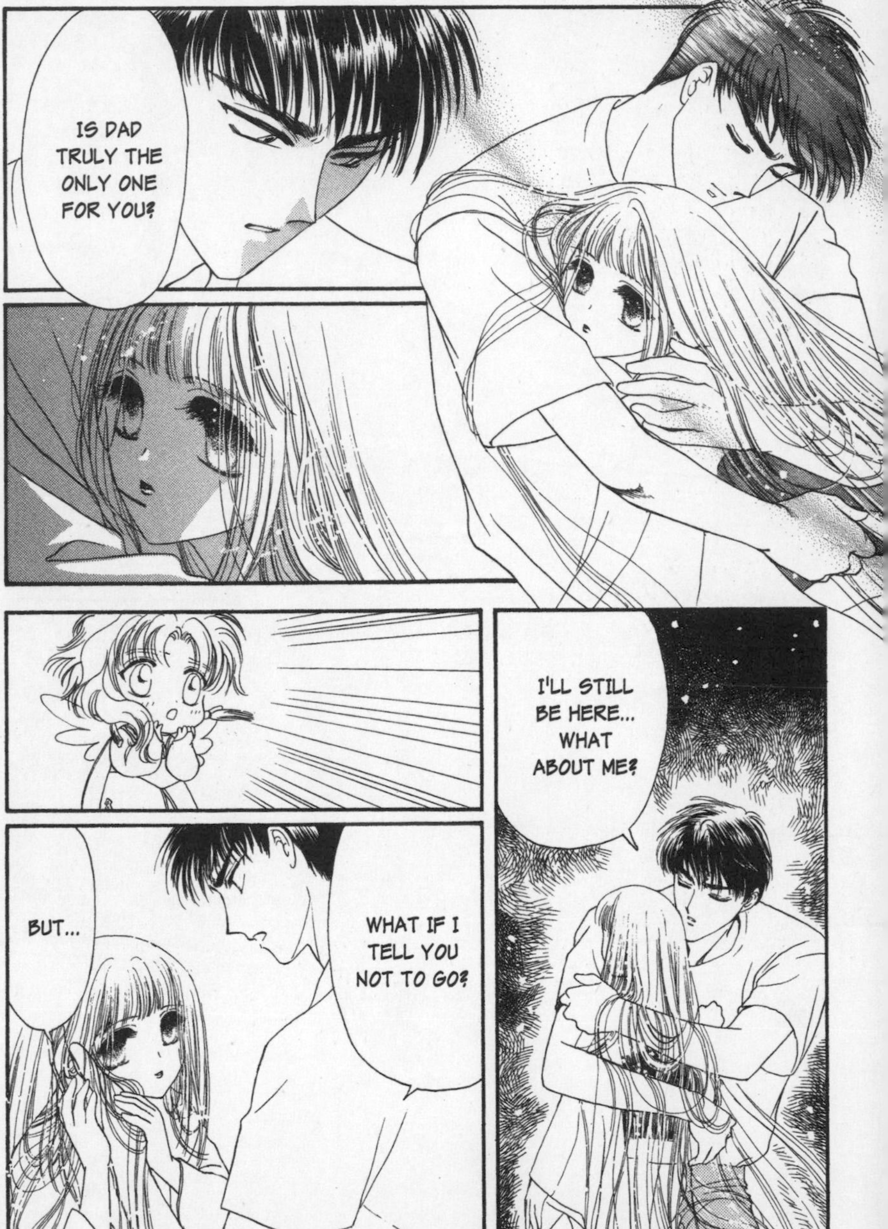
IS DAD TRULY THE ONLY ONE FOR YOU?
I'LL STILL BE HERE... WHAT ABOUT ME?
WHAT IF I TELL YOU NOT TO GO?
BUT...

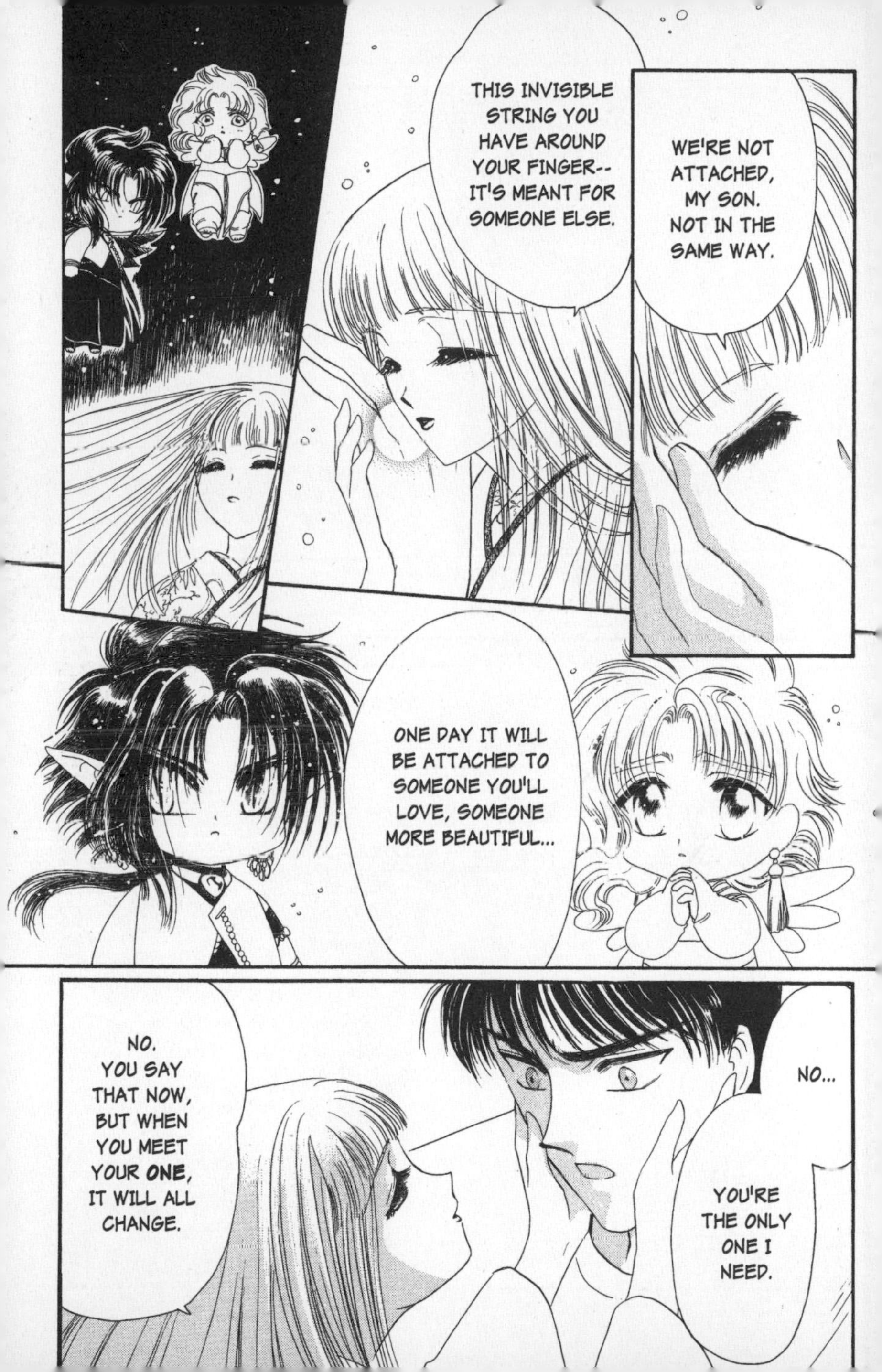
WE'RE NOT ATTACHED, MY SON. NOT IN THE SAME WAY.
THIS INVISIBLE STRING YOU HAVE AROUND YOUR FINGER-- IT'S MEANT FOR SOMEONE ELSE.
ONE DAY IT WILL BE ATTACHED TO SOMEONE YOU'LL LOVE, SOMEONE MORE BEAUTIFUL...
NO...
YOU'RE THE ONLY ONE I NEED.
NO. YOU SAY THAT NOW, BUT WHEN YOU MEET YOUR **ONE**, IT WILL ALL CHANGE.

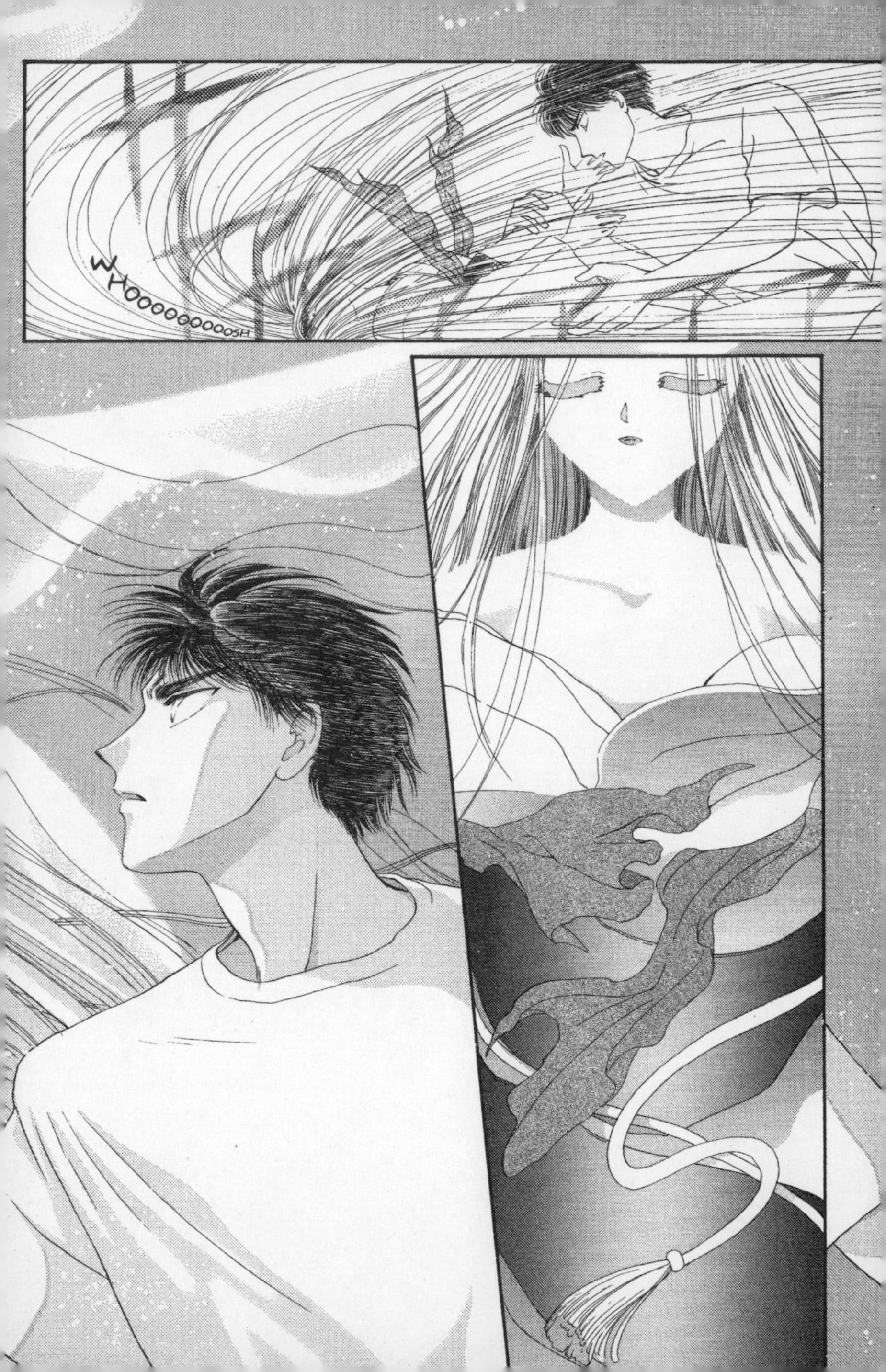
WHOOOOOOOOOSH

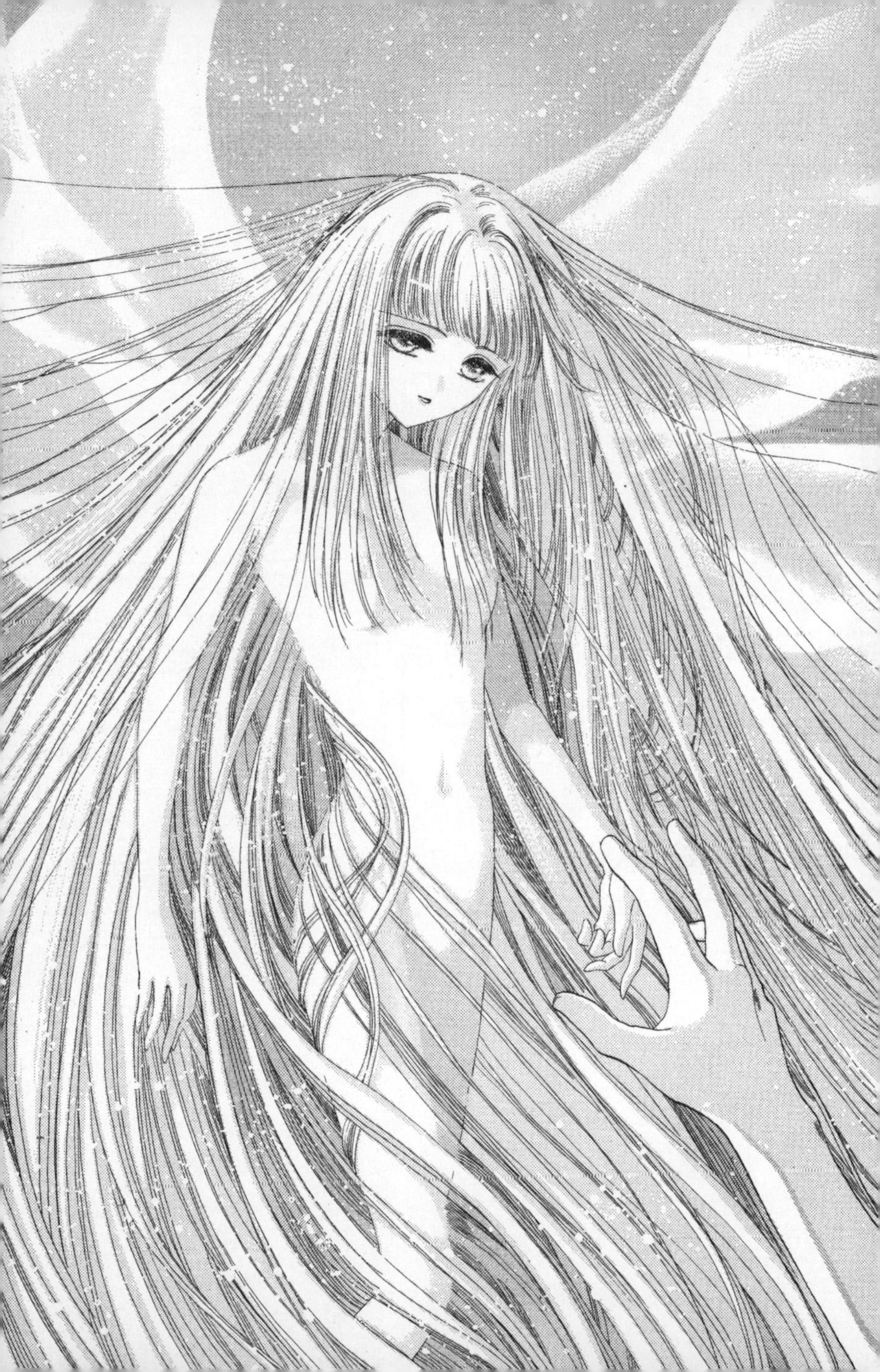

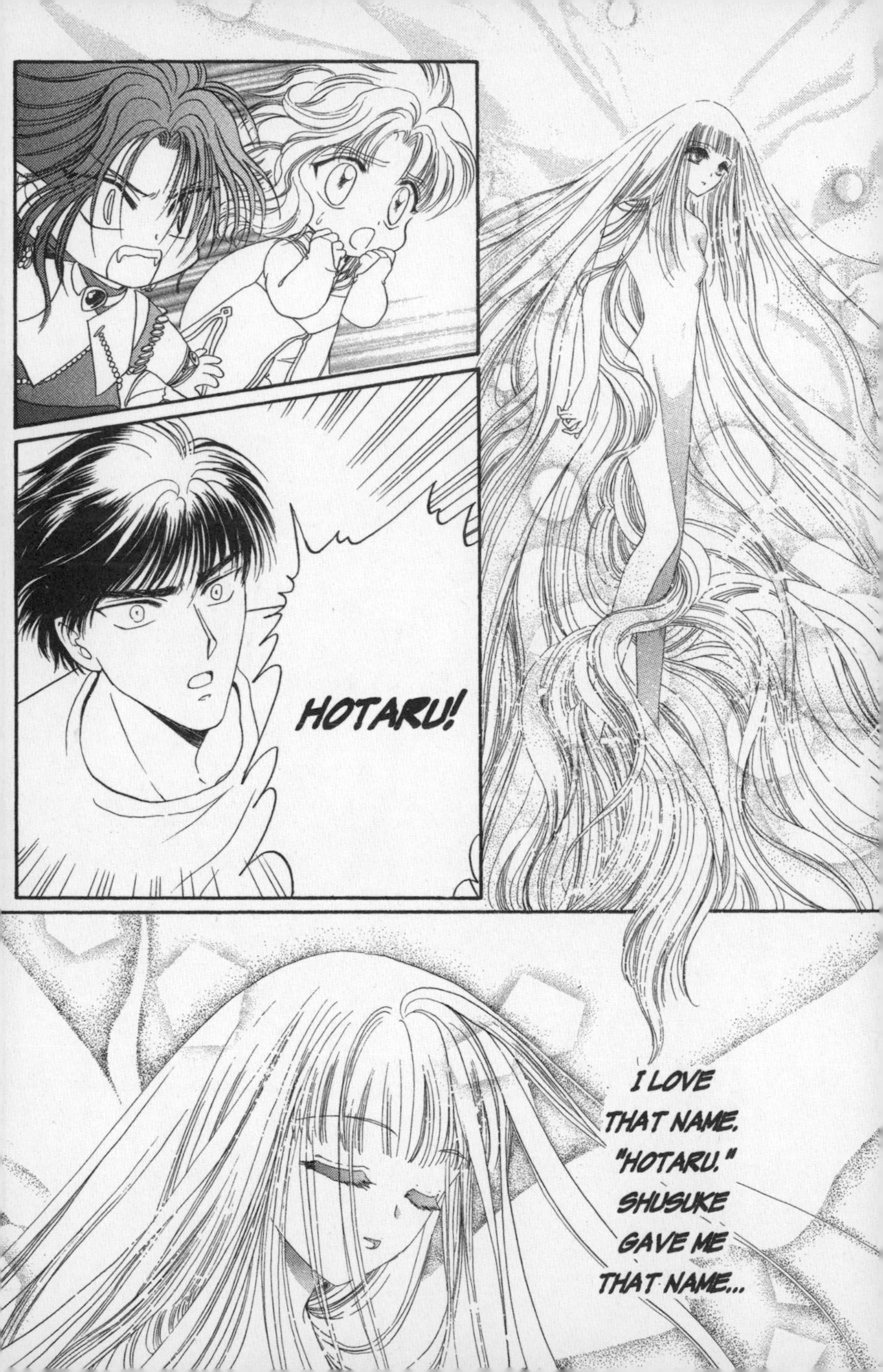
HOTARU!
I LOVE THAT NAME. "HOTARU." SHUSUKE GAVE ME THAT NAME...

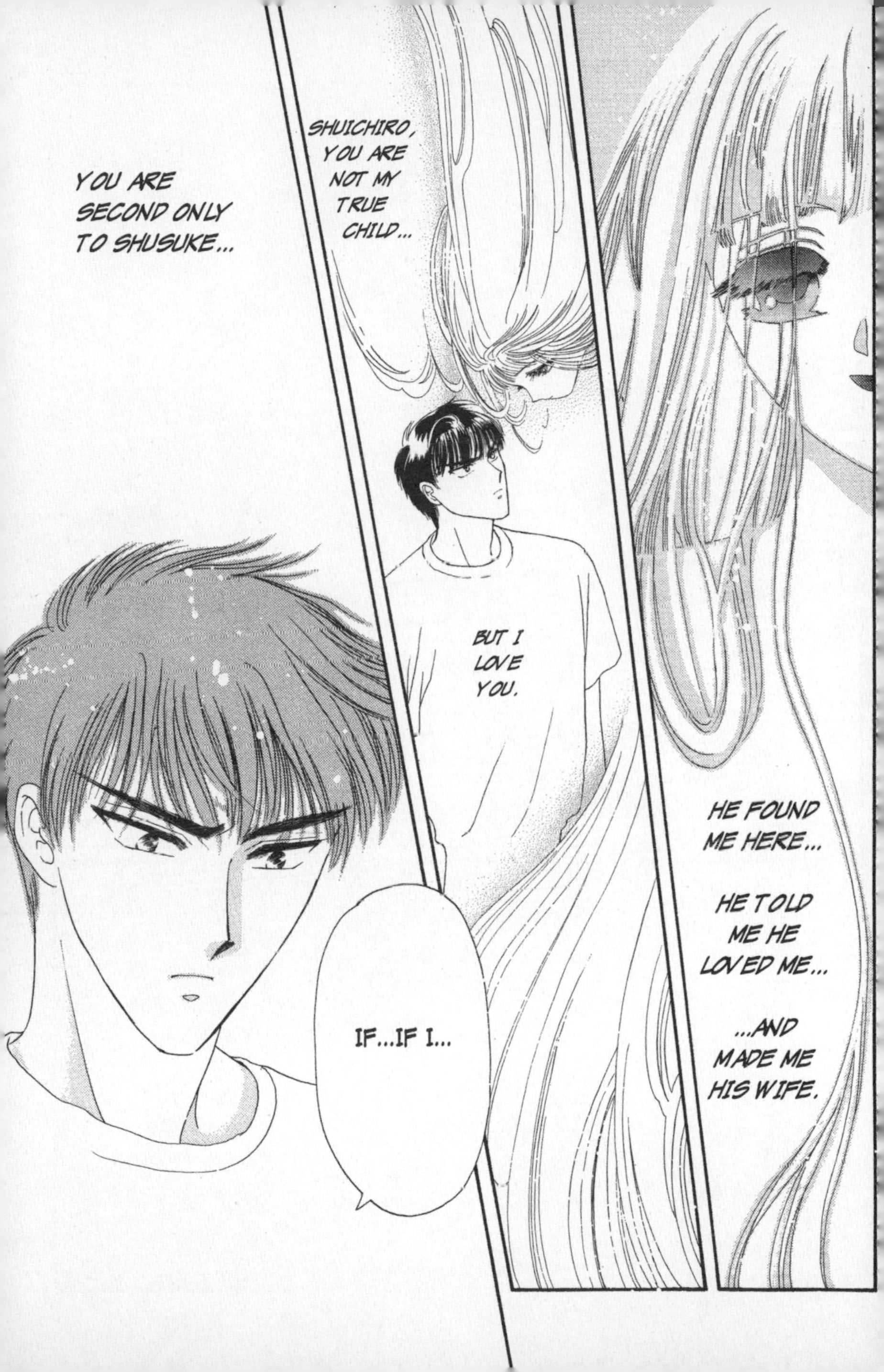
HE FOUND ME HERE...
HE TOLD ME HE LOVED ME...
...AND MADE ME HIS WIFE.
SHUICHIRO, YOU ARE NOT MY TRUE CHILD...
BUT I LOVE YOU.
YOU ARE SECOND ONLY TO SHUSUKE...
IF...IF I...

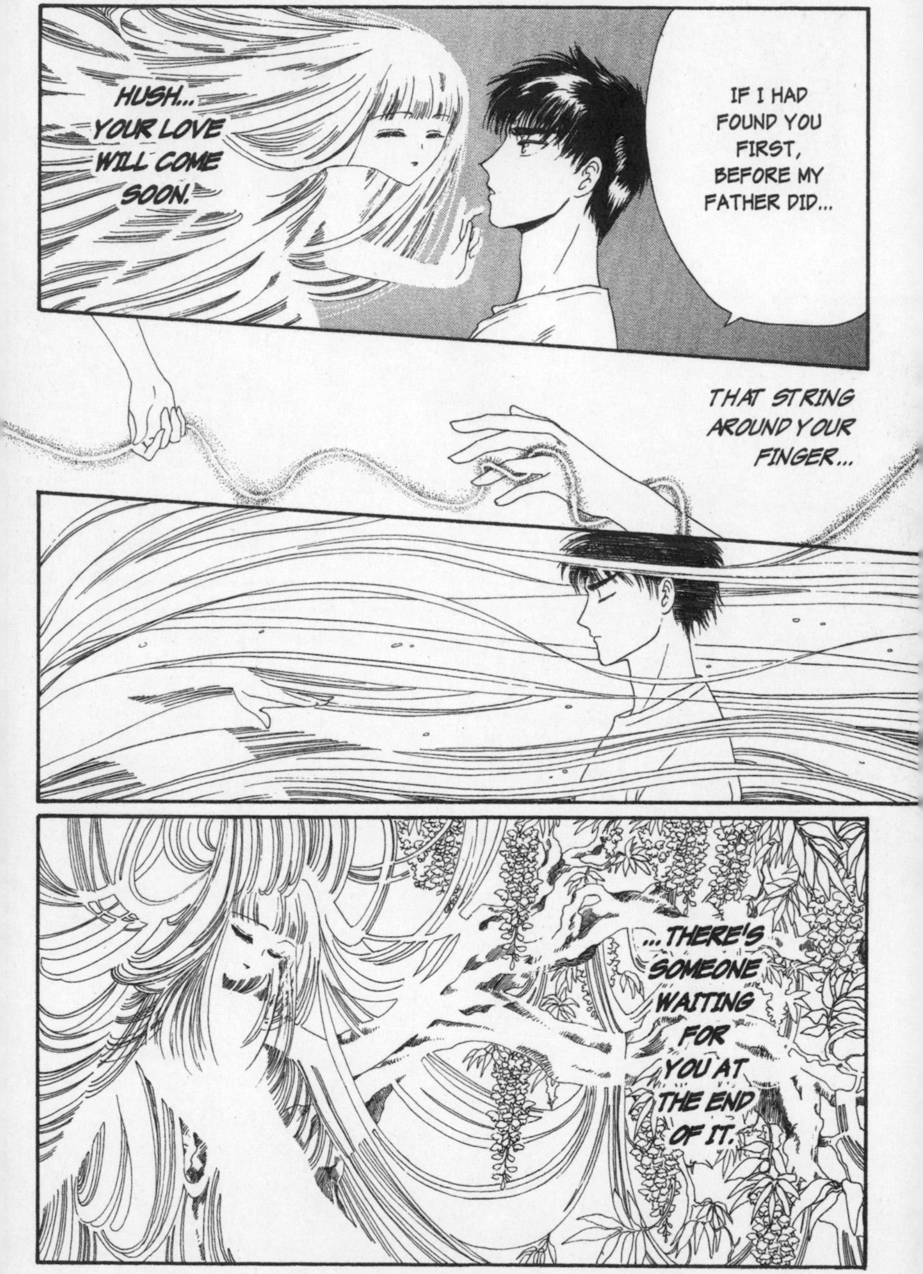
IF I HAD FOUND YOU FIRST, BEFORE MY FATHER DID...
HUSH... YOUR LOVE WILL COME SOON.
THAT STRING AROUND YOUR FINGER...
...THERE'S SOMEONE WAITING FOR YOU AT THE END OF IT.

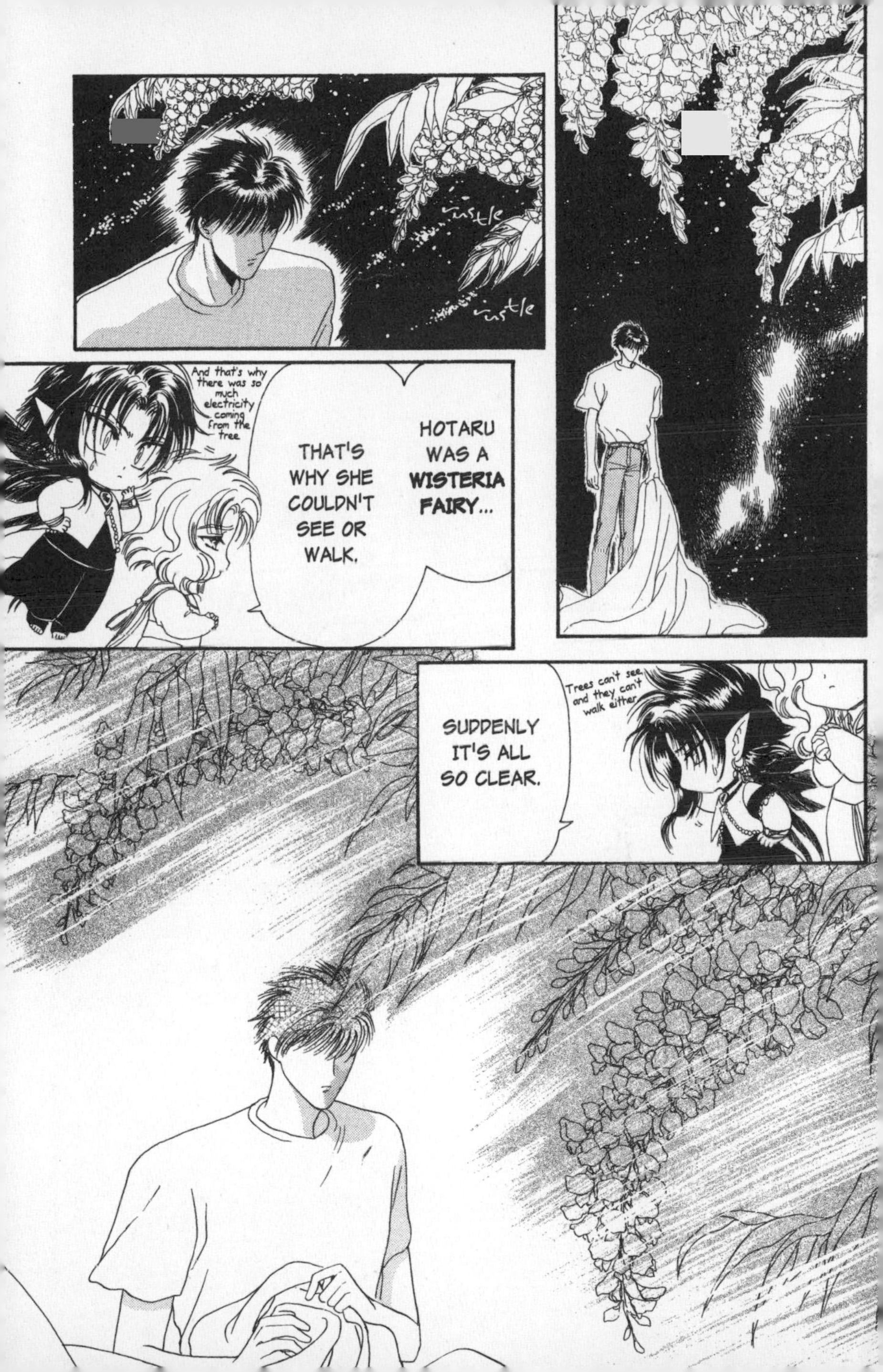
rustle
rustle
HOTARU WAS A WISTERIA FAIRY...
THAT'S WHY SHE COULDN'T SEE OR WALK.
And that's why there was so much electricity coming from the tree
Trees can't see and they can't walk either
SUDDENLY IT'S ALL SO CLEAR.

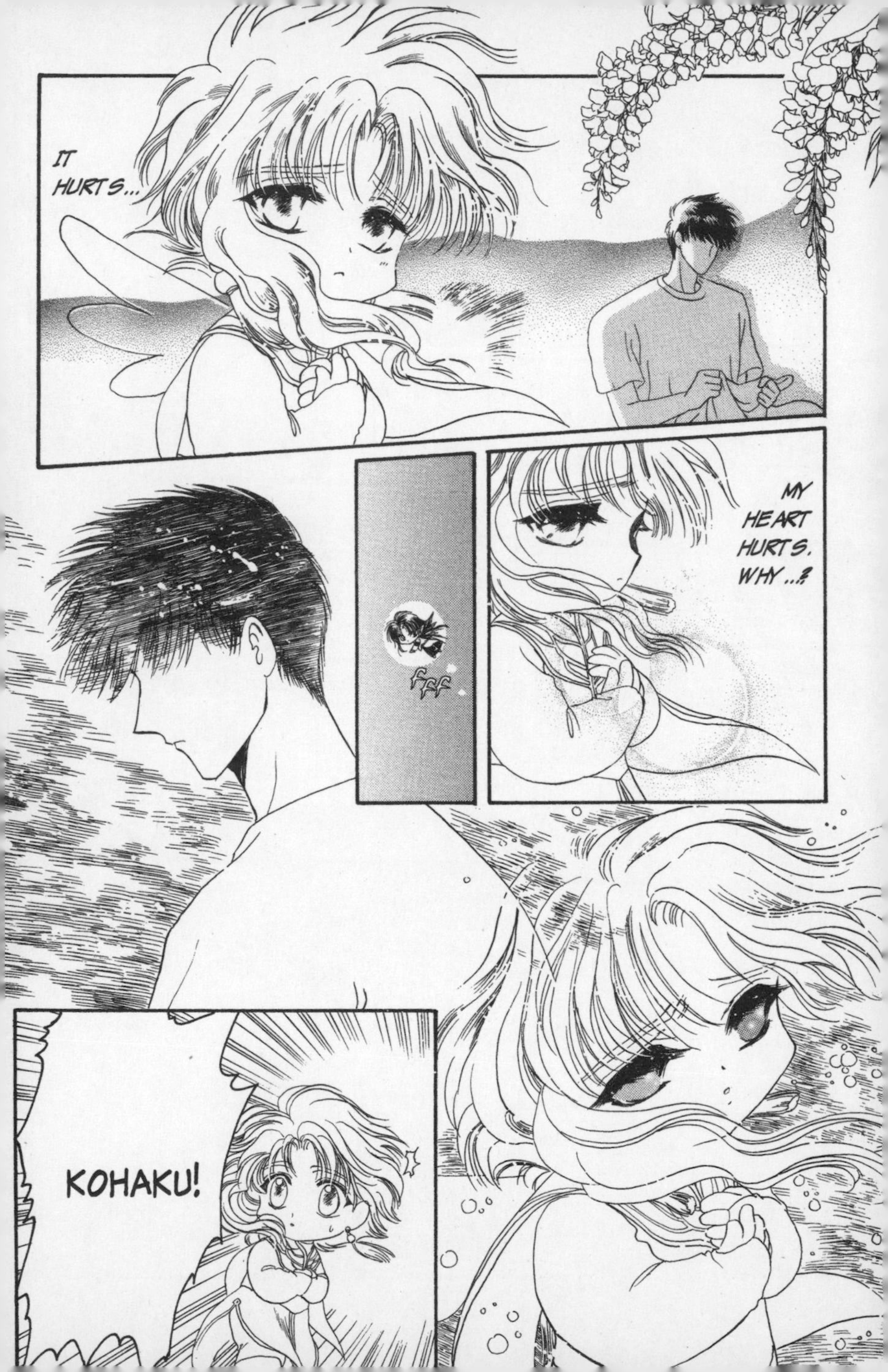
IT HURTS...
MY HEART HURTS. WHY...?
fff
KOHAKU!

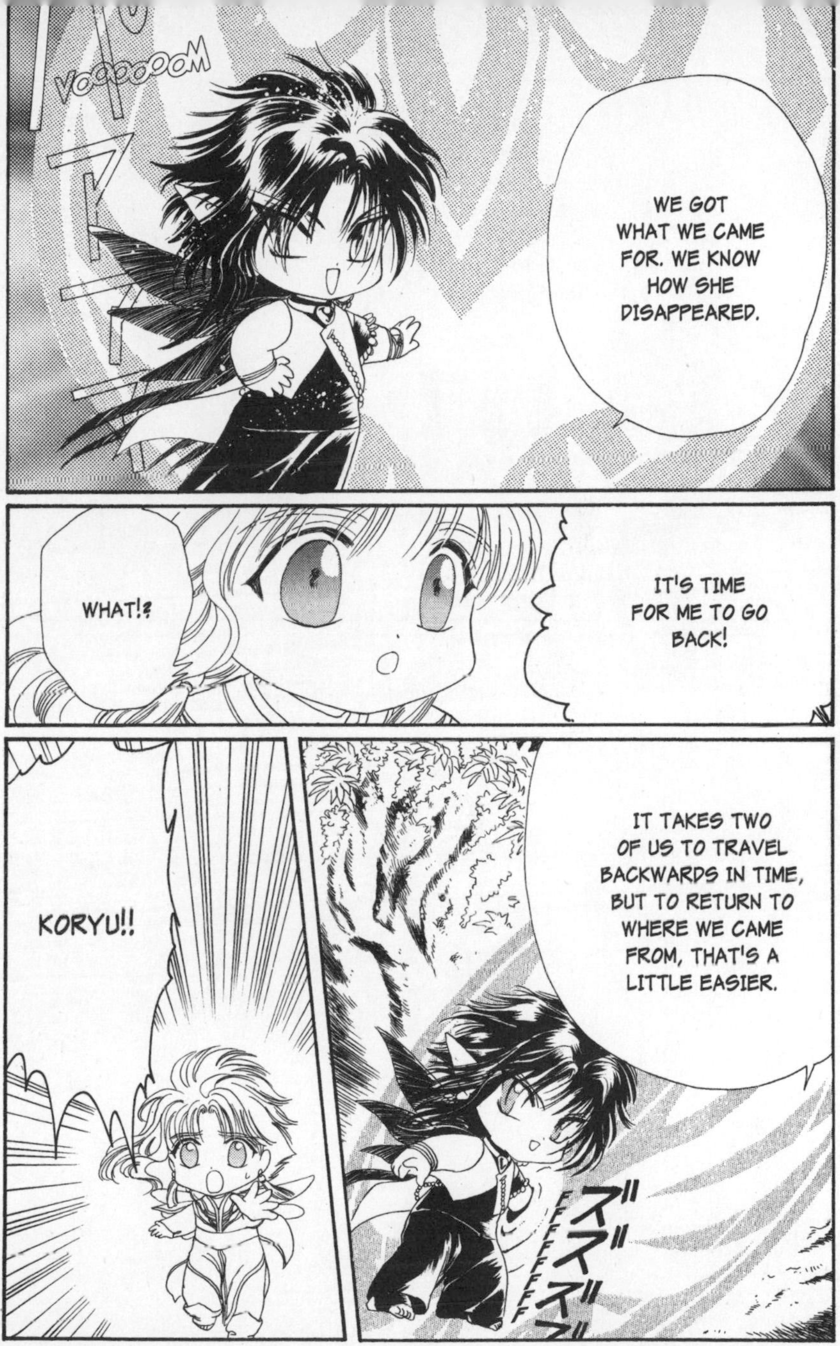
VOOOOOOM
WE GOT WHAT WE CAME FOR. WE KNOW HOW SHE DISAPPEARED.
IT'S TIME FOR ME TO GO BACK!
WHAT!?
IT TAKES TWO OF US TO TRAVEL BACKWARDS IN TIME, BUT TO RETURN TO WHERE WE CAME FROM, THAT'S A LITTLE EASIER.
KORYU!!

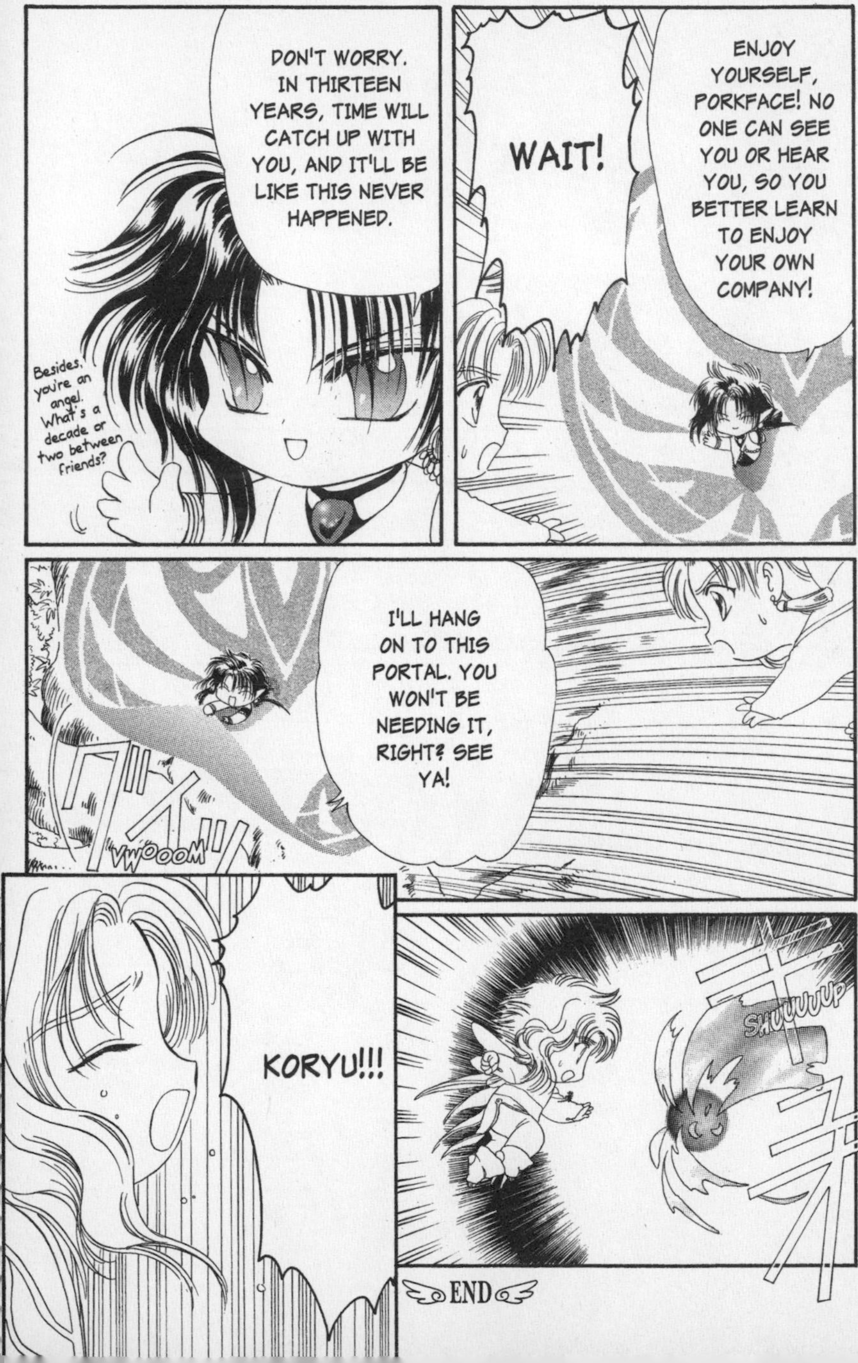
ENJOY YOURSELF, PORKFACE! NO ONE CAN SEE YOU OR HEAR YOU, SO YOU BETTER LEARN TO ENJOY YOUR OWN COMPANY!
WAIT!
DON'T WORRY. IN THIRTEEN YEARS, TIME WILL CATCH UP WITH YOU, AND IT'LL BE LIKE THIS NEVER HAPPENED.
Besides, you're an angel. What's a decade or two between friends?
I'LL HANG ON TO THIS PORTAL. YOU WON'T BE NEEDING IT, RIGHT? SEE YA!
VWOOOM
SHUUUUUP
KORYU!!!
END

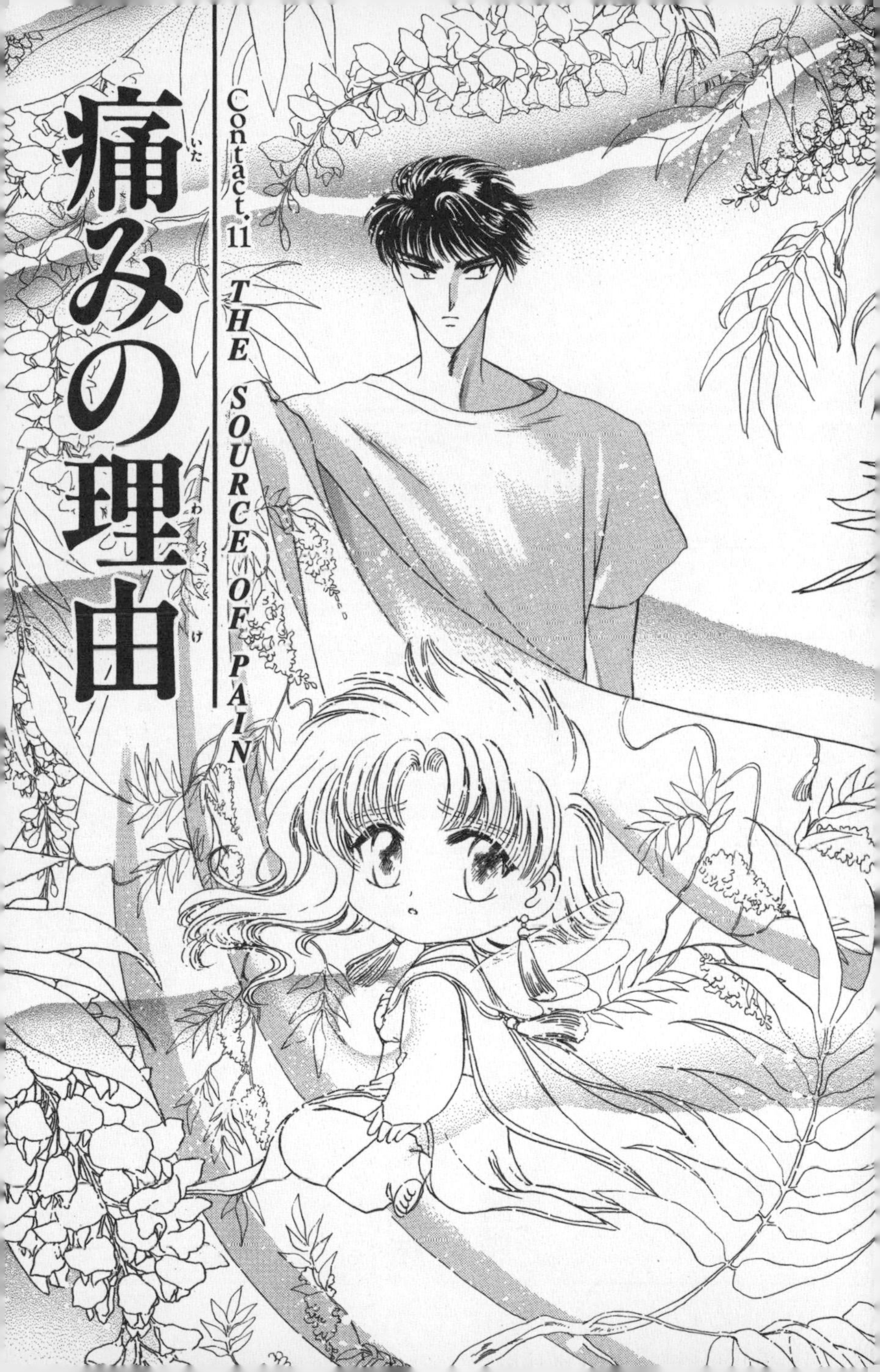
Contact.11 THE SOURCE OF PAIN
痛みの理由

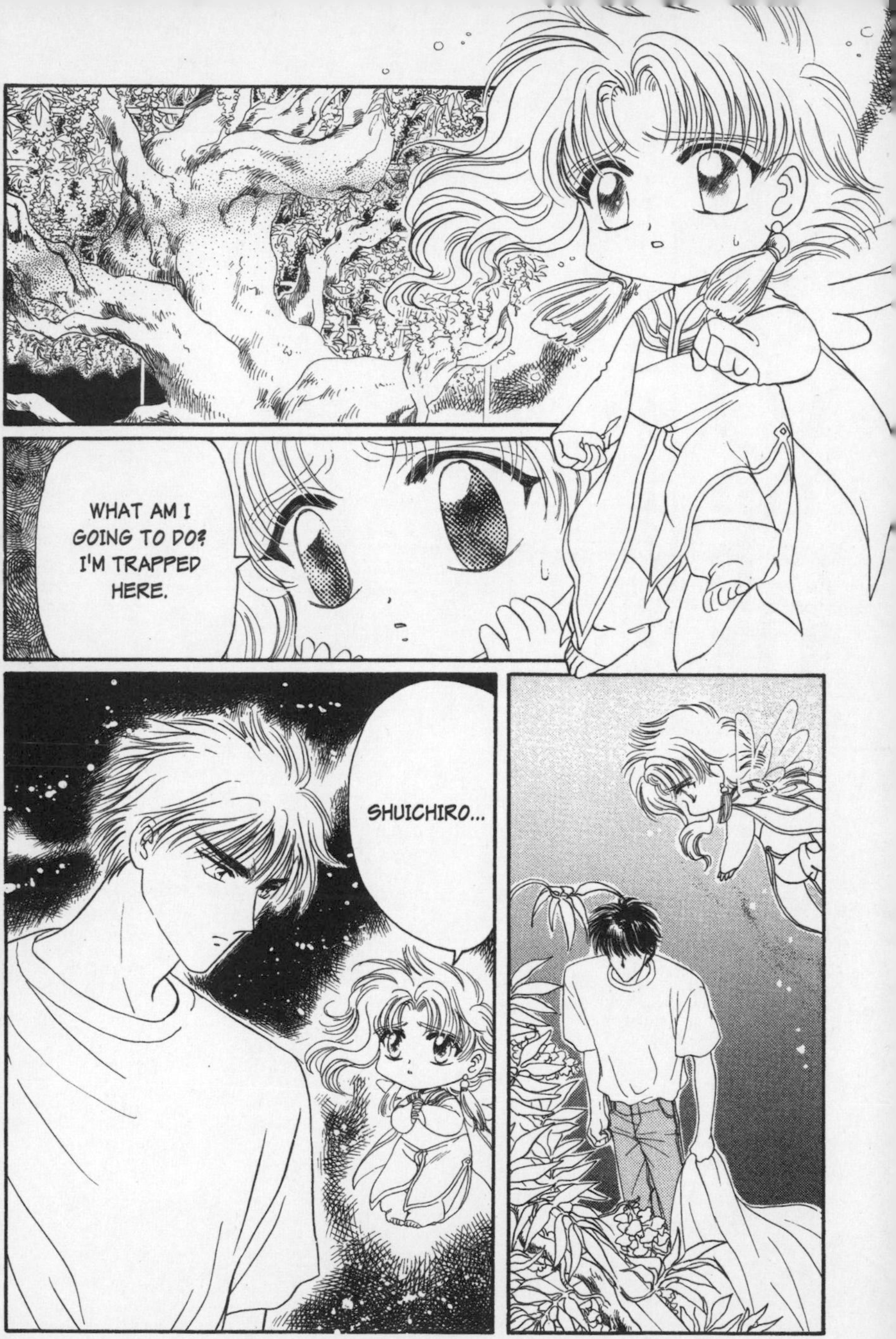
WHAT AM I GOING TO DO? I'M TRAPPED HERE.
SHUICHIRO...

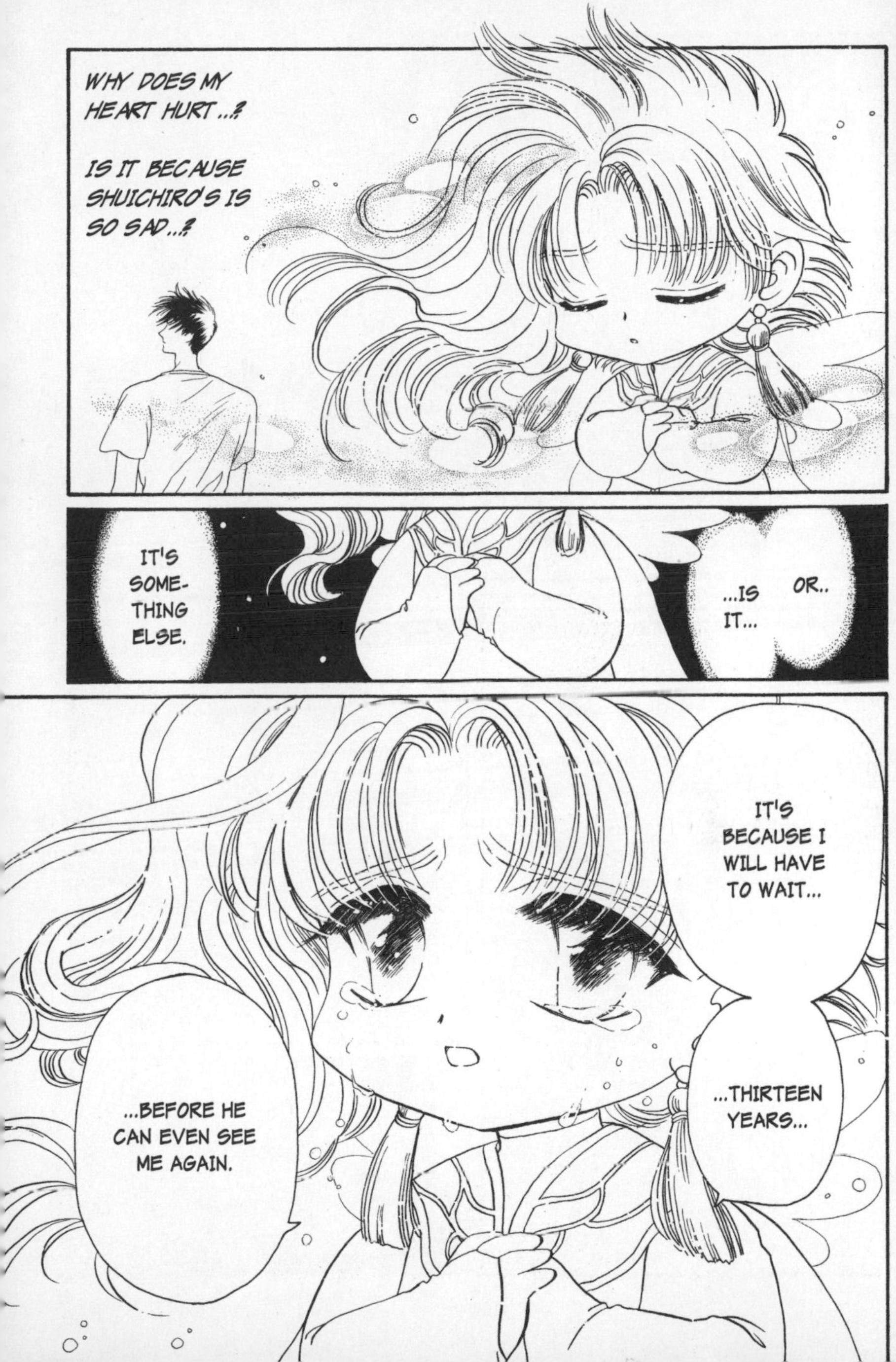
WHY DOES MY HEART HURT...?
IS IT BECAUSE SHUICHIRO'S IS SO SAD...?
OR..
...IS IT...
IT'S SOME-THING ELSE.
IT'S BECAUSE I WILL HAVE TO WAIT...
...THIRTEEN YEARS...
...BEFORE HE CAN EVEN SEE ME AGAIN.

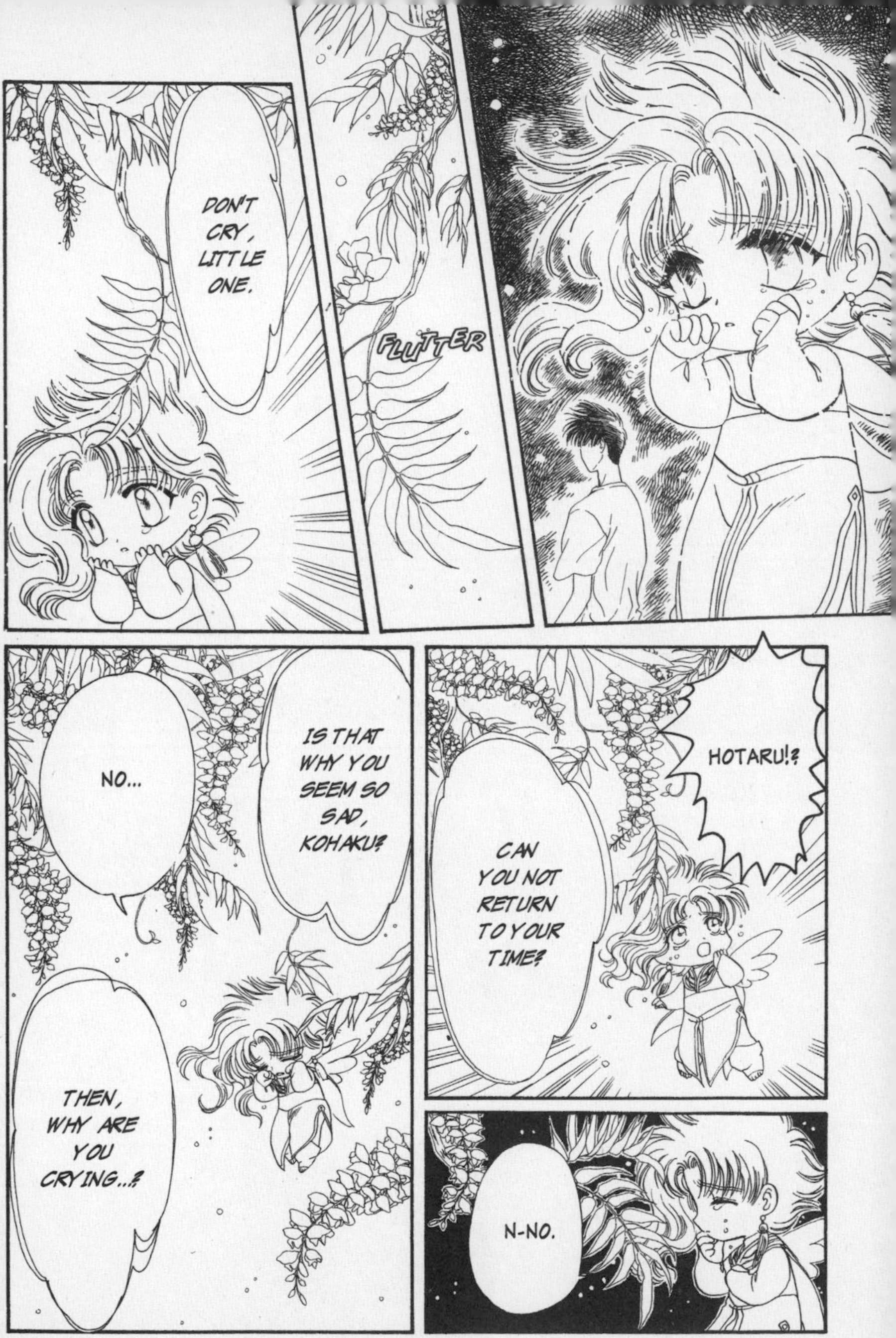
FLUTTER
DON'T CRY, LITTLE ONE.
HOTARU!?
CAN YOU NOT RETURN TO YOUR TIME?
N-NO.
IS THAT WHY YOU SEEM SO SAD, KOHAKU?
NO...
THEN, WHY ARE YOU CRYING...!?

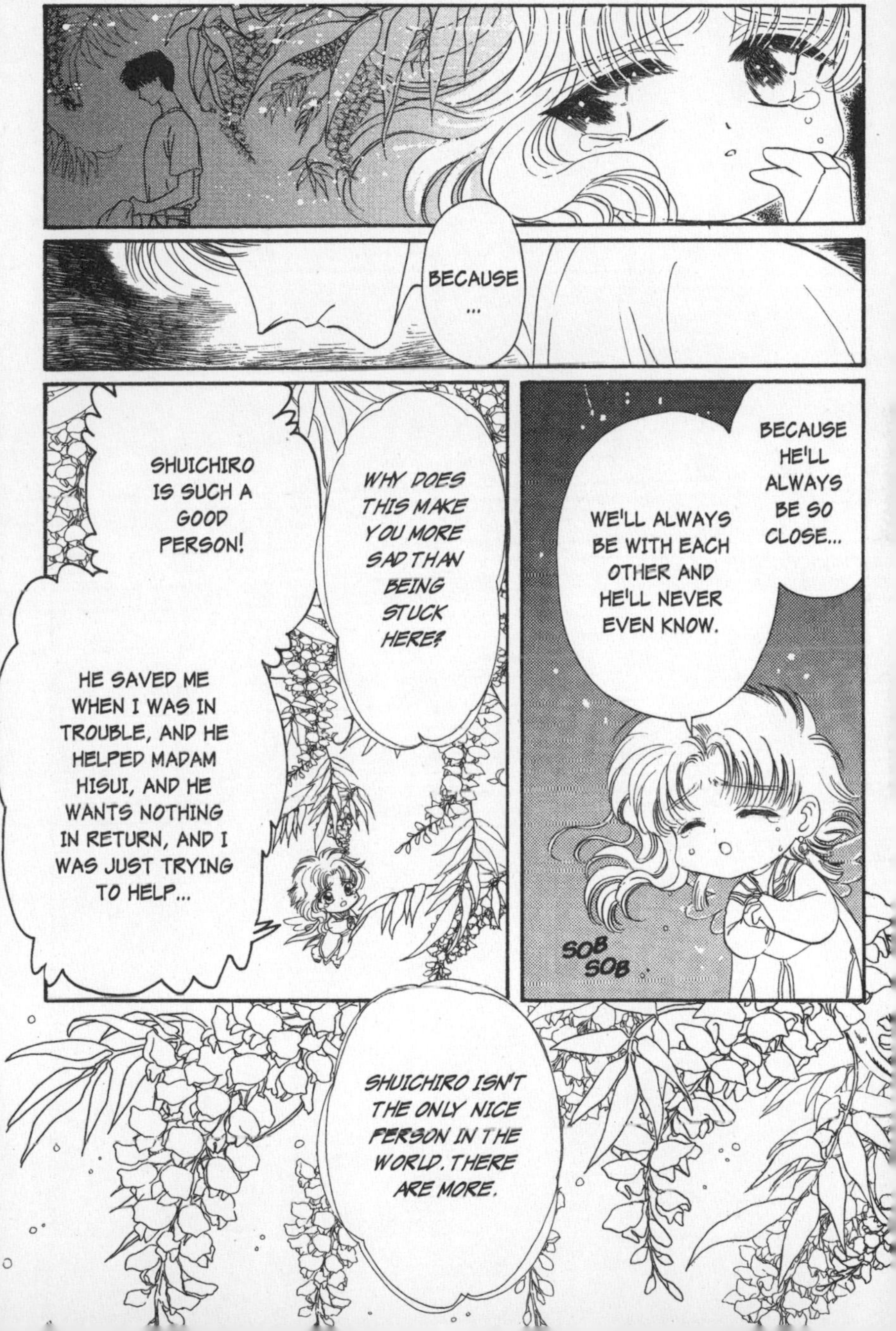
BECAUSE ...
BECAUSE HE'LL ALWAYS BE SO CLOSE...
WE'LL ALWAYS BE WITH EACH OTHER AND HE'LL NEVER EVEN KNOW.
SOB SOB
WHY DOES THIS MAKE YOU MORE SAD THAN BEING STUCK HERE?
SHUICHIRO IS SUCH A GOOD PERSON!
HE SAVED ME WHEN I WAS IN TROUBLE, AND HE HELPED MADAM HISUI, AND HE WANTS NOTHING IN RETURN, AND I WAS JUST TRYING TO HELP...
SHUICHIRO ISN'T THE ONLY NICE PERSON IN THE WORLD. THERE ARE MORE.

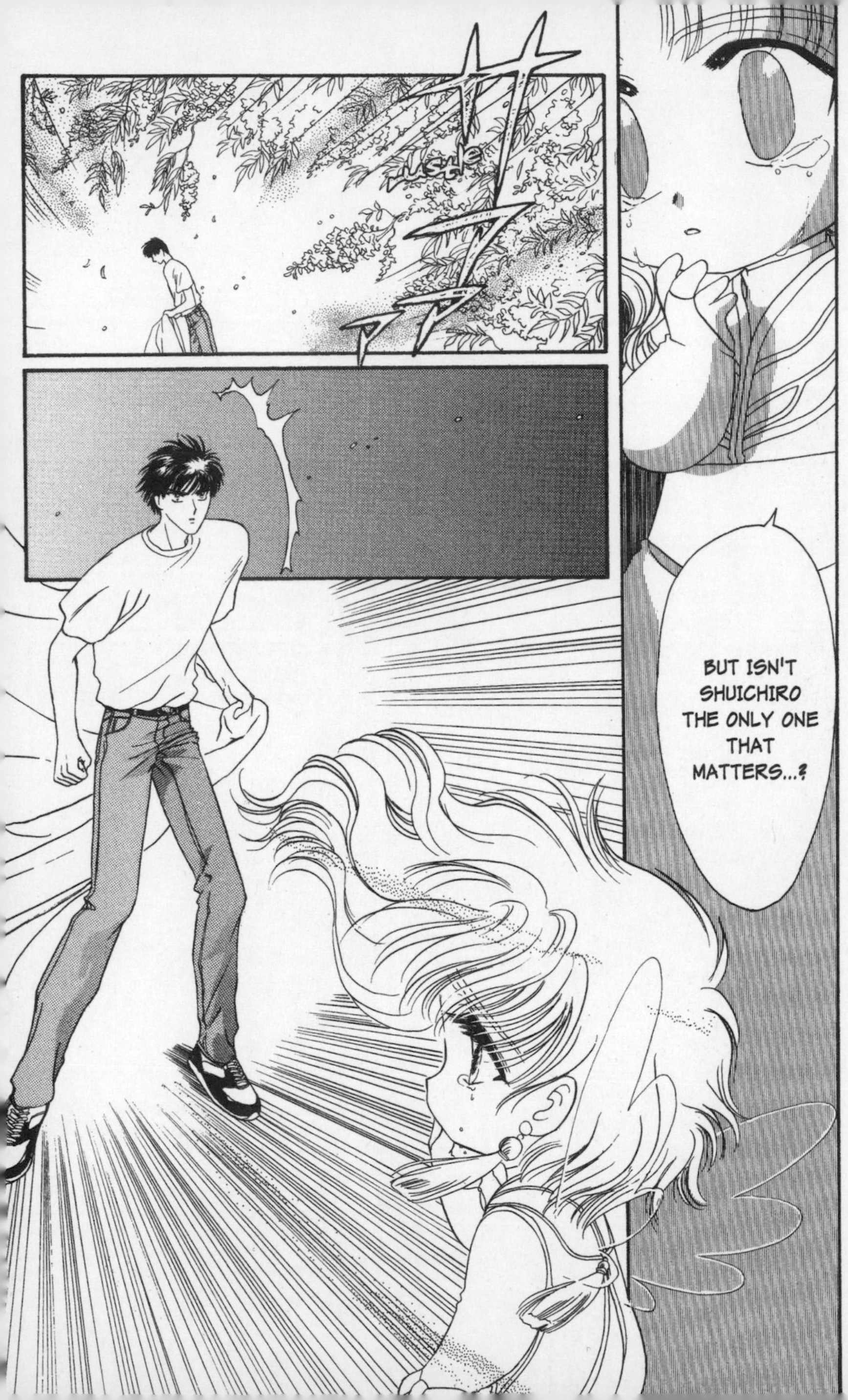
BUT ISN'T SHUICHIRO THE ONLY ONE THAT MATTERS...?
rustle

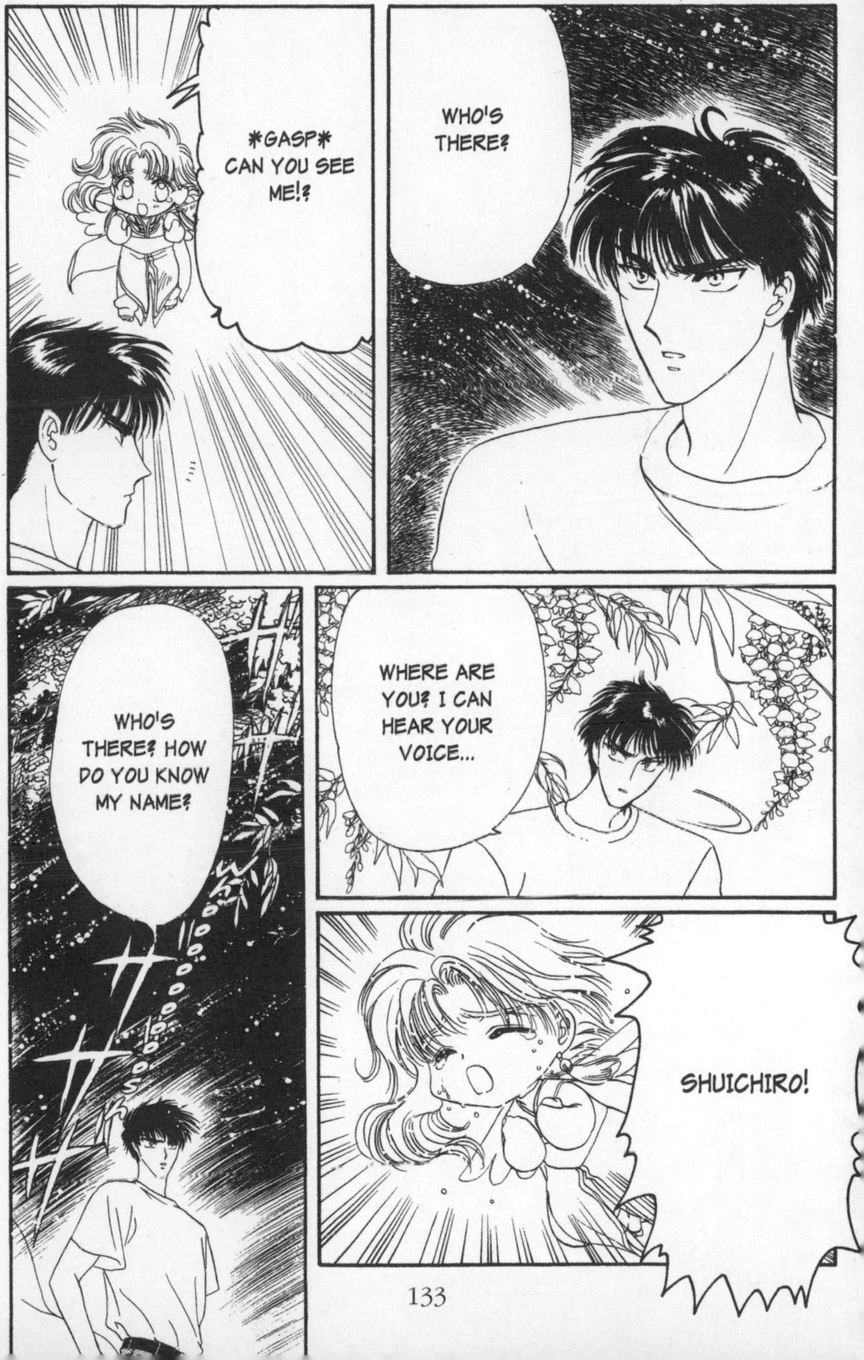
WHO'S THERE?
GASP CAN YOU SEE ME!?
WHERE ARE YOU? I CAN HEAR YOUR VOICE...
SHUICHIRO!
WHO'S THERE? HOW DO YOU KNOW MY NAME?

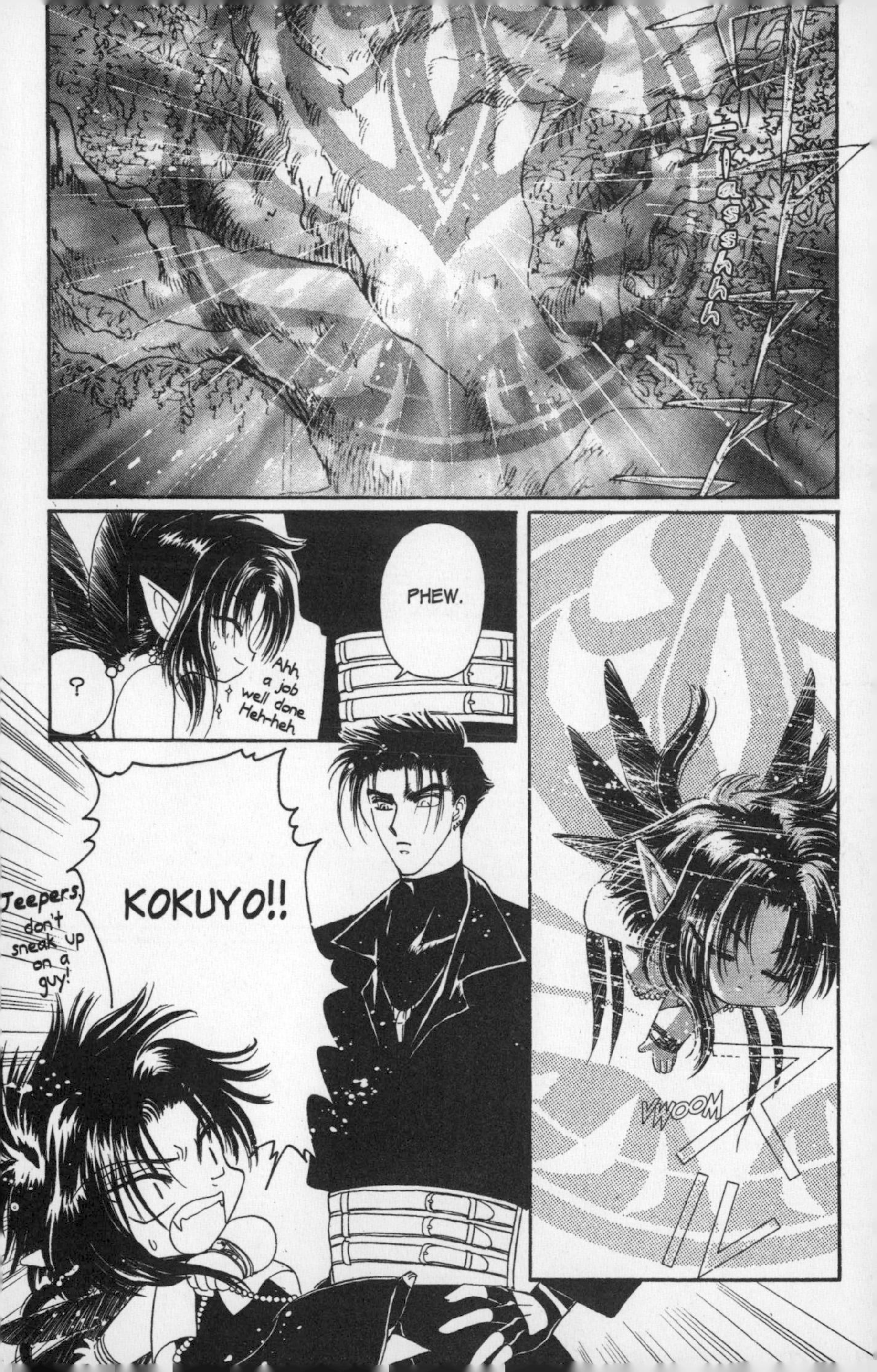
Flasshhh
VWOOM
PHEW.
Ahh, a job well done Heh-heh
?
KOKUYO!!
Jeepers, don't sneak up on a guy!

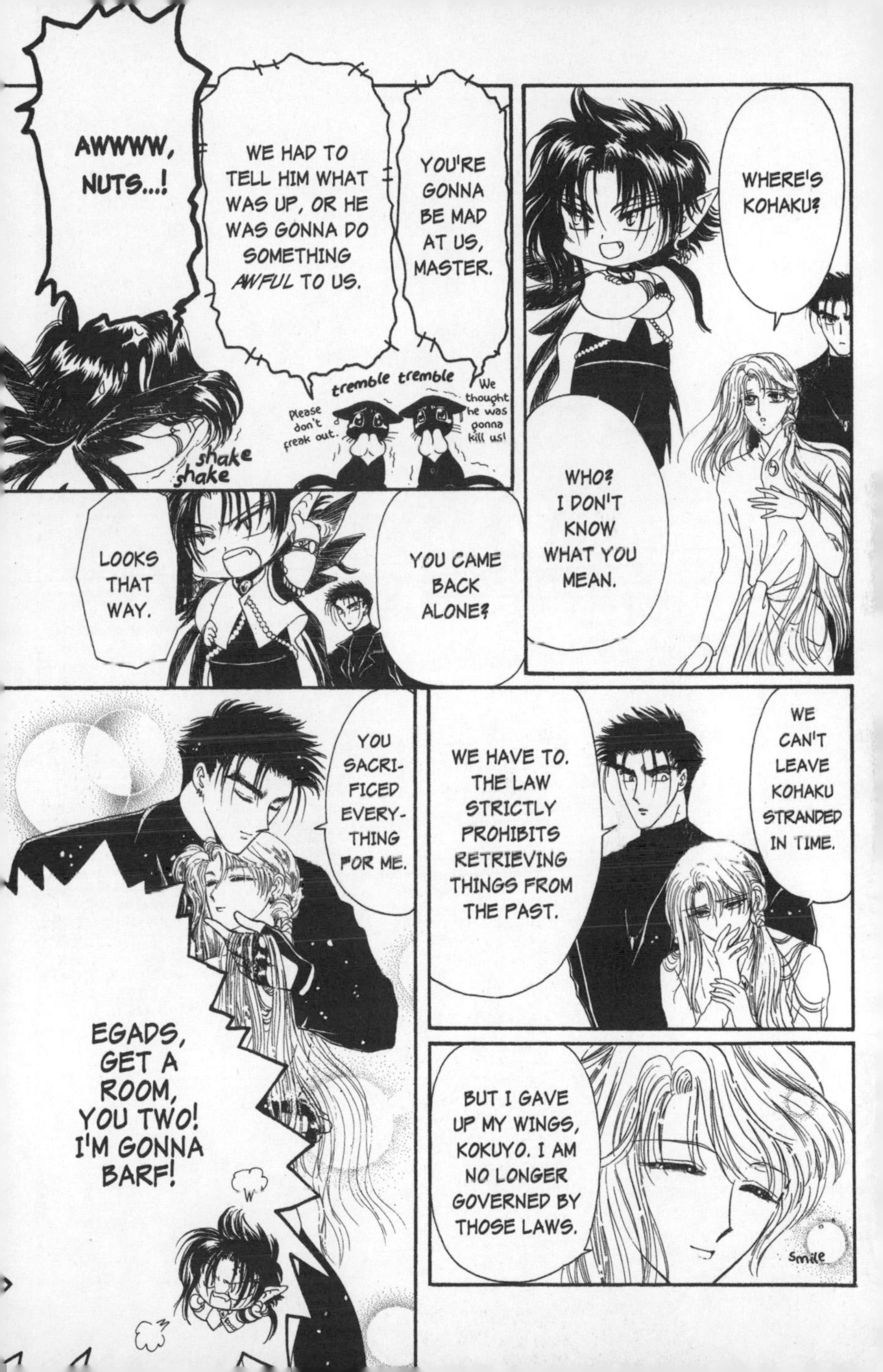
WHERE'S KOHAKU?
WHO? I DON'T KNOW WHAT YOU MEAN.
YOU'RE GONNA BE MAD AT US, MASTER.
WE HAD TO TELL HIM WHAT WAS UP, OR HE WAS GONNA DO SOMETHING *AWFUL* TO US.
AWWWW, NUTS...!
We thought he was gonna kill us!
tremble tremble
Please don't freak out.
shake shake
YOU CAME BACK ALONE?
LOOKS THAT WAY.
WE CAN'T LEAVE KOHAKU STRANDED IN TIME.
WE HAVE TO. THE LAW STRICTLY PROHIBITS RETRIEVING THINGS FROM THE PAST.
BUT I GAVE UP MY WINGS, KOKUYO. I AM NO LONGER GOVERNED BY THOSE LAWS.
Smile
YOU SACRI-FICED EVERY-THING FOR ME.
EGADS, GET A ROOM, YOU TWO! I'M GONNA BARF!

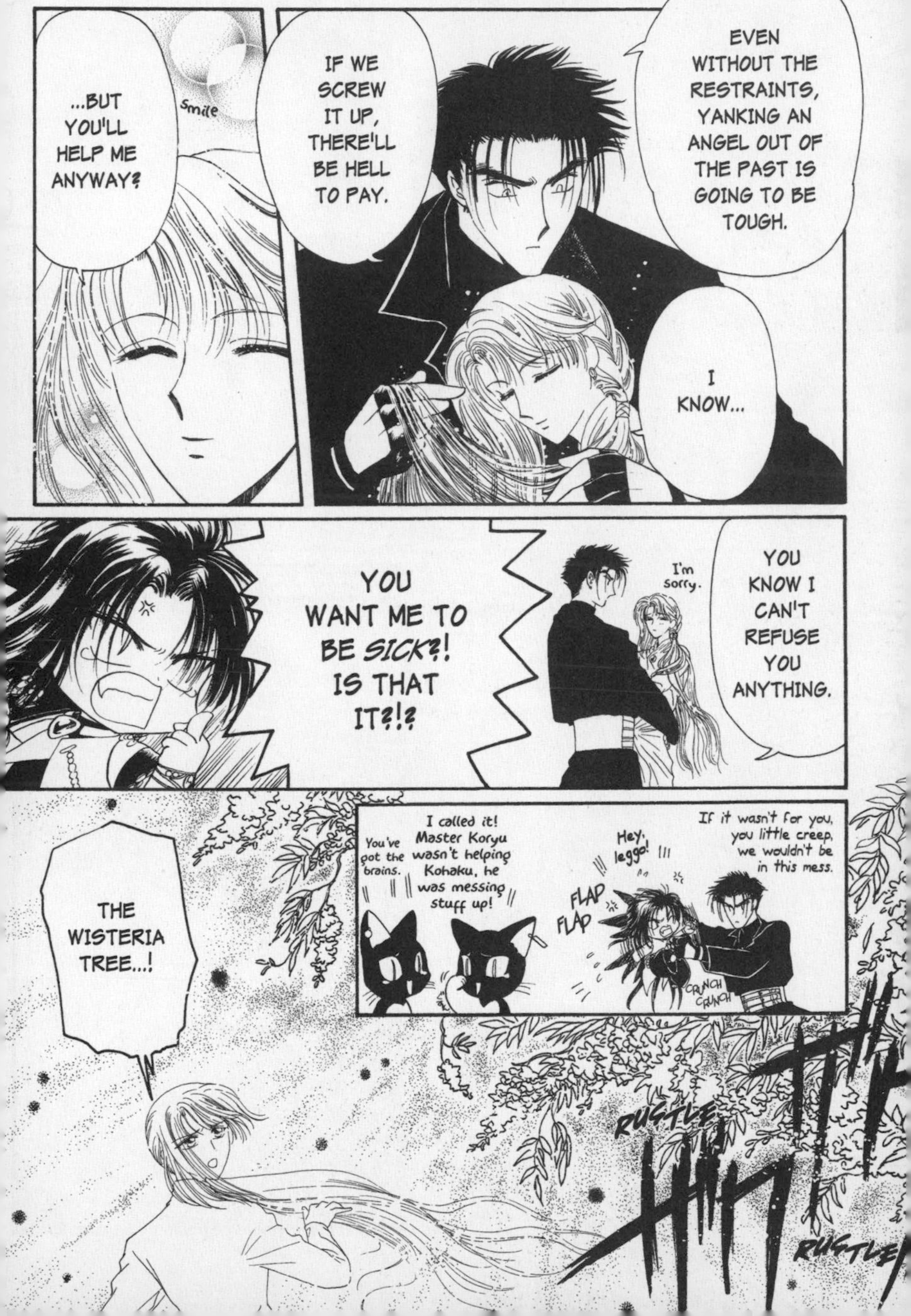
EVEN WITHOUT THE RESTRAINTS, YANKING AN ANGEL OUT OF THE PAST IS GOING TO BE TOUGH.
IF WE SCREW IT UP, THERE'LL BE HELL TO PAY.
I KNOW...
Smile
...BUT YOU'LL HELP ME ANYWAY?
YOU KNOW I CAN'T REFUSE YOU ANYTHING.
I'm sorry.
YOU WANT ME TO BE SICK?! IS THAT IT?!?
If it wasn't for you, you little creep, we wouldn't be in this mess.
Hey, leggo!
CRUNCH CRUNCH
FLAP FLAP
I called it! Master Koryu wasn't helping Kohaku, he was messing stuff up!
You've got the brains.
RUSTLE
RUSTLE
THE WISTERIA TREE...!

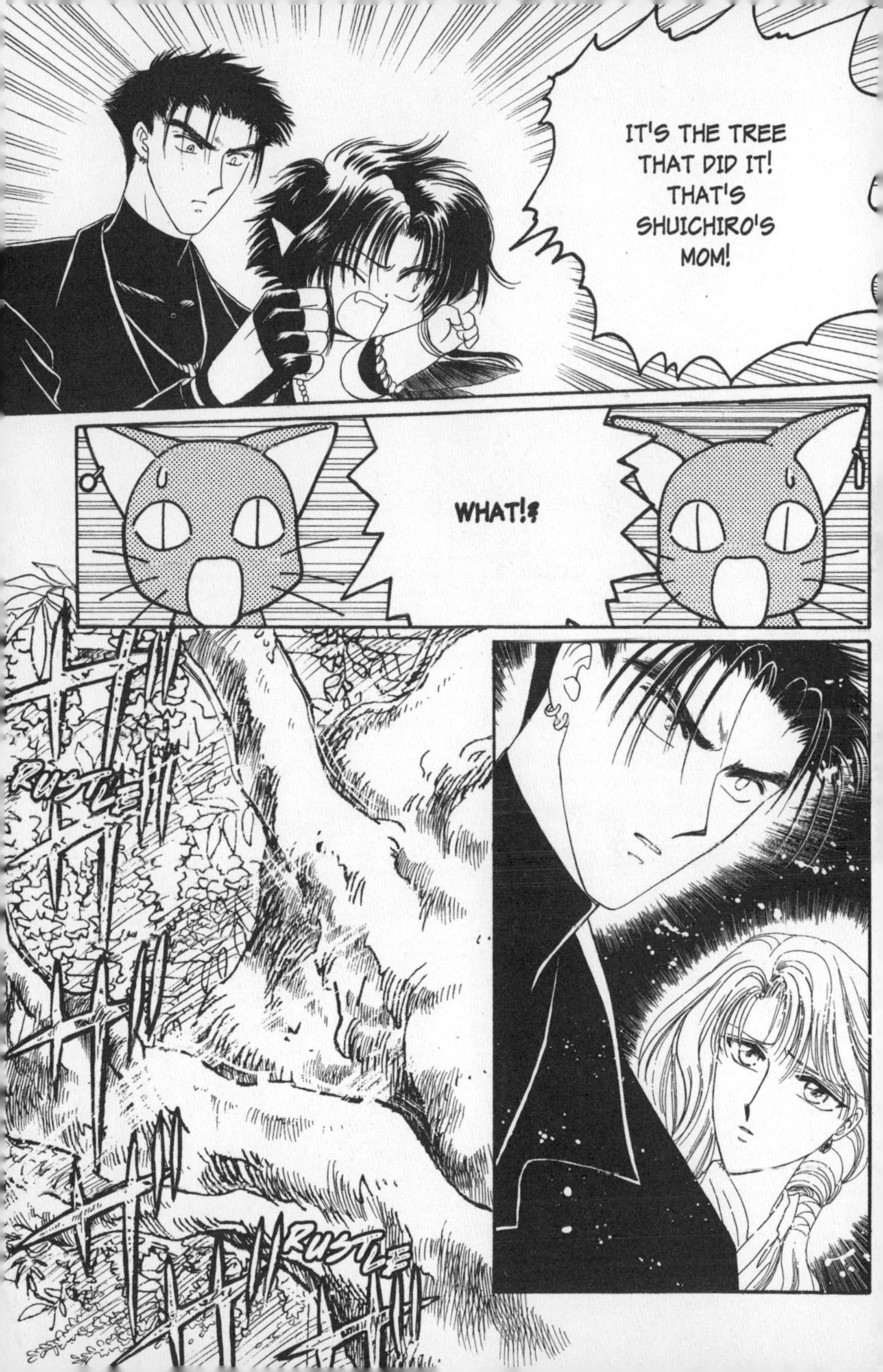
IT'S THE TREE THAT DID IT! THAT'S SHUICHIRO'S MOM!
WHAT!?
RUSTLE
RUSTLE

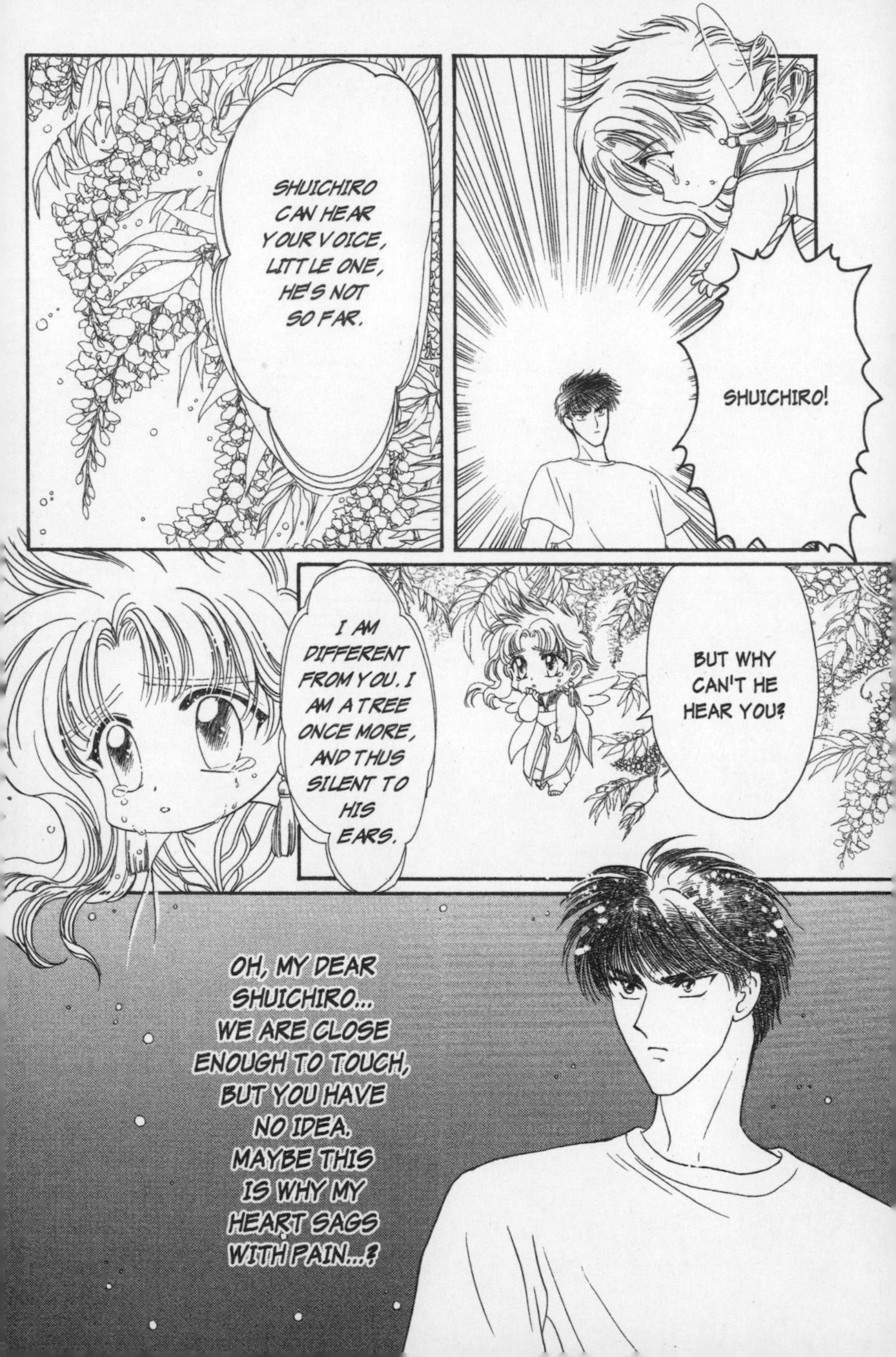
SHUICHIRO!
SHUICHIRO CAN HEAR YOUR VOICE, LITTLE ONE, HE'S NOT SO FAR.
BUT WHY CAN'T HE HEAR YOU?
I AM DIFFERENT FROM YOU. I AM A TREE ONCE MORE, AND THUS SILENT TO HIS EARS.
OH, MY DEAR SHUICHIRO... WE ARE CLOSE ENOUGH TO TOUCH, BUT YOU HAVE NO IDEA. MAYBE THIS IS WHY MY HEART SAGS WITH PAIN...?

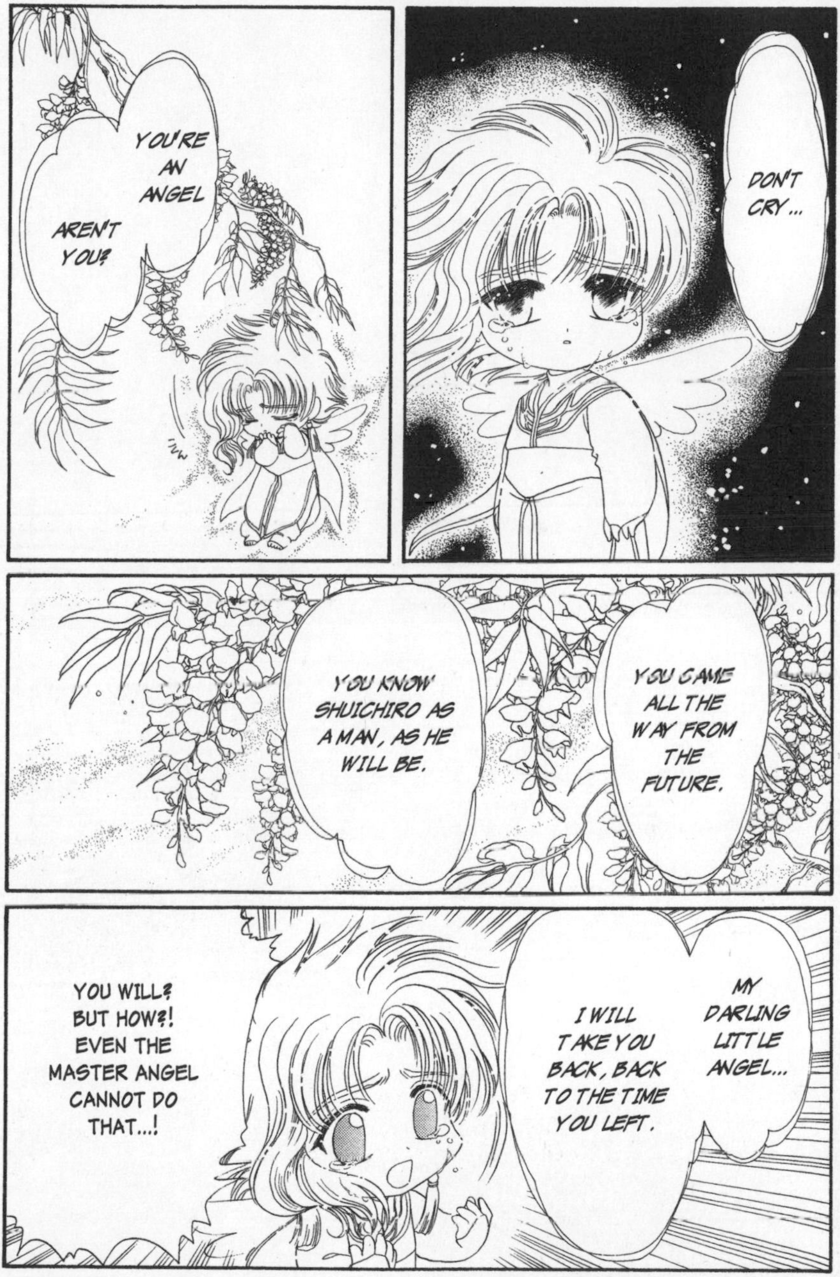
DON'T CRY...
YOU'RE AN ANGEL
AREN'T YOU?
YOU CAME ALL THE WAY FROM THE FUTURE.
YOU KNOW SHUICHIRO AS A MAN, AS HE WILL BE.
MY DARLING LITTLE ANGEL...
I WILL TAKE YOU BACK, BACK TO THE TIME YOU LEFT.
YOU WILL? BUT HOW?! EVEN THE MASTER ANGEL CANNOT DO THAT...!

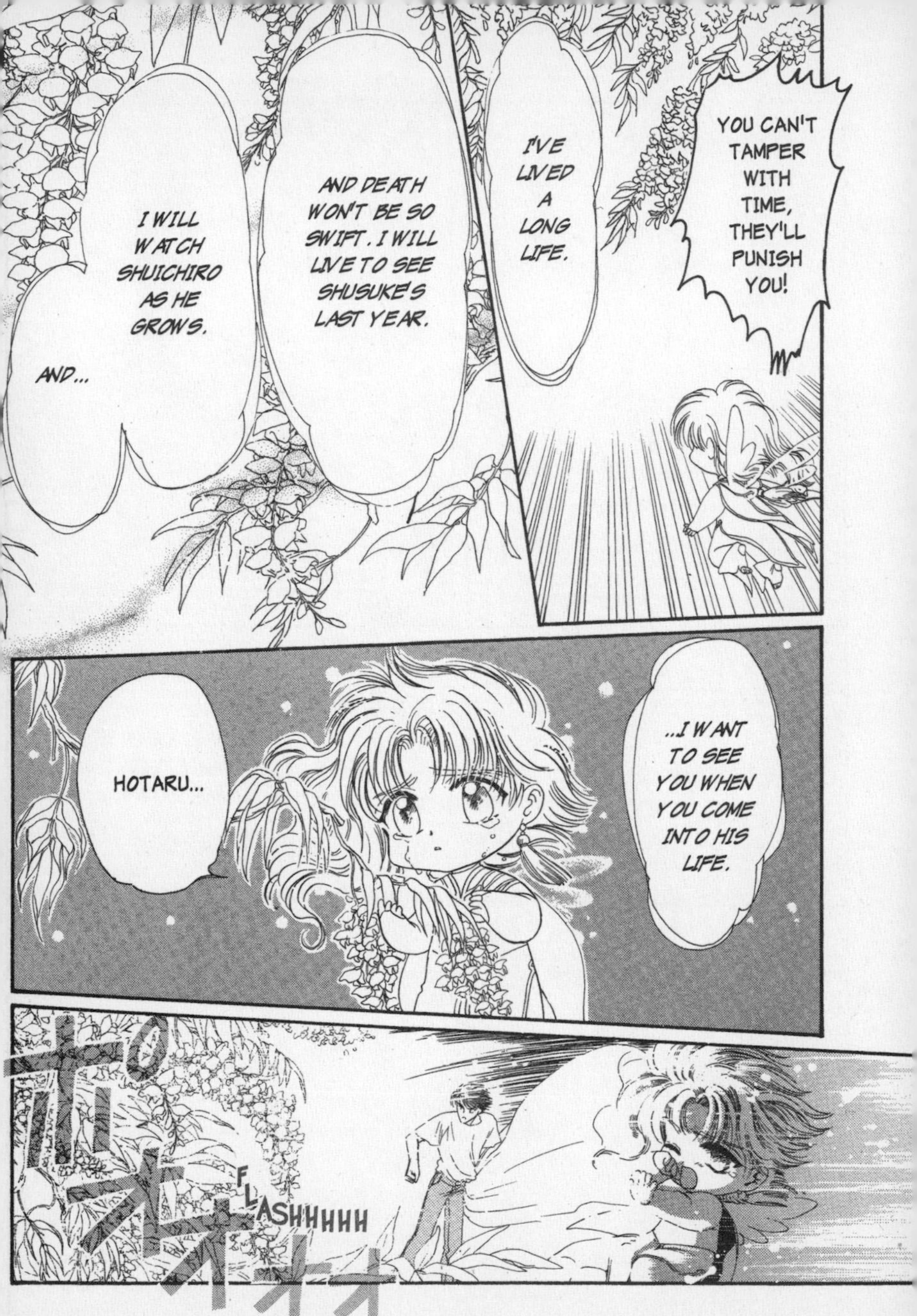
YOU CAN'T TAMPER WITH TIME, THEY'LL PUNISH YOU!
I'VE LIVED A LONG LIFE.
AND DEATH WON'T BE SO SWIFT. I WILL LIVE TO SEE SHUSUKE'S LAST YEAR.
I WILL WATCH SHUICHIRO AS HE GROWS.
AND...
...I WANT TO SEE YOU WHEN YOU COME INTO HIS LIFE.
HOTARU...
FLASHHHHH

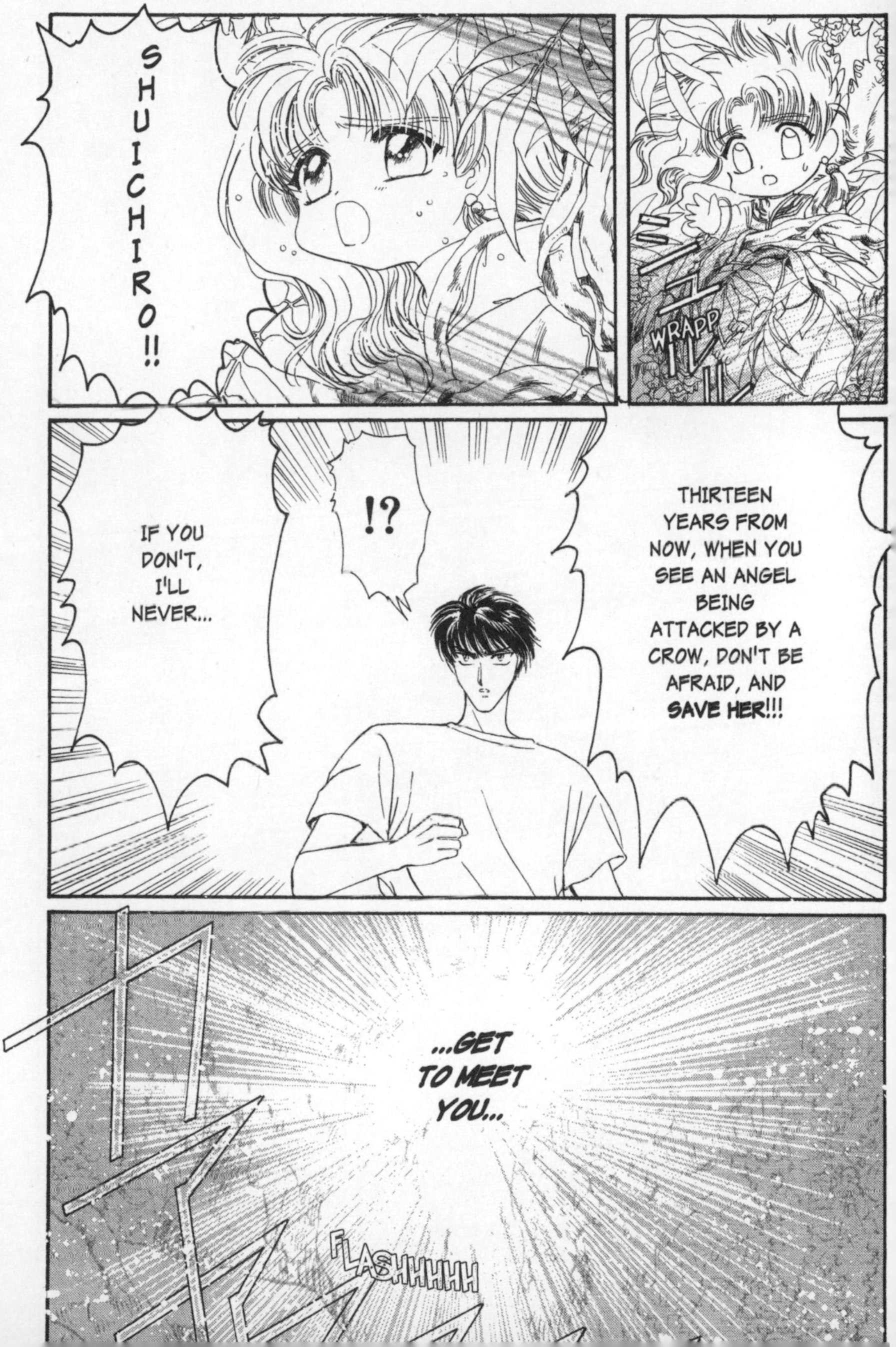
WRAPP
SHUICHIRO!!
THIRTEEN YEARS FROM NOW, WHEN YOU SEE AN ANGEL BEING ATTACKED BY A CROW, DON'T BE AFRAID, AND SAVE HER!!!
!?
IF YOU DON'T, I'LL NEVER...
...GET TO MEET YOU...
FLASHHHHH

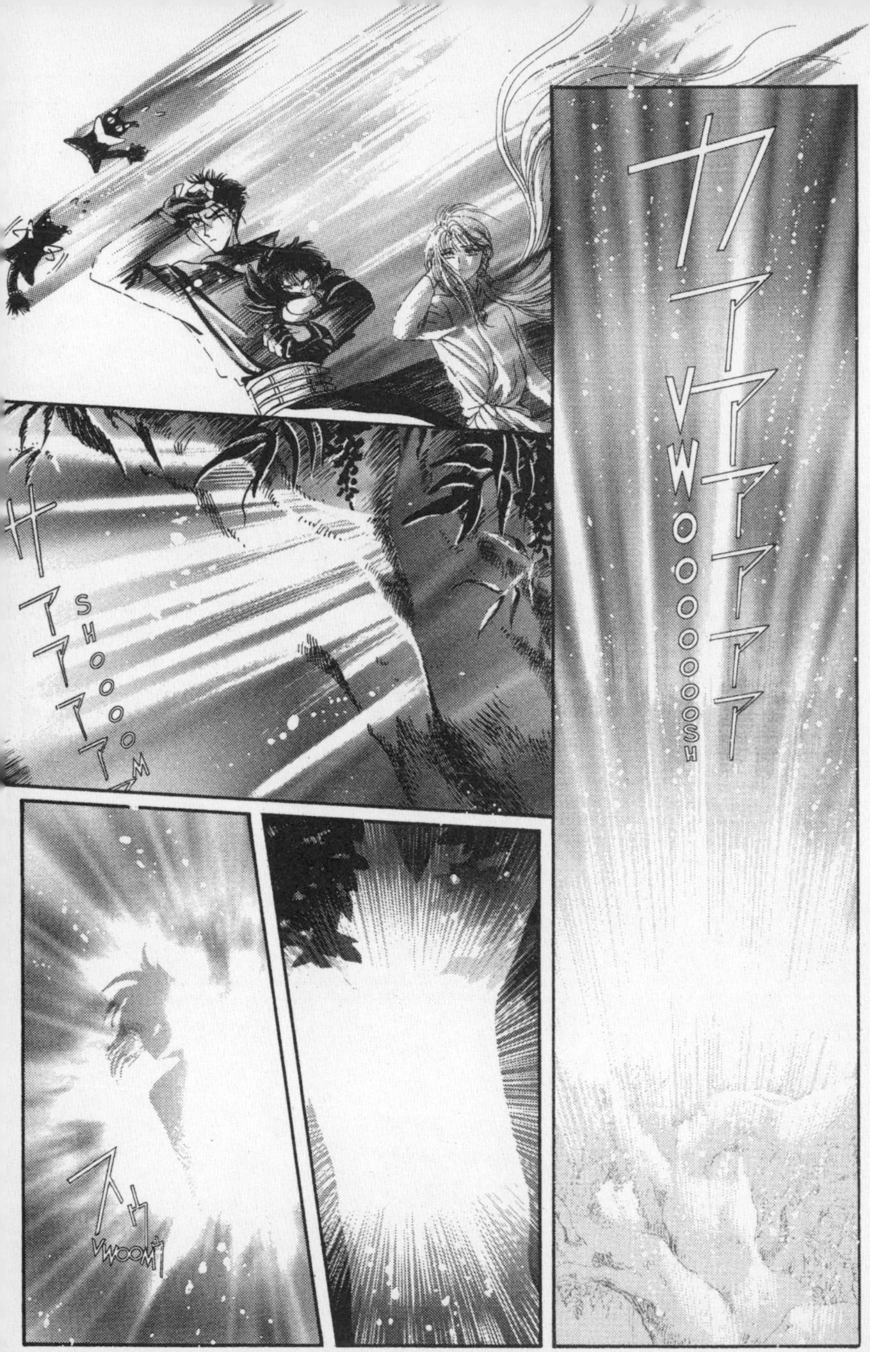

カァアァアァ
VWOOOOOOOOSH
サァァァァ
SHOOOOM
スゥ
VWOOM

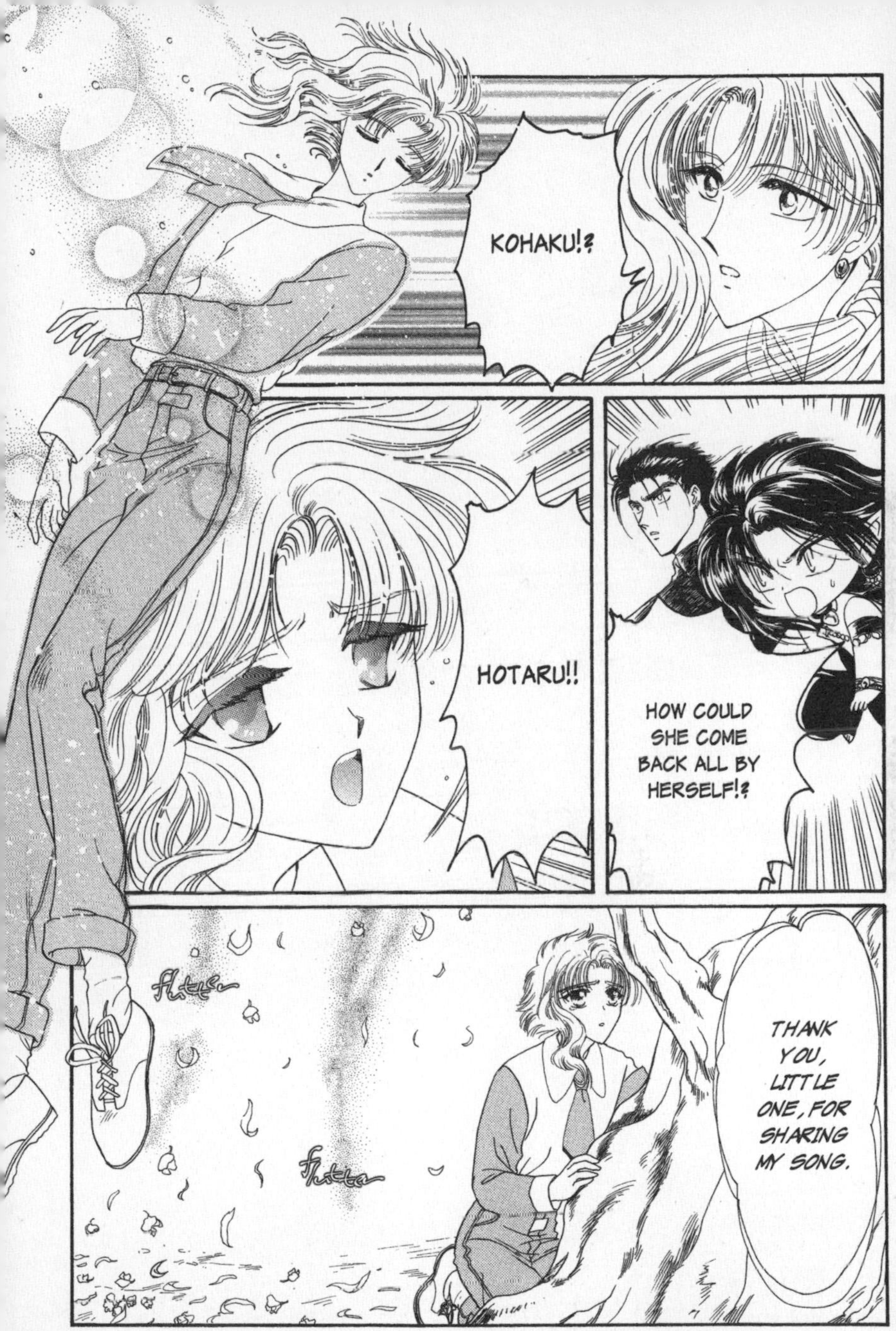
KOHAKU!?
HOW COULD SHE COME BACK ALL BY HERSELF!?
HOTARU!!
THANK YOU, LITTLE ONE, FOR SHARING MY SONG.

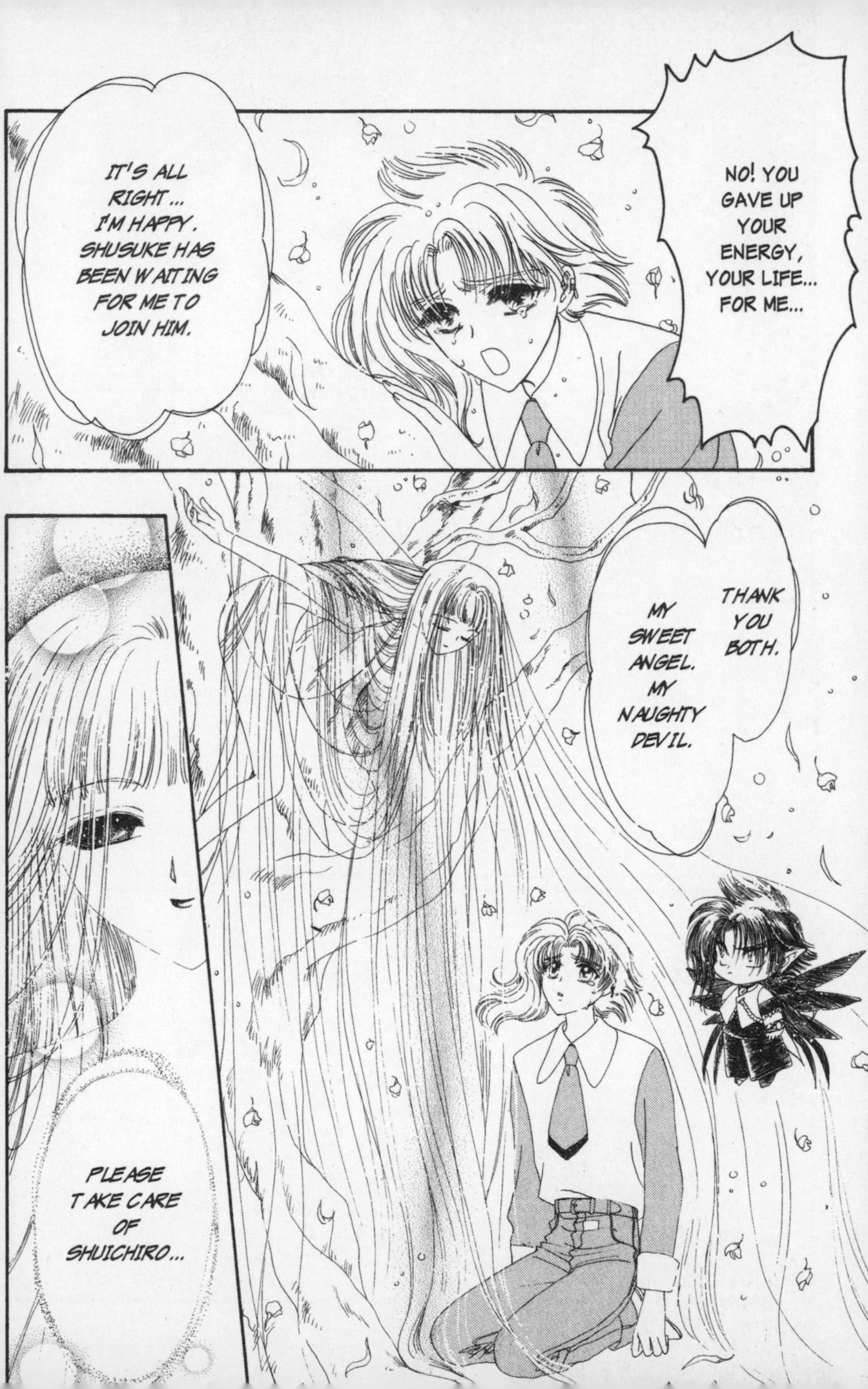
NO! YOU GAVE UP YOUR ENERGY, YOUR LIFE... FOR ME...
IT'S ALL RIGHT... I'M HAPPY. SHUSUKE HAS BEEN WAITING FOR ME TO JOIN HIM.
THANK YOU BOTH.
MY SWEET ANGEL. MY NAUGHTY DEVIL.
PLEASE TAKE CARE OF SHUICHIRO...

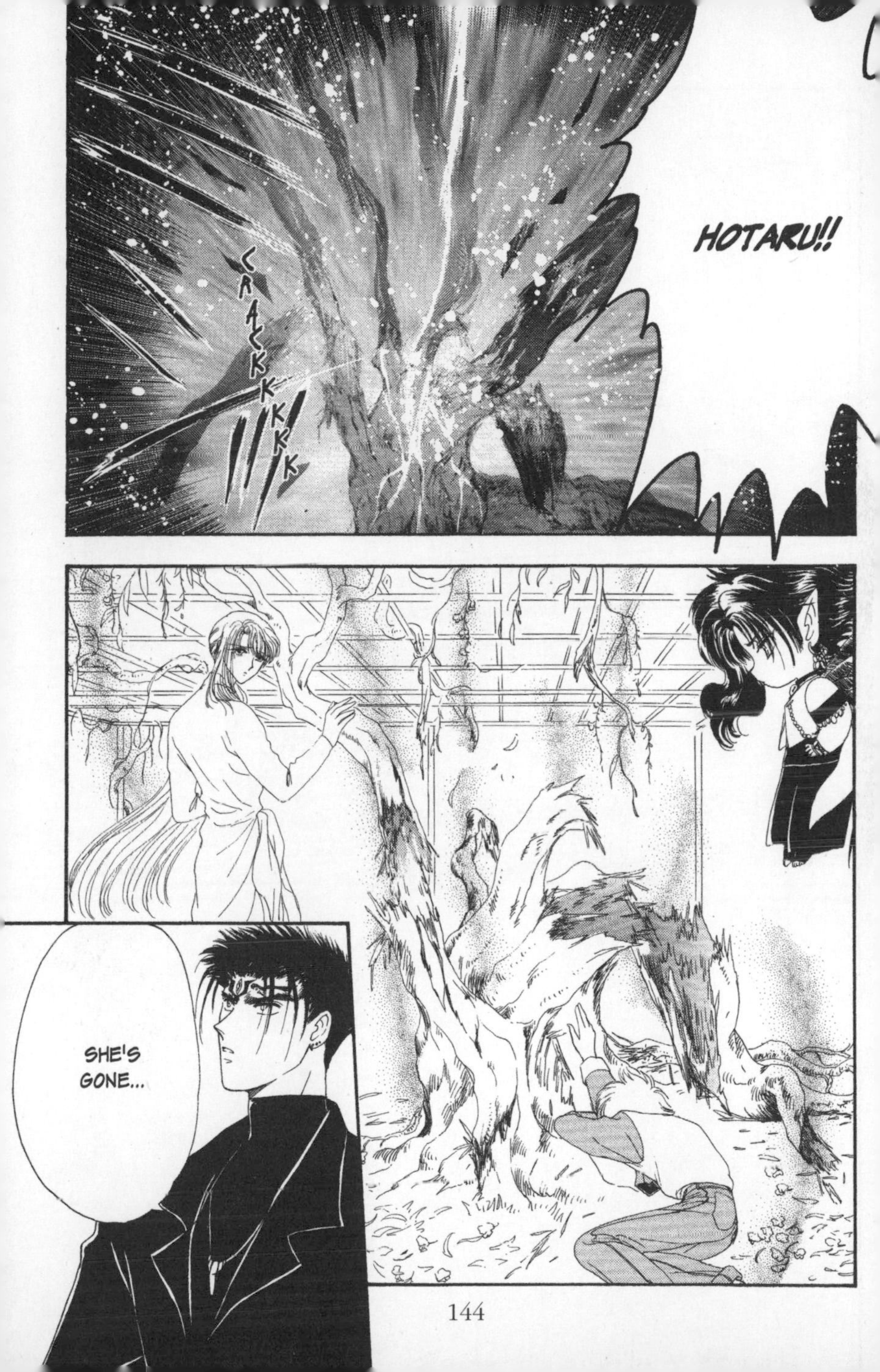
HOTARU!!
CRACKKKKK
SHE'S GONE...

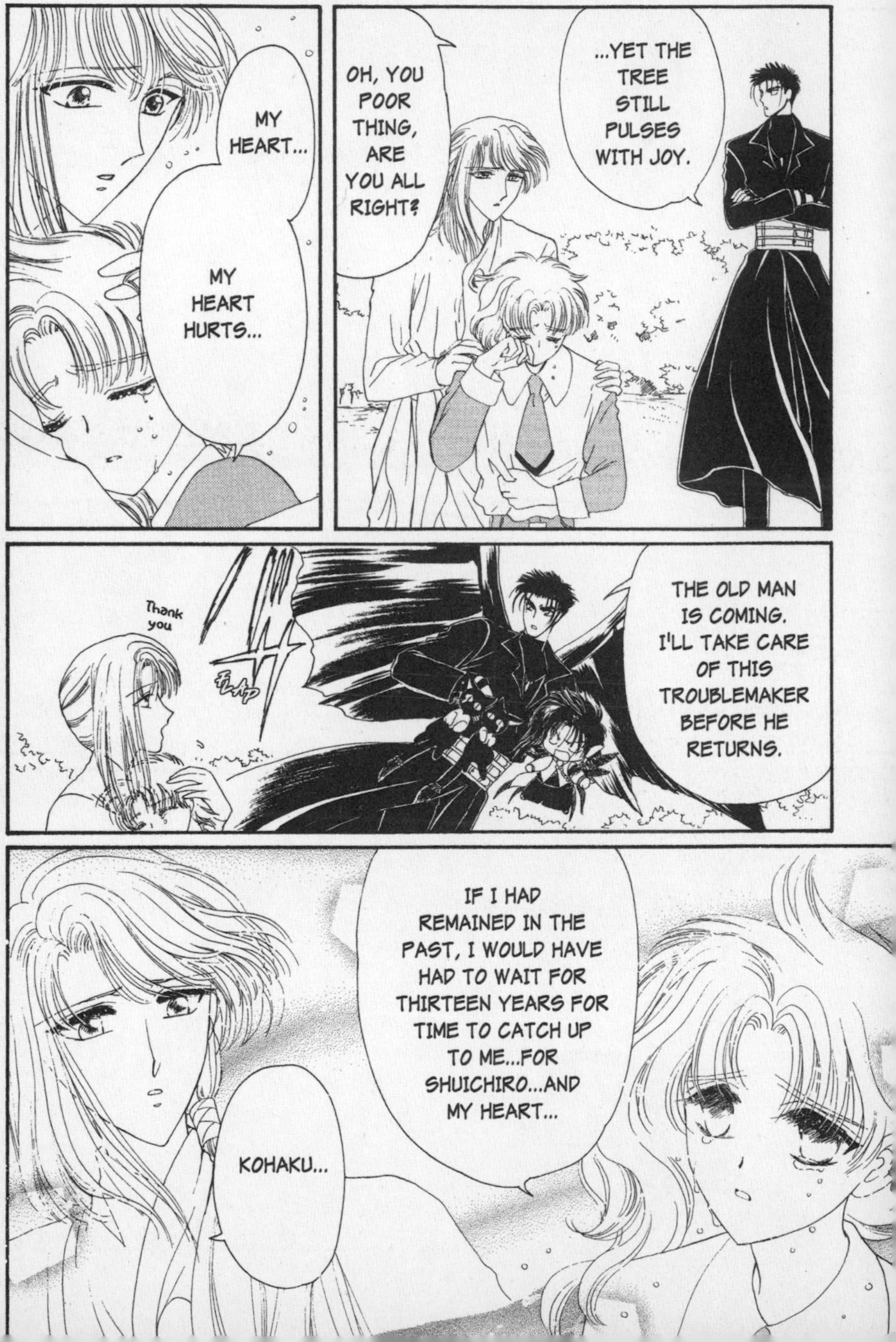
...YET THE TREE STILL PULSES WITH JOY.
OH, YOU POOR THING, ARE YOU ALL RIGHT?
MY HEART...
MY HEART HURTS...
THE OLD MAN IS COMING. I'LL TAKE CARE OF THIS TROUBLEMAKER BEFORE HE RETURNS.
Thank you
IF I HAD REMAINED IN THE PAST, I WOULD HAVE HAD TO WAIT FOR THIRTEEN YEARS FOR TIME TO CATCH UP TO ME...FOR SHUICHIRO...AND MY HEART...
KOHAKU...

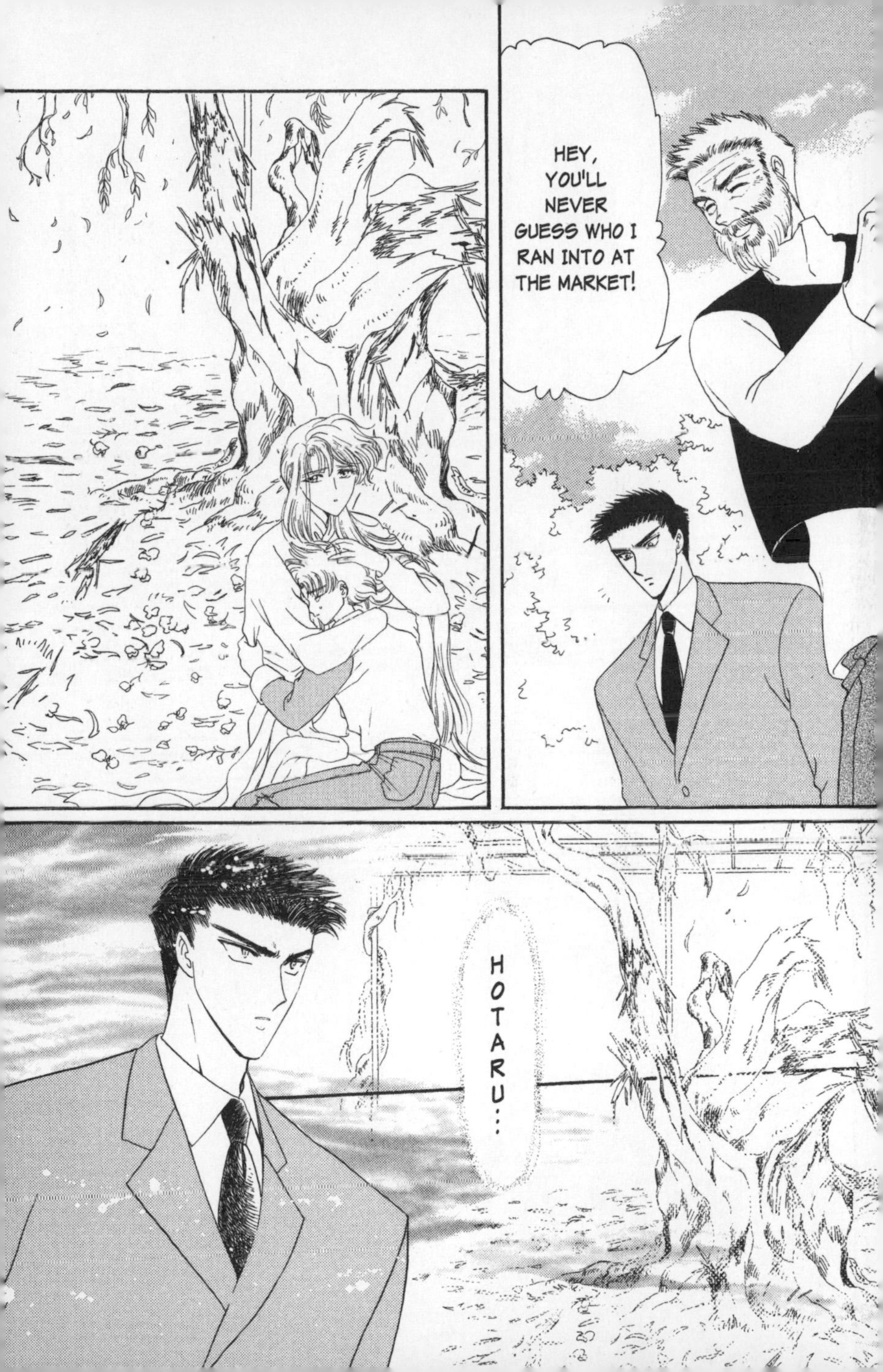
HEY, YOU'LL NEVER GUESS WHO I RAN INTO AT THE MARKET!
HOTARU...

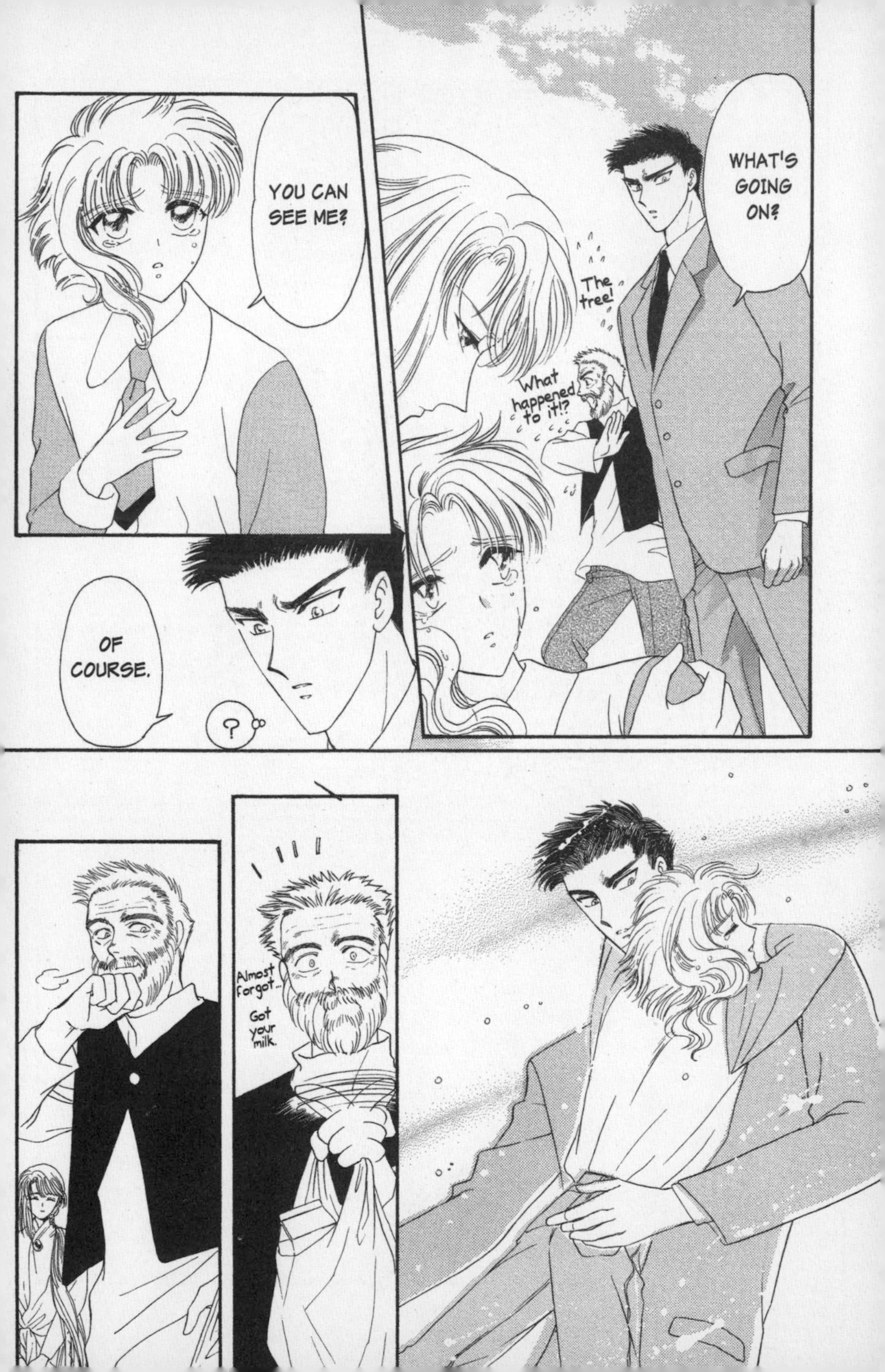
WHAT'S GOING ON?
The tree!
What happened to it!?
YOU CAN SEE ME?
OF COURSE.
?
Almost forgot...
Got your milk.

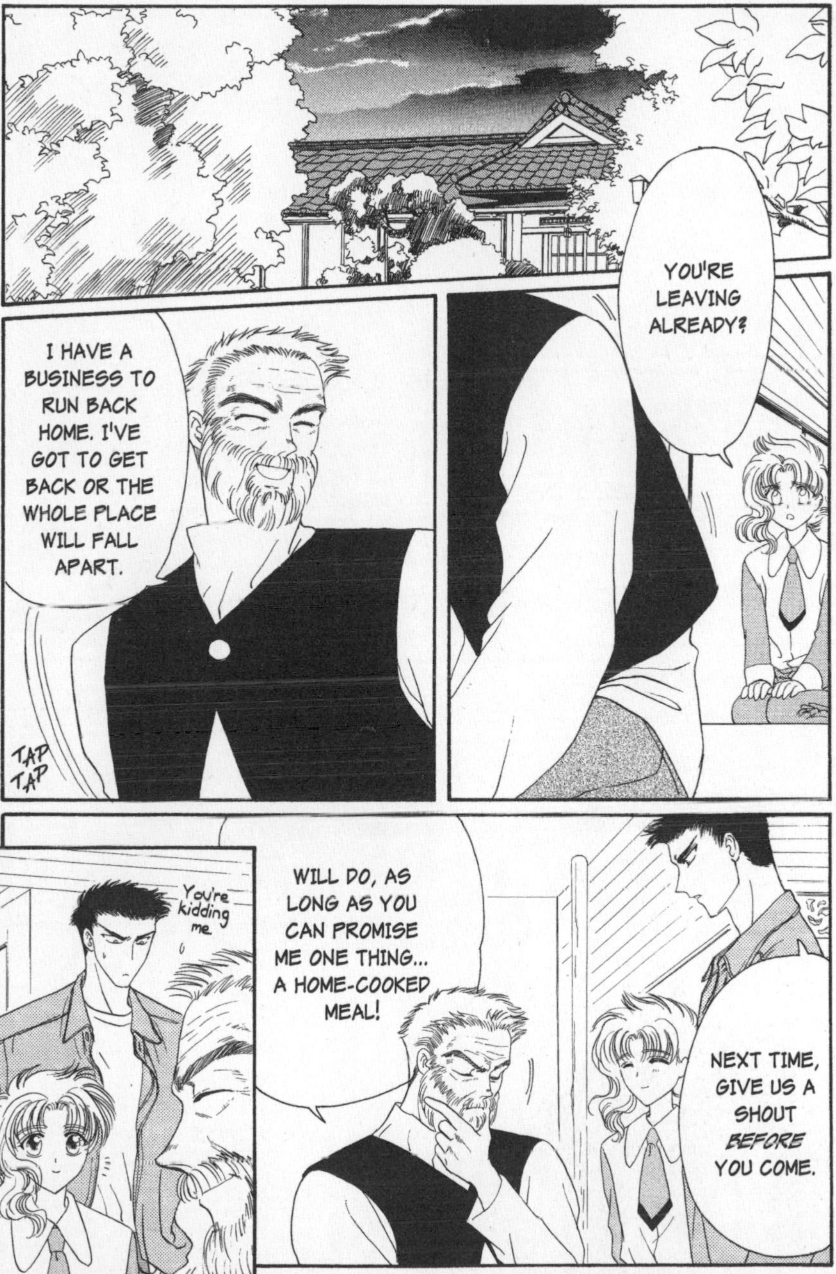
YOU'RE LEAVING ALREADY?
I HAVE A BUSINESS TO RUN BACK HOME. I'VE GOT TO GET BACK OR THE WHOLE PLACE WILL FALL APART.
TAP TAP
NEXT TIME, GIVE US A SHOUT *BEFORE* YOU COME.
WILL DO, AS LONG AS YOU CAN PROMISE ME ONE THING... A HOME-COOKED MEAL!
You're kidding me.

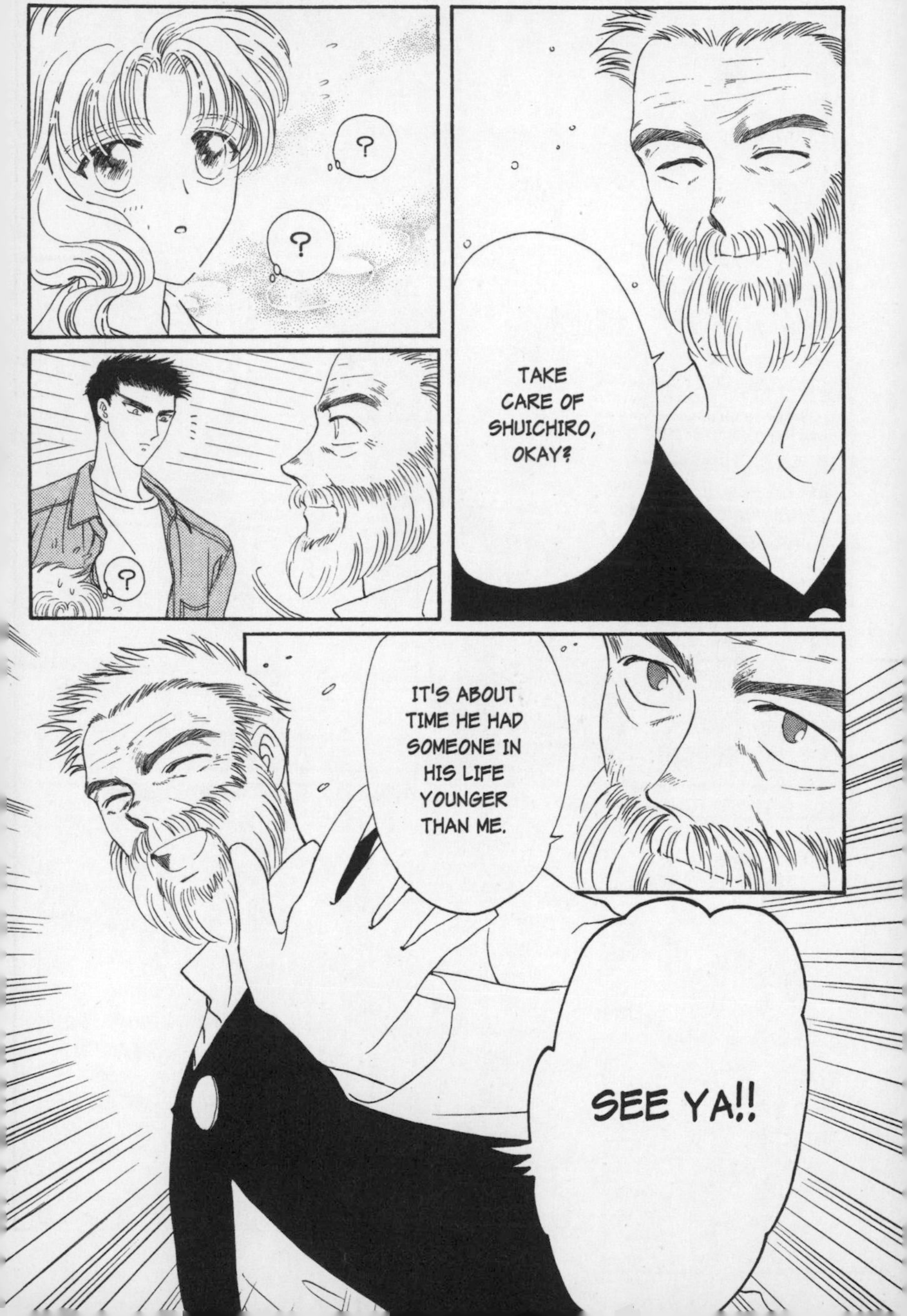
TAKE CARE OF SHUICHIRO, OKAY?
?
?
?
IT'S ABOUT TIME HE HAD SOMEONE IN HIS LIFE YOUNGER THAN ME.
SEE YA!!

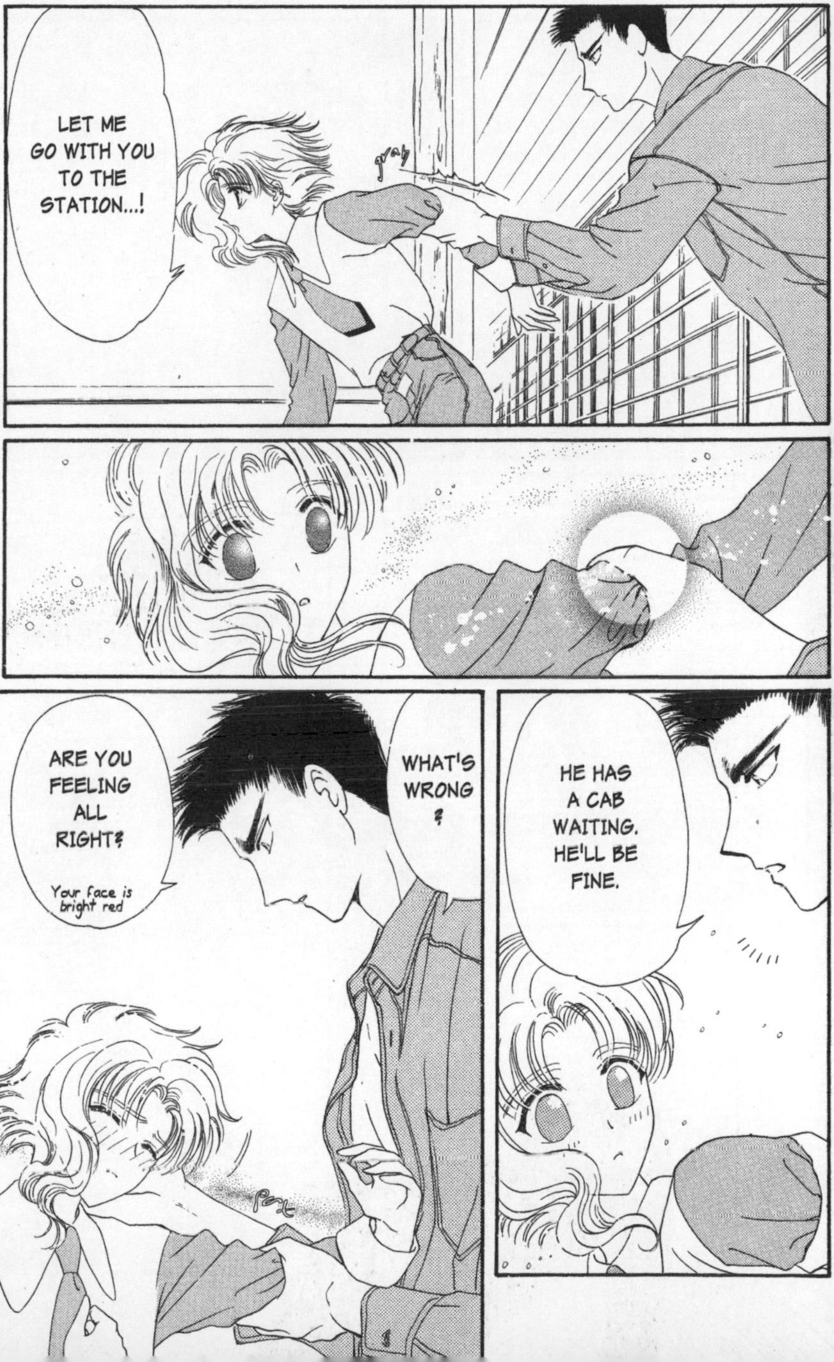
LET ME GO WITH YOU TO THE STATION...!
grab
HE HAS A CAB WAITING. HE'LL BE FINE.
WHAT'S WRONG?
ARE YOU FEELING ALL RIGHT?
Your face is bright red
pat

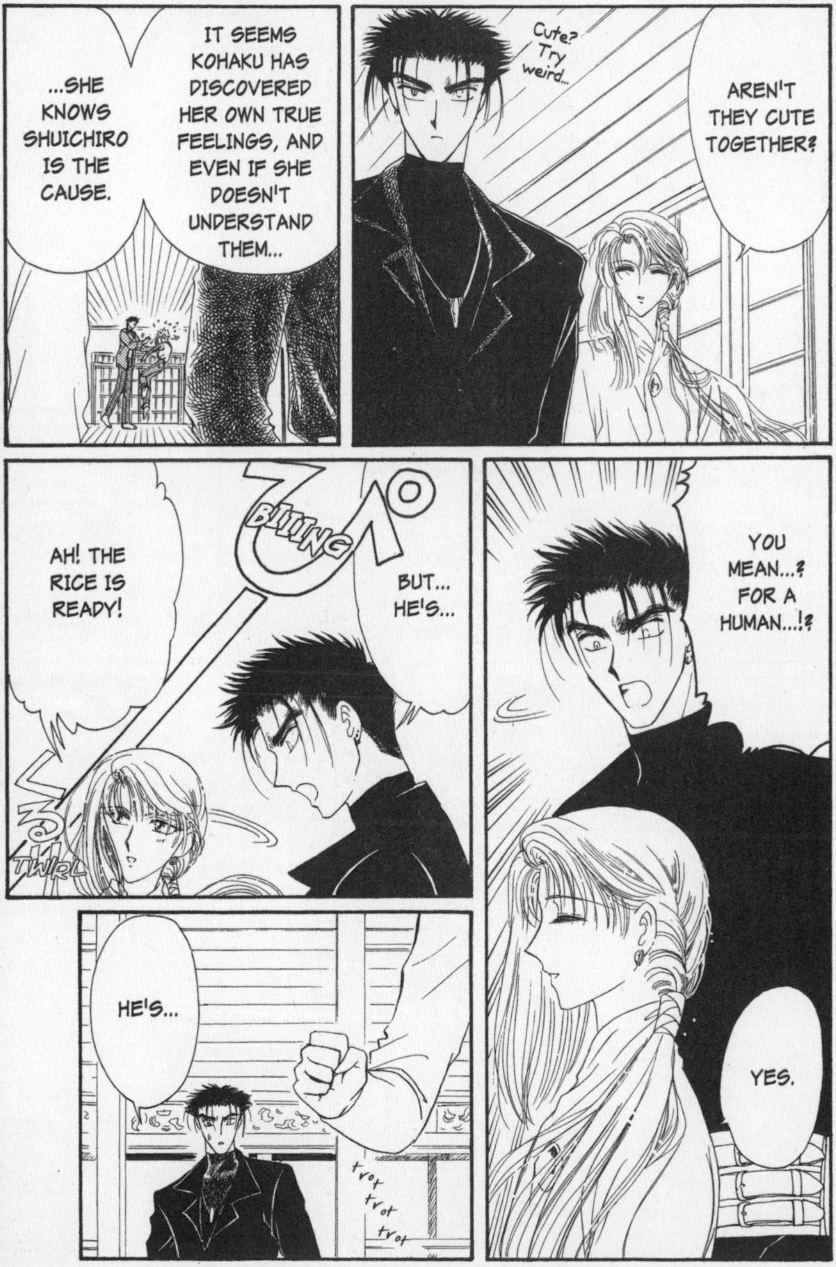
AREN'T THEY CUTE TOGETHER?
Cute? Try weird...
IT SEEMS KOHAKU HAS DISCOVERED HER OWN TRUE FEELINGS, AND EVEN IF SHE DOESN'T UNDERSTAND THEM...
...SHE KNOWS SHUICHIRO IS THE CAUSE.
YOU MEAN...? FOR A HUMAN...!?
YES.
BUT... HE'S...
BIIING
AH! THE RICE IS READY!
TWIRL
HE'S...
trot trot trot

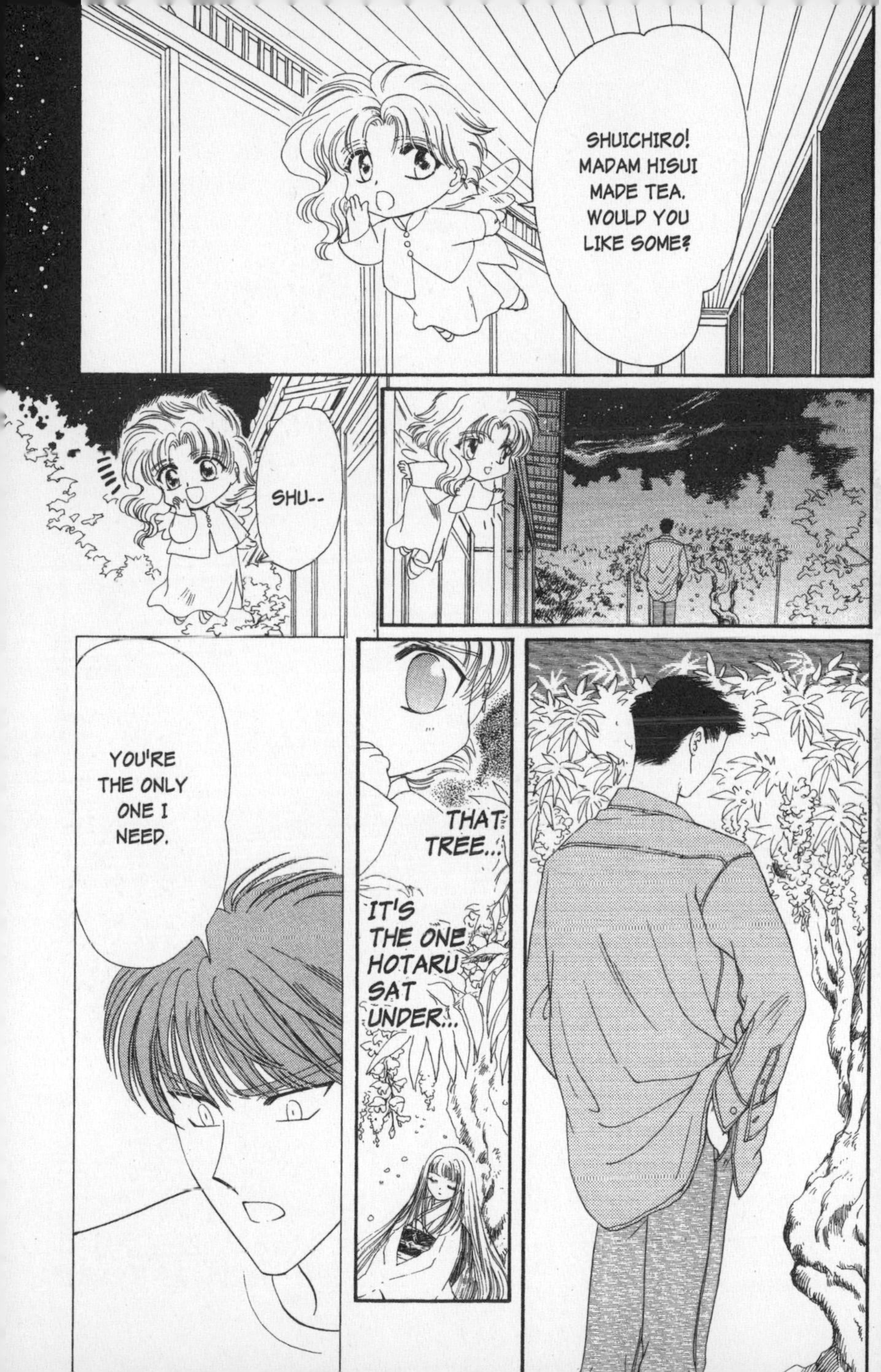
SHUICHIRO! MADAM HISUI MADE TEA. WOULD YOU LIKE SOME?
SHU--
THAT TREE...
IT'S THE ONE HOTARU SAT UNDER...
YOU'RE THE ONLY ONE I NEED.

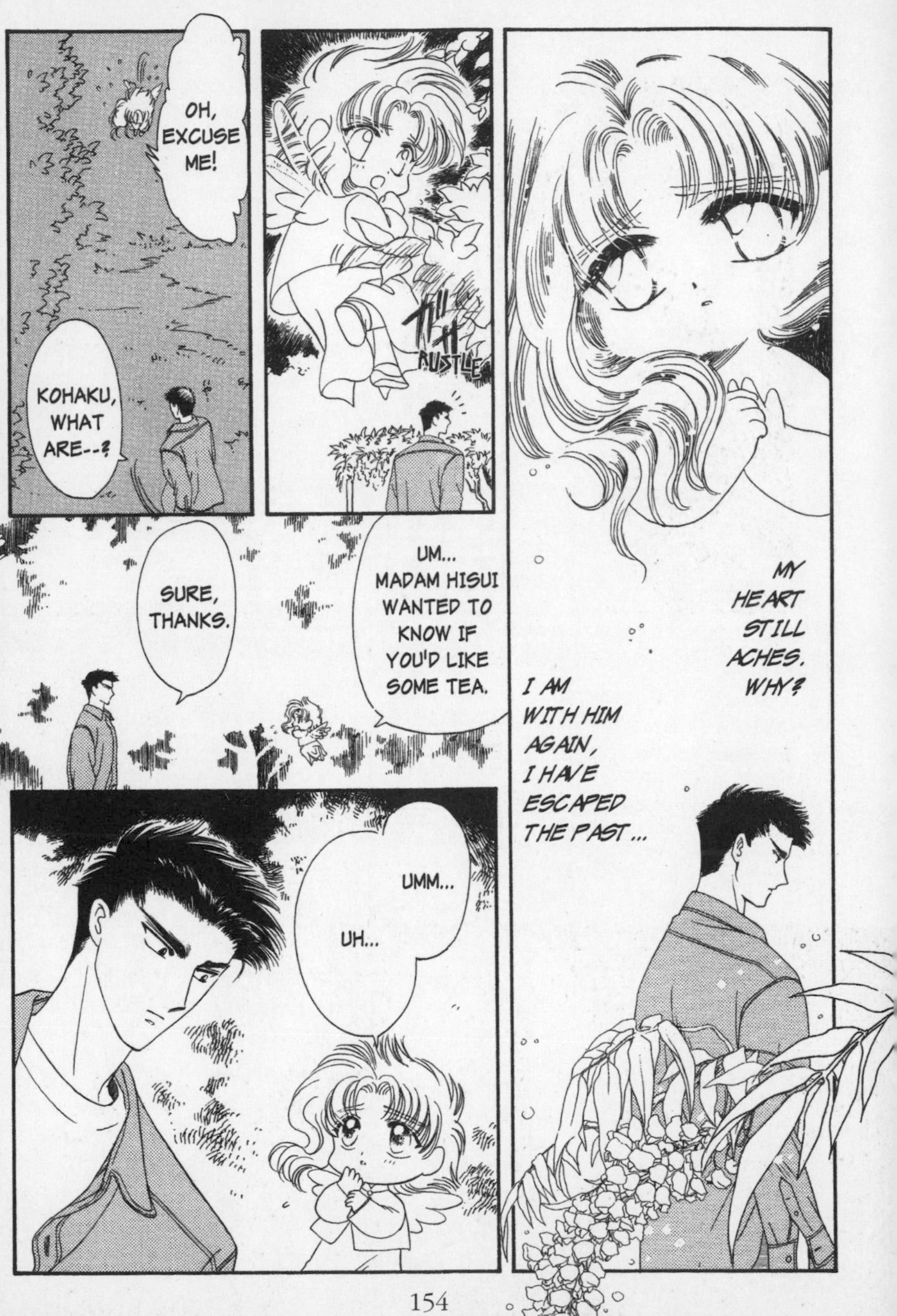

MY HEART STILL ACHES. WHY?
I AM WITH HIM AGAIN, I HAVE ESCAPED THE PAST...
RUSTLE
OH, EXCUSE ME!
KOHAKU, WHAT ARE--?
UM... MADAM HISUI WANTED TO KNOW IF YOU'D LIKE SOME TEA.
SURE, THANKS.
UMM...
UH...

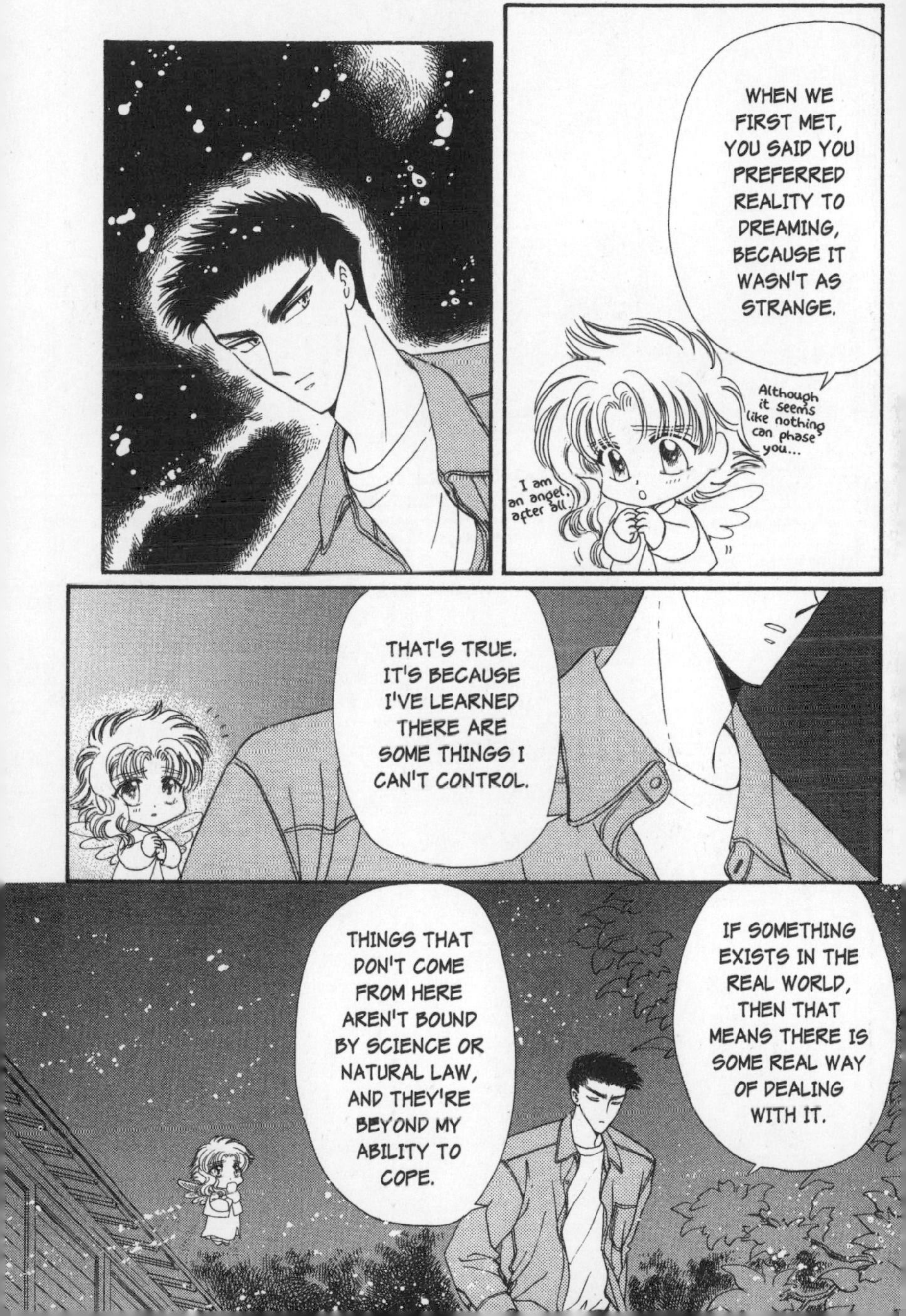
WHEN WE FIRST MET, YOU SAID YOU PREFERRED REALITY TO DREAMING, BECAUSE IT WASN'T AS STRANGE.
Although it seems like nothing can phase you...
I am an angel, after all.
THAT'S TRUE. IT'S BECAUSE I'VE LEARNED THERE ARE SOME THINGS I CAN'T CONTROL.
IF SOMETHING EXISTS IN THE REAL WORLD, THEN THAT MEANS THERE IS SOME REAL WAY OF DEALING WITH IT.
THINGS THAT DON'T COME FROM HERE AREN'T BOUND BY SCIENCE OR NATURAL LAW, AND THEY'RE BEYOND MY ABILITY TO COPE.

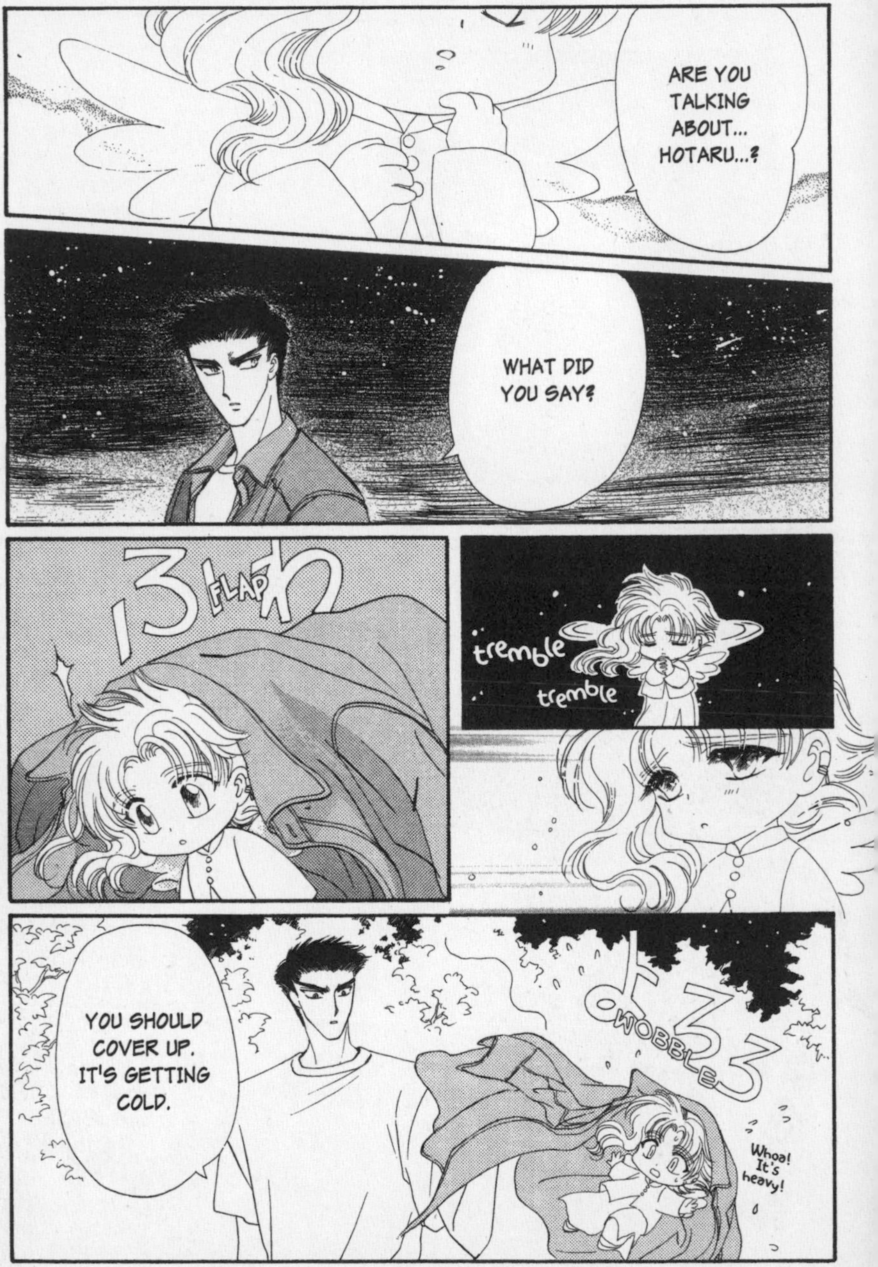
ARE YOU TALKING ABOUT... HOTARU...?
WHAT DID YOU SAY?
tremble
tremble
FLAP
WOBBLE
Whoa! It's heavy!
YOU SHOULD COVER UP. IT'S GETTING COLD.

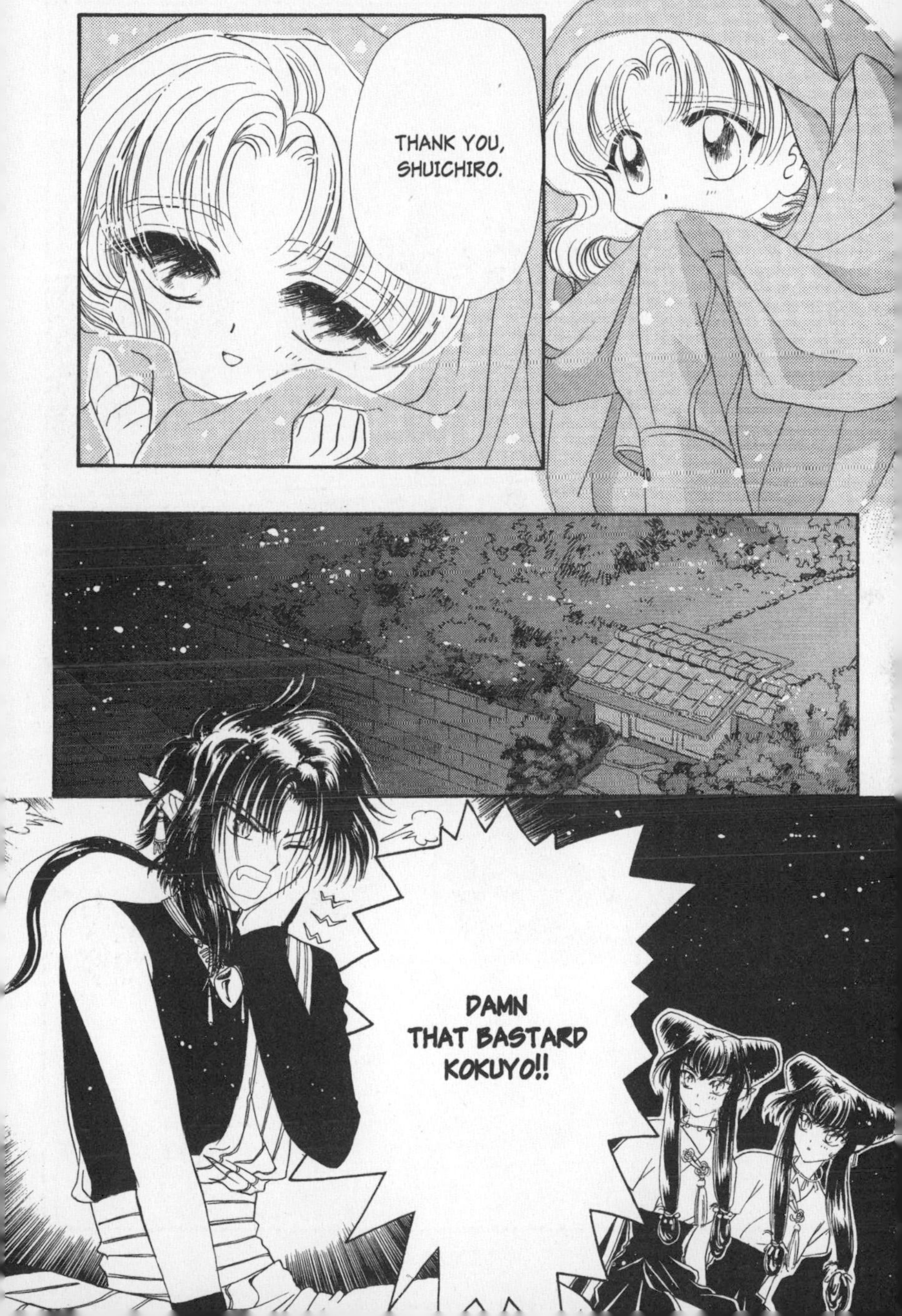
THANK YOU, SHUICHIRO.
DAMN THAT BASTARD KOKUYO!!

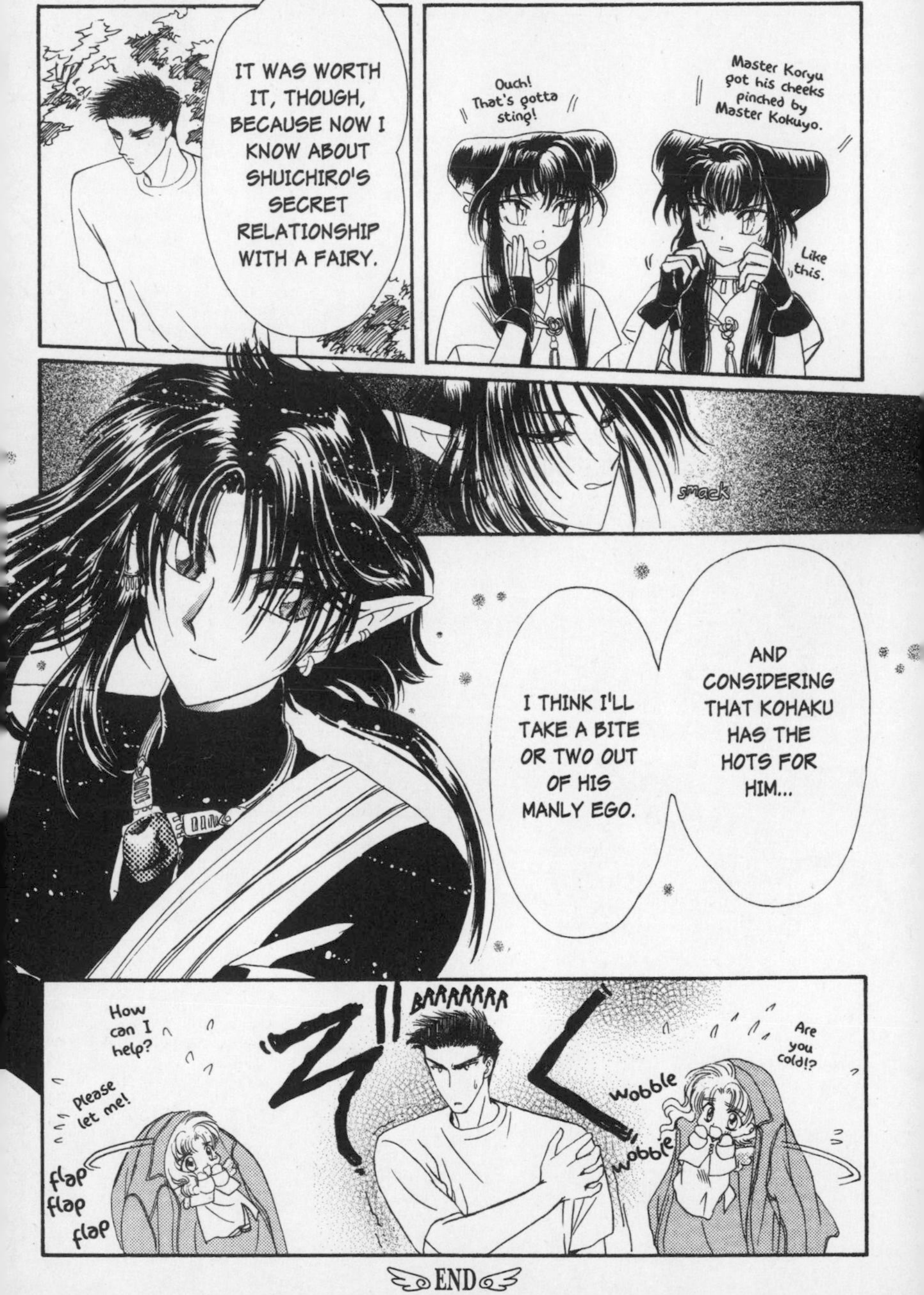
Master Koryu got his cheeks pinched by Master Kokuyo.
Like this.
Ouch! That's gotta sting!
IT WAS WORTH IT, THOUGH, BECAUSE NOW I KNOW ABOUT SHUICHIRO'S SECRET RELATIONSHIP WITH A FAIRY.
smack
AND CONSIDERING THAT KOHAKU HAS THE HOTS FOR HIM...
I THINK I'LL TAKE A BITE OR TWO OUT OF HIS MANLY EGO.
Are you cold!?
wobble
wobble
BRRRRRRR
How can I help?
Please let me!
flap
flap
flap

END

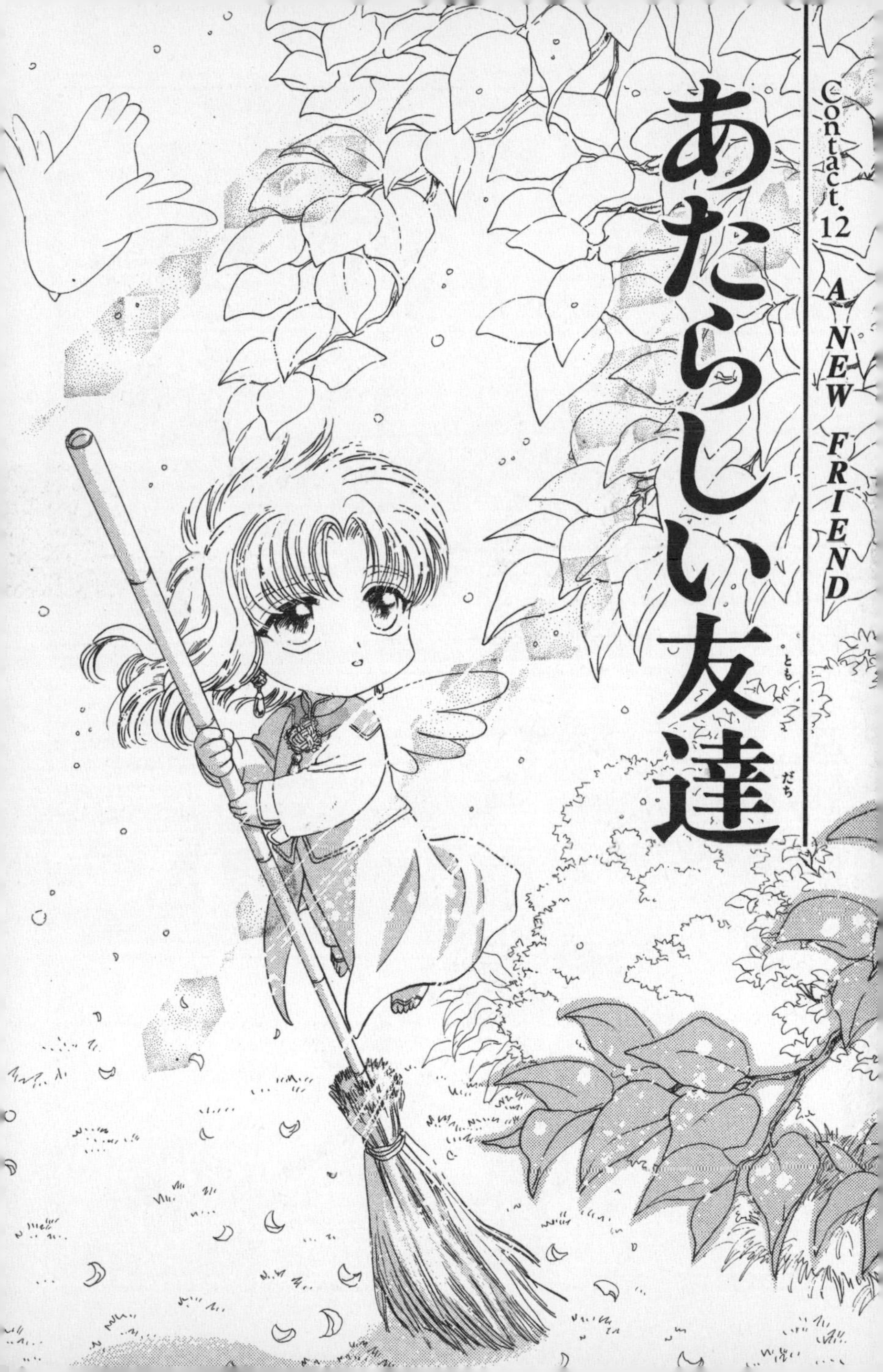
Contact.12
A NEW FRIEND
あたらしい友達

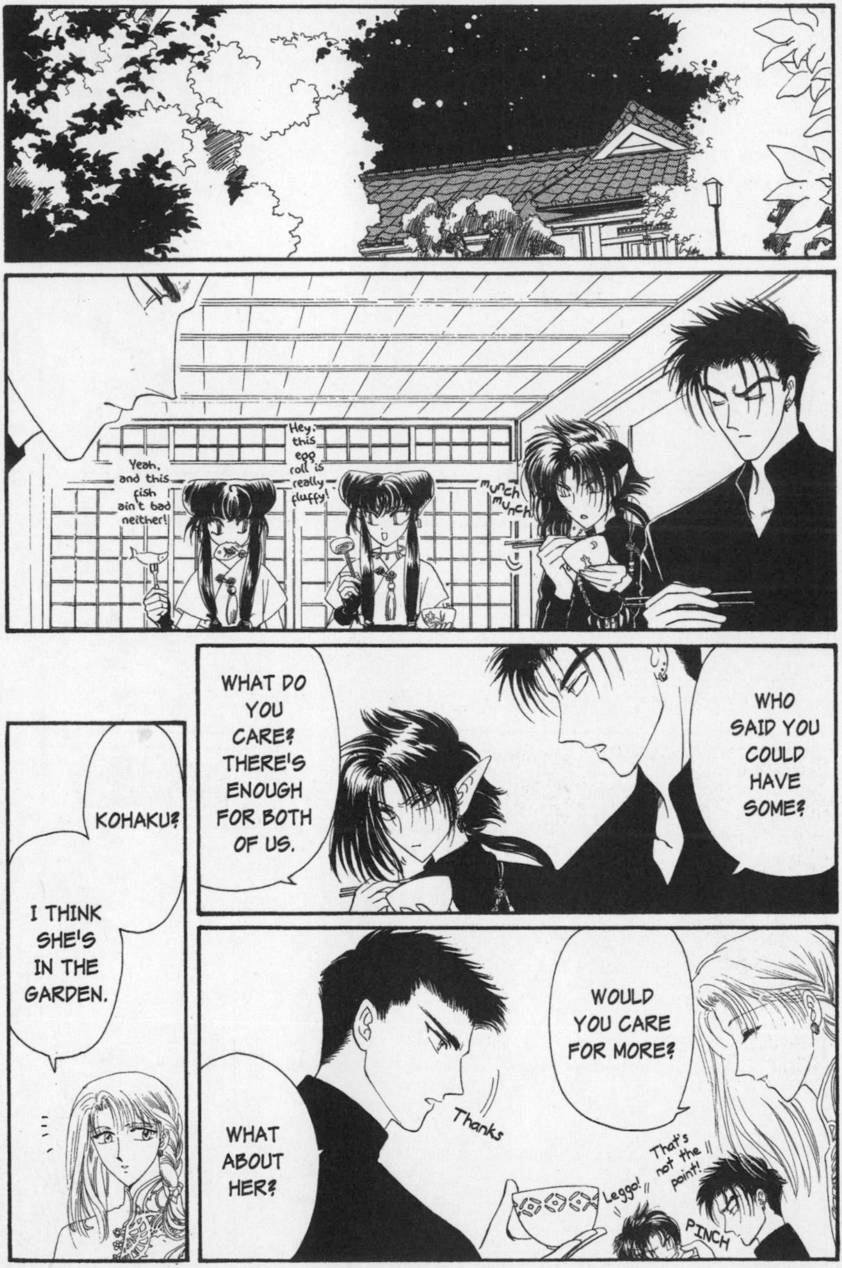
munch munch
Hey, this egg roll is really fluffy!
Yeah, and this fish ain't bad neither!
WHO SAID YOU COULD HAVE SOME?
WHAT DO YOU CARE? THERE'S ENOUGH FOR BOTH OF US.
WOULD YOU CARE FOR MORE?
That's not the point!
PINCH
Leggo!
Thanks
WHAT ABOUT HER?
KOHAKU?
I THINK SHE'S IN THE GARDEN.

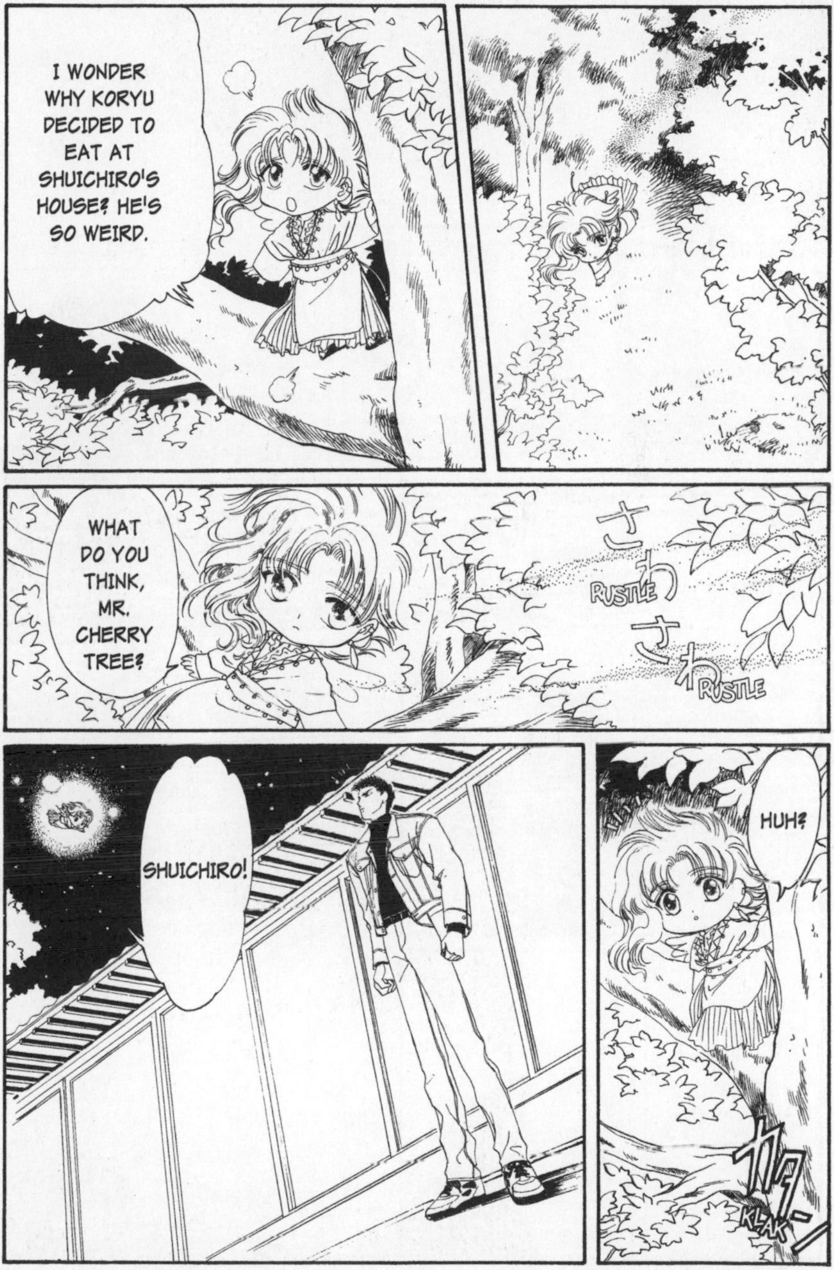
I WONDER WHY KORYU DECIDED TO EAT AT SHUICHIRO'S HOUSE? HE'S SO WEIRD.
さわ
RUSTLE
さわ
RUSTLE
WHAT DO YOU THINK, MR. CHERRY TREE?
HUH?
カタ
KLAK
SHUICHIRO!

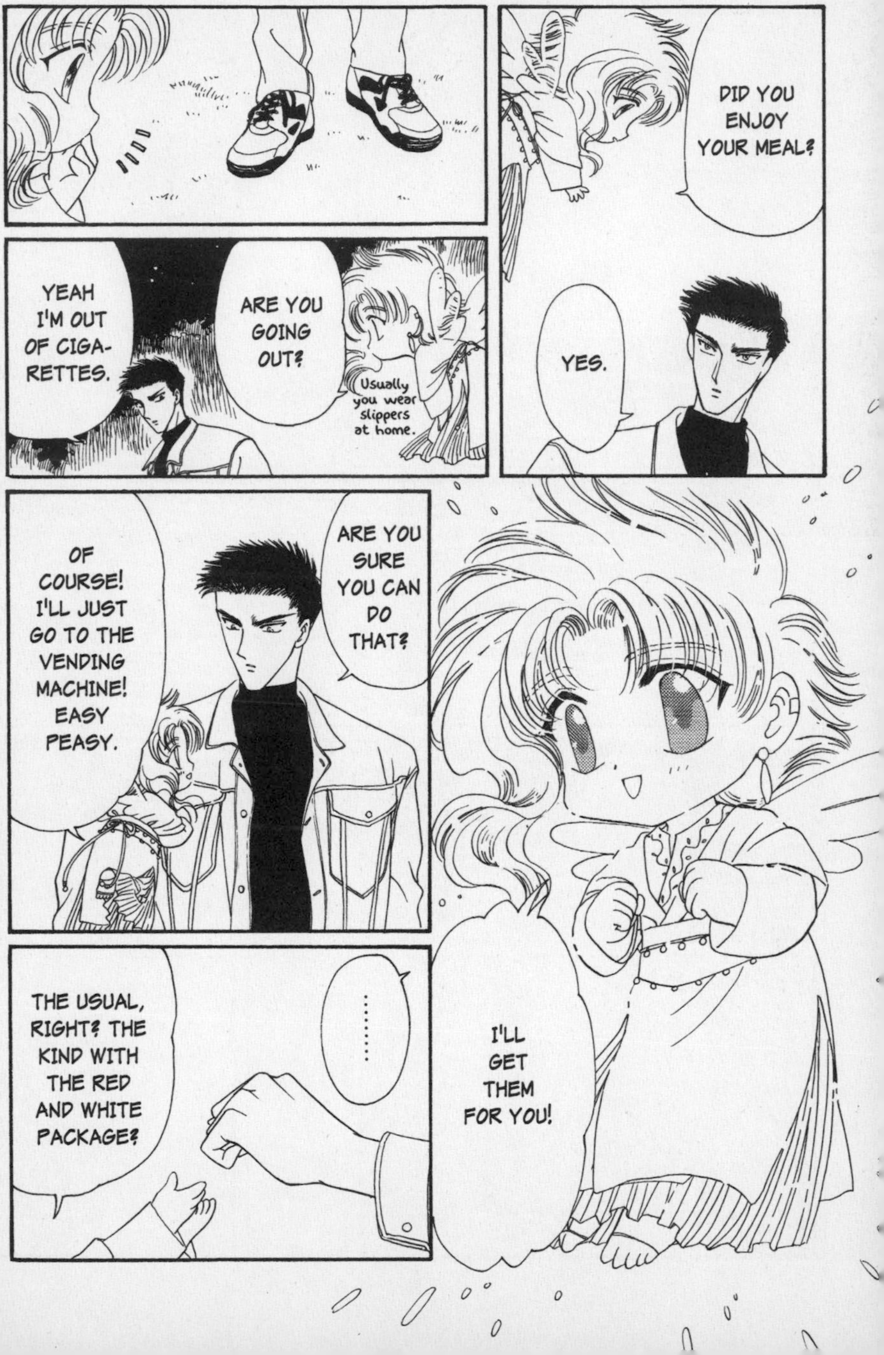
DID YOU ENJOY YOUR MEAL?
YES.
ARE YOU GOING OUT?
Usually you wear slippers at home.
YEAH I'M OUT OF CIGA-RETTES.
I'LL GET THEM FOR YOU!
ARE YOU SURE YOU CAN DO THAT?
OF COURSE! I'LL JUST GO TO THE VENDING MACHINE! EASY PEASY.
......
THE USUAL, RIGHT? THE KIND WITH THE RED AND WHITE PACKAGE?

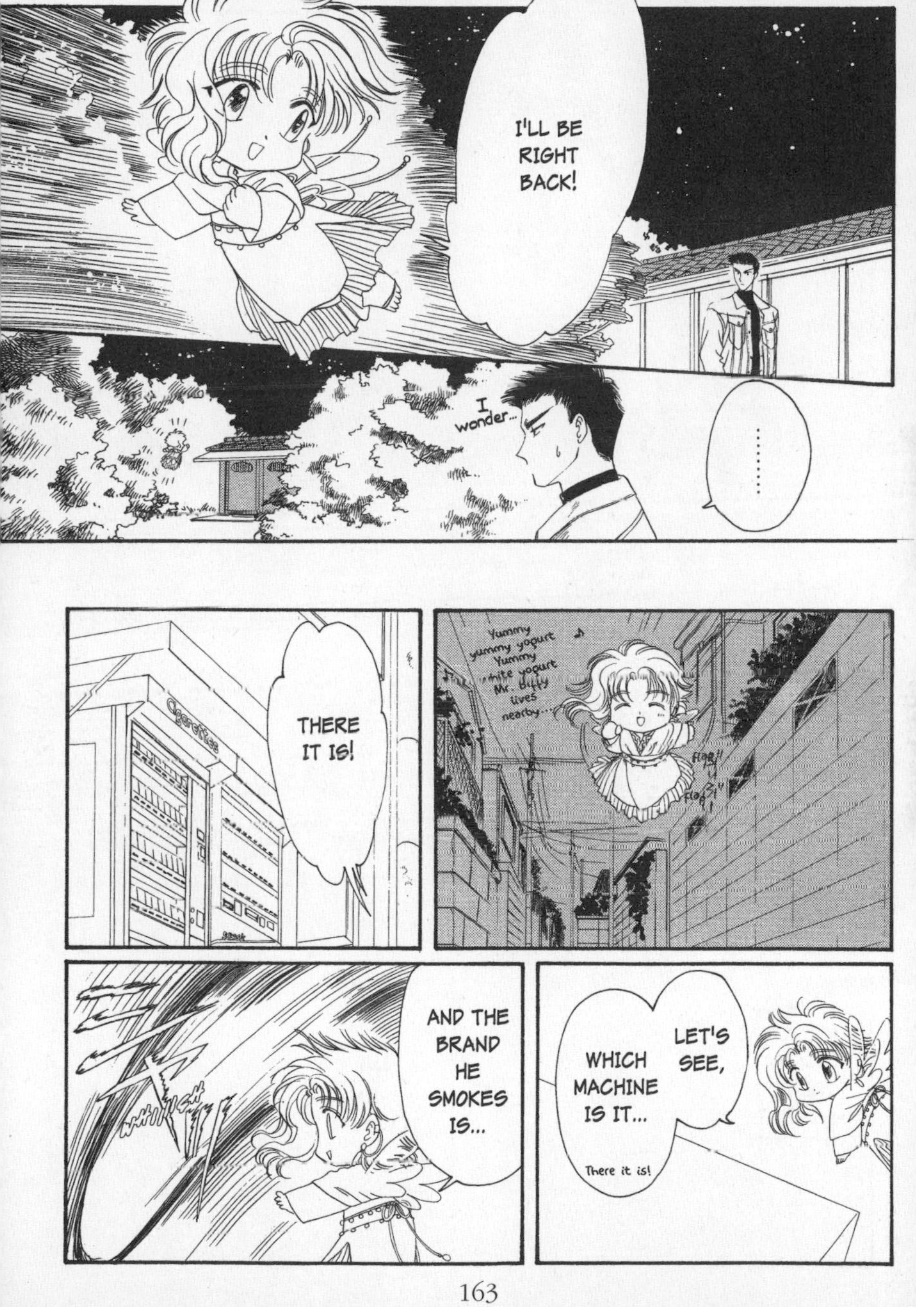
I'LL BE RIGHT BACK!
......
I wonder...
Yummy yummy yogurt Yummy white yogurt Mr. Bitty lives nearby...
Flap!! Flap!!
THERE IT IS!
LET'S SEE, WHICH MACHINE IS IT...
There it is!
AND THE BRAND HE SMOKES IS...
WHHIIICH

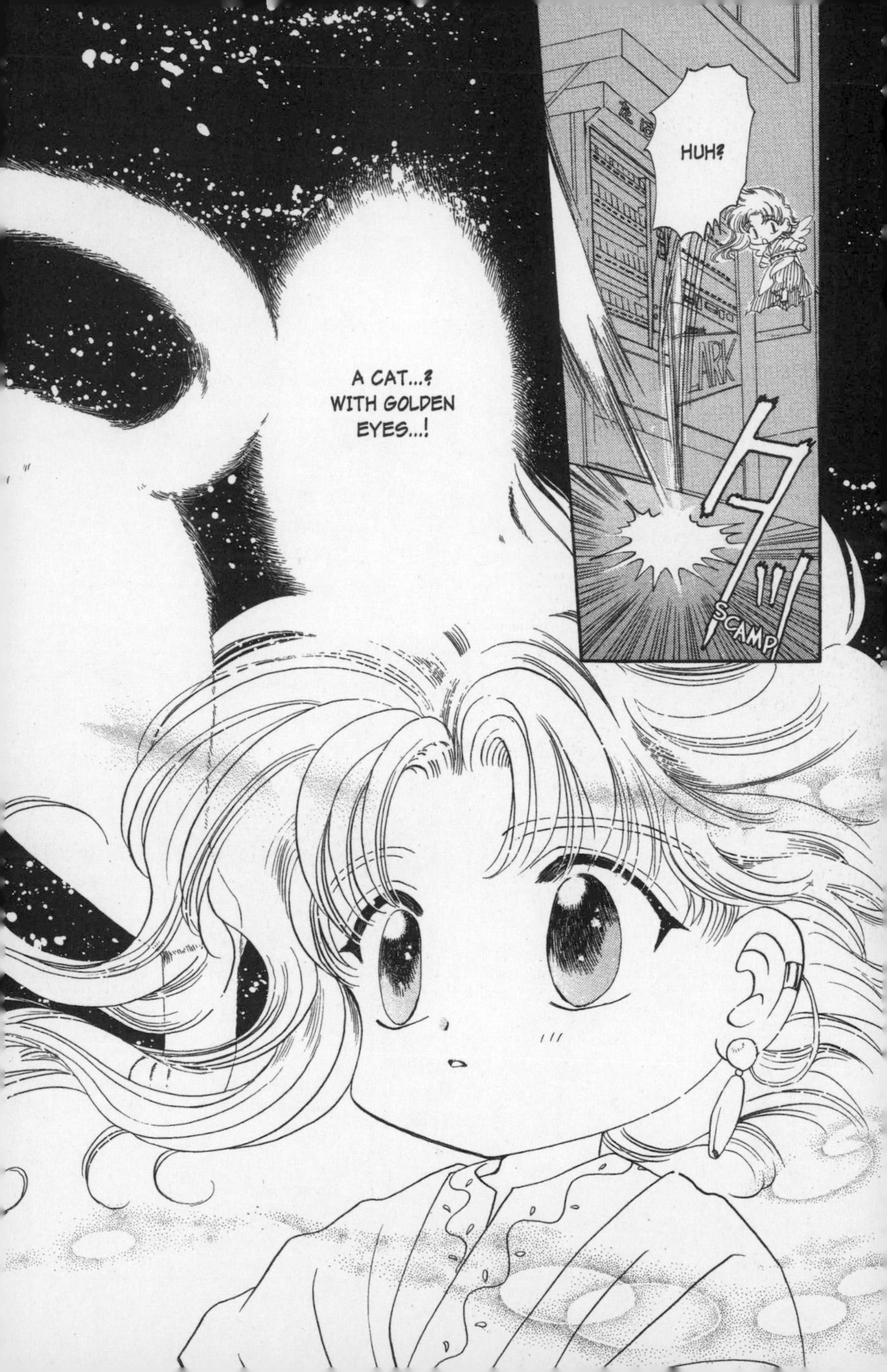
HUH?
SCAMP
A CAT...? WITH GOLDEN EYES...!

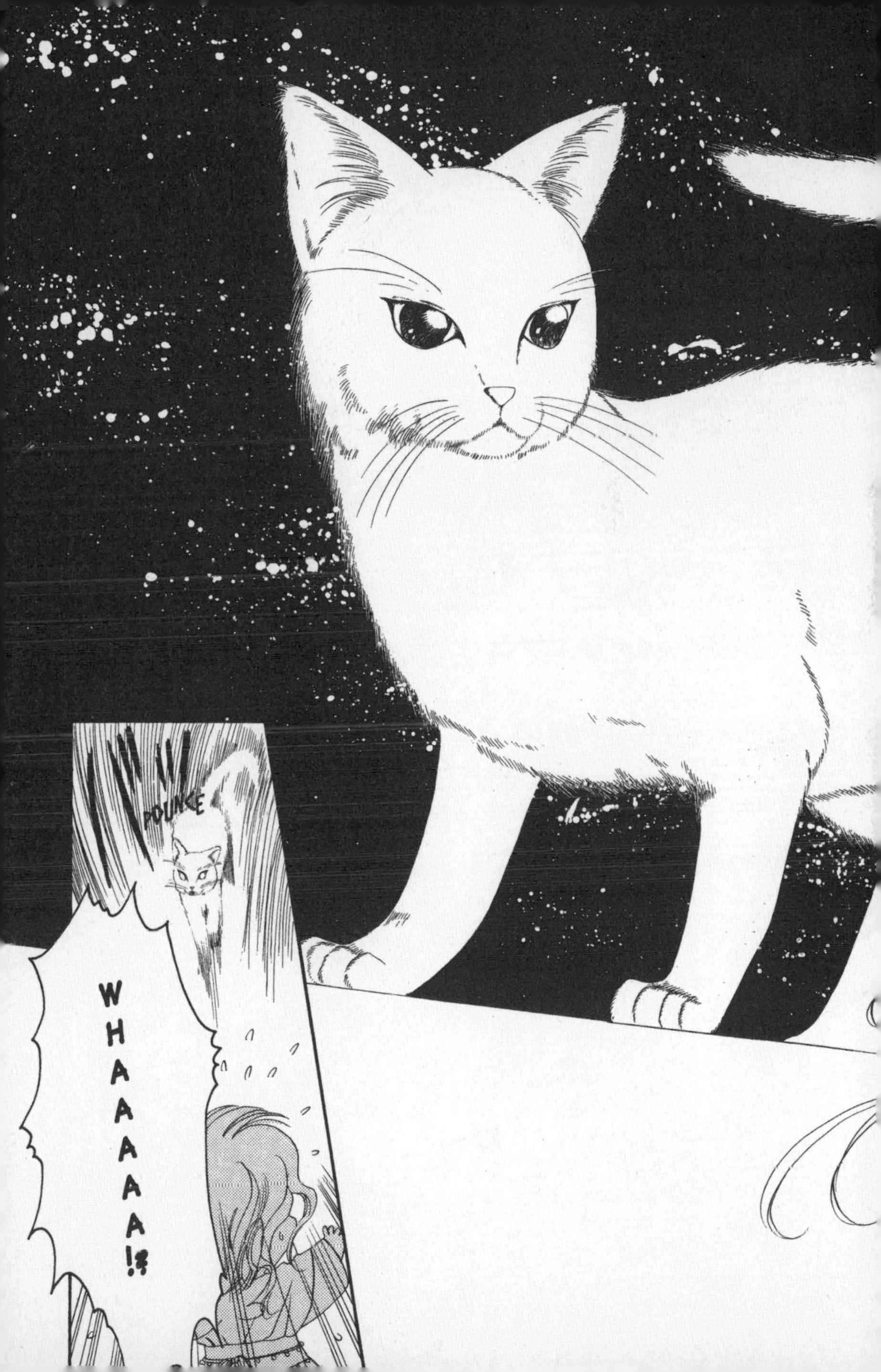
POUNCE
WHAAAAAA!?

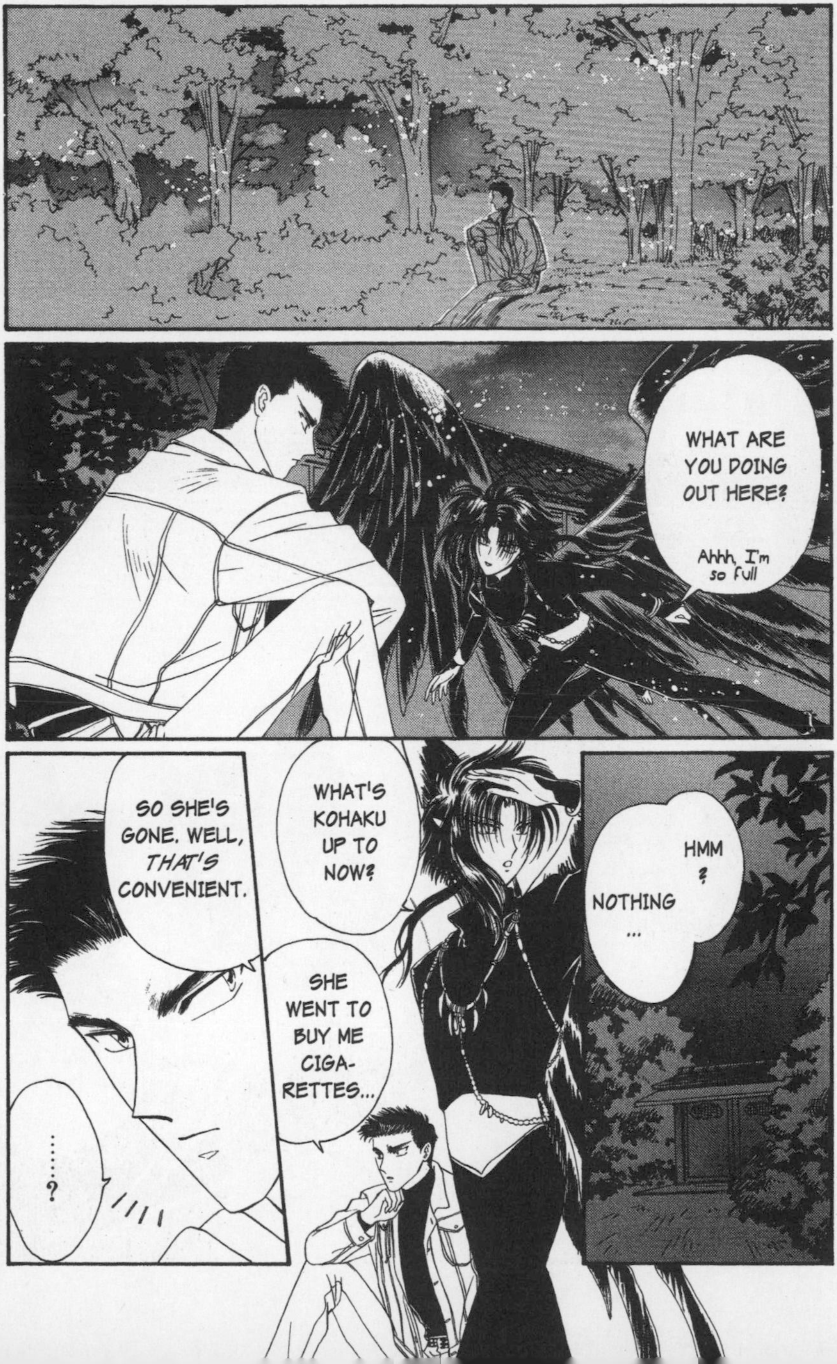
WHAT ARE YOU DOING OUT HERE?
Ahhh, I'm so full
HMM?
NOTHING...
WHAT'S KOHAKU UP TO NOW?
SHE WENT TO BUY ME CIGA-RETTES...
SO SHE'S GONE. WELL, *THAT'S* CONVENIENT.
......?

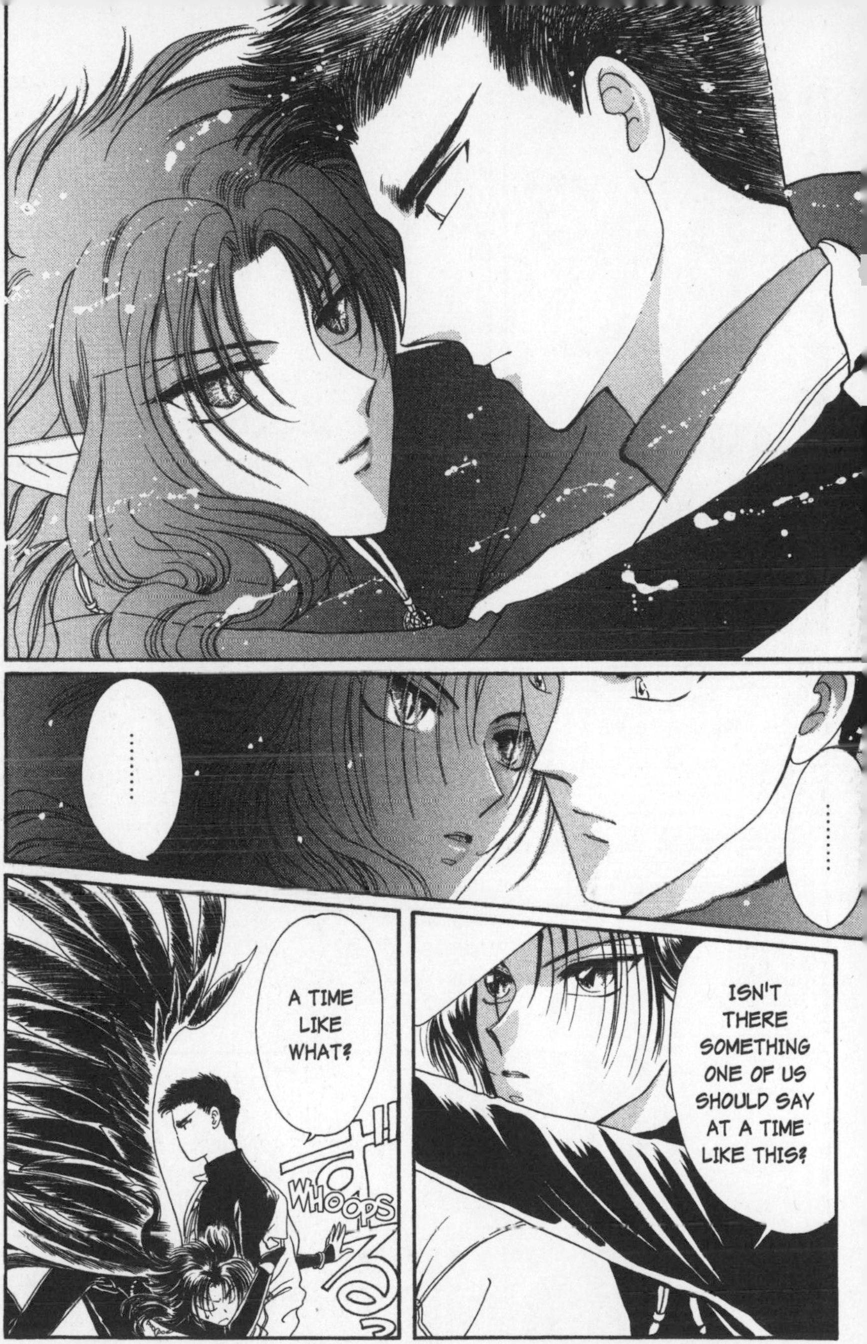
......
......
ISN'T THERE SOMETHING ONE OF US SHOULD SAY AT A TIME LIKE THIS?
A TIME LIKE WHAT?
WHOOPS

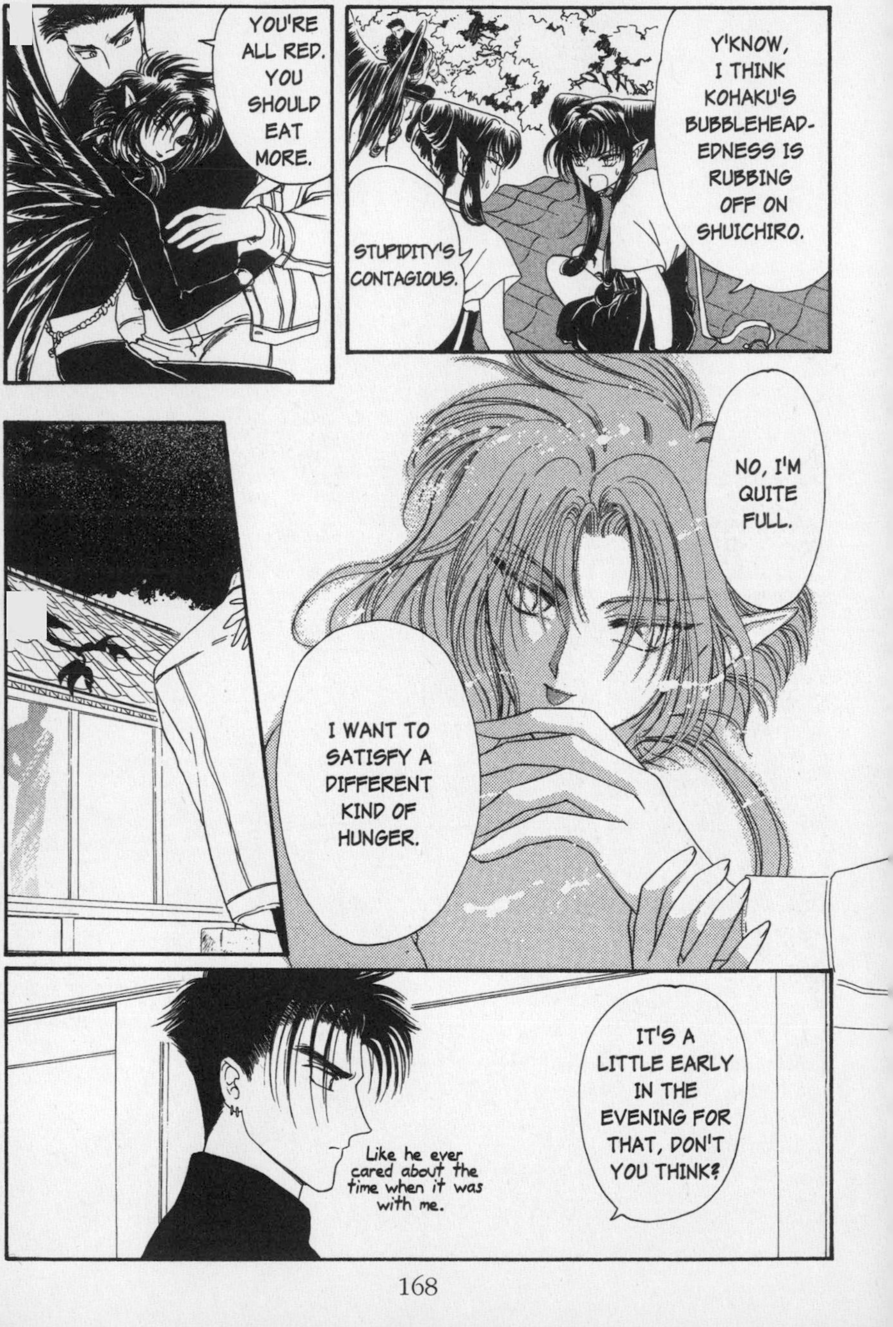
Y'KNOW, I THINK KOHAKU'S BUBBLEHEAD-EDNESS IS RUBBING OFF ON SHUICHIRO.
STUPIDITY'S CONTAGIOUS.
YOU'RE ALL RED. YOU SHOULD EAT MORE.
NO, I'M QUITE FULL.
I WANT TO SATISFY A DIFFERENT KIND OF HUNGER.
IT'S A LITTLE EARLY IN THE EVENING FOR THAT, DON'T YOU THINK?
Like he ever cared about the time when it was with me.

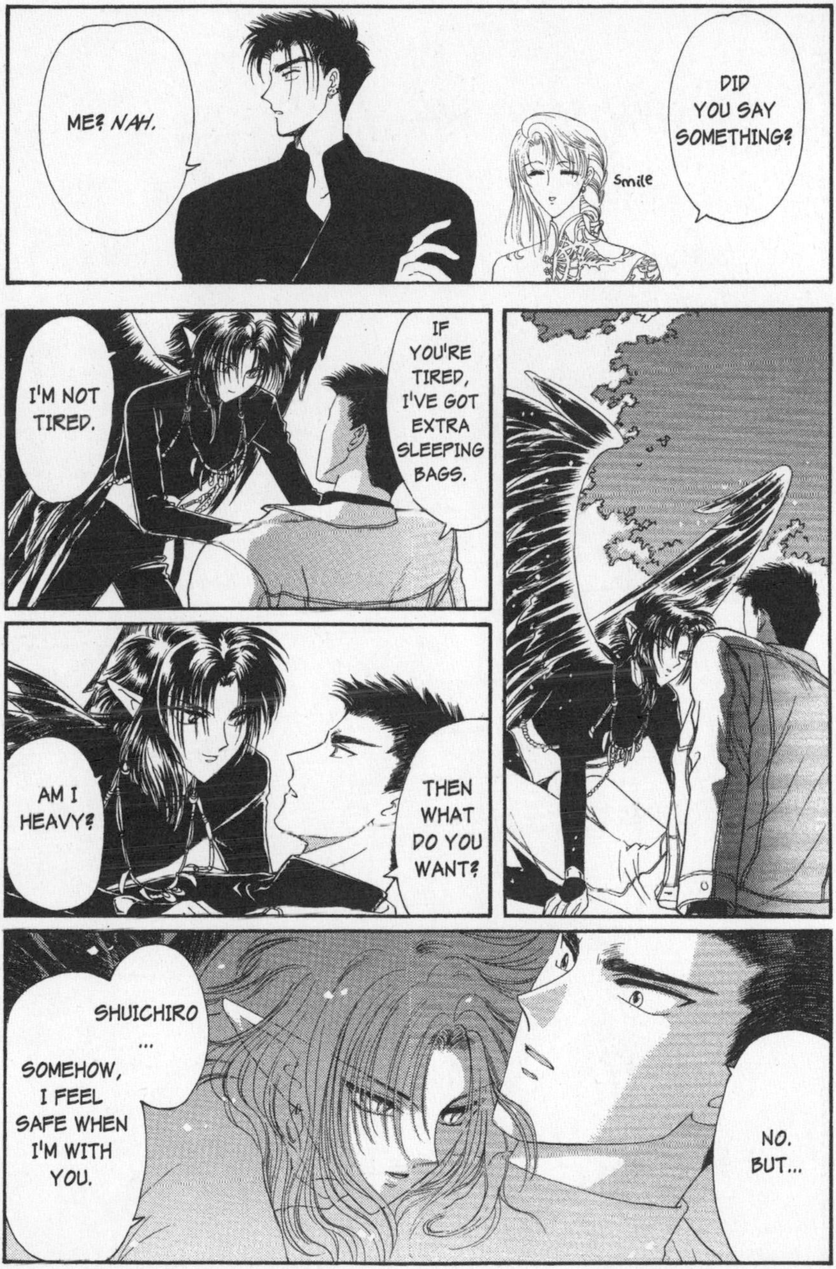
DID YOU SAY SOMETHING?
Smile
ME? NAH.
IF YOU'RE TIRED, I'VE GOT EXTRA SLEEPING BAGS.
I'M NOT TIRED.
THEN WHAT DO YOU WANT?
AM I HEAVY?
NO. BUT...
SHUICHIRO ... SOMEHOW, I FEEL SAFE WHEN I'M WITH YOU.

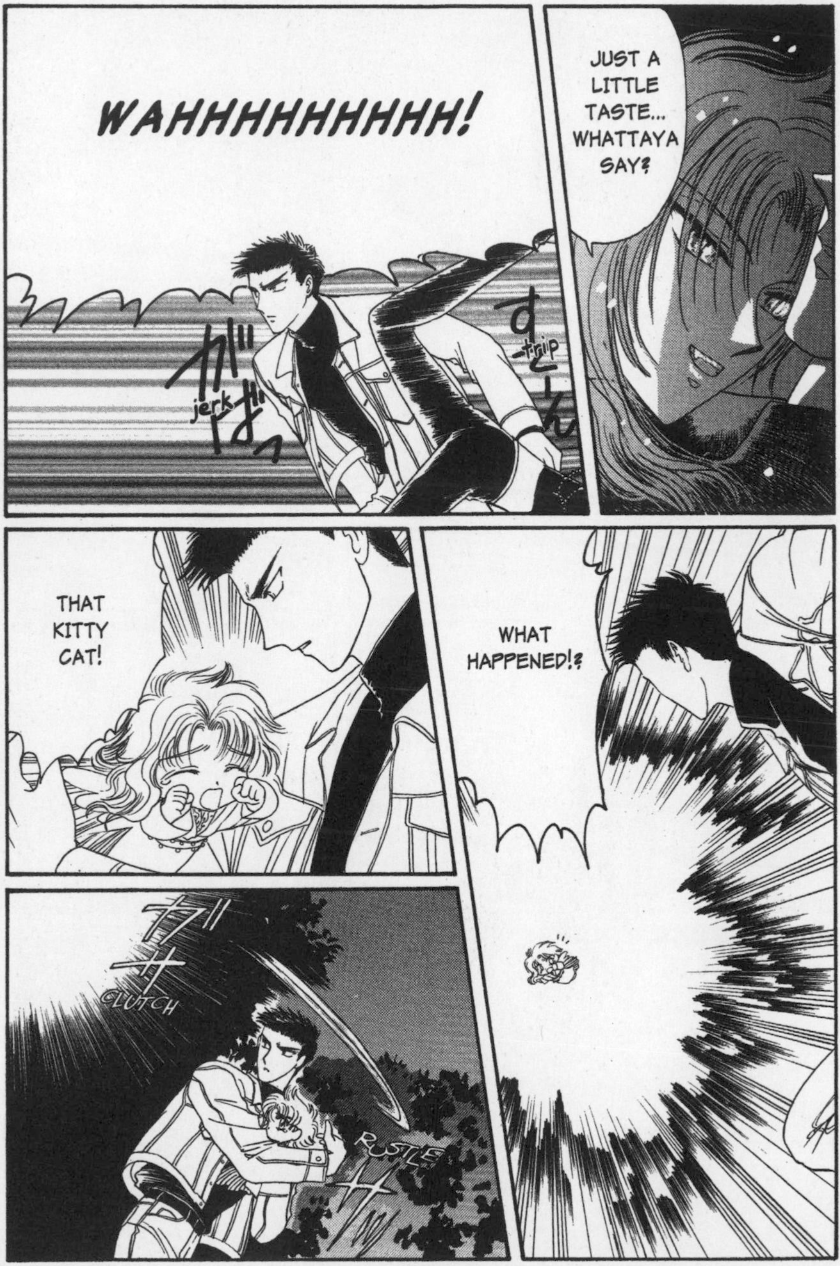
JUST A LITTLE TASTE... WHATTAYA SAY?
WAHHHHHHHHH!
trip
jerk
WHAT HAPPENED!?
THAT KITTY CAT!
CLUTCH
RUSTLE

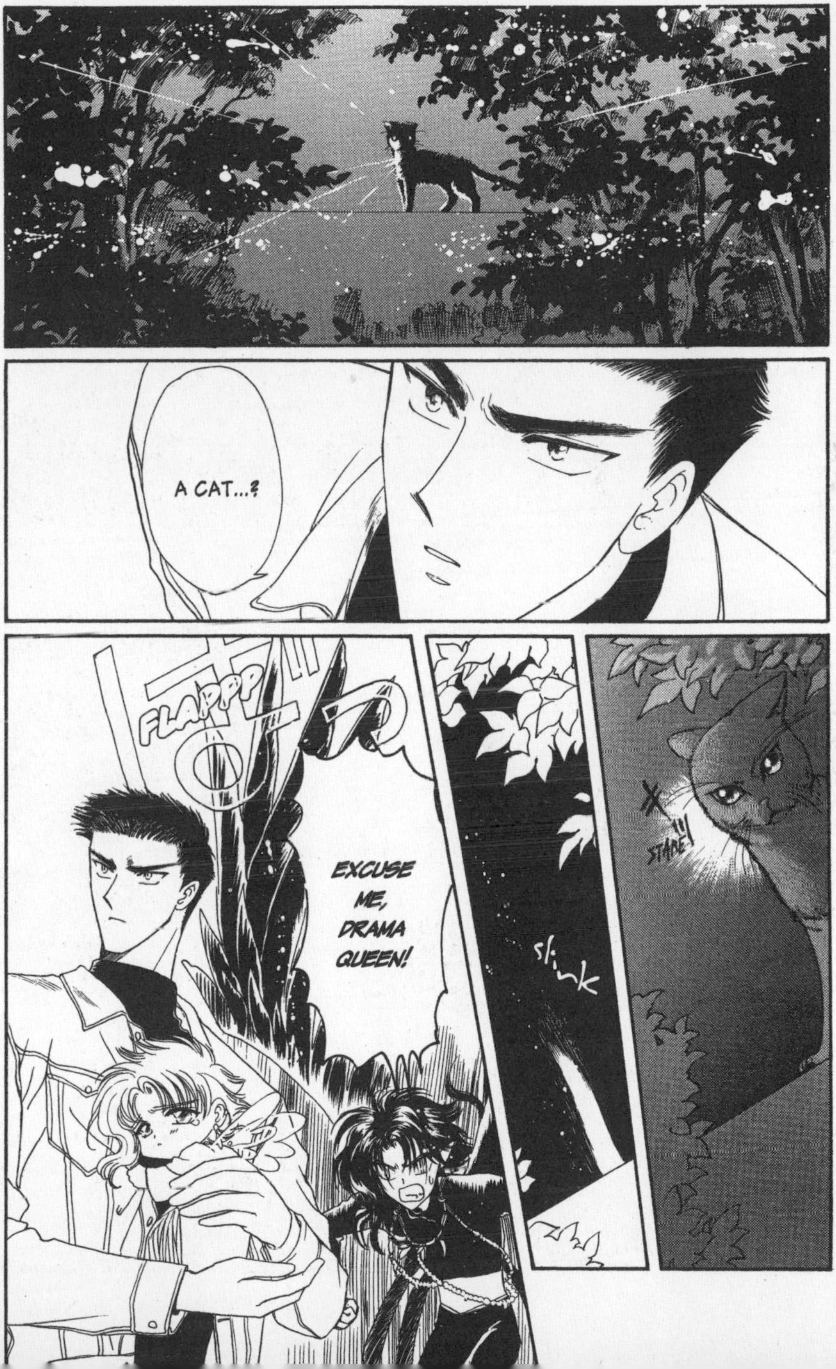
A CAT...?
STARE
slink
FLAPPP
EXCUSE ME, DRAMA QUEEN!

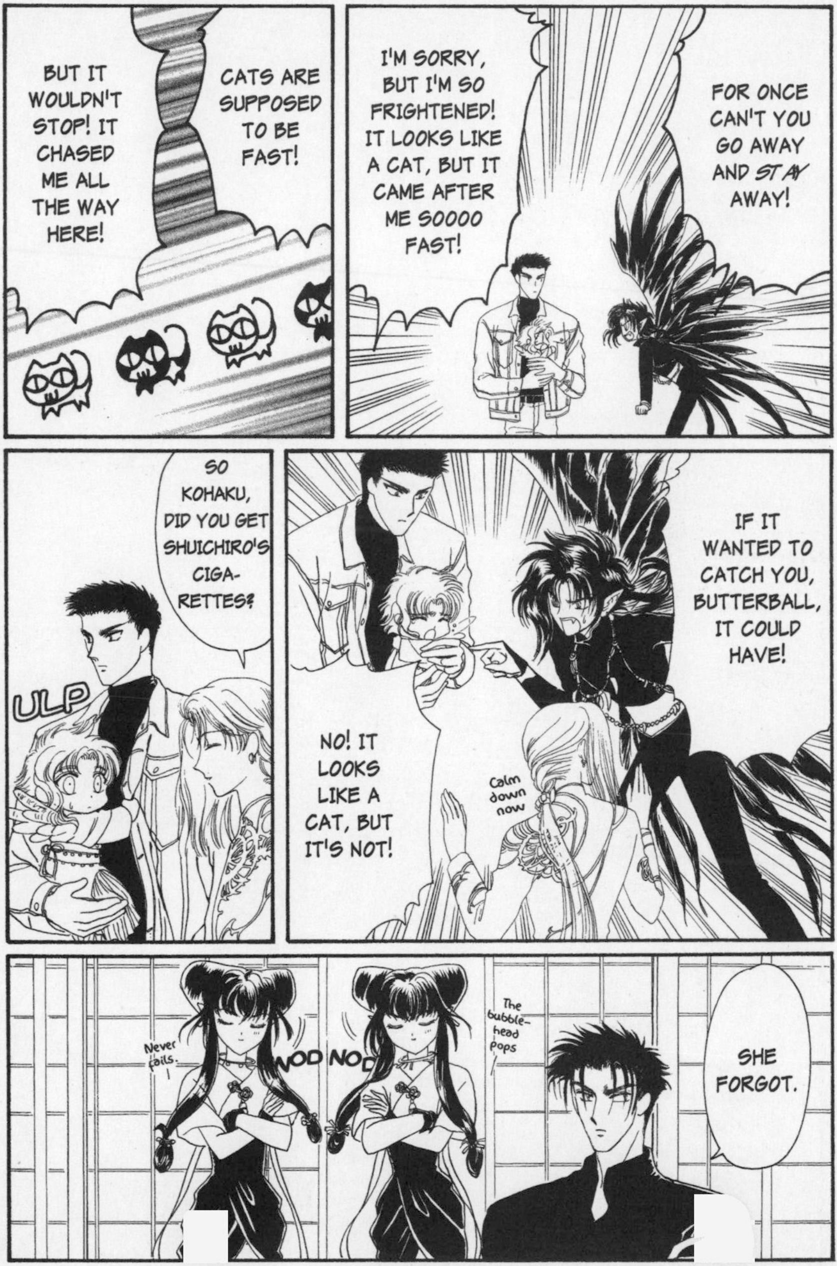
FOR ONCE CAN'T YOU GO AWAY AND STAY AWAY!
I'M SORRY, BUT I'M SO FRIGHTENED! IT LOOKS LIKE A CAT, BUT IT CAME AFTER ME SOOOO FAST!
CATS ARE SUPPOSED TO BE FAST!
BUT IT WOULDN'T STOP! IT CHASED ME ALL THE WAY HERE!
IF IT WANTED TO CATCH YOU, BUTTERBALL, IT COULD HAVE!
Calm down now
NO! IT LOOKS LIKE A CAT, BUT IT'S NOT!
SO KOHAKU, DID YOU GET SHUICHIRO'S CIGA-RETTES?
ULP
SHE FORGOT.
The bubble-head pops
NOD NOD
Never fails.

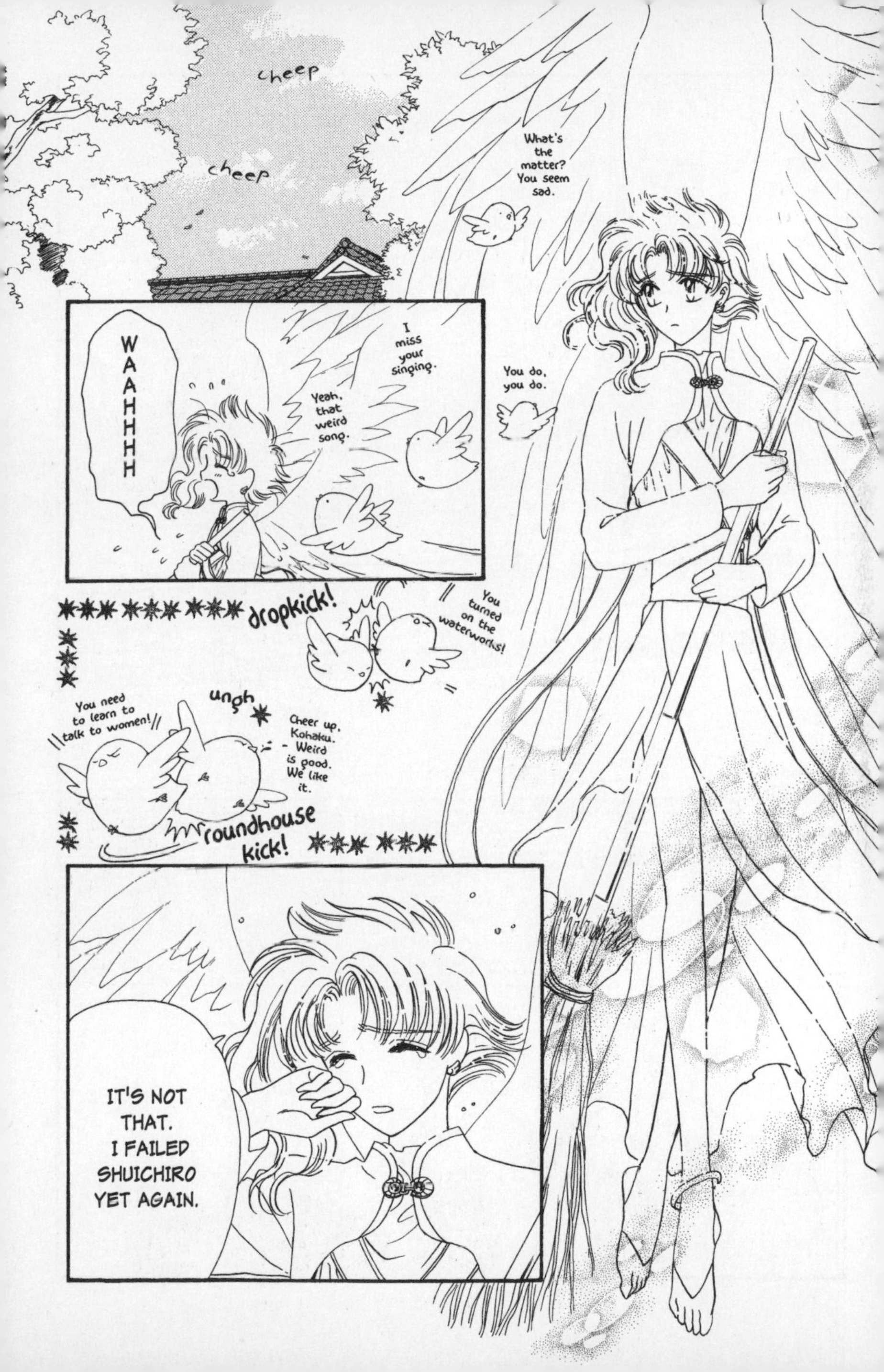
cheep
cheep
What's the matter? You seem sad.
You do, you do.
I miss your singing.
Yeah, that weird song.
WAAHHHH
You turned on the waterworks!
dropkick!
Cheer up, Kohaku. Weird is good. We like it.
ungh
You need to learn to talk to women!
roundhouse kick!
IT'S NOT THAT. I FAILED SHUICHIRO YET AGAIN.

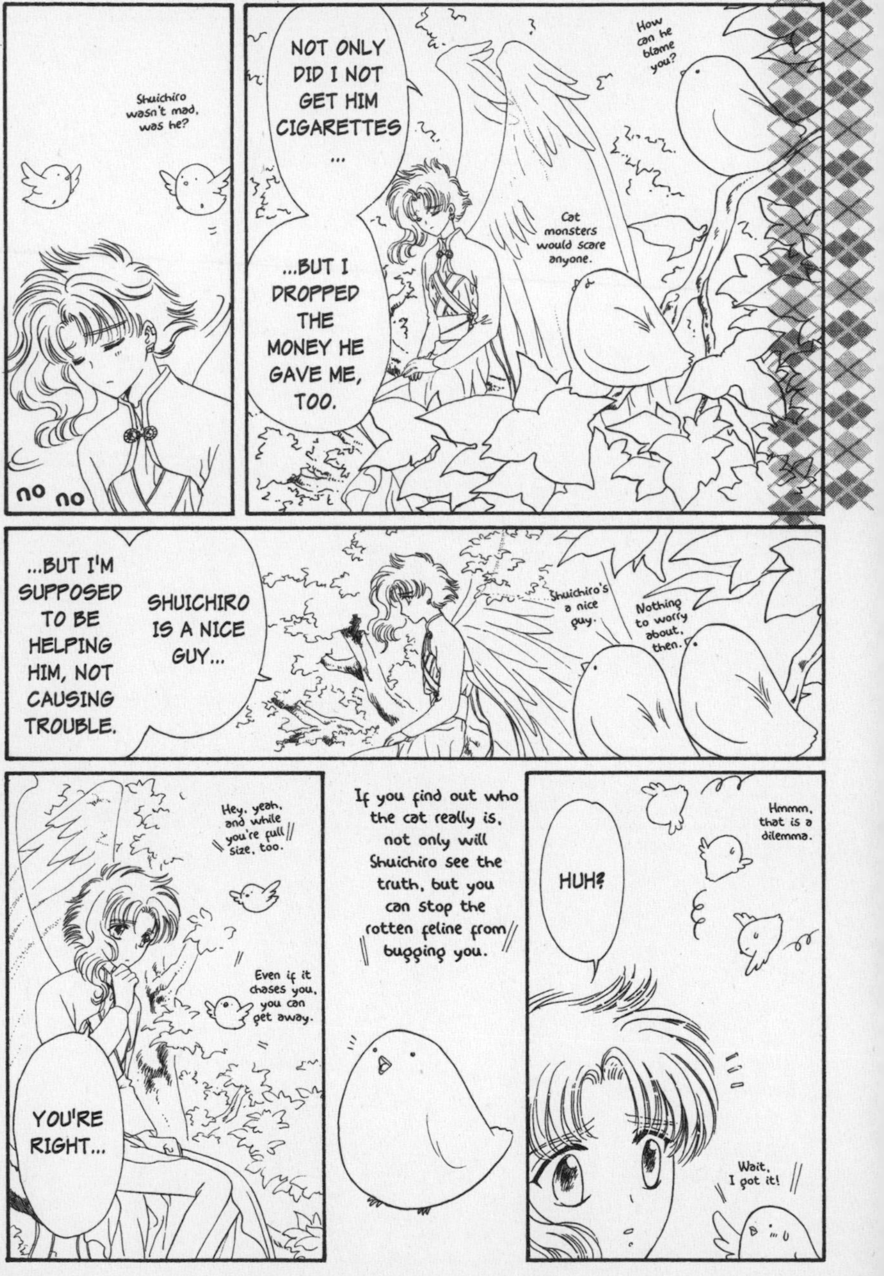
NOT ONLY DID I NOT GET HIM CIGARETTES ...
...BUT I DROPPED THE MONEY HE GAVE ME, TOO.
How can he blame you?
Cat monsters would scare anyone.
Shuichiro wasn't mad, was he?
no no
Shuichiro's a nice guy.
Nothing to worry about, then.
SHUICHIRO IS A NICE GUY...
...BUT I'M SUPPOSED TO BE HELPING HIM, NOT CAUSING TROUBLE.
Hmmm, that is a dilemma.
Wait, I got it!
HUH?
If you find out who the cat really is, not only will Shuichiro see the truth, but you can stop the rotten feline from bugging you.
Hey, yeah, and while you're full size, too.
Even if it chases you, you can get away.
YOU'RE RIGHT...

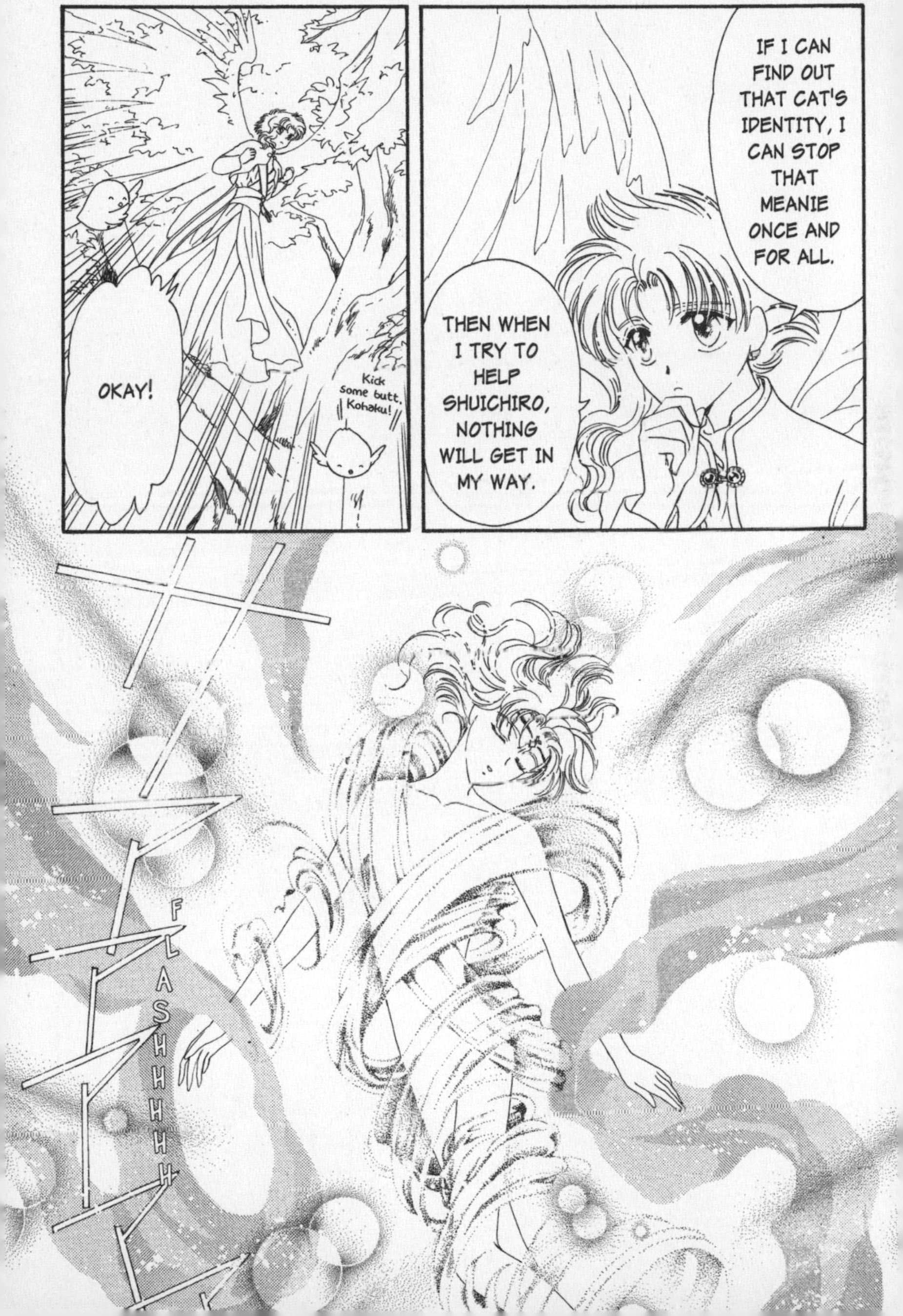
IF I CAN FIND OUT THAT CAT'S IDENTITY, I CAN STOP THAT MEANIE ONCE AND FOR ALL.
THEN WHEN I TRY TO HELP SHUICHIRO, NOTHING WILL GET IN MY WAY.
Kick some butt, Kohaku!
OKAY!
FLASHHHH

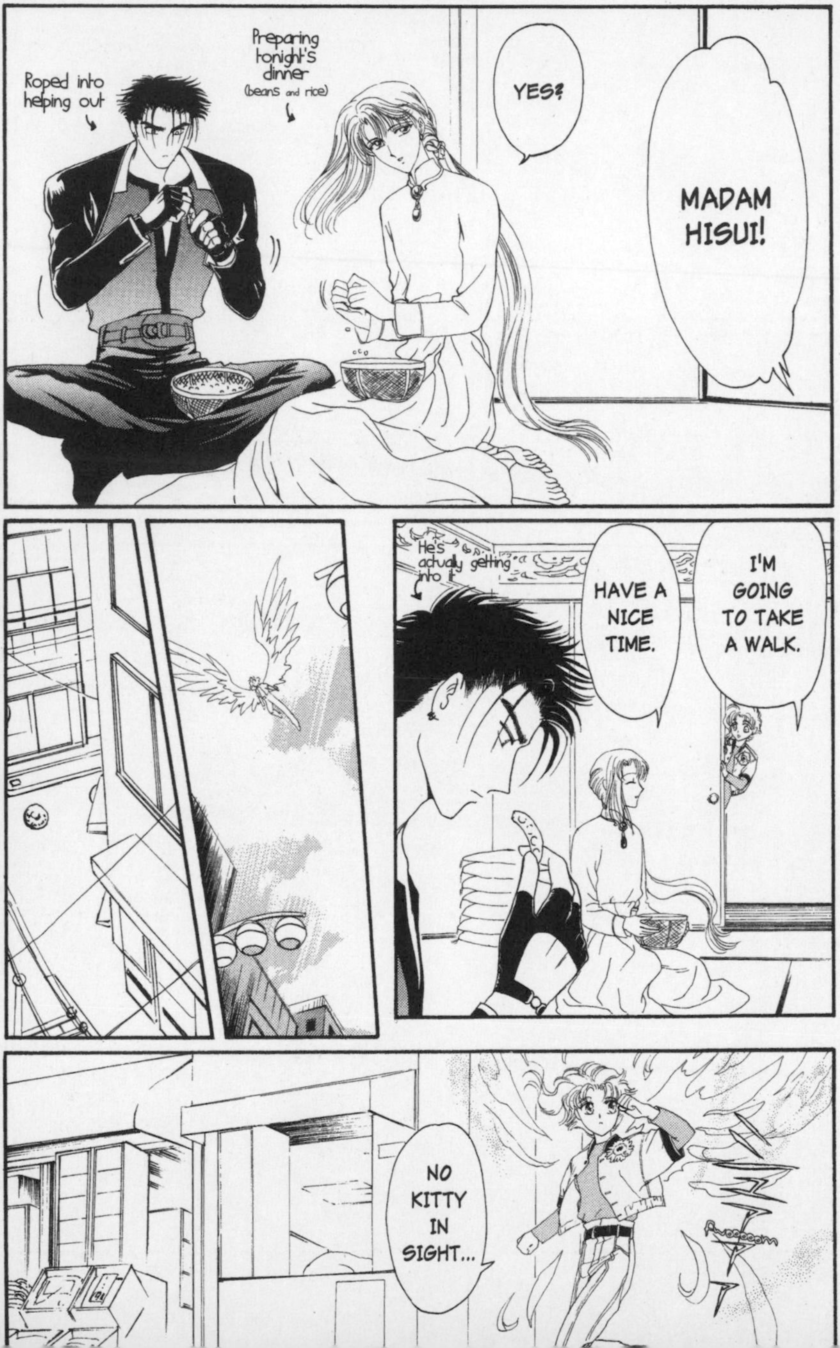
MADAM HISUI!
YES?
Preparing tonight's dinner (beans and rice)
Roped into helping out
I'M GOING TO TAKE A WALK.
HAVE A NICE TIME.
He's actually getting into it
NO KITTY IN SIGHT...
Fwoooooom

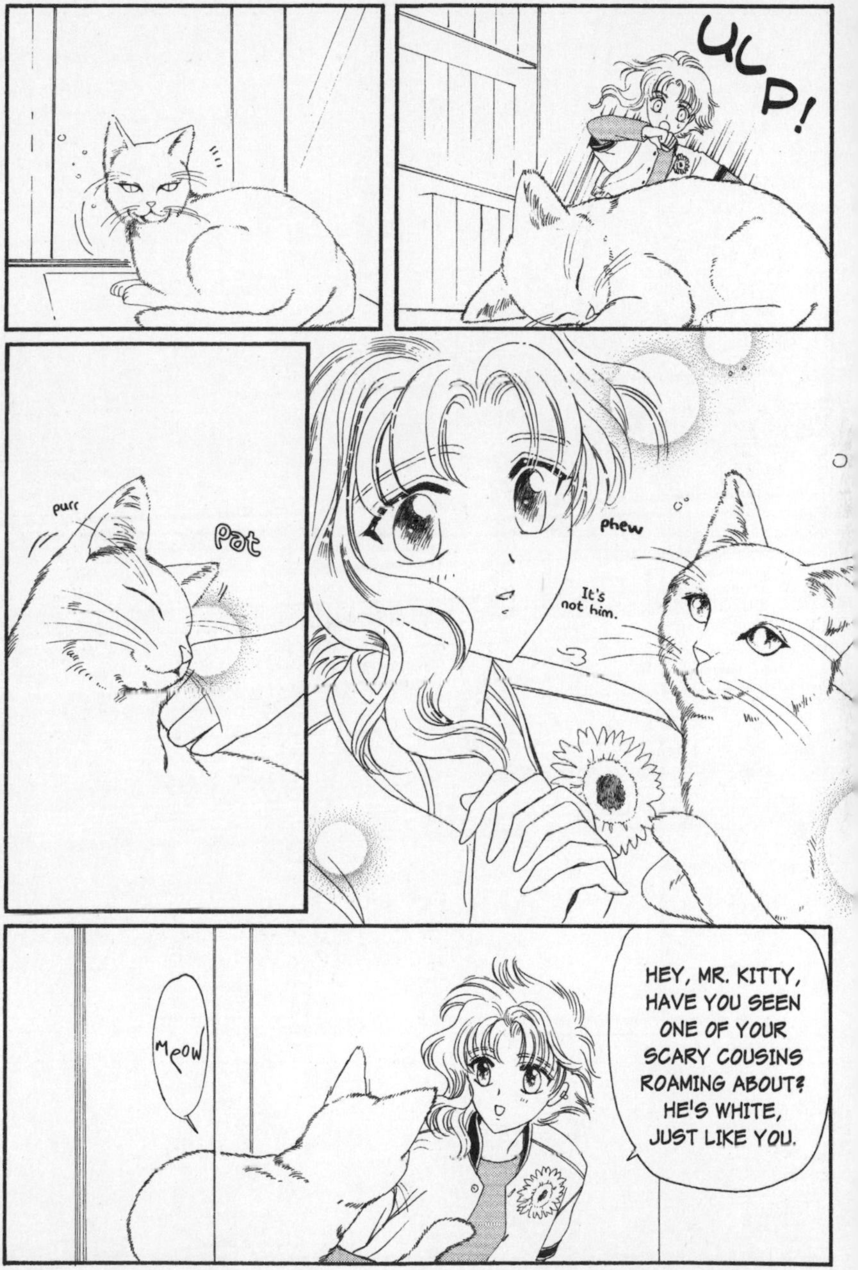
ULP!
phew
It's not him.
purr
pat
HEY, MR. KITTY, HAVE YOU SEEN ONE OF YOUR SCARY COUSINS ROAMING ABOUT? HE'S WHITE, JUST LIKE YOU.
Meow

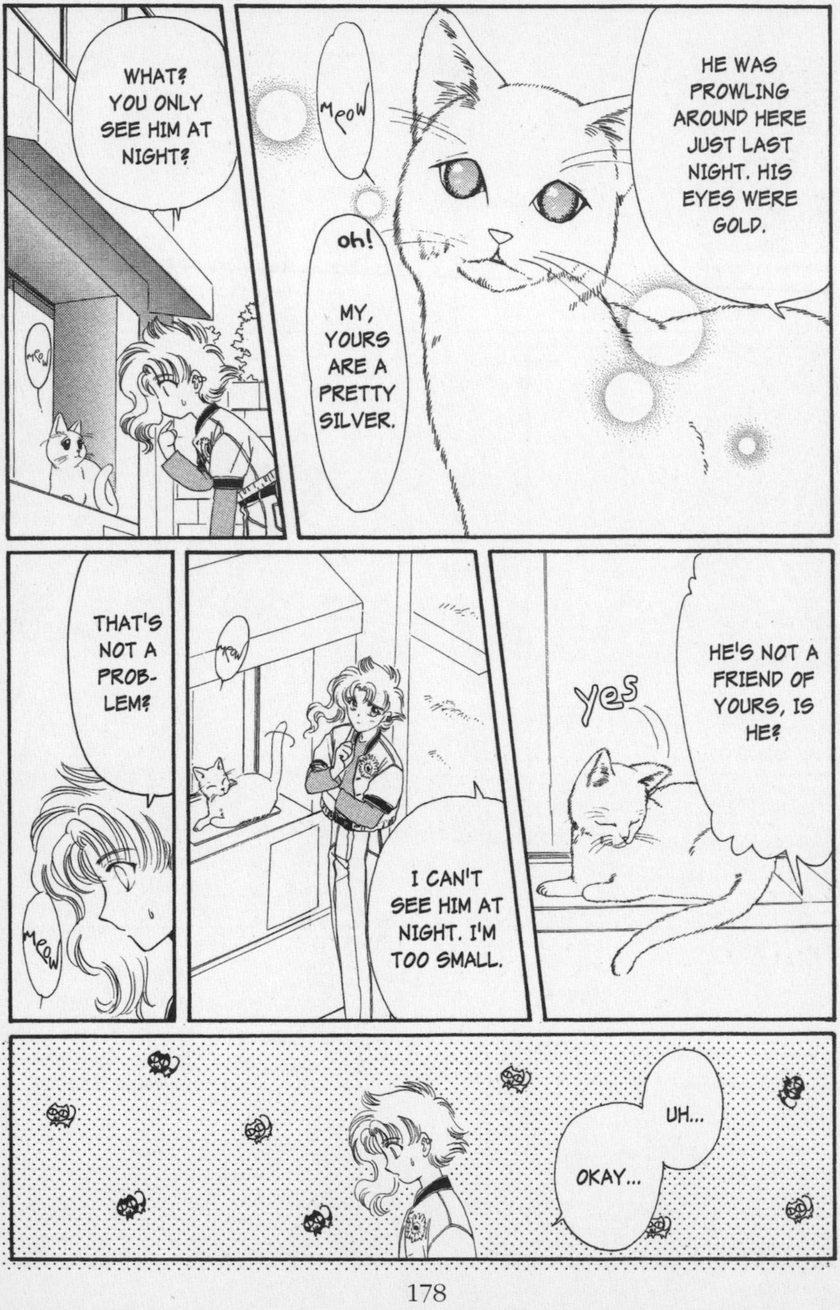
HE WAS PROWLING AROUND HERE JUST LAST NIGHT. HIS EYES WERE GOLD.
MEOW
oh!
MY, YOURS ARE A PRETTY SILVER.
WHAT? YOU ONLY SEE HIM AT NIGHT?
MEOW
HE'S NOT A FRIEND OF YOURS, IS HE?
yes
MEOW
I CAN'T SEE HIM AT NIGHT. I'M TOO SMALL.
THAT'S NOT A PROB-LEM?
MEOW
UH...
OKAY...

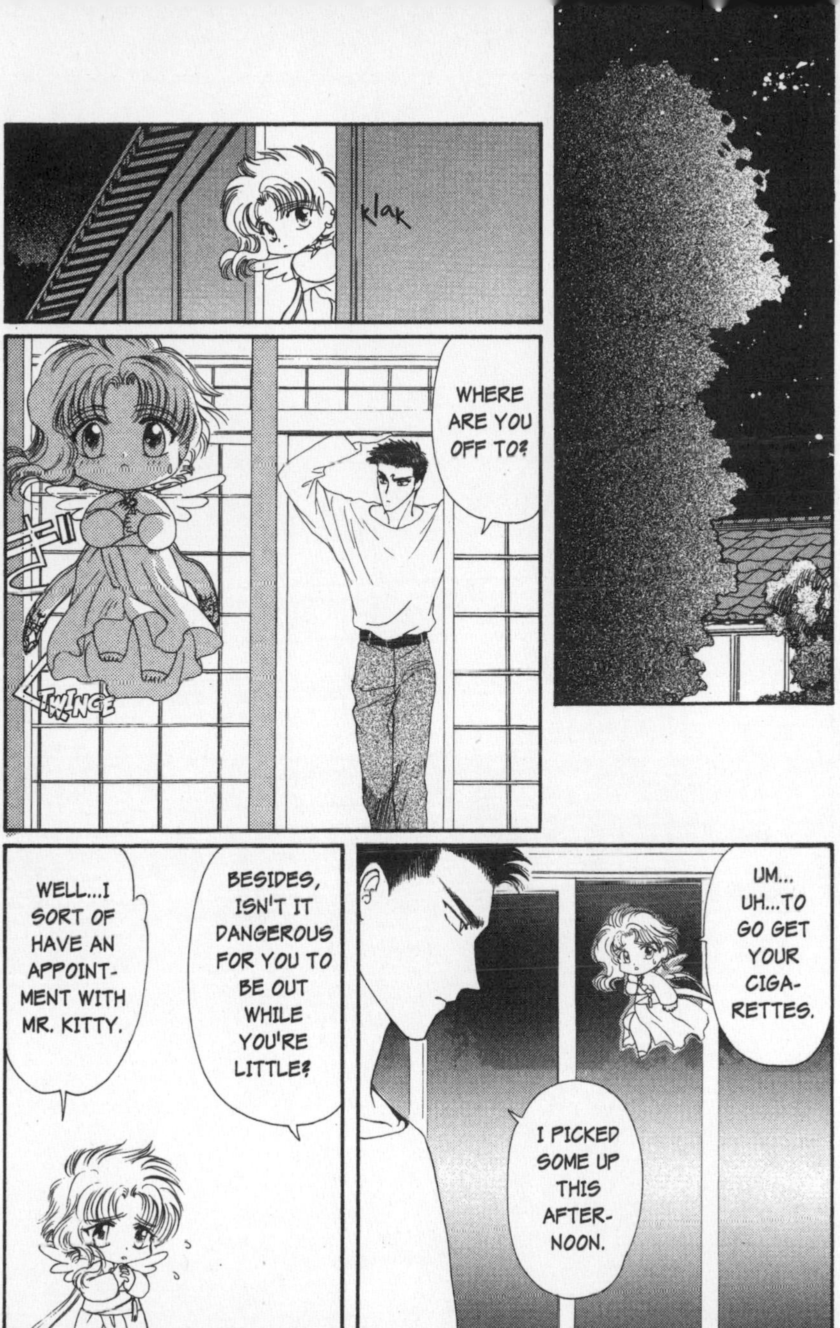

KLAK
WHERE ARE YOU OFF TO?
TWINGE
UM... UH...TO GO GET YOUR CIGARETTES.
I PICKED SOME UP THIS AFTERNOON.
BESIDES, ISN'T IT DANGEROUS FOR YOU TO BE OUT WHILE YOU'RE LITTLE?
WELL...I SORT OF HAVE AN APPOINTMENT WITH MR. KITTY.

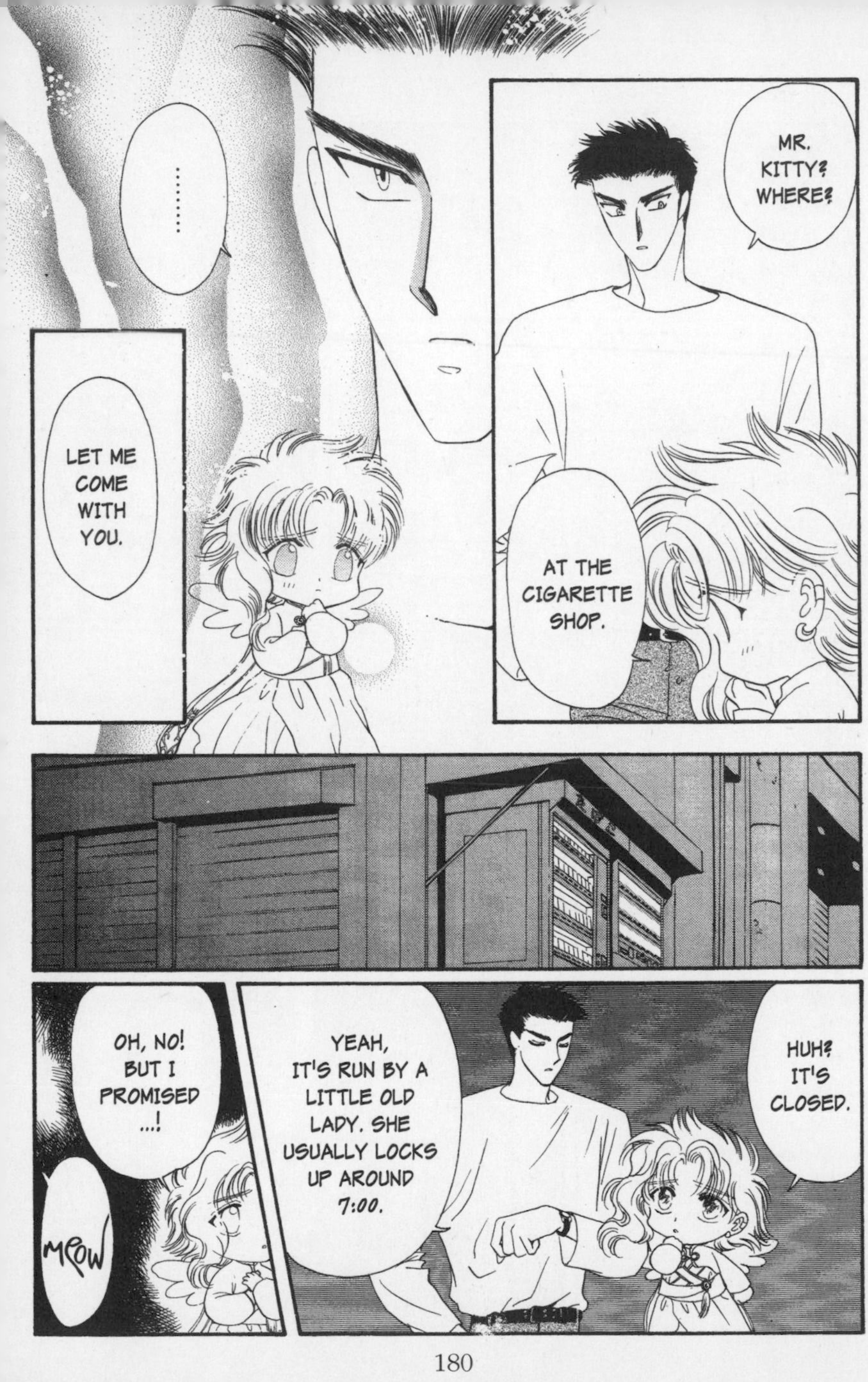
MR. KITTY? WHERE?
AT THE CIGARETTE SHOP.
......
LET ME COME WITH YOU.
HUH? IT'S CLOSED.
YEAH, IT'S RUN BY A LITTLE OLD LADY. SHE USUALLY LOCKS UP AROUND 7:00.
OH, NO! BUT I PROMISED ...!
MEOW

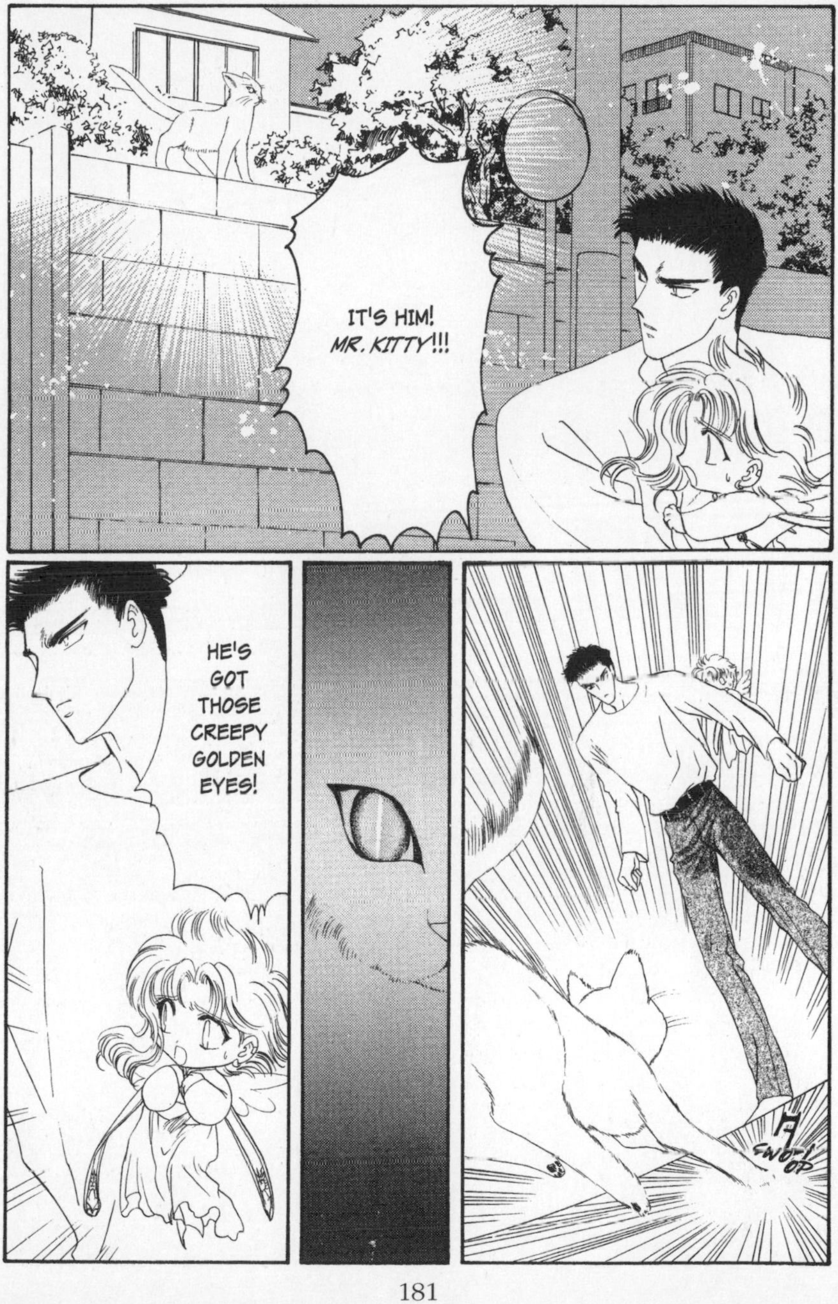
IT'S HIM! MR. KITTY!!!
SWOOP
HE'S GOT THOSE CREEPY GOLDEN EYES!

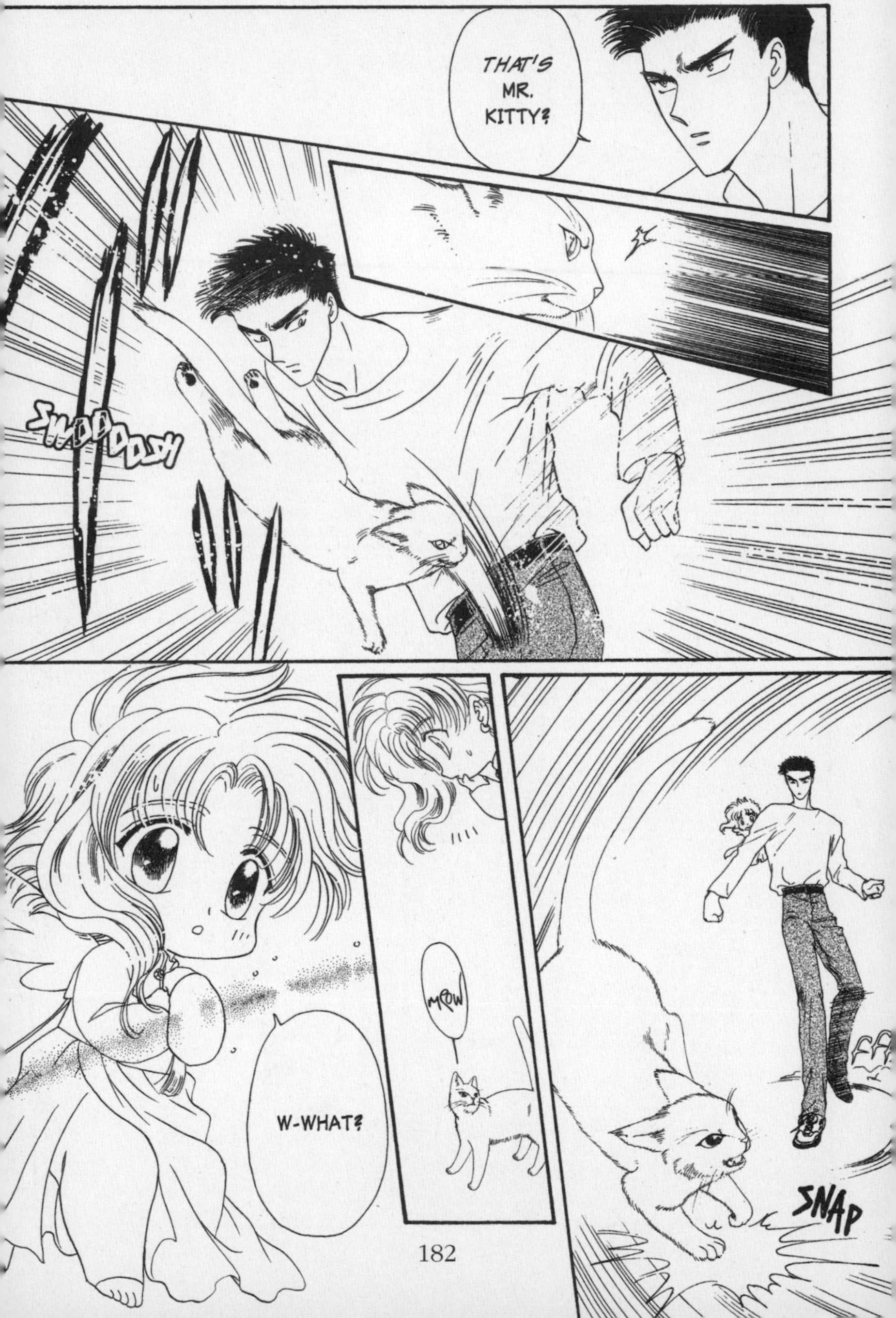
THAT'S MR. KITTY?
SWOOOSH
SNAP
MEOW
W-WHAT?

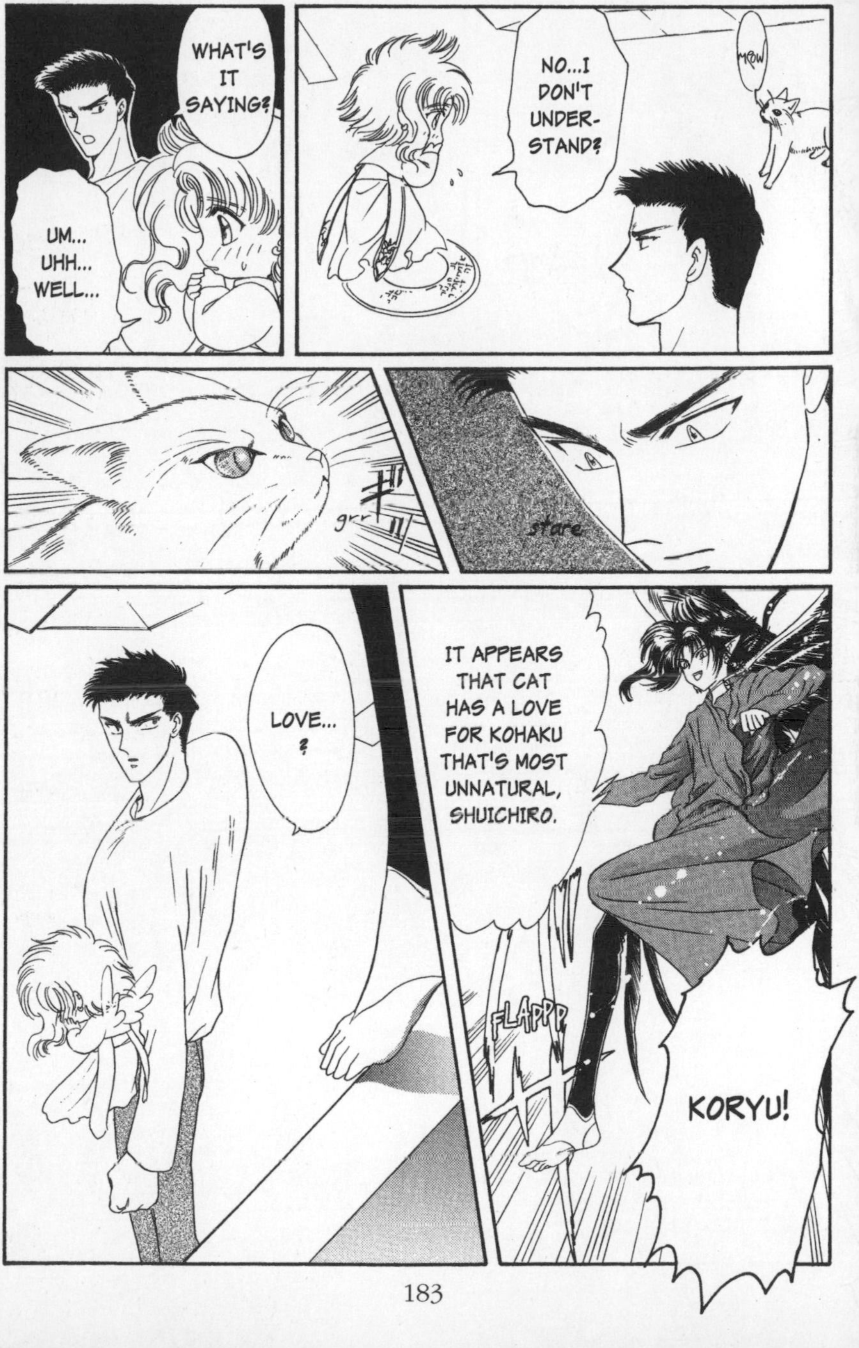
MEOW
NO...I DON'T UNDER-STAND?
WHAT'S IT SAYING?
UM... UHH... WELL...
stare
grr
IT APPEARS THAT CAT HAS A LOVE FOR KOHAKU THAT'S MOST UNNATURAL, SHUICHIRO.
FLAPPP
KORYU!
LOVE... ?

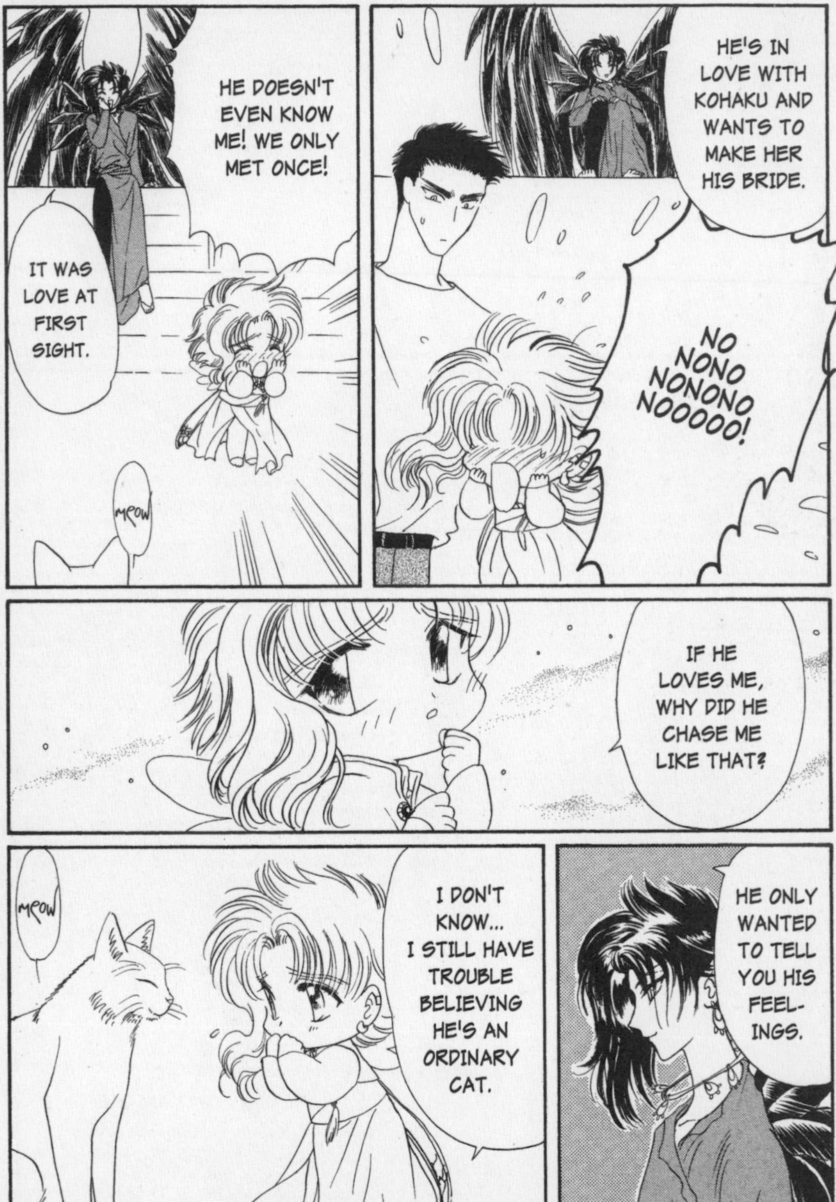
HE'S IN LOVE WITH KOHAKU AND WANTS TO MAKE HER HIS BRIDE.
NO NONO NONONO NOOOOO!
HE DOESN'T EVEN KNOW ME! WE ONLY MET ONCE!
IT WAS LOVE AT FIRST SIGHT.
MEOW
IF HE LOVES ME, WHY DID HE CHASE ME LIKE THAT?
HE ONLY WANTED TO TELL YOU HIS FEEL-INGS.
I DON'T KNOW... I STILL HAVE TROUBLE BELIEVING HE'S AN ORDINARY CAT.
MEOW

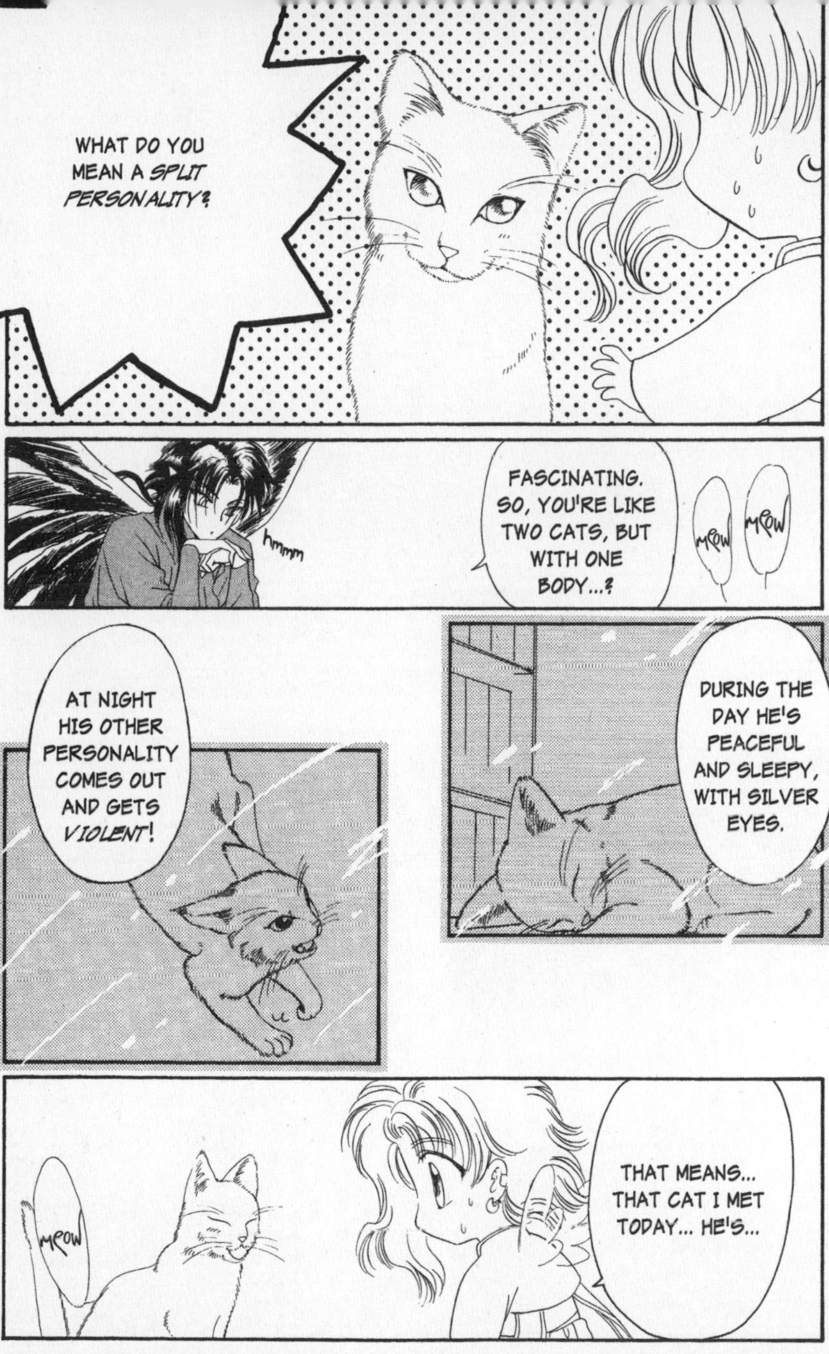
WHAT DO YOU MEAN A *SPLIT PERSONALITY*?
meow
meow
FASCINATING. SO, YOU'RE LIKE TWO CATS, BUT WITH ONE BODY...?
hmmm
DURING THE DAY HE'S PEACEFUL AND SLEEPY, WITH SILVER EYES.
AT NIGHT HIS OTHER PERSONALITY COMES OUT AND GETS *VIOLENT*!
THAT MEANS... THAT CAT I MET TODAY... HE'S...
meow

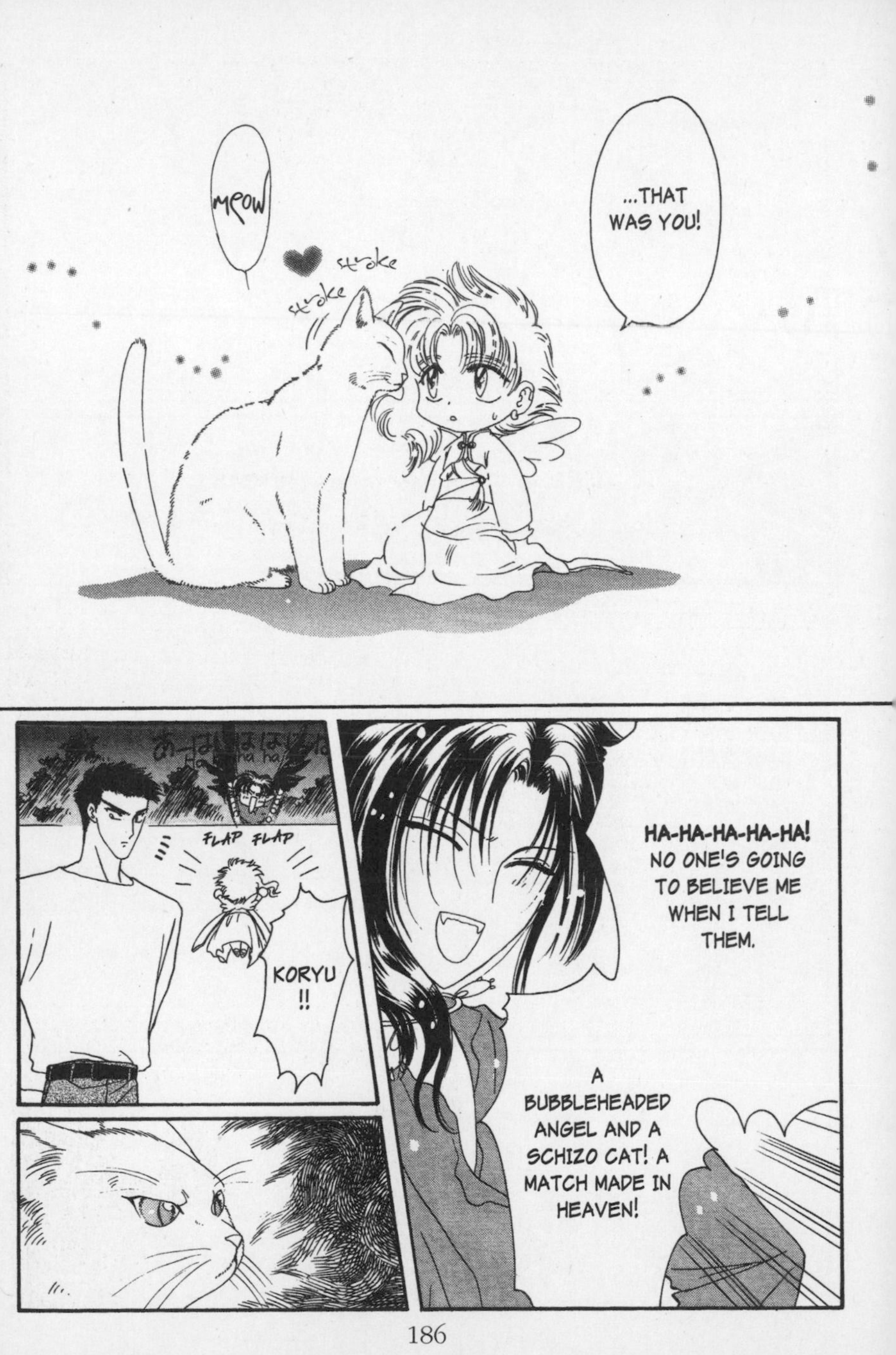
...THAT WAS YOU!
MEOW
stroke
stroke
HA-HA-HA-HA-HA! NO ONE'S GOING TO BELIEVE ME WHEN I TELL THEM.
A BUBBLEHEADED ANGEL AND A SCHIZO CAT! A MATCH MADE IN HEAVEN!
FLAP FLAP
KORYU !!

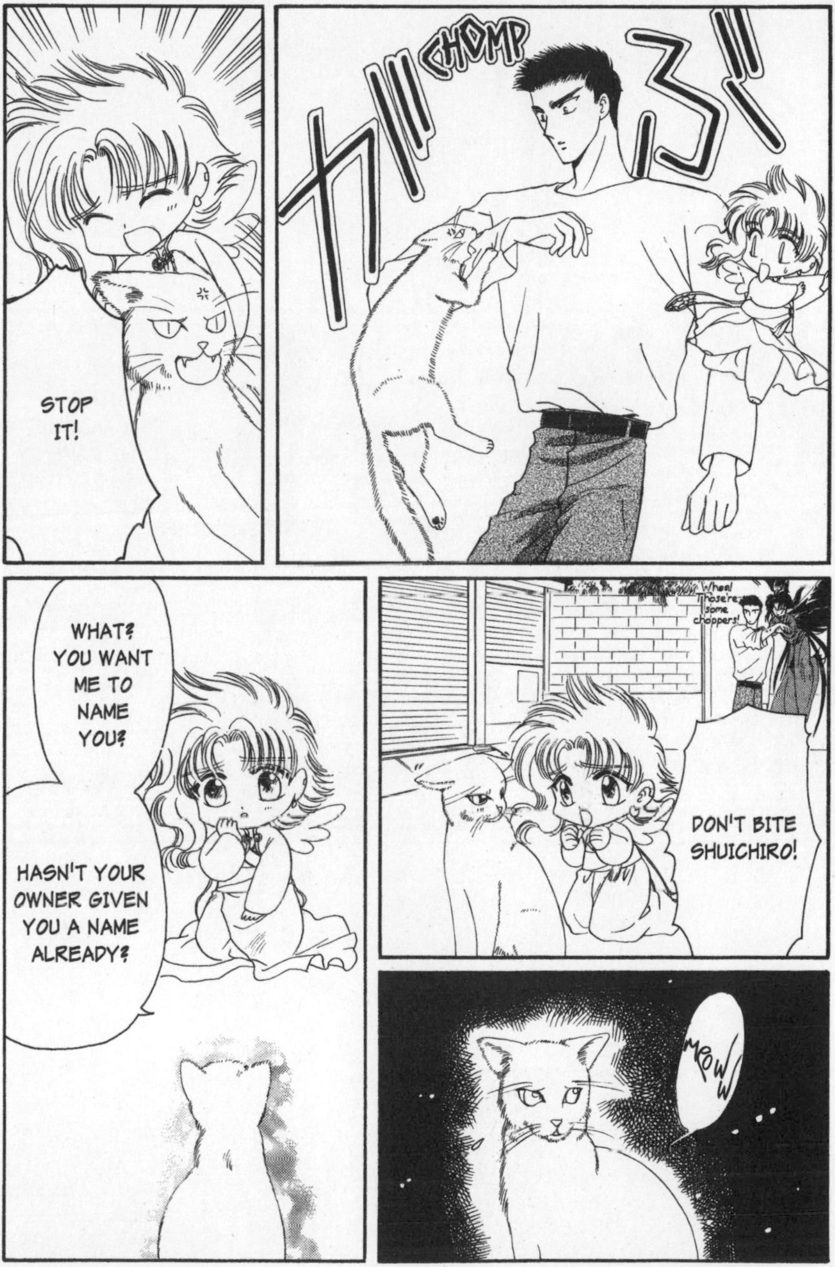
CHOMP
STOP IT!
Whoa! Those're some choppers!
DON'T BITE SHUICHIRO!
MEOW
WHAT? YOU WANT ME TO NAME YOU?
HASN'T YOUR OWNER GIVEN YOU A NAME ALREADY?

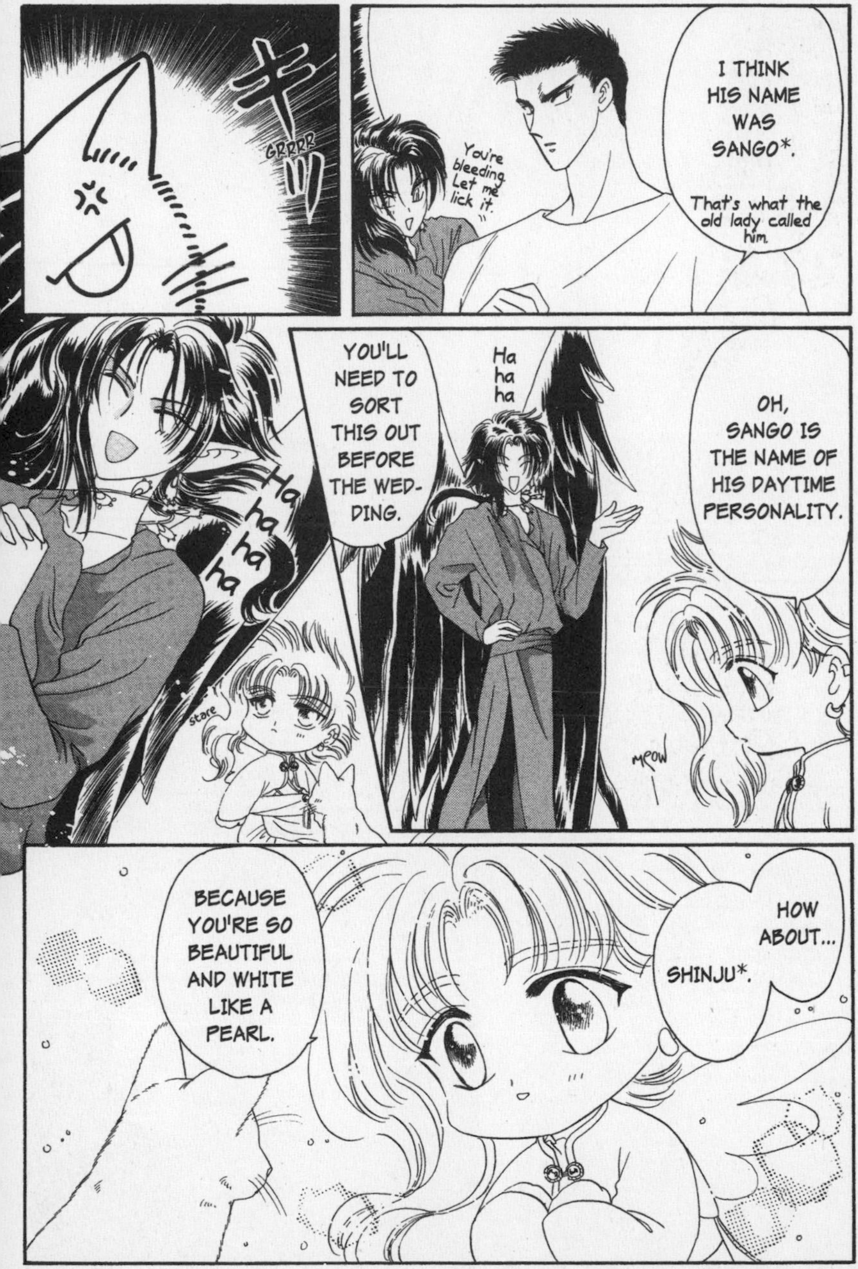
I THINK HIS NAME WAS SANGO*.
That's what the old lady called him.
You're bleeding. Let me lick it.
キ
GRRRR
ッ
OH, SANGO IS THE NAME OF HIS DAYTIME PERSONALITY.
meow
YOU'LL NEED TO SORT THIS OUT BEFORE THE WED-DING.
Ha ha ha
Ha ha ha ha ha
stare
HOW ABOUT...
SHINJU*.
BECAUSE YOU'RE SO BEAUTIFUL AND WHITE LIKE A PEARL.

* *Sango means coral, Shinju means pearl.*

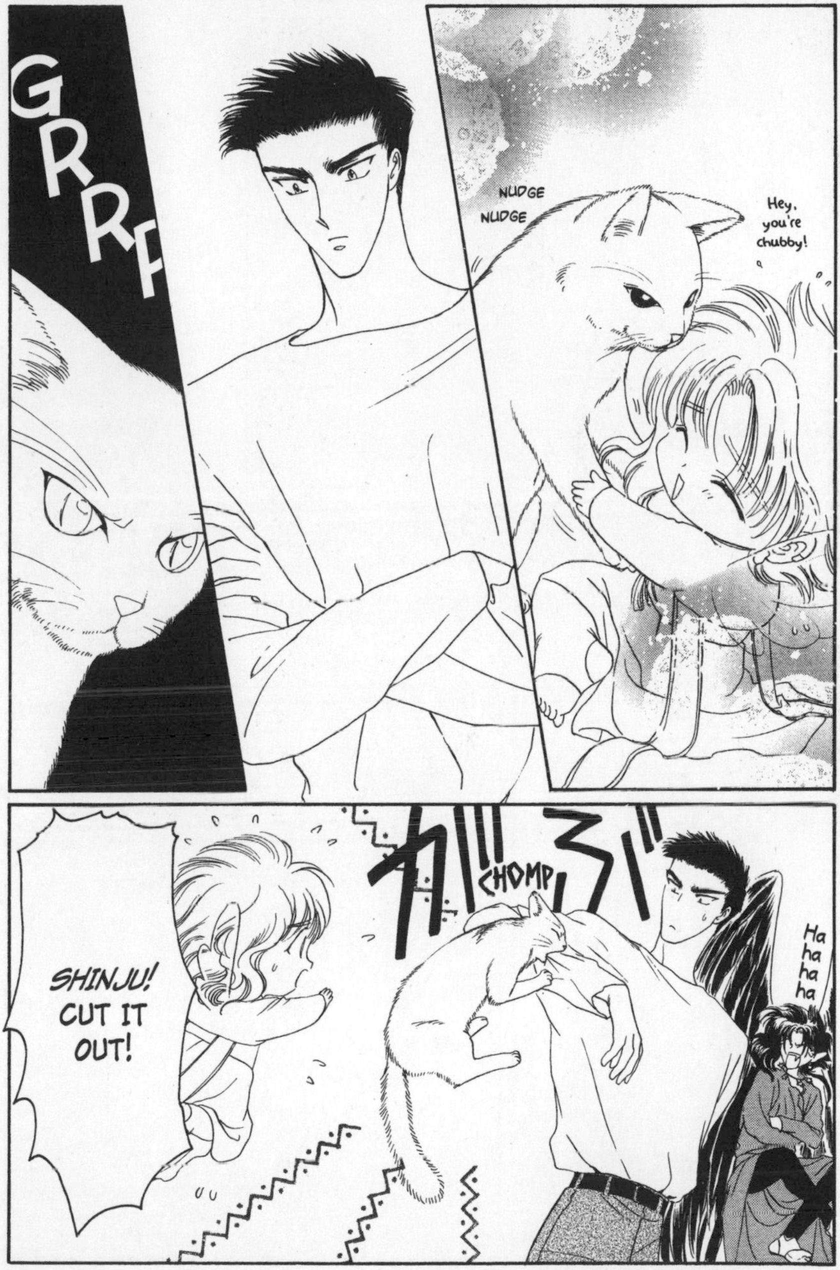
Hey, you're chubby!
NUDGE NUDGE
GRRR
Ha ha ha ha
CHOMP
SHINJU! CUT IT OUT!

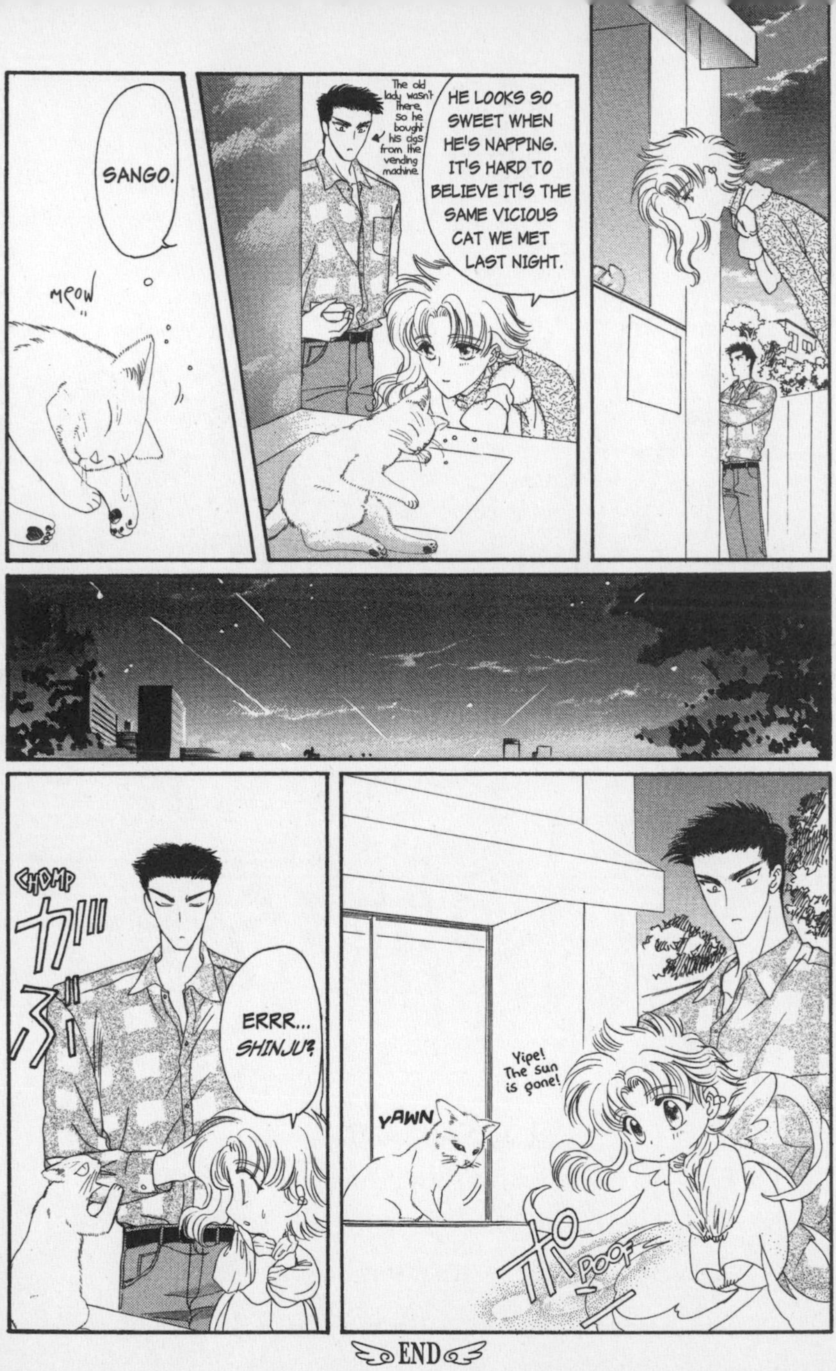
HE LOOKS SO SWEET WHEN HE'S NAPPING. IT'S HARD TO BELIEVE IT'S THE SAME VICIOUS CAT WE MET LAST NIGHT.
The old lady wasn't there, so he bought his cigs from the vending machine.
SANGO.
MEOW
Yipe! The sun is gone!
YAWN
POOF
ERRR... SHINJU?
CHOMP

END

Wish

See you again soon.

CLAMP staff
Art by Mick Nekoi
Story by Nanase Ohkawa
Design by Satsuki Igarashi and Nanase Ohkawa
Special Thanks to Mokona Apapa

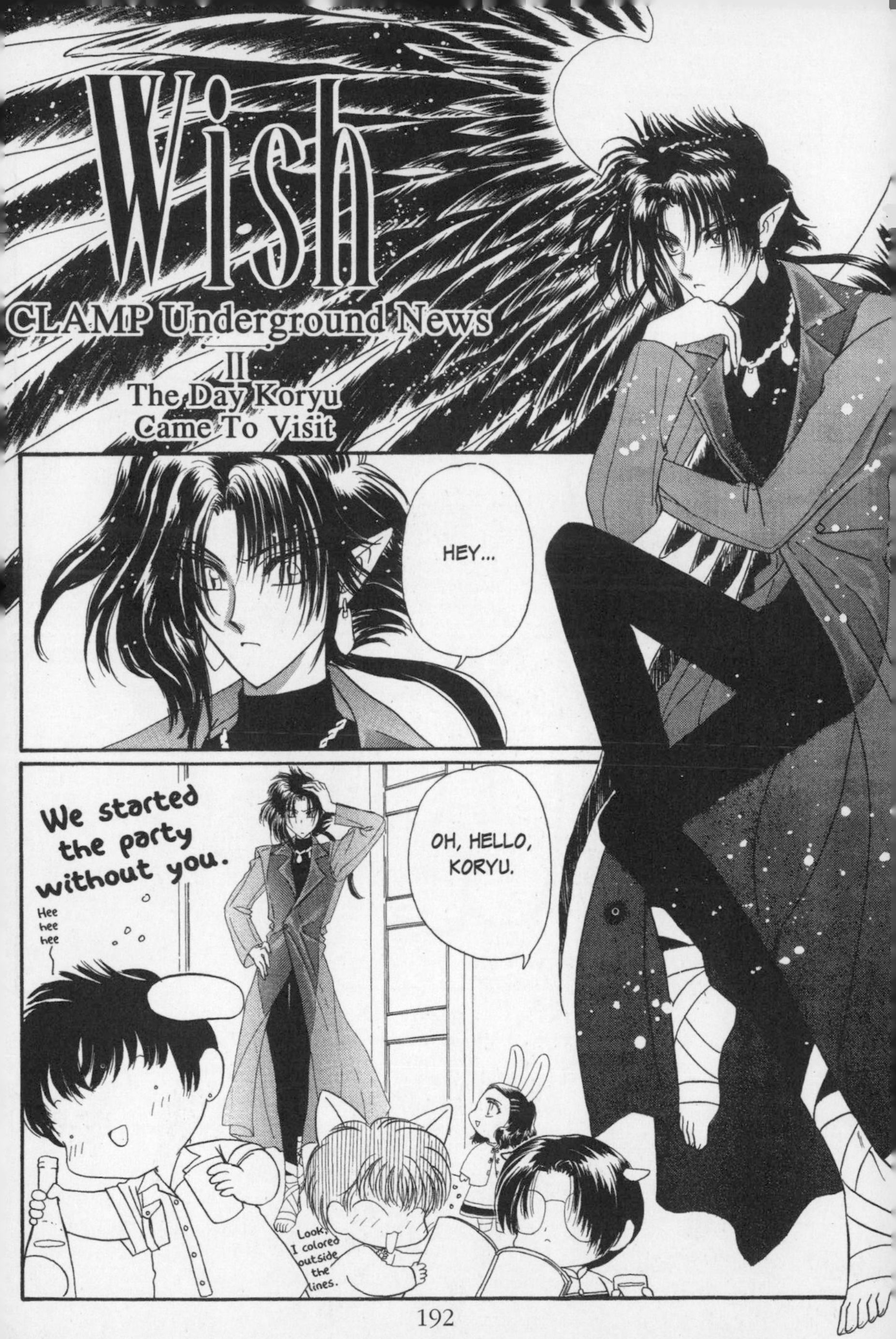
Wish
CLAMP Underground News
II
The Day Koryu Came To Visit
HEY...
OH, HELLO, KORYU.
We started the party without you.
Hee hee hee
Look, I colored outside the lines.

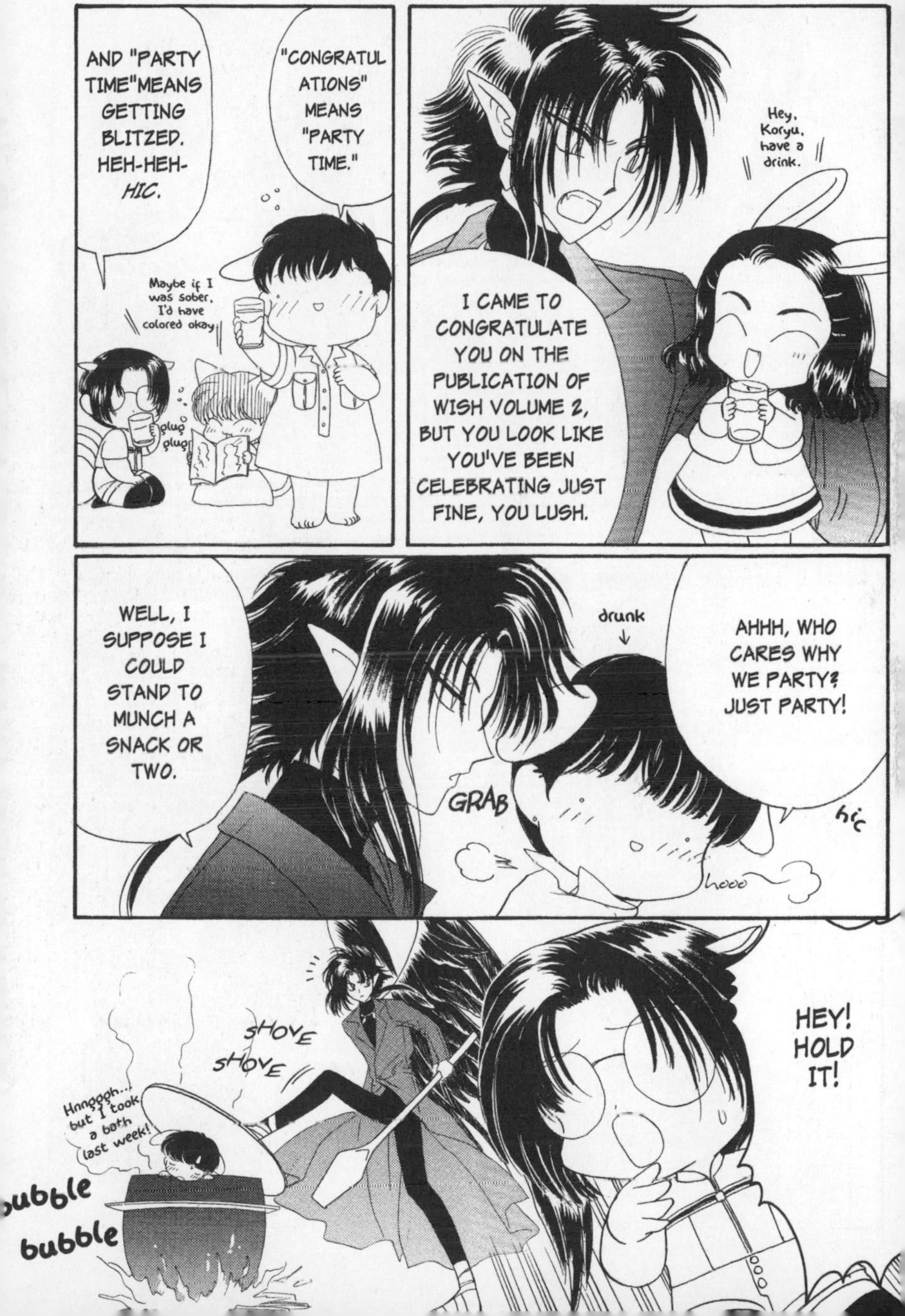
Hey, Koryu, have a drink.
I CAME TO CONGRATULATE YOU ON THE PUBLICATION OF WISH VOLUME 2, BUT YOU LOOK LIKE YOU'VE BEEN CELEBRATING JUST FINE, YOU LUSH.
"CONGRATULATIONS" MEANS "PARTY TIME."
AND "PARTY TIME" MEANS GETTING BLITZED. HEH-HEH-HIC.
Maybe if I was sober, I'd have colored okay
glug glug
AHHH, WHO CARES WHY WE PARTY? JUST PARTY!
drunk
hic
hooo
GRAB
WELL, I SUPPOSE I COULD STAND TO MUNCH A SNACK OR TWO.
HEY! HOLD IT!
SHOVE
SHOVE
Hnngggh... but I took a bath last week!
bubble
bubble

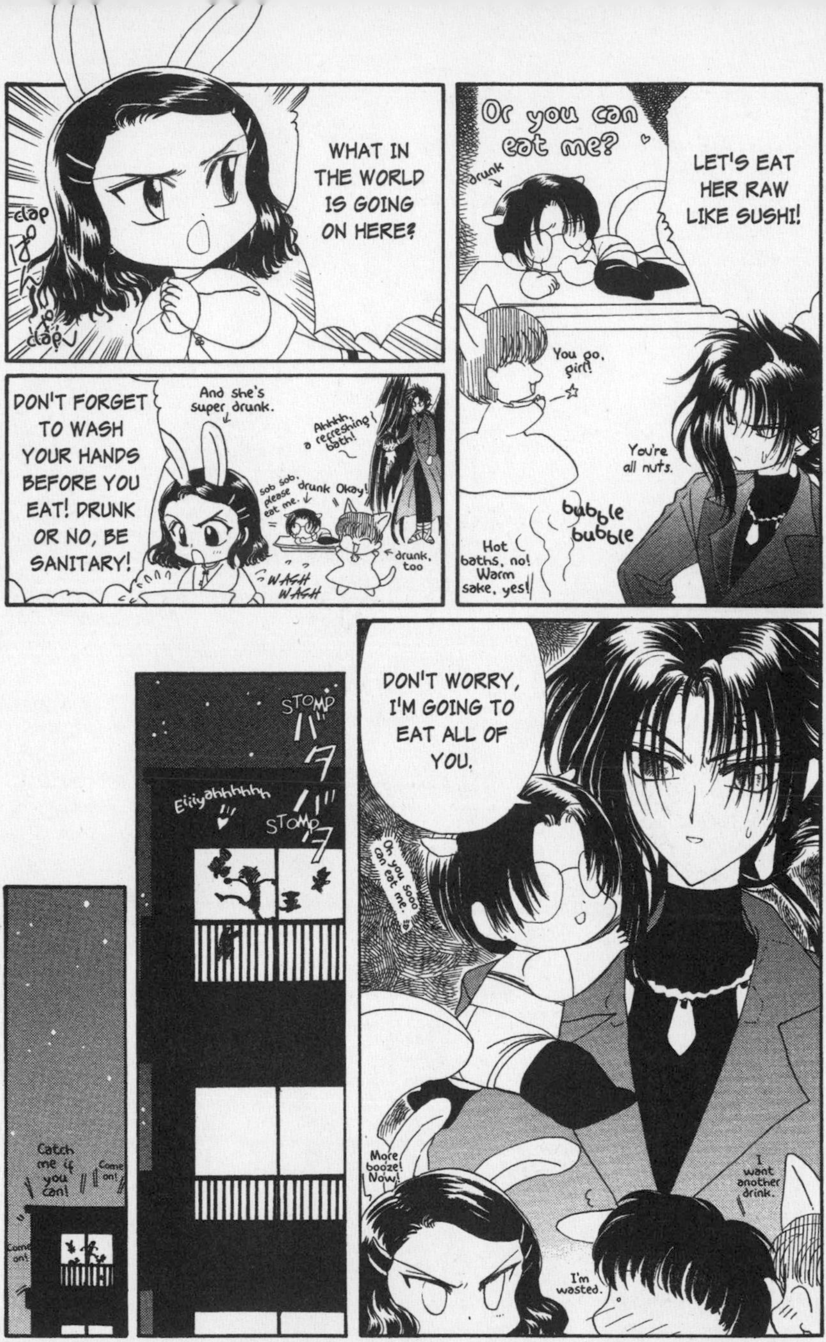

Or you can eat me?
drunk
LET'S EAT HER RAW LIKE SUSHI!
You go, girl!
You're all nuts.
bubble bubble
Hot baths, no! Warm sake, yes!
WHAT IN THE WORLD IS GOING ON HERE?
clap
clap
DON'T FORGET TO WASH YOUR HANDS BEFORE YOU EAT! DRUNK OR NO, BE SANITARY!
And she's super drunk.
Ahhhh, a refreshing bath!
sob sob, please eat me.
drunk
Okay!
drunk, too
WASH WASH
DON'T WORRY, I'M GOING TO EAT ALL OF YOU.
Oh you sooo can eat me.
More booze! Now!
I want another drink.
I'm wasted.
STOMP
STOMP
Eiiiyahhhhh
Catch me if you can!
Come on!
Come on!

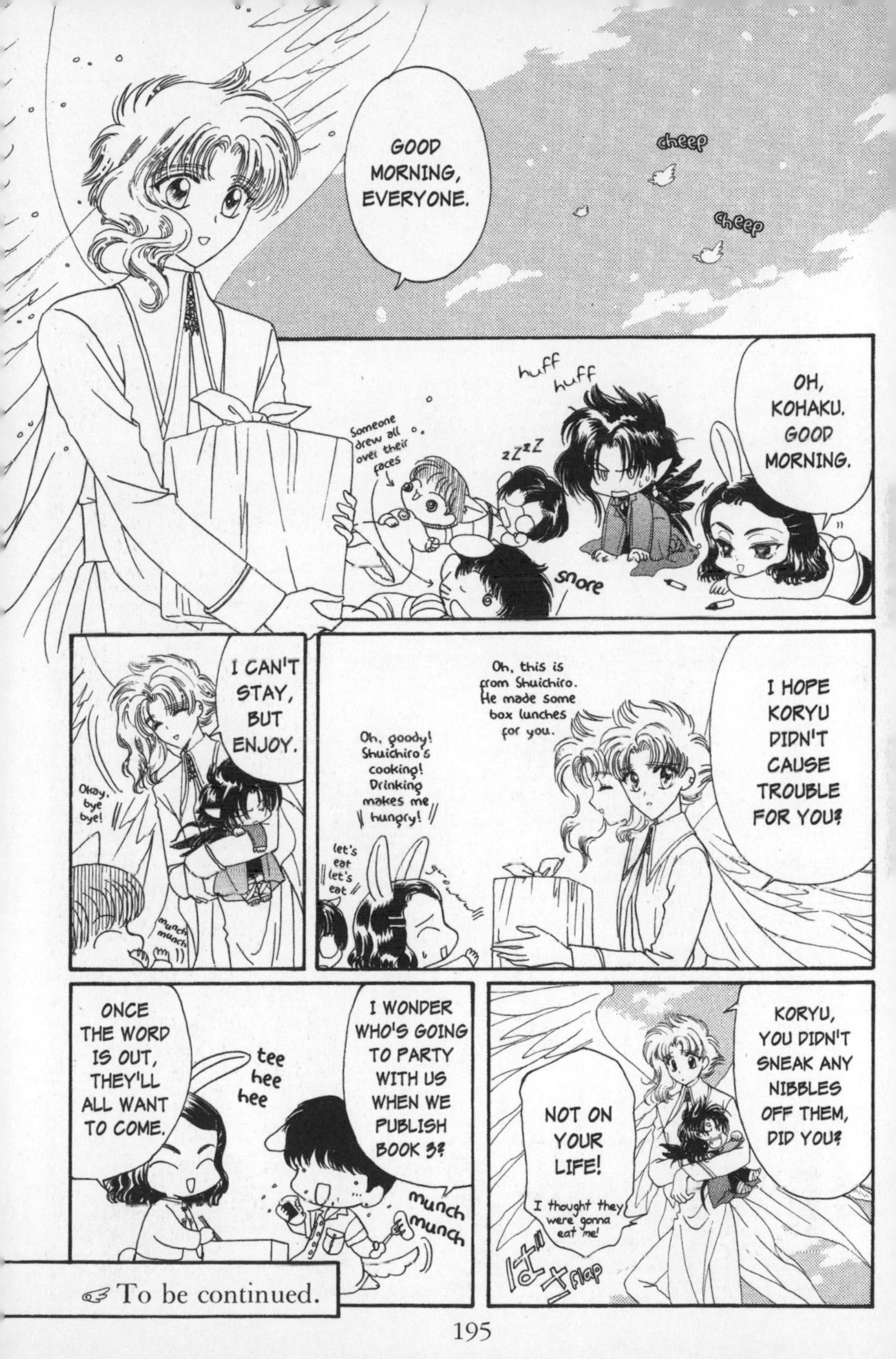
GOOD MORNING, EVERYONE.
cheep
cheep
OH, KOHAKU. GOOD MORNING.
huff huff
zZzZ
Someone drew all over their faces
snore
I HOPE KORYU DIDN'T CAUSE TROUBLE FOR YOU?
Oh, this is from Shuichiro. He made some box lunches for you.
Oh, goody! Shuichiro's cooking! Drinking makes me hungry!
let's eat let's eat
I CAN'T STAY, BUT ENJOY.
Okay, bye bye!
munch munch
KORYU, YOU DIDN'T SNEAK ANY NIBBLES OFF THEM, DID YOU?
NOT ON YOUR LIFE!
I thought they were gonna eat me!
flap
I WONDER WHO'S GOING TO PARTY WITH US WHEN WE PUBLISH BOOK 3?
ONCE THE WORD IS OUT, THEY'LL ALL WANT TO COME.
tee hee hee
munch munch
To be continued.

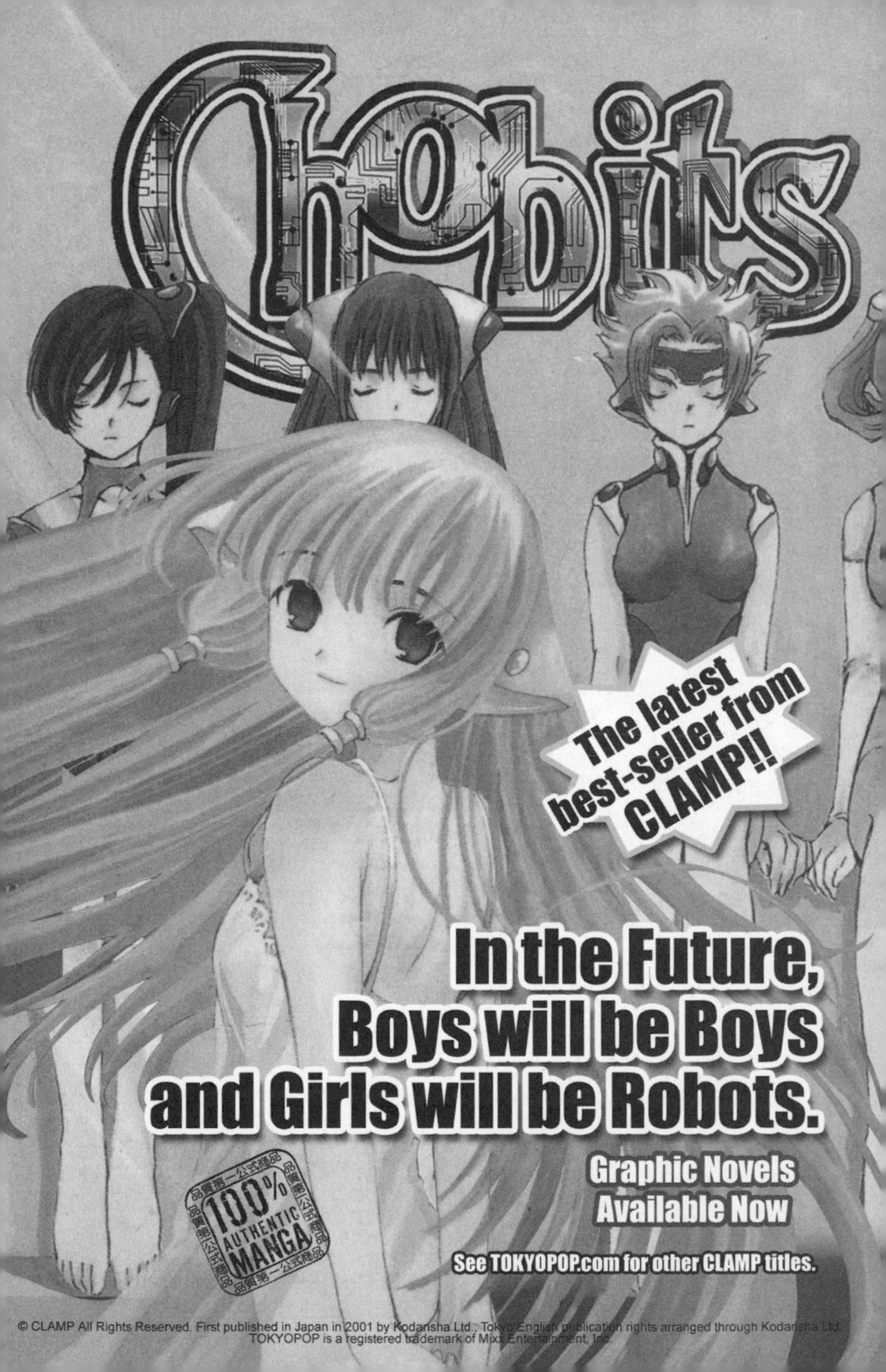
Chobits
The latest best-seller from CLAMP!!
In the Future, Boys will be Boys and Girls will be Robots.
Graphic Novels Available Now
100% AUTHENTIC MANGA
See TOKYOPOP.com for other CLAMP titles.
© CLAMP All Rights Reserved. First published in Japan in 2001 by Kodansha Ltd., Tokyo. English publication rights arranged through Kodansha Ltd.
TOKYOPOP is a registered trademark of Mixx Entertainment, Inc.